A Modern History of Southeast Asia: decolonization, nationalism and separatism

CLIVE J. CHRISTIE

Tauris Academic Studies
I.B.Tauris Publishers
LONDON · NEW YORK

Published in 1996 by Tauris Academic Studies
an imprint of I.B.Tauris & Co Ltd,
45 Bloomsbury Square, London WCIA 2HY
175 Fifth Avenue, New York NY 10010   .

In the United States of America and in Canada
distributed by St Martin's Press, 175 Fifth Avenue
New York NY 10010

A full CIP record for this book is available from the British
Library

A full CIP record for this book is available from the Library of
Congress

ISBN 1 85043 997 4

Library of Congress catalog card number: 95–61521

Set in Monotype Ehrhardt by Ewan Smith, London

Printed and bound in Great Britain by
WBC Ltd, Bridgend, Mid Glamorgan

A Modern History of
Southeast Asia

Contents

Maps

Preface and Acknowledgements

The intention of this book is to study the general process of decolonization in Southeast Asia, its antecedents and consequences, from the perspective of the separatist movements and other rebellions that were an intrinsic part of that decolonization process. Its point of view is strictly historical, and its basic argument is that the varied separatist movements that emerged in Southeast Asia in the wake of the Second World War sprang from a common historical experience: namely, the development of nationalist resistance to the European colonial powers, the definition of the respective national identities of the region, the upheaval of the period of Japanese intervention, and the establishment of independent states.

There are manifest dangers in attempting a general approach of this kind. A proper study of the phenomena of nationalism and separatism must necessarily concentrate on the specific, inherent characteristics of the identity of the group seeking self-determination, and the unique circumstances and historical events that helped forge that identity. Generalizations across a range of disparate examples may well lose this essential historical depth. Equally, ahistorical attempts to elicit the common characteristics and 'laws of behaviour' of movements for self-determination, using the methods of social and political science, run the risk of culminating in definitions so obvious and bland as to be completely unhelpful. Wide-ranging books on nationalist and separatist movements tend, therefore, either to descend into vapid generalizations, or merely to end up as a compilation of unconnected narratives written by specialists of the respective areas concerned, in which synthesis is sacrificed for the sake of area expertise.

There are other difficulties that confront those who would wish to write on the related issues of separatism and religious, ethnic and national identity. It need hardly be said that these are extremely sensitive issues for most states, including those of the West, but particularly for those that have recently gained independence. Any area specialist, therefore – whether writer, journalist or academic – who plans to tackle

vii

these subjects will find great difficulty in gaining access to and co-operation in the region concerned. Any cooperation that is given is liable to be extremely partial, and carries with it the great danger of enticing the writer to become involved in special pleading rather than strictly impartial investigation. For the professional area specialist there is the associated danger that research in this hazardous field – however anodyne – will incur the suspicion of, loss of contacts in, and possibly even loss of access to, the state concerned. There is practically no way that the issue of separatism can be addressed in a manner that is acceptable to sensitive governments. This is a serious consideration, and it helps explain why academic area specialists often allow separatist issues to remain shrouded in a veil of silence, leaving the field open to shrill and often ignorant polemics.

The manner in which separatism is treated also depends on the prevailing orthodoxy of a particular period. Generally speaking – and for reasons that will be examined in greater depth later – the period between 1945 and 1990 was one in which there was a discernible consensus against what might be called the 'legitimacy' of separatist aspirations, particularly in the 'Third World'. Analyses of separatist movements in the Third World during that time tended to view such movements from the perspective of, and through the perceptions of, the central state; as 'problems' to be resolved by appropriate policies of development and pacification. There was, in effect, a tendency to treat separatism as a pathological problem: to try to see separatist movements not from the point of view of their own agendas and aspirations, but rather as a symptom of illnesses within the body-politic of the central state, where it is the responsibility of the regional expert to identify the causes and symptoms and, perhaps, prescribe appropriate cures.

Since 1990, however, the global taboo on separatism has broken down, at least in Eastern Europe and Central Asia. Separatism is 'on the agenda', and, as the rapid recognition of Croatia and Bosnia reveals, has acquired a legitimacy in international affairs undreamt of in the immediately preceding decades. Although this change of perception has scarcely touched Southeast Asia as yet, it is possible that future studies of separatist movements in the region will regard these movements in a different way, with more respect for and interest in their agendas and aspirations.

There is, in fact, a danger that, as the pendulum of global respectability shifts towards separatism and away from the desirability of maintaining the unity of states, academic perspectives will once again become skewed. As issues of separatism and ethnicity become fashionable, objective analysis will be imperilled in new and entirely different ways. Just as it is necessary to challenge the view that dealing with separatist movements is simply a matter of judiciously adjusting the bribes and threats of the central state, so it is necessary to challenge the view that it is right or inevitable that every ethnic group should live within its own state. It is a fundamental thesis of this book that the success or failure of separatist movements in Southeast Asia is not the consequence of irresistible and immutable 'laws' of ethnicity and nationalism, but rather reflects identifiable failures or successes of statecraft at a critical stage of the history of the states concerned.

This book is the culmination of a number of years spent teaching and writing on the issues of national identity, ethnicity, separatism, religious identity and 'loyalism' in Southeast Asia and Asia in general. Reading and research for the diverse chapters of this book has been spread over a decade, but it was not until recently that this wide variety of research seemed almost of its own accord to coalesce into a common theme. Invaluable help was provided by people both inside and outside the academic world. I am particularly grateful to the members of the History Department at Universiti Sains Malaysia, Penang; academic colleagues both in Hull University and in the University of London with whom I have discussed in one form or another the issues addressed in this book; various anonymous informants in southern Thailand; and a wide range of people in the Special Province of Aceh, Indonesia. I am indebted in particular to Ali Hasjmy, leader of the Council of Ulamas in Aceh, and Haji Muhammad, owner of the Toko Buku Haji Muhammad in Banda Aceh.

I am very grateful for the help that I have received in libraries and record offices: in London, the Public Record Office, the India Office Library, the British Library, the Colindale Newspaper Library, and the library of the School of Oriental and African Studies; in Penang, Malaysia, the library of the Universiti Sains Malaysia, the Penang Public Library and the library of the Chinese Chamber of Commerce in the Chinese Town Hall; and in Hull, the Hull University Library.

Thanks to travel grants which I have received from the Centre for Southeast Asian Studies in Hull University between 1979 and 1992, regions which would have been mere academic abstractions have come alive. This has helped to focus the historical imagination. I have been able to see most of Aceh except the western coastal region, and have travelled through the Patani region from Narathiwat to Satun. I spent one year teaching at Universiti Sains Malaysia, and have since paid a number of visits to Penang. I have at least made a foray into Karen territory across the Thai border. In late 1992 I paid an all too short visit to central Vietnam; two decades earlier, I had had the good fortune to visit southern Laos, and to see for myself the strategic position of the Bolovens Plateau in the Central Highlands region. Arakan and Ambon remain, regrettably, *terra incognita*.

I owe a special debt of thanks to my wife Jan, both for advice and support while producing the various chapters of the book, and for giving me absolutely crucial support in the final stages of its production. Without her help, it is difficult to see how the book could ever have seen the light of day.

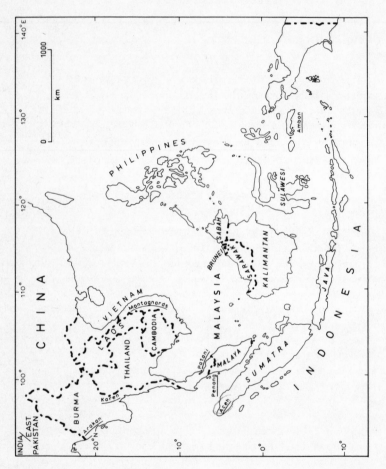

Map 1 Southeast Asia

I

Introduction

The plot of history is written, retrospectively, by the 'winners'. As a consequence, the actions of the 'losers' appear in hindsight to be fragmented, illogical and incoherent. This book seeks to redress the balance by presenting a history of modern Southeast Asia from the losers' point of view, and by attempting to construct out of their disparate experiences a connected, unified and intelligible story.

Winners and losers in modern Southeast Asian history

In April 1947, demands by Malay-Muslim community leaders for autonomy for the Patani region of Thailand started an era of revolt and dissidence on the Thai–Malay border. In April 1948, Muslim clerics in north Arakan declared a *jihad*, or holy war, against the newly independent Burmese government. In December 1948, a committee was set up in Penang with the aim of bringing about the secession of Penang from the Federation of Malaya. In January 1949, after months if not years of tension and skirmishing, the Karens of Burma came out in revolt against the central government. On 25 May 1950 the *Republik Maluku Selatan* (South Moluccan Republic) declared itself independent of the Indonesian Republic. And, in September 1953, the Acehnese joined the Indonesia-wide *Darul Islam* rebellion that had begun in 1948.

In addition to these rebellions and separatist movements, the year 1948 saw the outbreak of communist insurgencies in Burma, Malaya and the Philippines, and a communist *putsch* in Indonesia. This general upheaval sprang out of disparate circumstances and diverse objectives, mainly ideological or separatist. But it clearly reflected a common set of historical experiences in Southeast Asia, namely, the consolidation in the nineteenth century of European colonial rule, the subsequent revolution in national consciousness, the process of decolonization and the establishment of independent nation-states. The ideological and separatist rebellions of the period 1945 to 1953 reflected the disappointed hopes of the 'losers' in this historical process.

It is the objective of this book to consider the separatist and what might be called 'separatist-ideological' rebellions of this period, within the general historical context of decolonization. However, in order to understand the process of decolonization, it is first necessary to examine the phenomenon of nationalism and the European roots of the nationalist idea.

Identity and community: the European origins of the terminology of nationalism

All human societies, from the most rudimentary to the most sophisticated, have tended to coalesce around varying forms of identity. In all but the most primitive forms of community, the individual will adhere to a complex network of competing and coexisting identities, from the family to widening layers of community identity and political organization.

In traditional European thinking, there has been a tendency to distinguish between what might be called 'organic' and 'acquired' forms of identity and community. 'Organic' forms of community include what is inherent and what one inherits: birth, family, local community, and the land and culture in which one is born and brought up. These organic forms of identity can in reality, of course, be overcome by choice or necessity, but they are generally seen as intrinsic and to a degree inescapable. The Latin words *patria*, *natio*, *tribus* and the Greek words *patris*, *ethnos*, *ethné* and *genos* – even though they contain a subtle range of meanings – all have this common implication of an organic or rooted community.[1]

Against this, 'acquired' identities imply communities that have been created as the consequence of deliberate thought and organization from above. In these cases, the binding identity is to a degree 'conceived' rather than inherent, and may indeed challenge or subsume rooted forms of identity. Classic examples of such 'created' or 'organized' communities are the ideal states conceived by Plato and Aristotle as the guiding model for the Greek city-states; the Roman Republic, forged together, according to myth, from a variety of local and migrant communities, and gradually stabilized through a series of constitutional expedients;[2] and the universal religious community created by the followers of Jesus Christ. Traditional signs of these acquired identities are the Greek and Latin words *politeia*, *respublica*, *civitas* and *ecclésia*.

Classical European thinking on the issue of identity has always recognized the existence and strength of the 'organic' community. What was not generally accepted – in theory at least – was the idea that the 'civilized' state or polity should be based upon these organic identities.

The historical basis of the European nation-state

It is only in the nineteenth and twentieth centuries that we have seen the creation – first in Europe and then throughout the world – of a global system of sovereign nation-states. This period has witnessed the collapse of multi-*ethnic* empires under the pressure of ethnic groups claiming a separate *national* identity, and demanding the creation of their own *nation-state*. Subsequent attempts to create a supra-national global authority – the United Nations – have not seriously diminished the sovereign authority of the nation-state; and efforts in Europe to create a new 'super-state' are only in the formative stages.

Compared to this modern, uniform world of nation-states, the Europe of the mid-eighteenth century was composed of a jumble of states that were not dependent on any single principle of legitimacy. Kingdoms and empires that were based on the dynastic principle coexisted with aristocratic republics and ecclesiastical states. Moreover, the extent of the authority of these various states was not always clearly defined; the consequence was an almost permanent condition of dynastic competition and conflicting claims of sovereignty.

This situation was transformed in Europe and North America by two profound revolutions, the first in the concept of the state, and the second in the relationship between identity and the state. The stimulus for the first of these upheavals was the new challenge in the late eighteenth century to the legitimacy of traditional government. The fundamental question asked in the American and French Revolutions was: by what authority do governments govern? The revolutionary answer to this question was that the only legitimate form of government over states was that based on 'popular sovereignty' (or – ultimately – democracy). In a state based on popular sovereignty, the dynastic *subject* was replaced by the equal *citizen,* and ultimate authority resided in the collective citizenry. This concept of popular sovereignty clearly follows the classical European political tradition, both in attempting to found government on universal political principles (the 'Rights of Man'), and in asserting the notion that the educated, responsible citizen should form the basis of the state. This transformation did not, however – except in the wilder reaches of utopian thought – involve the creation of a universal state. Rather, existing 'illegitimate' dynastic entities were to be transformed by the principle of popular sovereignty into legitimate *nations*. In the French revolutionary concept of *la nation,* the essential foundation of the new state was a matter not of identity, but of political principle.[3]

Running parallel, however, to this revolution in political ideas were other equally profound upheavals in the areas of science and history. It is this vital linkage between science and history that provides the basis for the revolution in racial and ethnic awareness – in other words, in identity – of the late eighteenth and nineteenth centuries. The rapid advances of this period in understanding the laws of nature and the origin, classification and transformation of the natural world naturally stimulated enquiries into the scientific laws governing the human species. There was, therefore, an explosion of interest in the origins of humanity, the definition of its racial subdivisions, its linguistic and cultural diversity, and the laws governing the survival, dominance and decline of races and civilizations.[4] This interest in the origin of *races* (defined here as the major subdivisions of the human species) and *ethnic* groups (defined as subdivisions within the separate races) was bolstered by linguistic and historical investigations, and legitimized by scientific or pseudo-scientific 'laws'.[5]

Put simply, the modern phenomenon of nationalism springs from the dynamic contact between ethnic consciousness and the concept of popular sovereignty, or democracy. The revolution in ethnic conscious-ness led inevitably to the demand that ethnic identity be given a legitimate political expression. In a new political environment increas-ingly dominated by the concept of popular sovereignty, the natural medium through which ethnic rights could be expressed was the democratic process. To the old question: by what right do existing governments govern? was added a new question: by what right do existing states exist? In his analysis of the operation of popular sovereignty, John Stuart Mill got to the nub of the problem when he pointed out that, just as it was a fundamental right of the people of a state to choose their government, so it was a fundamental right, within the limits of feasibility, for a community within that state to decide whether it wished to share a state with others, or form a state of its own.[6] National consciousness could be said to come into being when ethnic consciousness crystallizes into a desire to create a state based on that ethnic consciousness: the prize at the end of this process of national 'self-determination' is the modern nation-state.

The key to the phenomenon of nationalism and the programme of national self-determination was the revolution in ethnic consciousness. The all-important point to note here is that, although ethnic conscious-ness – the consciousness, that is, of roots and origins – existed before, it was only now that it took a self-conscious political shape. It is also important to note, however, that nationalism as a political programme often – particularly in Western and Central Europe and North America – involved more than the mere expression of ethnic identity and rights. Any nationalist movement laying claim to the right to create a nation-state would also have to claim a national territory. And – because ethnic groups do not arrange themselves on the map for the convenience of nationalist aspirations – this territory would almost invariably contain ethnic minorities. In order to win broad support, therefore, and head off counter-nationalist claims by ethnic minorities inhabiting the same space, nationalist movements were often forced to define their programmes in broader terms than the mere assertion of the rights of an ethnic group. The dynamic for nationalism may have been the assertion of ethnic identity and rights, but its political success normally depended on a generous, inclusive definition of national belonging that involved respect for minority rights and the concept of the equality of rights of all citizens. The classic European notion that the state should be founded on political principle rather than mere identity managed to retain a foothold, therefore, in the ideology of nationalism.

If these are the ideological foundations of nationalism, how was the programme of nationalism realized in the actual history of Europe? One can detect, in the eighteenth, nineteenth and twentieth centuries, two fundamental processes: one where pre-national dynastic states (like Britain) forged a national identity from above to match the contours of the existing state – in other words, where states became nations; and one where ethnic communities created a nation-state for themselves – where the nations became states. The whole history of Europe in the nineteenth and twentieth centuries has been dominated – and nearly destroyed – by this process of consolidation, fragmentation and co-alescence. Multi-ethnic empires have broken up and, out of their ruins, new nation-states have been created; elsewhere, as in the German and Italian regions of Europe, mini-states have been linked together to create nation-states. Today, even as Western and Central Europe are trying to evolve new political entities that would modify the sovereignty of nation-states, further to the east, new nation-states are struggling to emerge out of the ruins of the communist empires.

The consolidation of European empires in Southeast Asia

It is a testimony to the uneven development of world history that, at the very time that nation-states were emerging from the fragmenting empires within Europe, European nations were themselves consolidating global empires. In an astonishing period of compressed political, military, diplomatic and administrative activity roughly stretching from the 1820s to 1900, Britain, the Netherlands and France were able to push out from their scattered possessions and trading-posts in Southeast Asia and establish empires over the whole region (see Map 1). In the Philippines, the United States in similar fashion dispossessed Spain at the end of the nineteenth century, and incorporated the islands into their growing Pacific and Caribbean empire.

The dynamic behind this extraordinary phenomenon was the huge but temporary divergence between Europe's and North America's technological progress, and that of the rest of the world. The immediate stimulus was a competitive search for markets, raw materials, sources of investment, political prestige, and the creation of naval–military networks designed to protect and promote these interests. In the prevailing economic and political thinking of the nineteenth century, empire was seen as an indispensable extension of national power and status. It is interesting to note, however, that although the rapid expansion of empire in Southeast Asia in the late nineteenth century was provoked by competitive fear of other European powers gaining a decisive advantage, the growing convergence of French and British interests in *Europe* ensured that the final stages of imperial consolidation in the area were achieved with a measure of consensus. All things considered, the phase of imperial expansion in Southeast Asia in the last part of the nineteenth century was a remarkably smooth process.

In maritime Southeast Asia, the imperial process involved the steady takeover by a combination of negotiation and force of a number of small, dispersed states and statelets. This diversity was determined by the geography of the region: the main settlements were scattered along the principal rivers of the various islands and through the remoter uplands that had trading contacts with these riverine states. Only on the island of Java was the shape of the terrain suitable for the establishment of large, agriculturally based states.

In the course of the nineteenth century, the British established a general control over the Malayan peninsula and the northern coast of Borneo. The Dutch at the same time gradually completed their occupation of the rest of the East Indian archipelago.[7] The boundaries of Dutch and British imperial influence were determined by the complex evolution of diplomatic relations between these two states between 1789 and 1824, in the course of which respective spheres of influence were broadly agreed. In this sense the two colonial states – British Malaya and the Dutch East Indies – were arbitrary creations that made no effort to follow the existing political or ethnic contours of the region: the Malay world, for example, was divided between British Malaya and Dutch-controlled Sumatra.

The colonial powers, therefore, created large polities out of a bewildering diversity of states and communities. These colonial states were to form the basis of the modern nation-states of Indonesia and Malaysia. It is worth noting, however, that beneath the apparent disunity there were certain common characteristics binding the region together. Primary among these were Islam – particularly in the main trading areas; the general use of a *lingua franca*, the Malay language, along the coasts and ports of the region; and broadly similar cultures, systems of law and political structures.

The dominant colonial powers in mainland Southeast Asia were France and Britain. The pre-colonial political shape of this region was entirely different from insular Southeast Asia. Here, in the course of the late eighteenth and early nineteenth centuries, three major ethnic groups and three dynasties consolidated their control over the whole region: in Burma, the ethnic Burmans and the Konbaung dynasty; in Siam, the ethnic Thai and the Chakkri dynasty; and in Vietnam, the ethnic Vietnamese and the Nguyen dynasty. In all three cases, this era of empire-building was the culmination of a long process of expansion that would, in all probability, have ended with the final absorption of the statelets of Laos and the kingdom of Cambodia. This process was, however, interrupted by the colonial intervention that effectively began in the mid-nineteenth century. To the east, the French in the period between 1858 and 1900 gained control of Vietnam, Laos and Cambodia, and welded them into a colonial super-state, French Indochina. In the west, between 1826 and 1886, the British seized control of the state of Burma, dismantled its political structure, and turned Burma into a province of British India. Situated in between, the kingdom of Siam was able to benefit from the colonial *rapprochement* reached between Britain and France at the beginning of the twentieth century, and maintain a precarious independent existence as a buffer state between British India and French Indochina.

These mainland Southeast Asian states had all been subject to religious and cultural influences of external origin. In Burma, Siam, Laos and Cambodia, Theravada Buddhism was the official religion and dominated the social and political culture. In Vietnam, the whole civilization was overwhelmingly Sinicized. Despite these external cultural and religious influences, however, the three dominant states – Burma, Siam and Vietnam – were fiercely independent, and sustained by a clear sense of ethnic as well as religious identity. This dual inheritance of a strong state and a clear ethnic identity would inevitably form a powerful basis for the modern nationalist movements that began to take shape in Burma and Vietnam at the beginning of the twentieth century.

None of these pre-colonial states, however, could be described as 'nation-states' in the European sense. They could more accurately be described as 'ethnic empires', where a dominant ethnic group governed a wide range of minorities, normally at the periphery of the state, but where no serious attempt was made to integrate them into a common national identity. The sustained effort to create an inclusive national identity in the European sense was only to begin systematically in the early twentieth century.

Patterns of colonial rule in Southeast Asia in the late nineteenth century

The period roughly between 1870 and 1900 saw a number of resistance movements directed against this colonial takeover. The most significant were the belated rebellions – both of which began in 1885 – designed to protect the dynasties of Burma and Vietnam. The Dutch faced a similar resistance war in Aceh in 1873; in this case, however, the aim of defending the Acehnese sultanate was linked to a wider *jihad*, which saw the struggle in pan-Islamic as well as solely local terms. In general, these wars were strictly conservative in their objectives and political rhetoric.[8] Despite the self-sacrificing bravery that was shown by the rebels, they revealed in the starkest possible manner the weakness of traditional Asian states in the face of European power and technology.

The structures of colonial administration introduced by the colonial powers were varied. The traditional system of government was eliminated in Burma, and it became a province of British India. As has often been noted, British rule in Burma was doubly alien: not only did the new colonial rulers introduce the British Indian structure of provincial administration, but they filled up lowly administrative posts with Indians, protected their interests with Indian soldiers and police, and – through the agency of mass Indian immigration – created the basis for a new export economy in Lower Burma.

In the Malayan peninsula, Britain created a dual colonial structure. On the one side, the three Straits Settlements of Singapore, Malacca and Penang were directly administered by Britain as a colony. With the Malay States, however, the British concluded separate protectorate treaties, where the traditional system of government remained intact, but where the administration was effectively put into British hands, and the sultan deferred to a British Adviser or Resident on matters of policy. Although this complex arrangement ultimately came under a single British authority in Singapore, the British maintained a precarious balance between the two systems right up to the Japanese invasion of Malaya in 1941. But the fact that the modern economy created by the British – along with its immigrants, its roads and its railways – spanned the Straits Settlements and the traditional Malay States made this dual structure ever more difficult to sustain.

The French used a similar dual system in Indochina. Cochinchina, the southernmost part of Vietnam – the first to come under French rule, and the area with the greatest economic potential – was administered directly as a colony of France. The remainder of Indochina, however – the two Vietnamese regions of Annam and Tonkin, the kingdom of Cambodia and the principalities of Laos – were taken over by France on the basis of protectorate agreements concluded with the local monarchies. In the protectorates, the traditional indigenous administration was maintained, but the French exerted real control through a parallel administrative structure – the *résident* system – that penetrated to the provincial level. Despite the apparent diversity of political structures, the whole Indochina system was in fact dominated by the French Government-General in Hanoi.

The administration of the Dutch East Indies was systematized at the end of the nineteenth and the beginning of the twentieth centuries. Basically, it imposed a single, direct colonial administration while at the same time co-opting traditional indigenous administrators at the local level. Rather than build on a series of protectorate arrangements with a bewildering array of local states and statelets, the Dutch created a uniform administrative structure, but, at the district level, they retained the authority of the local hereditary nobility – the traditional administrators of the pre-colonial states – and incorporated them into the colonial system. This 'regent' or *bupati* class became the key to the Dutch administration in the East Indies.

Southeast Asia up to the First World War: from resistance to reform

As the European nations consolidated their empires in Southeast Asia towards the end of the nineteenth century, so imperial 'philosophies' took shape – explicitly in the case of the Dutch 'Ethical Policy' and the French *mission civilisatrice,* implicitly in the case of Britain. In essence, these philosophies asserted that imperial rule should involve reciprocal benefits: colonial empires should no longer be seen simply as a source of profit and national power, but as a responsibility, where white civilization had the duty to provide better government, education and general welfare for the native population, and – above all – access to the culture, ideas and technology of Europe. To this generally altruistic concept was added the practical concern that the elite 'collaborator' stratum of the indigenous population – on which the whole system of colonial administration ultimately depended – should be introduced to Western education and ideas. It was hoped that the creation of a European-orientated native elite would provide the basis for a greater indigenous participation in government that would help strengthen the foundations of empire.

Many members of the local elites, either individually or, as in the case of the Straits Chinese of the Malayan peninsula, collectively, enthusiastically took up this idea of imperial participation. It is during this pre-First World War period, indeed, that the phenomenon of loyalism, which is dealt with in the first part of this book, began to flourish. Generally speaking, though, the explosion in the late nineteenth and early twentieth centuries of native elite interest in European ideas, educational and social reform, and the reform of indigenous religions and cultures, had a different foundation. Throughout Asia and the Islamic world, the educated elite of this period were acutely aware of the ossification of their local cultures and political systems, and indeed of their apparent helplessness before the European threat. Their reading of Darwin and the Social Darwinians warned them that a civilization that failed to adapt to the challenges of a changing world was doomed to decay and eventually perish.[9]

It was basically this line of thinking that stimulated the pre-1914 reform movement in Southeast Asia. In the area of religion, Islamic and Buddhist reform movements sought – in line with organizations in the wider Asian and Islamic world – to clear away the accretions of local practices and superstitions, restore the pure essence of original religious doctrine, and to adapt that doctrine to the modern challenges of democracy and technological progress.[10] In the educational field, schools were established, and linguistic reforms – such as the romanized *quoc-ngu* Vietnamese writing system – were popularized; greater access was gained to the literature of Europe; and at the same time, interest was re-ignited in the classical literature of Asia.[11] Organizations for the encouragement of cultural and social change proliferated, and whole areas of traditional life were opened up for discussion.[12] It is important to note that the overall rationale behind this reforming activity was that of 'self-strengthening'; its programme was not – at this stage – anti-colonial.

1914–41: Anti-colonialism and nationalism in Southeast Asia

It was during the period of the First World War and the ensuing interwar years that a national consciousness and a nationalist programme in the European sense began to take shape in Southeast Asia. As has already been noted, nationalism has its foundations in ethnic consciousness, but transforms it by attempting to draw the inhabitants of the conceived 'nation' together with a transcending social, political and sometimes even religious-based ideology. It is noticeable that these Southeast Asian nationalist ideologies, as they gradually emerged, drew heavily on European concepts and models. But the ideology of nationalism by no means won absolute, uncontested dominance in Southeast Asia during these years. In this era of intensifying anti-colonial organization, rhetoric and action, nationalism had to compete with two other major ideological forces: communism and Islam.[13]

This competition of ideologies was a symptom of a growing political upheaval during these inter-war years – an upheaval that was based on a rejection of the colonial agenda. The impact of anti-colonialism was, however, uneven: while the tranquillity of the Malayan region or of the outer islands of the Dutch East Indies remained relatively un-disturbed, other areas, such as Java and Vietnam, were becoming hotbeds of political and social agitation.[14] Undoubtedly this growing anti-colonialism was stimulated by the global events that were triggered by the First World War. The war itself seriously dented the notion of the innate superiority of European civilization, and revealed the potential vulnerability of the European empires. Even though it did not become a theatre of war, there was a significant upsurge of anti-colonial organization and activity in Southeast Asia, and indeed Asia as a whole, during the war years. It was evident to the politically aware that if Japan had been an enemy rather than an ally of Britain in this period, it would have been difficult if not impossible for the French, Dutch and British to defend their empires in Southeast Asia.[15]

The imperial situation was made even more precarious by the fact that the United States – grudgingly followed by Britain and France – chose to put an ideological gloss on the Allied war aims. If the Allies claimed that they were fighting for the right to 'self-determination' of all the peoples of Europe, it was natural that the peoples of the colonial regions would demand a similar right. The hopes of the colonized regions – even those that had been under German or Ottoman control – were in the event disappointed at the end of the war. But the notion that the legitimate foundation for a future world order was one of sovereign nation-states based on the right of peoples to self-determination had been established, even if it was imperfectly realized.[16]

This had a profound impact on the European imperial systems. It is true that, with the exception of the institution of very limited representative structures and occasional periods of liberalization, there were few administrative or constitutional changes in the Dutch East Indies, French Indochina or British Malaya in the period up to 1941. Imperial *stasis* was the rule – a *stasis* that was, indeed, justified by growing anti-colonial and revolutionary activity. But in British India – and thereby Burma, as a province of British India – significant changes took place in the inter-war years. Faced by the rhetoric of self-determination that had been generated by the First World War and by the growing demand of India for political rights, Britain speeded up the process – already begun in the White Dominions – of trying to redefine its empire as a free association of self-governing states. The principle of the right of Indians to accelerated political participation was recognized in the Montagu Declaration of 1917, and, after the war, India and Burma – the latter first as part of India, and after 1937 as a separate state – began the tortuous constitutional process of realizing this principle.[17] In theory at least, if this process had not been interrupted by the Second World War, the culmination would have been self-government as Dominions within the British Empire. By the outbreak of the Second World War, Burma had a Burmese prime minister and cabinet, and a Burmese-dominated legislature; ultimate authority and reserve powers, however, still lay in the hands of Britain. A more adventurous process of transition to self-government took place at roughly the same time in the Philippines.

Outside of Burma and the Philippines, however, there were no avenues presented for serious political and constitutional change, let alone moves to self-government, in the Southeast Asian colonies. It is this fact above all that explains the popularity and influence of the revolutionary doctrines that emerged from the Bolshevik Revolution in Russia in 1917. Lenin and the Bolshevik leadership argued that, since imperialism was at the root a global extension of capitalism, the interests of the working class in the industrialized world and of the colonized peoples naturally coincided. Successful revolution in the industrialized world would therefore destroy the capitalist basis of imperialism; conversely, successful anti-colonial revolutions would destroy the imperial networks on which metropolitan capitalism fundamentally depended.[18] Accordingly, the Bolshevik leadership rapidly set about creating a global revolutionary network, based on the Communist International, or Comintern, founded in 1919. In the course of the 1920s and 1930s, communist parties and subsidiary revolutionary organizations were established throughout Southeast Asia.

These inter-war years, therefore, saw an ideological struggle in Southeast Asia for dominance over the respective anti-colonial movements. After its zenith in the pre-war reform era and a short period during and immediately after the First World War, Islam tended to decline as a mass ideological force, and to retreat to the safer havens of educational and social reform. Communism, on the other hand, flourished, and for a time dominated the radical political agenda of the

1920s. Comintern policy, however – to some extent reflecting the imprecisions of the Leninist theory of 'national-liberation' – was not able to fix a clear position on the relationship between communism and nationalism or, indeed, between communism and religion. Between the early 1920s and 1927, the Comintern – using the alliance between the Chinese communists and Chinese nationalists as a general model – encouraged the creation of political 'fronts' and the highlighting of broad national and anti-colonial issues. After the Chinese débâcle of 1927, however, in which the Chinese nationalist party, the Kuomintang, turned on and virtually destroyed the Chinese communists, all nationalist rhetoric used by the communists was subordinated to a primary concentration on the 'class struggle' – a largely unrealistic policy in an area like Asia, where the working class was in an embryonic stage of development. It was only in the face of the global threat of fascism that communist-nationalist 'patriotic' alliances were resumed in the mid-1930s. These shifts in policy had a devastating effect on the communist movements of Southeast Asia, which found themselves at crucial moments – as with the Indonesian Communist Party (PKI) revolts of 1926–27, or the Indochinese Communist Party (ICP) revolts of 1930–31 – isolated and vulnerable.[19]

The whole strength of nationalism, as opposed to other ideologies, lay in its overriding emphasis on unity above all else. Nowhere is this more evident than in the Dutch East Indies. The pre-colonial states of Burma and Vietnam had been strong enough to give a clear sense of identity to the Burmese and Vietnamese anti-colonial movements. In the case of the Dutch East Indies, Indonesian nationalism literally had to be created. The inter-war years saw a self-conscious, sustained effort to forge a united identity out of the hotch-potch of islands that made up the Dutch empire in the East. The Malay *lingua franca* was turned into a national language, and a national literature was created on the basis of that language.[20] A national political elite was beginning to be created from the children of wealthy Indonesians from all over the archipelago, who found themselves thrown together in the schools and colleges of Java or the Netherlands. Above all, political leaders like Achmed Sukarno and Mohammad Hatta began the process of trying to forge a nationalist ideology that would incorporate, and at the same time harness, the ideas of Islam and socialism.[21]

The impact of the Second World War in Southeast Asia

In the autumn of 1940, Japan established a military foothold in Indochina, a foothold that the French government – recently defeated in

Europe – was in no position to deny. In December 1941, Japan began a series of assaults on the remainder of colonized Southeast Asia, assaults that rapidly culminated in complete domination of the region. There can be no doubt that these events were the key to the decolonization process in Southeast Asia.

In the first place, and crucially, the colonial administrations were removed. In the case of Britain, the Netherlands and the United States, this occurred rapidly in early 1942. France managed to hang on to its Indochina possessions by the simple expedient of allowing the territory to be used for strategic purposes by Japan; but French rule was eventually obliterated by a brutal Japanese *putsch* in March 1945. These events dealt a blow to colonial rule in Southeast Asia from which it was never able to recover. Whatever the form of administration that was subsequently imposed by the Japanese authorities, it was inevitable that they came to rely very heavily on the indigenous populations for support. As part of this process of winning support for their war effort, they expanded the administrative responsibilities of the indigenous administrators. They encouraged – under conditions of strict scrutiny – the formation of a variety of 'pan-Asian' associations and militias, and gave considerable scope for mass organization and activity to prominent political and religious leaders who were prepared to take a pro-Japanese and anti-Allied stand. Furthermore, after an initial period of hesitation, they countenanced, and to an extent encouraged, the creation of independent governments, first in Burma and the Philippines in 1943, and later in Vietnam, Laos, Cambodia and – towards the very end of the war – in Indonesia.

Despite the fact that political activity was always strictly controlled by the Japanese, and the 'independent' governments of Southeast Asia had to subordinate their policies to Japanese war aims, this marked a decisive and ultimately irreversible change in the fortunes of the Southeast Asian anti-colonial movements. But, at the same time, the Japanese presence exacerbated ethnic and ideological differences within the respective Southeast Asian states and nationalist movements. In the first place, the Japanese ideological model that dominated this period, along with being militarist and anti-white in its rhetoric, also uncompromisingly emphasized unitary national identities under authoritarian governments. This ideology undoubtedly affected the Siamese–Thai nationalist programme of the early 1940s, with its attempt to create an exclusive 'Thai' identity at the expense of all forms of cultural, ethnic and religious diversity. To a greater or lesser degree, the Japanese ideology also influenced the constitutions and ideologies of the other states and anti-colonial movements of Southeast Asia at this time. In such circumstances, it was inevitable that there would be a dramatic rise in tension between dominant ethnic groups on one side, and ethnic minorities and 'loyalist' groups that had worked with the colonial powers on the other. Examples of this tension are chronicled in the ensuing chapters of this book.

The Japanese presence also stimulated ideological tensions within the respective nationalist movements. Despite the fact that Japan encouraged political activity and organization to a degree undreamt of in the colonial era, they tended to compartmentalize this activity by encouraging separate – and to some degree competing – religious, ideological and communal organizations. In Java, for example, they carefully maintained distinct nationalist and Islamic mass movements and militias; this was to have serious repercussions in the post-war era.[22] Just as dangerous for the maintenance of the unity of Southeast Asian nationalist movements was the ideological division between the pro-Japanese and pro-Allied factions of the various nationalist movements. While the core of the nationalist movements – with the exception of those in Vietnam – were prepared to work within the restricted political framework provided by the Japanese, the socialist Left in general, and the communist parties of the region in particular, provided the basis for indigenous resistance to the Japanese.

For their part, the Allied military were prepared to accept all the local help they could get; and the result was an incongruous military alliance between, for example, the British armed forces and the communists of Malaya and Burma. In addition, the colonial powers sought to establish military links with strategically important ethnic groups, particularly in mainland Southeast Asia. Minority regions – like the Hmong regions of Laos, the Kachin region of north Burma, or the Arakanese, Chin and Naga regions of west Burma – which had hitherto been neglected backwaters, now assumed a considerable military significance. This too, as this book will attempt to show, had substantial repercussions for the nationalist movements of Southeast Asia.[23]

It was, however, precisely because of this danger that the pressures of war would irrevocably divide and weaken Southeast Asian anti-colonialism, that strenuous efforts were made by key nationalist leaders to build solid mass organizations bolstered by an inclusive nationalist programme. This is particularly the case in the key states of Burma, Vietnam and Indonesia. In all these cases, pre-war ideological squabbles were substantially resolved by the end of the war with the creation of united nationalist movements sustained by an inclusive strategy and ideology. In Burma, Aung San's Anti-Fascist Peoples Freedom League (AFPFL), formed in 1945, united pro- and anti-Japanese, communist and nationalist, soldier and civilian, and – at least in intention – ethnic Burman and non-Burman, in one all-embracing mass movement with a single objective: the immediate and unqualified independence of Burma.[24] In Vietnam, the Indochina Communist Party formed in 1941 a patriotic 'front', the Viet-Minh; its core organization was communist, but its political programme was strictly nationalist, calling as it did for the unity of all classes and ethnic groups ('nationalities') in Vietnam in the struggle for independence and unity. After the Japanese surrender in mid-1945, this movement had become sufficiently strong to brush aside the government hastily created by the Japanese, declare the independence of Vietnam, and establish the Democratic Republic of Vietnam. In Indonesia, where the Japanese in early 1945 had encouraged the nationalist and Islamic leaders to begin the process of preparing for independence, Sukarno was able to entrench his so-called *pancasila* principles – national unity, social justice, democracy, humanitarianism and belief in God – as the foundation stones of the national ideology of the Indonesian Republic, which declared its independence in August 1945. In each of these cases, a conscious effort was made to draw together political ideologies (including communism) and religious and ethnic groups through a broadly based nationalist ethos.

The post-war strategies of the colonial powers

At the end of the Second World War, the colonial powers found themselves confronted by a completely changed political environment. To varying degrees, they were unprepared for this change, and it was only gradually that they were able to adapt to the realities of the new post-colonial era that had emerged in Southeast Asia during the Second World War. Only in the Philippines was the transition of sovereignty from the United States to an independent government carried out rapidly and relatively smoothly.

Although Britain was aware that there would have to be a drastic restructuring of its empire in Asia, British imperial policy was still inhibited by a number of constraints and even delusions. In general, Britain hoped that the imperial framework – in the sense of a genuine unity in the constitutional, political, economic and defence spheres – could be maintained, even if states such as India evolved into self-governing dominions. In the Southeast Asian sphere, it was felt that certain preconditions would have to be met before the process of moving towards self-government could even begin. Burma, which had twice been overrun as a battlefield in the period 1942–45, would need a long period of economic and social recuperation before the scars of war had healed and the political process could start again.[25] In Malaya, the complex tangle of the pre-war system of administration would have to be ended, and a united nation would have to be created on the basis of the equal right to citizenship of all its inhabitants under direct British control; only then could more adventurous political steps be considered.[26] The states of Sarawak and North Borneo, which had hitherto had only a loose form of British government supervision, came – like Malaya – under direct Colonial Office control, but the question of their long-term future was held in abeyance.

Britain at least had the advantage of being able to take over authority of its Southeast Asian possessions directly from the Japanese. To that degree, it had control of the political agenda. The big powers, however, had delegated Britain and Nationalist China to supervise the post-surrender arrangements in Indochina, Sumatra and Java. France and the Netherlands were, therefore, left on the sidelines in their own colonial territories. The main post-war priority of both these countries was hence the simple one of regaining control of these possessions. Given their own military and – probably more important in the long run – economic weakness, and the extent to which the Democratic Republic of Vietnam and the Republic of Indonesia were able to en-trench themselves administratively and politically in the vital months after August 1945, this objective was never fully achieved by either France or the Netherlands.

It would be unfair to suggest, however, that France and the Nether-lands returned to Southeast Asia having, like the Bourbon courtiers, 'forgotten nothing and learnt nothing'. Both were aware that the concept of empire would have to be redefined. In the case of the Netherlands, a plan was drawn up during the course of the war for the creation of a new imperial partnership between the Netherlands and a self-governing Indonesia under the Dutch crown.[27] In the spring of 1945, France put forward a more restricted plan for greater native political participation in a federal Indochina, but without any serious suggestion of self-government. By March 1946, however, political and military realities had forced the French to concede an autonomous status to the Democratic Republic of Vietnam within a wider Indo-chinese Federation.[28]

Both the Dutch and French post-war policies, however, were clearly designed to hold together the imperial unit and retain the ultimate sovereignty of the imperial metropolis. This crucial objective involved attempts to restrict the degree of self-governing rights that were conceded to their colonies, which helps to explain their strategy of encouraging regional and minority rights. For Britain as well as France and the Netherlands, this latter strategy was to some degree the result of an opportunistic attempt to fragment – or at least weaken – the nationalist movements, and to strengthen the hands of the respective colonial powers in negotiations with those movements. But it also reflected a sense of residual obligation, and a genuine belief that the rights of minority communities should be protected.

When Britain returned to Burma in 1945, it resumed its pre-war obligation to protect the peripheral minority regions and administer them. It undoubtedly felt an additional responsibility for those minorities, such as the Kachin and Karen, who had helped Britain during the war and had endured a considerable degree of hardship as a consequence. In its immediate post-war negotiations with Burmese nationalists, therefore, Britain made it clear that a united self-governing Burma could be achieved only with the consent of those peripheral minorities. In the case of Malaya, the Malayan Union plan was based on a guarantee of equal citizenship rights to all people of whatever race who 'regarded Malaya as their true home and the object of their loyalty'.[29] This, inevitably, strengthened the position of the Chinese and other communities in Malaya against the Malays. As shall be seen in Chapter 5, the Dutch in Indonesia tried in the period 1945–49 to build up a federated structure based on regional *negara*, or states. Their strategy had a dual purpose: first, to guarantee the rights of areas and peoples that had had a long association with the Netherlands and feared subordination to nationalist Java; second, to weaken the authority of the unitary Republic of Indonesia. A similar combination of motives influenced the decision of the French in the summer of 1946 to create autonomous political units in the Cochinchina region of Vietnam and in the Central Highlands.[30]

These various imperial strategies undoubtedly had the effect of forcing the nationalist movements of Indonesia, Burma and Vietnam to widen their political appeal and compete for the loyalties of ethnic minorities and peripheral regions. This strengthened the move, already apparent after the Japanese defeat, away from ethnic-dominated nationalism towards an all-embracing vision of the nation that would include all minorities, religions and ideological tendencies.

Negotiations, independence and post-independence rebellions

For a variety of reasons, the European colonial powers in Southeast Asia were forced in the ensuing years to abandon their respective constitutional plans. In the course of 1946, the British government realized that it simply did not have the resources to impose its will on the Burmese nationalist movement and its mass organizations. In the same year, the implementation by Britain of the Malayan Union plan stimulated the unanimous hostility of the ethnic Malays and the creation of the United Malays National Organization, or UMNO. In the face of this comprehensively powerful and unprecedented display of Malay unity, the British were forced to go back to the drawing-board and formulate a new constitutional structure that guaranteed the primary political rights of the Malays in Malaya.

With the Dutch in Indonesia, the process was more drawn out. After years of alternating negotiation and military action, however, the Dutch were finally forced by a combination of international pressure and the prospect of endless guerrilla war to accept a political settlement with the Indonesian Republic in 1949. In Vietnam, the French came to the belated realization in 1947 that their policy of fragmentation – embodied in the creation of the 'republic' of Cochinchina – would bring few political benefits. Accordingly, they switched from an ethnic-regional strategy of weakening the Democratic Republic of Vietnam to what might be described as an ideological strategy. This involved opening negotiations with anti-communist Vietnamese politicians with a view to creating a self-governing State of Vietnam that would, it was hoped, challenge the legitimacy of the communist-dominated Democratic Republic of Vietnam.[31]

With the exception of the case of Vietnam, which needs to be considered separately, these switches in imperial policy had remarkably similar consequences for the countries concerned. The priority of the colonial powers was now no longer one of using expedients to sabotage or, at the very least, slow down the progress towards self-government. Considerations of prestige and economic interest now demanded that the colonial powers should enter into a kind of partnership with the dominating nationalist movements in order to facilitate moves towards independence. It was hoped that thereby the colonial powers would be able to retain at least a measure of their political influence and their economic position, and safeguard the interests of residual European colonial communities and businesses.

In the rush of colonial powers to cement good relationships with the respective nationalist movements, the rights of minorities and loyalist communities, and the political structures that were designed to protect their interests, tended to be forgotten. The story of this abandonment forms a major part of this book.

If the obvious winners of the decolonization process were the major nationalist movements, there were also inevitably 'losers' that rapidly became aware of their increasingly marginal position. First of all, there were the 'loyalist' communities that had in one way or another played a key role in, and in some cases hinged their very collective identity on, the imperial structures that had been created in Southeast Asia.[32] Then there were the ethnic minorities and peripheral regions that had reason to fear – despite the assurances of the nationalist movements –

that their rights and interests would be ignored in the newly emerging nation-states. Finally, there were the ideological or religious-based movements – such as the communist or Islamic parties – that saw their power and influence steadily eroding as the nationalist movements sought to create all-embracing political programmes in the era of anti-colonial struggle. This erosion of influence was accelerated in the period of independence negotiations – a key period when the main nationalist organizations needed simultaneously to reassure the international community and the departing colonial powers that their governments would be 'responsible' and broad-based, and also to ensure firm control of the new state apparatuses that were being created.

It is not surprising, therefore, that this crucial phase of decolonization between 1945 and 1954 saw a whole series of communist, Islamic, loyalist and ethnic minority rebellions. The most significant loyalist and minority rebellions and secession movements form the subject of this book. The most important Islamic rebellion – the *Darul Islam* rebellion of Indonesia – started in 1948 in West Java, and spread subsequently to Sulawesi, Kalimantan and Sumatra. The communist parties of Burma, Malaya, the Philippines and Indonesia turned from a strategy of cooperation with the main nationalist movements to one of confrontation and rebellion in the course of 1947 and 1948. The rebellion of the Malayan Communist Party – which was dominated by ethnic Chinese – is of particular interest, since it was stimulated by the marginalization in the political negotiations over the future of Malaya not only of the communists, but also of the Chinese community.

The process of decolonization followed a different pattern in Vietnam. Here the main nationalist movement, the Viet-Minh patriotic front, and the main nationalist political entity, the Democratic Republic of Vietnam, were dominated by the communist party. In the years between 1947 and 1951, as the guerrilla war between France and the Viet-Minh intensified, the patriotic rhetoric of the Democratic Republic – a rhetoric that had been designed to win broad support from all classes, regions, religious movements and ethnic groups – began to make way for a more overtly communist programme.[33] France was able to exploit anxiety, both within Vietnam itself and internationally, over the more and more overtly communist character of the Democratic Republic in order to build up an alternative anti-communist, 'nationalist' Vietnamese state, namely the State of Vietnam headed by ex-emperor Bao Dai.

In the normal course of events, it can safely be predicted that this latter state would have been quietly abandoned by the French in 1954 when they realized that they had no alternative but to negotiate for a political and military settlement with the Viet-Minh. That this did not happen, and that the ideological division of the Vietnamese nationalist movement continued for another twenty years after 1954, was a direct result of the intrusion of the Cold War into Southeast Asia.

National unity, ideological divisions, separatist rebellions and the impact of the Cold War on Southeast Asia

The conflict between communism and the West in Europe theoretically became global in 1947, when the Soviet Union's 'Two Camp' doctrine stated that the world had been divided into two irreconcilable communist and capitalist camps; and when, for its part, the United States identified communist ideology as an international threat. The fact that four communist insurgencies broke out in 1948 in Southeast Asia suggested – at the very least – that a worldwide communist conspiracy was taking shape. The most important events bringing the Cold War to East and Southeast Asia were, however, the victory in 1949 of the communists over the nationalists in the Chinese civil war; the launching in 1950 of an attack by communist North Korea on non-communist South Korea; the emergence in 1950–51 of the Democratic Republic of Vietnam as a fully fledged communist state; and the launching by the Viet-Minh of full-scale military assaults on the French in and around the Tonkin Delta region.

By the early 1950s, therefore, the United States in particular and the West in general saw Southeast Asia as *the* crucial front-line in the global Cold War. The confrontation between the West and communism in Southeast Asia, and the attempts of the United States to develop a security network in the region, were to have a profound effect on the ideological and ethnic divisions within the new nation-states of Southeast Asia.

In the Indochina region, the ideological division in the Vietnamese nationalist movement was sustained, and the United States inherited France's role in propping up what in 1954 became – after the partition of Vietnam at the Geneva Conference – non-communist South Vietnam. This ideological conflict divided the Laotian nationalist movement as well, and helped bring about civil war in 1959.[34] The same destructive process was repeated in Cambodia in 1970.

In the whole northern area of mainland Southeast Asia, the Cold War confrontation badly destabilized the local nation-states. Both ideological camps – the Chinese, Vietnamese, Laotian, Thai and Burmese communists on one side, the Americans and their regional allies on the other – sought to build a network of alliances through, among other means, the exploitation of local ethnic grievances. This process gave a new lease of life to old separatist movements, like that of the Karens, and sustained new separatist movements like those of the Shans and Kachins, which emerged in the late 1950s and early 1960s. In its increasingly desperate attempts in the early and mid-1960s to hold the line against the communist threat in Vietnam and Laos, the United States developed a network of special military relationships with the Indochinese minorities who inhabited the strategically vital highlands that divided Laos and Vietnam. These special relationships helped stimulate a separatist movement among the minorities of the Central Highlands of Vietnam in 1964, and separatist sentiments – if nothing more – among the Hmong minority of Laos.[35]

When the Cold War in the Far East drew to an end in the late 1980s, however, and the dust began to settle in the region, it was discovered that the local nation-states had, against the odds, survived intact. In fact, with two exceptions, all the political entities of Southeast Asia that emerged from the decolonization process have maintained their territorial integrity. The exceptions are the Federation of Malaysia – formed in 1963 by an amalgamation of Malaya, Singapore, Sarawak and Sabah – which Singapore left in 1965; and Portuguese Timor, which was swallowed up by Indonesia in December 1975, while the territory was in a chaotic transitional stage between colonial rule and full independence. It could also be said that, with the possible exception of Burma, the unity of the nation-states of the Southeast Asian region does not appear to be threatened in the immediate future.

Compared to the situation in the Indian sub-continent, it may reasonably be asked why – particularly given the fact that the region was a front-line in the Cold War – this regional stability has been sustained.

Even at the height of the Cold War, it is noticeable that both sides of the ideological divide maintained an unspoken consensus in favour of the unity of the nation-states of the region. Though the United States was occasionally tempted to exploit separatist sentiments in its search for effective allies in building an anti-communist alliance – its 'special relationship' with the minorities of Laos and Vietnam provides a good example – its overwhelming concern was for 'nation-building'. It was a fundamental tenet of the American Third World strategy of the 1960s that communism fed above all on the weaknesses and instabilities of the newly independent states of Asia. The primary task of the West and the United States, therefore, was that of encouraging the unity and strength of these states, in order to counter what were seen as the destabilizing tactics of communism.

For their part, the communists of the region had as much to fear – if not more – from ethnic rebellions and separatist movements as from the Americans. The primary division of the Cold War era was ideological, not ethnic. There may have been communist rebellions in Burma, Thailand, Laos, Cambodia and South Vietnam; but in each country, if the opposing sides were agreed on one thing, it was on maintaining the unity of their respective nations. This basic fact helped create an equilibrium in favour of the unity of those states through all the vicissitudes of the Cold War.

There is no doubt, also, that a collective feeling of regional threat in the 1960s and 1970s – particularly after the unification of Vietnam in 1975, and the apparent global victories of communism in the same period – helped to hold most of the Southeast Asian states together. Overriding security concerns imposed a discipline and a realization that a threat to one state could rapidly mean a threat to all. The ensuing chapters will show many examples where ethnic problems have stretched over national borders. In these circumstances, there is always the temptation for one state to make short-term internal political gains by exploiting the ethnic difficulties of a neighbouring state. But a sense of mutual vulnerability, a fear that the beginning of such a process could lead to a general ethnic and political unravelling that would destabilize the whole region, has helped sustain the sense of a common interest in regional stability.

PART I

Decolonization, Separatism and Loyalism

Introduction

In the lexicon of terms used to define colonialism, 'collaboration' and 'loyalism' are closely connected. However, the term 'collaboration' is normally used to describe a general phenomenon throughout colonized societies: a tendency of certain individuals, families, classes or groups within that society to work with the colonial power. The motives of such collaborators – the term itself has become very loaded – may be varied, and range from ideological conviction to a simple desire for personal gain. The point is that such collaboration is a matter not so much of *identity* as of *inclination*. Loyalism, however, is defined here as a special relationship between a colonial power and a particular community with a distinct identity, normally ethnic or religious, or a combination of both.

Some loyalist communities are created by the very conditions of colonial rule. The most obvious examples are the Eurasian communities throughout Southeast Asia. The Eurasians, however, were unable to develop either any real political coherence or separatist aspirations because of their lack of a territorial base. Most loyalist communities existed as distinct ethnic groupings before the arrival of the respective colonial powers. The circumstances that led to the development of a special and privileged relationship between the colonial power and such groups varied – the chance of long historical contact, a group's history of antagonism to the pre-colonial state, or successful missionary and educational activity – but in all cases they depended on a confluence of perceived interest.

The success or failure of a separatist movement depended on its peripheral position in relation to the nationalist entity claiming independence. 'Peripherality' implies backwardness, and indeed the traditional picture of loyalist communities in Southeast Asia is that of remote, secluded and primitive groups that had often had a hostile tributary relationship with a dominant pre-colonial state. During the colonial era, these groups would normally have maintained a 'special relationship' with the colonial power and would thus have been shielded from the mainstream of economic and political life. During the crucial period of the Second World War and the independence struggles thereafter, these loyalist groups looked to the colonial powers for protection in a period of turbulence, and in return provided the colonial power with military assistance.

This model certainly fits the history of the Kachins, the Chins, the Arakanese Muslims and the Nagas living along the India–Burma border, who provided valuable help for the British in the war against the Japanese. These loyalist connections created local tensions that had very long-lasting consequences after the Second World War. A similar loyalist relationship was developed between the French and some at least of the diverse minority groups living in the mountainous regions between Vietnam, Laos and Cambodia. These so-called *montagnards* were generally insulated, during the period of French rule, from the lowland areas of Laos, Cambodia and Vietnam with which they had traditionally had an uneasy, and sometimes downright hostile, relationship. During the period of revolutionary and nationalist turbulence that lasted in Indochina from 1945 up to 1975 and beyond, the French and the Americans were able to rely on a considerable degree of armed assistance from these *montagnards*. This, too, has had long-term consequences in the region.

The notion that there was a natural link between loyalism, peripherality and economic, cultural and political backwardness would not fit the case of the Straits Chinese of Penang, however, or that of the Karens of Burma, or indeed that of the Christian Ambonese. In the cases of the Straits Chinese of Penang and of the Christian Ambonese in particular, peripherality is a historically relative description of their condition. Penang and Ambon were early epicentres of what later became the British and Dutch empires in Southeast Asia. It was in these conditions that the special relationships developed between the colonial powers and the groups concerned. It was only later, as the colonial power expanded and new political and economic imperatives developed for the colonial powers, that these two regions and groups were marginalized, both geographically and in terms of colonial policy.

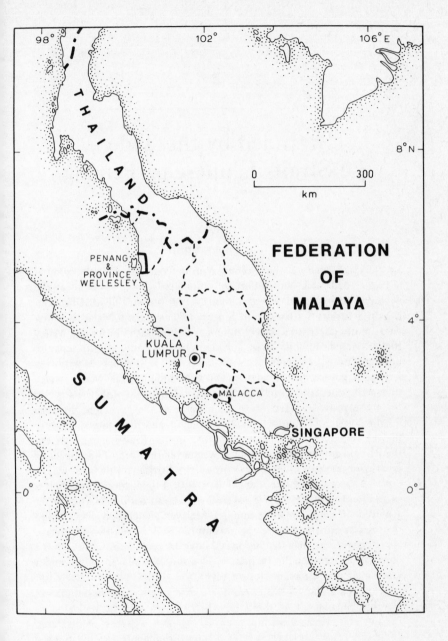

Map 2   The Straits Settlements and Malaya

Stranded by the Tide:
the Straits Chinese of Penang

The background

In the years before the Second World War, the British colonial authority had made some effort to 'rationalize' the government of the Malayan peninsula. However, administration was still divided between the three Straits Settlements of Singapore, Penang and Malacca, which were jointly governed as direct colonies of Britain; the Federated Malay States, comprising four Malay sultanates that had entered into separate protectorate agreements with Britain, but now worked within a federated government structure; and five 'unfederated' Malay States that maintained their exclusive bilateral relationship with Britain.

In the pre-war years, the tension between the economic pressure for the creation of a united, 'modern' Malaya, and the political pressure for the retention of the special identity of the Malay states that the British had undertaken to protect, was never resolved. The impact of the Japanese invasion of Malaya forced the British, on their return, to evolve a long-term policy for Malaya with a view to creating first a united, and ultimately a self-governing Malayan nation. In 1948, after a period of considerable turmoil, a Malayan Federation was created that was essentially an attempt to compromise between the imperative of safeguarding Malay rights in a Malay land, and the desire at the same time to ensure the foundation of a united Malayan nation and a more inclusive Malayan national identity.

A crucial aspect of this attempt to create a new Malayan nation was the dismemberment of the Straits Settlements and the inclusion of Penang and Malacca within a united Malaya. Because of its large Chinese population and powerful economy, Singapore was felt to be – for the time being at least – too indigestible to be absorbed within the Malayan Federation. For a number of economic, geographical and political reasons, but mainly because of the natural instinct to 'tidy up' hitherto disparate systems of government once the decision to expedite national unity and self-government had been reached, Penang and its adjunct territory of Province Wellesley were included within the Malayan Federation (see Map 2). This decision was taken despite its large Chinese majority[1] and the very different character of its society, economy and traditions of government from those of the Malay States.

The economic and political elite of Penang witnessed these developments with growing alarm. Their anxieties focused principally on the questions of economic status and citizenship rights, and, above all, on the perceived dangers of being cut loose from their traditional ties with Singapore and Britain, and swallowed up by an ethnic Malay-dominated nation. These anxieties were given voice through the formation on 13 December 1948 of the Penang Secession Committee.[2] The primary demands of the Committee were that Penang should be excluded from the Malayan Federation, and that it should revert to its former status within the Straits Settlements and retain its traditional links within the British Empire. These demands were formally expressed in a motion put forward in the Penang Settlement Council on 10 February 1949, and subsequently in a petition sent to the government in London in November 1949.[3]

The response of the British government to these demands was polite and sympathetic, but ultimately implacable. There were many cogent reasons why the British were determined to resist the demands of the secession movement, but underlying them all was the central fact that, once the momentum towards Malay nationalist self-assertion had begun in 1946, Britain inevitably pursued a policy of least resistance. Put simply, Britain would have needed to expend more cost and energy, and would have had to confront far more formidable political forces, if it had chosen to disrupt the process of consolidating the Malayan Federation rather than expedite it. The Penang Secession movement fell foul of this iron law governing the process of decolonization, as did secession movements in Burma, Indonesia and Indochina during the same period. The Penang Secession movement soon drifted into obscurity, but the fears for the future that it embodied were substantially justified in the years after independence.

Defining Straits Chinese identity

What, then, were the forces – ethnic, economic and political – and the circumstances that helped forge the Penang Secession movement of 1948–51? As in Hong Kong and Shanghai, the dominating feature of both Singapore and Penang in the nineteenth and early twentieth centuries was the dynamic combination of British administration and an overwhelmingly Chinese immigrant population.[4] With their entrepôt economy and free-port status and their immigrant populations, Singapore and Penang were very distinct – administratively, economically and in ethnic composition – from their neighbouring Malay states, and they were kept separate until after the Second World War by the British colonial administration. But along with the Chinese majority there was in the Straits Settlements a kaleidoscope of disparate ethnic groups and cultures. These distinct cultures existed side by side, and the binding elements of unity were provided by the economy itself, and by the British administration, to which members of the business and professional elite among the Chinese and other ethnic groups were selectively co-opted. Singapore and Penang were, in fact, plural or 'multi-cultural' societies, and they confirm the view that multi-cultural societies thrive best in conditions of imperial rule. Harmony in such a system was guaranteed by an informal alliance of interest and allegiance between the imperial government and the business elites of the various racial groups, and the severe discouragement of all political activity among the rest of the population.[5]

To some degree, the membership of the Penang Secession movement in the late 1940s reflected the diverse ethnic elements of this elite, who were determined to resist any attempt to destroy the special status that Penang and its mixed elite had achieved within the British Empire. In practice, however, the Penang Secession movement was primarily influenced by the Chinese community of Penang. To understand the roots of Penang separatism, therefore, it is necessary to analyse the characteristics of the Chinese business elite that dominated the society, economy, and even ultimately the politics of the Straits Settlements in general, and of Penang in particular.

The majority of the Chinese in the Straits Settlements were recent immigrants from China, non English-speaking and owing primary loyalty to a tangled web of family, clan and regional dialect organizations that had links to the homeland.[6] The elite of Chinese society were, however, very separate. They were defined – and defined themselves – as a special category, generally called the 'Straits Chinese'. Straits Chinese identity was complex. Essentially, however, members of this group possessed the following general characteristics: their families had been living in the region in general, and in the Straits Settlements in particular, for generations; they had acquired the status of British subjects within the Empire; though they had generally maintained their clan and dialect-group links, they tended to speak English and to give their children an English education at one of the prestigious local private schools; and they ran a network of business organizations that were highly influential, even if only informally, within the Straits Settlements.[7]

In his discussion of the 'Baba' Chinese of the Straits Settlements – Chinese, that is, who had at an earlier period intermarried with local Malays, but who were part of the Straits Chinese elite – John Clammer has suggested that the key to their identity was 'political'. The same could be said *a fortiori* of the Straits Chinese as a whole. A 'political' identity implies primarily an identity that is created by special circumstances at a special time, rather than one that has evolved naturally over time. Straits Chinese identity was essentially the confluence of three different foci of loyalty: to China, by blood and roots; to the Malayan region by territorial settlement; and to the British Empire by a combination of interest and sentiment. Straits Chinese identity was a specific affinity forged in a specific place, at a specific time, and as a by-product of a specific role played in a specific political system, the global *Pax Britannica*. Or, as John Clammer puts it:

> they were originally a product of the social relations of a colonial society based on a rigid system of stratification, which however encouraged a certain degree of accommodation from groups who were prepared to take the step (which was not in those days a risky step) of identifying their interests with those of the colonialists.[8]

The search for an identity and a role

In the late nineteenth and early twentieth centuries the Straits Chinese established institutions that were to consolidate their substantial, if informal, position in Straits society. In 1900, Straits Chinese British Associations (SCBAs) were formed, first in Singapore and then in Malacca. In 1903, the Penang Chinese Chamber of Commerce was created; this institution was led by Straits Chinese, even if the bulk of its membership was composed of non English-speaking Chinese.[9] These institutions, among others, played a key role as the Straits Settlements subsequently inched towards greater representative government.

The Straits Chinese were at this time an informal elite trying to stabilize an identity and discover a role in colonial society. As such, they were not very different from other native elite groups in the colonial world at that time. In the space between resistance to the colonial takeover and the development of mass nationalist movements, there was, in the 'golden age' of colonialism before the First World War, an interval of relative political stability. It was during these years that the native intelligentsia – normally sons and daughters of the traditional indigenous elites – underwent what could be called a 'revolution of cultural awareness'. In essence, this revolution was a response to the overwhelming power and apparent cultural, political and economic superiority of European civilization. It was an attempt to adapt traditional civilizations and religions to this new all-conquering presence, in the hope that indigenous societies could thereby be 'dynamized' and made capable of responding to the challenges of the modern world. Because this 'revolution' was largely non-political, the colonial powers themselves – or at least their more enlightened officials – were happy to encourage this process of cultural rediscovery and redefinition.

Examples of this 'revolution of cultural awareness' are to be found everywhere in the colonial world. The years before the First World War formed the high period of pan-Islamic reform in the Middle East and in Muslim India.[10] This was matched, though at a slightly earlier period, by the Bengali cultural and literary renaissance. In Burma and Ceylon, young intellectuals saw the reformation of Theravada Buddhism as the key to the regeneration of their respective societies.[11] In this same pre-war period, movements for Islamic reform were established in the Malayan region and the Dutch East Indies, while Princess Kartini's life came to embody the aspiration to reform and rejuvenate Javanese culture, a process that was carried forward by the 'Budi Utomo' movement formed in 1908.[12]

It is significant that this 'revolution in cultural awareness' was primarily religious and cultural in form, and was only tangentially political. Above all, this revolution was pre-national. Pre-colonial states such as Burma and Vietnam had recently been absorbed into colonial super-states. It was only gradually that modern nationalist movements were formed, and national identity restored and redefined. In other areas, such as the Dutch East Indies, the definition of national identity itself was only beginning to take shape. Nevertheless, the cultural revolutions of pre-1914 were to determine the whole course of politics in the subsequent nationalist era. In some senses, these movements of religio-cultural reform could be described as ranging shots in the development of subsequent nationalist mass movements. They also, however, represented that narrow emphasis on religion and culture that came to be linked with racial or communal exclusiveness. As such, they were sidelined by the secular nationalism of the 1930–60 period, and their influence was only to be reasserted when ethnic and religious tensions re-emerged in the post-colonial era. From yet another perspective, however, the 'revolution of cultural awareness' also helped to shape the ideals and aspirations of the indigenous elite that worked within, and in effect sustained, the colonial system.

The Straits Chinese underwent precisely such a revolution in the years before the First World War, the early stages of which are delineated in the *Straits Chinese Magazine*, started in 1897. The primary objectives of this periodical were to define Straits Chinese identity, to instil a sense of pride in that identity, and, from this all-important base, to encourage a commitment to educational and social reform within the community. The ultimate objective was to persuade both the Straits Chinese community itself and the British authorities that the former could play a positive role in the empire as loyal and well-educated citizens. At the same time, however, contributors to the *Straits Chinese Magazine* were anxious to emphasize their Chinese roots, and to retrieve what was best in Chinese culture from the perceived decayed condition of Chinese civilization.

Straits Chinese identity was, therefore, poised in a delicate balance between Chinese origins on one side, and commitment to citizenship within the British Empire on the other. The *Straits Chinese Magazine* was clearly anxious to dissociate the Straits Chinese from the terminal decay of the Manchu Empire in China – embodied in the xenophobic Boxer Rebellion – and the essentially backward peasant culture of the bulk of the Chinese immigrants in Malaya and the Straits Settlements – embodied in the Secret Society organizations that so alarmed the British authorities.[13] Against the traditional insistence on the part of the Chinese government that all Chinese – whether inside the empire or not – were irrevocably tied to China by the laws of blood affiliation (*ius sanguinis*), it was a central part of the Straits Chinese political programme that *ius soli* should have priority over *ius sanguinis*.[14] In other words, the fact of Chinese origins should not imply an overriding loyalty to the Chinese state for those Chinese communities that found themselves, through choice or circumstance, outside the Manchu Empire.

Ius soli, the notion that primary loyalty should be focused on one's land of abode rather than the affiliation of blood links, lay at the very heart of Straits Chinese identity. The loyalty of the Straits Chinese was directed not towards Britain as such, but towards the British Empire as a political entity; it was focused on the specific territory of the Straits Settlements and British Malaya within that greater political entity.[15] The development of this empire citizenship would depend not on the assertion of loyalty alone, but on a genuine 'cultural revolution' among the Straits Chinese. This would involve, among other things, an emphasis on educational improvement for women as well as men, the shedding of 'backward' and discreditable traditional customs (concubinage, for example), and, above all, a commitment to participation in public affairs.[16]

At the same time, the editors of the *Straits Chinese Magazine* were anxious that the cultural roots of the Straits Chinese should not be abandoned in the rush for progress. It was by no means the intention of the Straits Chinese elite of the early twentieth century to create a deracinated, de-cultured community.[17] What they aspired to was the best of both worlds, where a modern, Westernized education would be combined with an appreciation of the Chinese cultural inheritance. This involved an emphasis not on the provincial dialects and demotic cultures of Overseas Chinese society in Southeast Asia, but on the Mandarin language and the teachings of Confucius.[18] The Straits Chinese sought only a purified and reformed version of what their Chinese inheritance had to offer.

The emphasis on 'Chinese-ness', however, was not merely a matter of cultural pride or nostalgia. At the root of the political vision of the Straits Chinese at this time was their assertion that the British Empire was a multi-racial empire where, ideally, all races could play an equal role. As loyal subjects of the empire, the Straits Chinese resented the fact that, despite their relative prestige at the local level, their colour barred them from equal status, representation or access to administrative posts in the colonial system. The *Straits Chinese Magazine* revealed the indignation that Straits Chinese felt at such manifestations of racial discrimination or anti-Chinese actions as, for example, the ill-treatment of Chinese workers in South Africa, or the pillage of Peking after the Boxer Rebellion.[19] It was a key assertion of the Straits Chinese, reflected in the *Straits Chinese Magazine*, that the conferring of rights and privileges within the empire should be based on loyalty, not racial origin:

> if any man (whether he be Aryan, Mongolian, Turanian or Ethiopian in race) be true, heart and soul, to the British Constitution, and bear perfect allegiance to Her Majesty, then he is a loyal subject of the Queen, a fit member of the British Empire, entitled to all its immunities and privileges.[20]

The inter-war period: political developments among the Straits Chinese

Up to the First World War, the Straits Chinese of Singapore had tended to dominate the agenda and the outlook of the Straits Chinese of the Settlements generally. After the First World War, however, there was a surge of political debate and activity among the Straits Chinese of Penang. The latter already had considerable local influence through the two key Chinese institutions of the colony, the Penang Chinese Chamber of Commerce and the Chinese Town Hall, and these institutions in their turn exercised considerable advisory influence in local government, particularly in the Georgetown Municipal Commission formed in 1913.[21] In 1920, however, it was proposed that the Legislative

Council, which, along with the Executive Council, was the main advisory body in the Straits Settlements, should be expanded to include more unofficial representatives. This proposal stimulated the creation in late 1920 of a Penang Straits Chinese British Association, modelled on that of Singapore, since it was felt by some Straits Chinese at least that the Chinese Town Hall and the Penang Chinese Chamber of Commerce – both of whose memberships contained a large number of Chinese residents who had not yet acquired British Subject status – were inappropriate vehicles for selecting Penang Chinese for the Legislative Council.[22] From 1921 onwards, therefore, the Singapore, Malacca and Penang SCBAs were the principal bodies representing exclusively Straits Chinese interests and concerns in the Straits Settlements.

However, although unofficial representation in the Legislative Council was increased after 1923, it remained limited, with thirteen unofficial representatives overall out of a council of twenty-six, and only three Chinese.[23] Moreover, perhaps because the British, while recognizing the leading role of the Straits Chinese among the Chinese of the Straits Settlements, wanted those leaders to represent all the Chinese and not merely exclusively Straits Chinese interests, the SCBAs did not succeed in gaining any exclusive or dominant position in the inter-war years. Rather, Straits Chinese influence – in Penang and elsewhere – was percolated through business organizations, newspapers such as the *Straits Echo* of Penang, or magazines like the *Malayan Chinese Review*, founded in Penang in 1932. It is in the inter-war years that we see the emergence of a Straits Chinese elite that was to dominate Penang in the 1930s and 1940s. They shared many characteristics: education in the local elite schools, particularly St Xavier's and the Penang Free School; important roles in banking and import–export businesses in Penang; and key positions in the Chinese Town Hall, the Penang Chinese Chamber of Commerce, the Straits Chinese British Association (SCBA) and the Georgetown Municipal Commission.[24]

From these positions of influence, the Straits Chinese of the Settlements campaigned throughout the 1920s and 1930s for a larger say in the government of the Straits Settlements. Their principal objectives were greater unofficial and Chinese representation in the Straits Legislative Council; unofficial representation in the Executive Council; and Straits Chinese access to jobs in the civil service of the Straits Settlements.[25] Though the Straits Chinese were constantly frustrated by the niggardly and belated concessions made by the British authorities, it was clear by the 1930s that their influence was steadily, if slowly, increasing.

When one looks at the writings and speeches of the Straits Chinese during this period, however, it is easy to detect a recurrent note of anxiety and doubt. This reflects that fact that, in the inter-war years, the political climate of Malaya as a whole was beginning to change. These years saw a burgeoning of political activity among the non-elite Chinese in the Malayan peninsula as a whole, and of ethnic consciousness and organization among the indigenous Malays. Much of the non-elite Chinese political activity was, in fact, related not to circumstances in Malaya itself, but rather to the growing political turmoil back in China. This intrusion of radical, 'alien' politics into Malaya alarmed both the Malays and the British authorities. The latter reacted in the late 1920s and 1930s by strictly controlling Chinese political activity, restricting Chinese immigration, taking measures to protect Malay rights to land, and entrenching the 'special relationship' between the Malay sultans and their colonial protectors.[26] At the very time that the Chinese immigrant community in Malaya was being stabilized and domiciled, and was increasingly cut off from the turmoil of the motherland in practical terms, the radical rhetoric of non-elite Chinese politics in Malaya was having the effect of pushing the Chinese community as a whole to the margins of Malayan politics.

These developments cruelly exposed the central dilemmas of Straits Chinese identity that had been apparent ever since the attempt had been made to define that identity in the late nineteenth century. On the one side, Straits Chinese lobbying for greater representation and influence in the Straits Settlements was designed to strengthen the notion that the Straits Chinese had a special, exclusive role within the Settlements and the empire, and to insulate them from the rest of Malaya and the rest of the Chinese community.[27] On the other, the Straits Chinese leaders were well aware that their political influence with the British depended on their links with the whole Chinese community, not only in the Straits Settlements, but throughout the Malayan peninsula. Any marginalization of the Malayan Chinese would, therefore, dramatically weaken the political clout of the Straits Chinese.

It is probably because of this dithering between the notion of themselves as a loyalist elite, and as the natural leaders of the whole Chinese community in Malaya, that the Straits Chinese give an impression of indecisiveness and relative ineffectuality in the inter-war years. Straits Chinese political commentators themselves lamented what was seen as a tendency to factionalism and political apathy, and openly wondered whether the community had the necessary dedication to responsible citizenship that could match their aspirations.[28]

During the course of the inter-war years, the most prescient Straits Chinese became aware that their political destiny was inextricably linked to that of the Chinese community throughout Malaya. Accordingly, we see the gradual emergence during these years of a pan-

Malayan, as opposed to mere Straits Settlements, political consciousness. As early as the 1920s, Tan Cheng Lock of Malacca was talking of the need to develop a 'Malayan consciousness' and to create a 'united self-governing British Malaya'.[29] The reluctance of the British to increase Straits Chinese representation in the Legislative Council beyond a very limited level, or, until 1933, to end the 'colour bar' in the Straits Civil Service, aroused the suspicion of the Straits Chinese that they were regarded not as equal partners, but very much as second-class citizens in the empire.[30] However, it was the attempt of the British in the 1930s to reinforce the concept of Malaya as *tanah Melayu* (the land of the Malays) and their consequent determination to exclude the Straits Chinese from the Malayan Civil Service that finally compelled other influential Straits Chinese leaders – particularly Heah Joo Seang, editor of the *Malayan Chinese Review*, president of the *Hu Yew Seah* (League of Helping Friends), and a leader of Straits Chinese opinion in Penang – to seek to defend Chinese interests on a Malaya-wide basis.[31] Against the British tendency in the 1930s to emphasize a Malaya composed of separate Malay sultanates, Heah Joo Seang, like Tan Cheng Lock, increasingly talked of a united Malaya in which all races would play a role.[32] In some senses, the notion of a united Malaya and the campaign for Chinese access to the Malayan – as opposed to merely Straits Settlements – civil service was simply a continuation of the aspiration expressed in the *Straits Chinese Magazine* at the turn of the century for an empire of multi-racial equality. But now the language was becoming more overtly nationalist and the concept of empire was being expanded beyond the Straits Settlements to the whole peninsula.[33]

The impact of the Second World War on the Straits Chinese on Penang

It seems that the Straits Chinese, and particularly the Straits Chinese of Penang, had reached a crossroads by the end of the 1930s. They might well have become an important part of an emerging Malayan nationalist elite, forging links with the domiciled overseas Chinese community in the Straits Settlements and beyond, and bargaining for political influence and power with the colonial authorities. Or they might have played a leading role in seeking to insulate the Straits Settlements from political developments in Malaya, and develop what might be called a 'Straits Polity'. The options they perceived for themselves were all, however, dependent upon the evolution of imperial policy, and tied to the continuing existence of the British Empire.

Thus, the Japanese invasion of Southeast Asia in December 1941 and the collapse of British imperial power in the region inflicted a blow on the Straits Chinese from which they never recovered as a united community. This successful Japanese takeover of Malaya immediately led to a phase of ruthless persecution of the Chinese community in Singapore, particularly those connected with anti-Japanese patriotic organizations and secret societies. This wave of terror hit Penang in mid-1942. Although the Straits Chinese in Penang escaped the worst of these persecutions, many were badly hit by the severe financial demands that the Japanese imposed as 'reparations' from the Chinese community. For example, Khoo Sian Ewe, a leading figure in the Penang community who had been nominated for the Legislative Council of the Straits Settlements in 1934, had to provide something like Straits $1 million out of the Straits $7 million demanded from the Chinese of Penang.[34] But it was not just a question of the drastic depletion of the inherited wealth of the Straits Chinese. More generally, this privileged community, adapted as it was to the solid tranquillity of the British Empire, found itself unable to adjust to the rough-and-tumble of economic life in war conditions.[35]

The tragedy is that, to the extent that the Straits Chinese *were* able to adapt to Japanese rule, this worked to their long-term disadvantage. As Japanese rule settled down, and they developed an uneasy *modus vivendi* with the native population, so they chose to exploit the Straits Chinese leaders' knowledge of English and administrative experience. The English-speaking Chinese of Malaya, for example, played an important role in the States' Councils that were set up by the Japanese to help their administration. The Penang State Council, which was established in December 1943, was dominated by the Straits Chinese elite, including Khoo Sian Ewe and Heah Joo Seang.[36] Heah Joo Seang also became chairman of the local Overseas Chinese Association, an organization established to facilitate the collection of 'voluntary contributions' to the Japanese war effort.[37] The Penang Straits Chinese, in other words, were drawn into collaboration with the Japanese.

In their switch from collaboration with the British to collaboration – of a sort at least – with the Japanese, the position of the Straits Chinese was no different from that of the *ilustrado* elite of the Philippines in relation to the Americans, or the *priyayi* elite of the Dutch East Indies. On top of this, given Penang's isolation from the centres of resistance to the Japanese in the heart of the Malayan peninsula, and given the huge ideological gap between the Straits Chinese and the Chinese communist guerrillas who led the resistance, it is difficult to see what else they could have done. Nevertheless, the Straits Chinese of Penang at the end of the war found themselves economically weakened and, to a degree, politically discredited. It was only in March 1946, for example, that Heah Joo Seang was finally cleared of charges of collaboration on account of his chairmanship of the Overseas Chinese Association.[38]

During the course of the war, the Straits Chinese were in effect increasingly marginalized in terms of political influence with the British. It is true that the eminent Malaccan Straits Chinese leader, Tan Cheng Lock, who spent the war in exile in South India, did, to a limited degree, 'have the ear' of the British authorities. From this vantage point, he formed in late 1943 his own 'Oversea–Chinese Association' and lobbied hard for his ideal of a united Malaya with equal rights for all races; to some extent, this aspiration was reflected in Britain's post-war plans for Malaya.[39] But in the crucial years between 1942 and 1945, Britain gave priority to military considerations, and was mainly interested in forging links with any group that could 'deliver' effective aid against the Japanese – hence the temporary alliance of convenience between the British and the guerrilla organization of the Malayan Communist Party (MCP). Although it would not be true to say that Britain's wartime planning for the shape of a post-war Malaya – which began in earnest in 1943 – was solely designed to 'reward' the Malayan Communist Party, it is clear that, until the very moment of the Japanese surrender, the British military was expecting to rely heavily on communist help in the event of an invasion of Malaya.[40] It is this key military imperative that explains Britain's willingness to bypass the old elites – Malay *and* Straits Chinese – on whom they had hitherto relied.

Post-1945: Penang and the slide to secession

The Malayan Union plan, which was formulated between 1943 and 1945, announced in October 1945 and implemented in April 1946, was anathema to the Malays, but at the same time did not meet the aspirations of the Straits Chinese.[41] The plan did at last create a united Malayan state, and it conferred equal citizenship rights on all inhabitants of that state, 'irrespective of race, who regarded Malaya as their true home and the object of their loyalty'.[42] However, Singapore, with its entrepôt economy and its huge Chinese population, was felt to be too economically and politically indigestible to be included in the new Malayan state. Singapore's crucial importance as a military base within the British Empire also determined Britain's decision to exclude Singapore from the Malayan Union.[43] Penang and Malacca were, however, included, and the Straits Settlements Repeal Bill of March 1946 put an end to the historic link between Singapore, Malacca and Penang.[44]

The Malayan Union plan highlighted not only the ambiguity of the political aspirations of the Straits Chinese but ultimately also the ambiguity of their identity. While they could only welcome the notion of equal citizenship and opportunities for all races in Malaya, they shrank from the prospect of being cut loose from the safe moorings of the Straits Settlements and thrown into the turbulent politics of the new Malaya. The privations of the Japanese occupation, coupled with the sheer struggle for survival of that period, had had the effect of turning the whole of the mixed Penang elite community – Chinese and non-Chinese alike – in on itself and away from the Malayan mainland, and had bred a special 'Penang patriotism'.[45] This sense of threat from the mainland was sharply increased by the decision of the British Military Administration in January 1946 to end Penang's duty-free status. It seemed to the whole economic elite of Penang that the very economic rationale of Penang's entrepôt economy was now at stake, and the Colonial Office received a torrent of protest from Penang at the beginning of 1946 against the plan to break up the Straits Settlements and impose the Malayan Union. The Penang Chinese Chamber of Commerce played a leading role in this protest, but it is significant that the Penang Indian Chamber of Commerce and even the Penang Muslim Chamber of Commerce joined the protest.[46] In the face of this united and influential opposition, the Colonial Office grudgingly restored Penang's free-port status in June 1946.[47]

At the very time, in fact, that the British government restored Penang's free-port status, they were already beginning to rethink the whole Malayan Union structure.[48] The informal alliance of interest that had drawn the British and the Malayan Communist Party together dissolved with the Japanese surrender, and Chinese radical movements, which in many senses dominated Malaya at this time, were not prepared to cooperate with any British 'colonialist' structure of government. Equally the Chinese elite – principally the Straits Chinese – had been too weakened and marginalized by the war to assert their authority in support of the plan. In any case, anxiety about the British policy of breaking up the Straits Settlements and detaching Singapore from Malaya merely added to the fatal hesitations of the Chinese leadership. Conversely, the Malays united in protest against a system of government that effectively ended the notion of *tanah Melayu*. In March 1946, the United Malays National Organization (UMNO) was formed, and the British found themselves confronted by a degree of political mobilization and unity among the Malays that they had never witnessed before.[49] Faced by the divided counsels or apathy of the Chinese community on one side, and by the determined stand of the Malays on the other, the British inevitably reacted by bowing to the prevailing wind and, in consultation with Malay leaders and in the teeth of belated protest by the Chinese community, replaced the Malayan Union with a new federated structure, the Malayan Federation.

Generally speaking, the new Federation proposals restored the concept of Malaya as a federation of Malay sultanates and as *tanah Melayu*. This latter was emphasized by the right of the Malay sultans to be consulted by the High Commissioner on immigration matters and by the new citizenship plans.[50] These plans gave priority to Malay culture and identity in the definition of Federal citizenship, since they conferred automatic citizenship on all Malay subjects of the respective Sultans. For non-Malays, citizenship was no longer – as in the original Malayan Union plan – available to all those 'who regarded Malaya as their true home and the object of their loyalty'. Eligibility now depended on certain stringent conditions. Even for British subjects living in Penang and Malacca – a definition that included the Straits Chinese – Federal citizenship would only be available if they had been born in those settlements and had lived there continuously for a number of years. The qualifications for citizenship for British subjects born outside Penang and Malacca were even more stringent.[51] Although the States' rights were emphasized, and Penang itself was provided with a 'Settlement Council' that had local legislative powers equivalent to those of the Malay States, real power resided in the centre at Kuala Lumpur, which was to be dominated by a British high commissioner, a Federal Executive Council, and a Legislative Council where Malays would have a majority of seats.[52] Singapore, which had been excluded from the Malayan Union, also remained outside the Malayan Federation, which officially came into being in February 1948.

Of the Straits Chinese leaders, only Tan Cheng Lock responded rapidly to Britain's obvious shift between 1946 and 1948 from a Chinese-orientated to a Malay-orientated policy. In July 1946, he played a leading role in sending a petition to the British government demanding that 'all sections of Malayan opinion' be consulted if any changes were to be made to the Malayan Union plan.[53] In the next month his local power base, the Malaccan Chinese Chamber of Commerce, created the Malacca Chinese Union, which in December 1946 formed the conservative wing of the All-Malayan Council for Joint Action, an organization which came into being with the specific objective of protecting the concept of a united democratic Malaya.[54] In December 1946, Tan Cheng Lock outlined in a memorandum his aspiration for a united Malaya, including Singapore, with an equal citizenship and a structure that would rapidly move towards democracy.[55]

In contrast, the Penang Straits Chinese leaders dithered between the attractions of a united Malaya composed of equal citizens on the one hand, and protection of their Straits identity and privileges on the other. Now they found themselves potentially confronted by the worst of both worlds: merger with an overtly Malay-dominated state that was clearly – whatever the intended time-span – on the road to self-government.

As the Federation plan moved from the drawing-board to actual realization in 1947 and 1948, the anxieties of the Penang Straits Chinese began to crystallize. The future of Penang's status as a free port remained uncertain through 1948, while the Colonial Office considered the tax structure of the whole Federation.[56] Wider than this consideration, however, was the fear that the interests of the entrepôt economy of Penang would be subordinated to those of the primary-producing export economy of the Malayan mainland, and that the wealthy, modern economy of Penang would become a 'milch-cow' for the more backward Malay States.[57] Penang, they also feared, would be not only economically burdened but politically marginalized. Already there were clear signs that the Malays would be able to entrench themselves in privileged positions in the administrative and educational systems of the Federation.[58] The Straits Chinese of Penang and Malacca would, in other words, become second-class citizens in an alien state, dominated by the Malays and run for Malay benefit, with no guarantee that this state would not in the future sever its links with the British Empire and drift towards racial partnership with the radical and unstable Indonesian Republic.[59] In the event of that happening, the final guarantee of the Straits Chinese – their British subject status – would become worthless.

The first clear sign of Penang Straits Chinese resistance to what was seen as a drift towards the creation of a Malay-dominated state came in December 1946, when the Penang Chinese Chamber of Commerce, the Chinese Town Hall and the Straits Chinese British Association of Penang united to form the Penang Chinese Constitutional Consultative Committee. In March 1947 this Consultative Committee sent a petition to the Secretary of State for the Colonies, pointing out that it would be a violation of the United Nations' Declaration on Non Self-governing Territories to change the status of Penang without the consent of its inhabitants.[60] The overriding anxiety expressed in the petition was that the Straits Chinese would become second-class citizens in a Federation based on the principle of *tanah Melayu*, and their principal request was that Penang be excluded from a united Malaya unless or until rights of equal citizenship could be guaranteed in that state.[61]

This petition, confined as it was to the Chinese, and principally Straits Chinese, elite of Penang, is perhaps the clearest expression of the anxieties and aspirations of the Straits Chinese at this time. It makes clear that these anxieties did not focus solely on the question of the economic status of Penang, but also on fundamental issues of political rights. Roughly a year later, in February 1948, Heah Joo Seang repeated this point in an article in the *Straits Times* entitled 'Federal misgivings of the Straits-born'.[62] In very strong terms, Heah Joo Seang protested against the idea that the Straits Chinese of Penang should trade their status as British subjects under the British Empire for an uncertain future within a Malay-controlled Federation. He called on all Straits Chinese to unite to protect Penang's status as a 'separate entity' and, in a subsequent letter to the *Straits Times*, he appealed to the spirit of interracial togetherness that had held Penang together during the war.[63] Even as the Federation was being set up, the Penang separatist agenda was taking shape.

During the summer of 1948, therefore, the accumulated fears of the Penang Straits Chinese might possibly in any case have led to a political crisis within the Federation. However, two major developments stimulated a shift to drastic action on the part of the normally timid Straits Chinese. The first was the outbreak of communist insurgent activity in Malaya in 1948 and the subsequent declaration of a state of emergency. In the first place, since the Malayan Communist Party and its ancillary organizations were almost entirely Chinese, the emergency had the immediate effect of weakening the political clout of the Chinese community in the Federation and further marginalizing them.[64] Secondly, and stemming from this, there was a real prospect that the whole Chinese community without distinction would be penalized and have their legal rights restricted by emergency measures. Indeed, by the end of 1948, it was proposed by the government of the Federation to extend to Penang a banishment ordinance and the right of the Public Prosecutor to appeal against acquittals in the courts.[65] Already, it seemed, the Straits Chinese were being given a dramatic example of the dangers of linking their prosperous and peaceful island with the turbulent ideological and racial politics of mainland Malaya.

On top of this, Dato Onn bin Jaafar, leader of UMNO and thereby *de facto* of the Malay community as a whole, made some highly provocative comments in an interview in London on 10 November 1948. He asserted that Malays, as the 'rightful owners' of Malaya, should have greater representation in government; that their 'paramount and special' position should be guaranteed in the constitution; that financial measures should be taken to alleviate the problem of indebtedness among the Malay peasantry; and that Malays should have a greater proportion of administrative appointments.[66] All these demands confirmed the worst fears of the Penang elite.

The Penang secession movement

As discontent in Penang came to a head in late 1948, so moves for secession took shape. The initial impetus for concrete steps was probably provided by the *Straits Echo* of Penang and the (European) Penang Chamber of Commerce under the leadership of D.A. Mackay.[67] In November 1948, the Penang Chamber of Commerce asked the Penang Chinese Chamber of Commerce whether they would be interested in forming a movement designed to get Penang out of the Malayan Federation, in order that it might rejoin Singapore as a Straits Settlement. The initial reaction of the Penang Chinese Chamber of Commerce was rather to favour a policy of working for Singapore's entry into the Federation.[68] However, by early December 1948 an almost irresistible momentum for secession was building up: on 4 December 1948, the Penang Straits Chinese British Association voted for a policy of secession, and this was unanimously backed by an emergency general meeting of the Penang Chinese Chamber of Commerce on 12 December 1948.[69] Support followed from the Settlement of Penang Association, the Penang Indian Chamber of Commerce and the Penang Eurasian Association – in effect, the bulk of the non-official professional and business elite of the island. At a meeting in the Chinese Town Hall on 13 December 1948, 200 against twelve of those present resolved to 'adopt all constitutional means to obtain the secession of the Settlement of Penang from the Federation of Malaya' and to set up a Secession Committee to implement these objectives.[70]

The names of those who voted for secession and thereafter formed the Penang Secession Committee at the meeting of 13 December reveal that all the major business and ethnic organizations, with the exception of those of the Malays, supported the idea of secession.[71] Leading figures in the Eurasian community and in the recently resuscitated Penang Indian Chamber of Commerce were clearly concerned about the political and, possibly more important, economic consequences of the absorption of Penang into the Federation. More surprisingly, perhaps – and certainly more annoying to the Malays – were the facts that the (mainly Indian) Penang Muslim Chamber of Commerce initially supported secession, and that its secretary, A.M. Abu Bakar, joined the Secession Committee.[72] This caused some embarrassment for the Penang Indian Muslims, since Abu Bakar was also their representative in the Settlement Council, and had been chosen as such at a meeting held by the Penang Muslim League.[73] Abu Bakar rapidly distanced himself from the Secession Committee when he saw the storm that his action had caused, and pointed out that the Penang Muslim Chamber of Commerce had supported secession for purely economic reasons. There was certainly some justification for this claim, since the Penang Muslim Chamber of Commerce had taken an equally strong line in early 1946 against the inclusion of Penang in a Malayan Customs Union.[74] Clearly, what particularly worried Indian business interests in late 1948 was the fact that, while Penang remained for the time being a free port, Province Wellesley had lost its free-port status. But it was a combination of Straits Chinese organizations and the European Penang Chamber of Commerce that dominated the Penang secession movement. The chairman of the Secession Committee was also the Chairman of the Penang Chamber of Commerce, D.A. Mackay, and the three key sub-committees of the Secession Committee for political, administrative and economic matters were headed by two Chinese and a European.[75]

Put together, these organizations and individuals represented the non-official elite of Penang, and their natural *modus operandi* was to negotiate at the elite level. After the forming of the Secession Committee, they made no effort to create a mass base of support in Penang, but rather tried to work through institutions susceptible to their influence. In the teeth of Malay threats and British pressure, leading members of the secession movement tried to push through a motion in favour of secession from the Federation in the Penang Settlement Council on 10 February 1949. The motion was narrowly defeated, fifteen to ten, by a combination of official votes and a few unofficial votes.[76] A few days later, the Penang Secession Committee decided to take their campaign to a higher level and petition the British Government itself.[77] After some considerable delay, during which the British High Commissioner, Sir Henry Gurney, tried to persuade the Secession Committee to modify the wording, the petition was finally sent to London at the end of November 1949.[78] Although the Colonial Office never contemplated conceding the demand for Penang's secession, the Penang Secession Committee and the Penang Chinese Chamber of Commerce were given a further chance to air their grievances directly to the Secretary of State for the Colonies at the end of May 1950, when he visited Penang in the course of a general tour of Malaya.[79]

From the petition itself, press comments on that petition, and the various representations made to James Griffiths, Secretary of State for the Colonies, it is possible to gain an overall idea of the anxieties and the aspirations of the Penang secession movement. The basic economic fear was that Penang's trading interests would become peripheral to the overall concerns of Kuala Lumpur; and that while Penang would be contributing disproportionately to the expenses of the Emergency and to the more backward economies of the Malay States, investment urgently needed for its own development would have a low priority.

To this general fear was added the specific grievance that Province Wellesley had been detached from the duty-free economy of Penang.[80] The main political fear was that the Malays would dominate the government of the Federation and use that power for the benefit of their own community. Fears that the Malayan Federation would effectively become a Malay nation appeared to be justified by the unequal citizenship proposals, and indications that Malays would have privileged access to educational scholarships and government jobs. More generally, the Penang secessionists anticipated that Malaya might drift away over time from the orbit of the British Empire, and into the turbulent waters of Asian nationalist politics.[81] As a Penang Chinese Chamber of Commerce memorandum of 30 May 1950 to the British government put it, the people of Penang and the Straits Chinese were afraid

> that in the future they may be handed over to the tender mercies of non-British subjects who are already showing signs of fostering that narrow type of nationalism which invariably carries with it discrimination against those who are not of their religion and race.[82] (See Appendix 1.)

The Penang secession movement was a classic separatist movement in that the bedrock of its demands was negative: that it should be excluded from a Malay-dominated Malaya. But what future did the separatist leaders envisage for a Penang that had been detached from the Federation? At first sight, their aims seem to contain a mixture of loyalism and nostalgia. Specifically, their petition requested that Penang's status as a 'colony of the Straits Settlements' be restored, and that the Straits Settlements should then be allowed to evolve a political future for themselves at their own pace.[83] At the core of this demand was a loyalist nostalgia for the stability and racial harmony of pre-war Penang: 'the people of this Settlement realize that British leadership is the only real factor that will weld together, into one complete whole, the various races who inhabit this Settlement'.[84] This combination of loyalism, nostalgia and Penang patriotism was most forcibly expressed by the *Penang Gazette and Straits Chronicle* at the time of the forming of the Secession Committee: 'A new Penang is waiting to be built – a Penang calling for courage. Let us hope that the courage which inspired and helped to create our great past will now move our present leaders in their endeavours to build a more glorious future for Penang.'[85]

Beneath this seeming unanimity of purpose, however, different priorities and agendas can be detected. While the European members of the Secession Committee, particularly D.A. Mackay himself, tended to cling to the maintenance of the British Empire link, one can detect a slightly different emphasis among some of the Straits Chinese.[86] This is particularly evident in the language used in its various representations by the Penang Chinese Chamber of Commerce, highlighting as it did Penang's right to self-determination.[87] Here, and elsewhere, there was at least a glimmer of ambiguity concerning their feelings about what might be called an imperial polity on the one hand, and a Chinese polity on the other. For the Penang Chinese Chamber of Commerce and the Chinese- and English-language newspapers of Malaya, the priority was not so much the maintenance of the imperial link *per se*, as the link with Chinese-dominated Singapore. As the Chinese-language newspaper *Kwong Wah* put it, the preferred solution was for Singapore to join the Federation and thus prevent the danger of a Malay-dominated Malaya. Only if this proved to be impossible should a separate Straits Settlements colony be reconstituted.[88]

The British response: new political perspectives

As has already been seen, circumstances dictated that the British government was bound to reject the idea of Penang's secession from the Federation. Although sympathetic to the anxieties of the Penang elite, and aware of Penang's sense of its special historical status, the British government had in the wake of the failure of the Malayan Union established a political partnership with the Malays that was far too valuable to be jettisoned for the sake of local sensitivities.[89] The Secretary of State for the Colonies did not formally reply to the petition for secession until 19 September 1951, but in the lengthy intervening period between the sending of the petition and the British reply, there was considerable discussion of the aspirations of the Penang separatists, both in London and in Kuala Lumpur.[90] The reply of September 1951 left no room for negotiation on the issue of the status of Penang in the Federation, but it argued that, since Penang had been given the equivalent constitutional rights of a state within the system, Penang's political leaders would be perfectly capable of negotiating to rectify any grievances they might have within the framework of the Federation. The British were able to point to the fact that, in the wake of a general survey of the tariff regime of Malaya, Penang's free-port status (minus Province Wellesley) had been guaranteed by the Federation of Malaya in 1949.[91] On top of this, there was at least a hint that Britain was prepared to consider amending the citizenship regulations in favour of the Malayan Chinese.[92]

The British trump card, however, was the question of Singapore. This was because it was above all the issue of Singapore that exposed the ambiguities and the divisions of the Penang secession movement. While the non-Chinese in the secession movement may have been quite happy in the end with a purely Penang-based political strategy, the Straits Chinese of Penang were throughout this period dithering between what might be called a 'Penang polity', a 'Straits polity' and a 'Malayan Chinese polity'. When the secession movement started at the end of 1948, it is significant that Chinese opinion, both in Penang and in Malaya as a whole, expressed a preference for Singapore to be included in the Federation as the ideal solution for Penang's discontents.[93] The British authorities were well aware that many sections of Chinese elite opinion in Penang – particularly the Penang Chinese Chamber of Commerce – regarded Penang secession as second-best to Singapore accession.[94] While, therefore, making sure that the question of Singapore's future integration was not publicly pushed to a degree that would alarm and alienate the Malays, the British were able at least to hint at the possible inclusion of Singapore in the future, and therefore to suggest that Penang's secession would be premature.[95]

It would, however, be incomplete to suggest – as this analysis of Britain's reaction to the secession movement might imply – that Britain had by 1948 simply opted for a 'Malay' Malaya, and were prepared to use any argument to inveigle Penang to accept this. In fact, developments in Malaya in 1948, particularly the beginning of the guerrilla campaign by the Malayan communists, persuaded the British of the need to look more closely at the whole question of 'nation-building' in Malaya. At first sight, of course, it seems clear that the overwhelmingly Chinese-dominated character of the communist insurgency drew the British ever closer to the Malay community; certainly the emergency was another powerful reason why the British were determined not to antagonize the Malays by making any concessions on Penang's secession demands.[96] On the other hand, the communist insurrection was a sign of the extent to which a section at least of the Chinese community in Malaya had become alienated from the political system. There was, therefore, a growing recognition by the British that national unity, political stability and economic welfare in Malaya depended on greater efforts to draw the Chinese into the political system as equals. The British saw both the communist emergency and the Penang secession movement as signs of the dangers that could arise if the Chinese became convinced that the Federation would lead to a Malay-dominated independent Malaya.

In 1948 and 1949, British policy began tentatively to move back to the notion that the Chinese needed to be given a greater political stake, and that the ultimate goal should be the creation of a united Malaya based on racial partnership. In this respect British policy was increasingly converging with the policy that had been advocated by Tan Cheng Lock since the 1920s, and that had attracted some of the Straits Chinese leaders in Penang before the Second World War. At the end of 1946 – just as the Malayan Union experiment was collapsing – Tan Cheng Lock had written a highly significant memorandum which suggested a political agenda for the future entirely different from that later pursued by the Penang separatists. The memorandum argued for the creation of a 'United Democratic Malaya' – including the Straits Settlements – with equal citizenship for those who lived in Malaya and regarded it as their single focus of allegiance; for the creation of a pan-Malayan Chinese organization to protect and promote Chinese interests in Malaya; for a united front between this organization and Malay political interests in order to negotiate with the British colonial authorities; and, above all, for the creation of a democratic Malaya where 'the different communities, while being politically united, can maintain their own intellectual, cultural and spiritual life'.[97] Not surprisingly, therefore, Tan Cheng Lock quickly and adamantly rejected the policy of the Penang separatists when they embarked on their venture two years later, and he recommended that the Straits Chinese should instead join with other Malayan Chinese to work for a new Malaya which would combine political unity with cultural diversity.[98]

That British policy was increasingly aware of the need to build a new consensus between the races of Malaya is best shown by the decision at the end of 1948 to encourage informal consultations between Malay and Chinese leaders. In January 1949, these meetings began under the chairmanship of Malcolm MacDonald, the British Commissioner-General in Southeast Asia, and the grouping, enlarged in subsequent meetings to include Indian, Eurasian, Sinhalese and European representation, became known as the Communities Liaison Committee.[99] The early meetings of the Communities Liaison Committee between January and March 1949 were almost sabotaged by the fact that the Penang Secession Committee was at the height of its activity at this very time; the fact that one Penang Straits Chinese leader, Lee Tiang Keng, was simultaneously a member of the Communities Liaison Committee and the Penang Secession Committee led to accusations of bad faith from the Malay members.[100]

But the survival of the Communities Liaison Committee, coupled with the formation in January 1949 of the Malayan Chinese Association by Tan Cheng Lock along the lines of his 1946 memorandum, was the clearest possible sign that a new policy of interracial partnership was taking shape.[101] In essence, the Malayan Chinese Association and the Communities Liaison Committee offered the Straits Chinese of Penang a way back to the centre of the political process. Even though the

Communities Liaison Committee did not immediately 'deliver' on the central issue of relaxing the citizenship rules, it did help to create a new political climate that was crucial for the Straits Chinese of Penang. In a sense, as far as the Straits Chinese were concerned, their support for secession had been an expression of their growing fear that the political agenda had been slipping away from their power to influence it. So long as there existed an opportunity to play an equal role in determining the future of Malaya as a whole, and a possibility that Singapore might be included in Malaya as a counter-weight to Malay political power, the idea of Penang's secession had not surfaced as an issue. It was only when the implementation and consolidation of the Federation plan and the concept of *tanah Melayu* seemed irreversible that the Straits Chinese had put their weight behind secession, and had thereby given the movement credibility.

Conclusion

In the face of British determination to maintain the Federation structure and the more encouraging climate created by the Malayan Chinese Association and Britain's clear recognition of the need to draw the Chinese leadership back to the centre of the political process, Penang separatism withered and died in the early 1950s. Thereafter the Straits Chinese were increasingly drawn into abandoning their 'Straits' polity, and into participating in a new 'Malaya' polity. The Straits Chinese played an important role in the Malayan Chinese Association in the 1950s and 1960s, and their cosmopolitan contacts, bolstered by their knowledge of the English language, compensated to some degree for their lack of a mass political base.[102]

But this shift of political orientation was just one measure of a profound transformation of Straits Chinese identity during the turbulent post-war years. The keystone of the identity of the Straits Chinese had been allegiance to and identification with the British Empire. With the removal of this keystone after the Second World War – of which Britain's refusal to support the idea of a revived Straits Settlements was the final and most brutal evidence – the traditional identity of the Straits Chinese simply collapsed. Straits identity gradually merged into Malayan Chinese identity, and the next generation of Straits Chinese were to become virtually indistinguishable in terms of identity and culture from their non-Straits Chinese elite counterparts. Tan Cheng Lock's vision of a pan-Malayan Chinese community, proud of their Chinese origin but owing their sole commitment and allegiance to Malaya, playing an equal role in the government of a democratic state, has been at least partially realized.[103]

It is also worth noting, however, that the fears expressed by the Straits Chinese in general and the Penang Secession Committee in particular were, in fact, to a great extent justified by the subsequent history of independent Malaya. Despite the creation of the Malaysian Federation in 1963, the Straits Settlements link between Penang and Singapore was in the end definitively severed; Malay inhabitants of Malaya did retain their privileged citizenship status; there has been discrimination in favour of the Malays in the administration, access to education, access to government credit and in other areas; Penang's free-port status, retained for a while, was finally terminated in 1968; the Commonwealth links came to mean less and less to a state which increasingly looked to the Pacific Rim or the Islamic Middle East for its natural links of affiliation; and, in sum, Penang did indeed become, as the secessionists had feared, a marginalized region in a Malay-dominated state.[104]

Despite the reassurances that the British government gave the Secession Committee, and despite the positive steps they subsequently took to try to make the Federation more palatable for the Straits Chinese, Colonial Office officials were well aware that they were throwing Britain's former loyal subjects into an uncertain future. The Straits Chinese of Penang would now have to defend themselves in a state where they would always be at an inherent disadvantage and where, possibly, the Malays, 'in order to preserve a position which they cannot hold by their own merits, may resort to desperate measures'. This was the basic fear that lay at the heart of the Penang secession movement, and, as one Colonial Office official further noted:

> nothing the Secretary of State could say to the Penang people could really allay this deep-seated fear. The short answer to these people is that there is no real practical alternative to Penang forming an integral part of the Federation and that it is up to them to make their voices felt in the counsels of the Federation. That is not very strong comfort.[105]

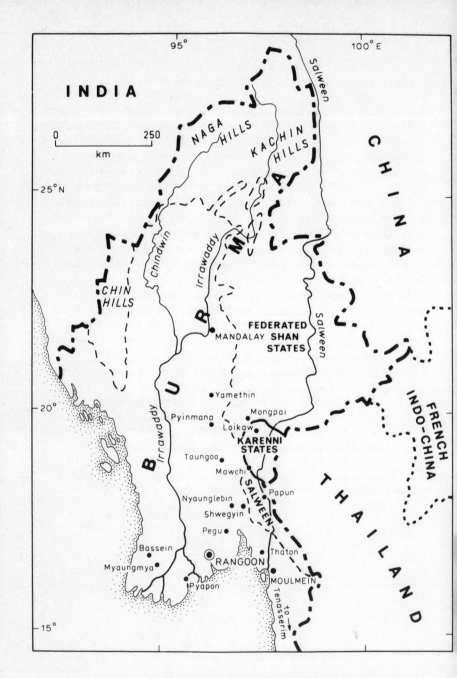

Map 3 Burma in the colonial period

3

Anatomy of a Betrayal:
the Karens of Burma

The Karens and the British: development of
a loyalist relationship

While the Penang Secession Committee was embarking at the end of 1948 on its constitutional campaign for separation from the Malayan Federation, another loyalist community, the Karen people – the largest ethnic minority group of Burma – was sliding towards an all-out separatist rebellion directed at the newly independent Union of Burma. The Penang secession movement gently slid into oblivion between 1948 and 1951; the Karen separatist rebellion has endured to the present day.

Although Karen identity is difficult to define, certain basic elements can be outlined. The broad generic term 'Karen' covers a number of sub-groups that share common linguistic (Sino-Tibetan, possibly related to the Tibeto-Burman sub-group) and cultural characteristics, and inhabit a common geographic region stretching from the southern Shan area on the Burma–Thailand border down to Tenasserim.[1] In the region between the Irrawaddy Delta and the foothills of the range dividing Burma and Thailand, Karen communities have in the modern historical era lived side by side – but not together – with ethnic Burmans and Mons (or Talaing). There were, however, no sophisticated or unified political organizations linking the dispersed Karen villages in the pre-colonial era, and there was no binding memory of a historic Karen state. The main feature distinguishing the condition of the Karen people was that of a subordinate, tributary and generally hostile and suspicious relationship with the Burmese state.[2]

The Karens' perception of their own history – so much more important for the development of a national identity than the objective definitions of ethnographers – certainly confirms this picture. The Karen Memorial of 26 September 1945 (see Appendix 2), presented to the British government as part of the campaign for the right to Karen self-determination, stated bluntly: 'Over a hundred years ago, before the British ever set foot in Burma, the Burmese kings and the Burmese people literally made slaves of the Karens, and persecuted them generally.'[3] 'Then came the British,' the Memorial continues, 'not only as a liberator, but also as a Guardian Angel, maintaining law and order, and preserving Peace and giving Protection.'[4]

Though modern Karen nationalists might not entirely agree with this rosy picture, there is little doubt that it was the British invasion of the region that defined Karen identity in the modern national sense and gave it coherence. The British were able to exploit Karen–Burman hostility in their step-by-step takeover of, first, Tenasserim, then Lower Burma, and finally Upper Burma, between 1826 and 1885. Because of their strategic territorial position, a friendly relationship with the Karens was enormously useful in the first stages of the British takeover of Lower Burma. The Karens also played a key role in the prolonged and difficult pacification campaigns of 1885 and 1886 in both Upper and Lower Burma.[5] Reciprocally, the Karens felt confident and safe within the new environment of British power. Very quickly, a classic 'loyalist' relationship developed between the British and the Karens.

This loyalist relationship, however, contained many ambiguities. In the first place, it would be a mistake to exaggerate the unity of Karen identity, even in the heyday of British rule. One can distinguish at least five different zones of separate Karen identity and community, which in itself emphasizes the geographic dispersal and cultural diversity of the Karen people. There were the Karen villages coexisting with other communities in the southern Shan States. To the south of the Shan States lay a tangle of Karen (or, as they were called, Karenni) statelets tucked away on the Thai border, so remote that they were never incorporated by the British into Burma proper, but entered into a separate feudatory agreement with the British.[6] Further south, along the highlands and foothills of the Burma–Thai border, was the Karen heartland: a patchwork of animist-Karen and Christian-Karen villages administered by the British on one side and the Siamese on the other. Then there were the Karen villages that intermingled with Burmese and Mon villages in a strip running parallel to the Karen heartland from Pyinmana to Tenasserim. Finally, there was the Karen population of the Irrawaddy Delta itself, particularly concentrated in the lower Delta towns of Bassein, Myaungmya and Pyapon.

The British–Karen relationship was not, therefore, a simple matter of an imperial power giving protection to, and gaining reciprocal loyalty from, a backward, oppressed and peripheral community. There were Karen communities at the very edge and at the centre of Burma; there were Karen areas that had scarcely been penetrated, let alone developed, and yet the Karen elite was disproportionately well-educated.[7] In some standard respects, however, the loyalist relationship between the Karens and the British hinged on the issue of security. The Karens provided vital military support for the British in the first two Burma wars, and, in 1885 and 1886, they were a crucial factor in the pacification of eastern Burma when the ethnic-Burman police proved to be unreliable.[8] The unsuitability – or, more important, the political unreliability – of ethnic Burmans, led the Indian government to pursue after 1925 a policy of recruiting ethnic minorities – particularly Karens, Chins and Kachins – for the armed forces in Burma.[9] Even among the minorities, the Karens played a disproportionate role in the army and the police: of the four battalions of the Burma Rifles, for example, two were exclusively Karen.[10] When the Karen leadership was making its claim for self-determination in 1945, it not unnaturally reminded the British government of the crucial role that Karens in the Burma Rifles had played in maintaining the very precarious peace of Burma in the whole period of British rule.[11]

However, the principal books that helped forge and define the modern Karen identity – D.M. Smeaton's *The Loyal Karens of Burma* (1887), H.I. Marshall's *The Karen People of Burma* (1922), Dr San C. Po's *Burma and the Karens* (1928) and Ian Morrison's *Grandfather Longlegs* (1947) – are all agreed that the key to the creation of a Karen national identity was the activity of American and other missionaries in the Karen region through the nineteenth century. Traditional messianic expectations among the Karens probably made them unusually receptive to the Christian message and, from the late 1820s onwards, the American Baptist Mission in particular was able to entrench itself among the Karen community. Not only was a pastoral network established in the Karen villages – a network that to some degree displaced the traditional pattern of village authority – but important educational institutions were set up, including Judson College in Rangoon. The need to translate the Bible into local languages led to the institution of writing systems for the two main Karen dialects.[12]

It is important to note the particular impact that this development had on Karen society and identity. Without the intervention of the British and of the missionaries, it is probable that the Karen communities in the plains areas would over time have converted to the dominant religion of Burma, Buddhism, and would gradually have merged into mainstream ethnic-Burman society. This process was already well under way by the time that the British took over Burma. Indeed, one of the main problems that contributed to the unreliability of the census that the British took in 1931 in Burma was the difficulty in distinguishing between Buddhist Burmans and Buddhist Karens in the villages of south Burma.[13] The arrival of the Christian Missions ruptured this process, and subsequently a new Christian elite emerged among the Karens, educated to a relatively high degree in the big local towns and in Rangoon itself. At the same time, many Karen villages in the more backward hill areas also converted to Christianity. Although Christian converts were never more than a minority of the largely Buddhist or animist Karen people, Christian Karens provided the leadership, the voice and the ballast of the new Karen identity.

In his *Burma and the Karens*, Dr San C. Po, the 'father' of the Karen nation, stated:

> The educational, social and spiritual progress of the Karens has been due, to a very great extent, to the missionaries who have worked so faithfully with them. The Karens are not ashamed or afraid to proclaim that they owe what progress or advancement they have made, to the missionaries whom they affectionately call their 'Mother' under the protection of the British Government whom they rightly call their 'Father'.

The latter, he concludes,

> as is usually the case with a father, never really knows, or if he knows often forgets, the special or peculiar needs of his individual child at home.[14]

The last part of this quote highlights a persistent ambiguity in the relationship between Britain and the Karens, of which Karen leaders were only too aware. Though the British authorities in Burma undoubtedly appreciated, and indeed were prepared to exploit, the support of the Karen community, they did not pursue a consistent policy of favouring the Karens. In the first place, the Karen community outside the hill and frontier areas was so closely intermingled with ethnic-Burman villages that any policy explicitly favouring the Karens would have imperilled rather than safeguarded political harmony in the countryside. Secondly, Karen leaders and their British supporters were probably correct in surmising that the British administration was not entirely comfortable with the close and rather exclusive relationship that the Karens had established with missionary organizations. British suspicion about this relationship was certainly apparent in the period of the Third Anglo-Burmese War in 1885–86 – when the British were manifestly reluctant to allow the missionaries to organize Karen self-defence organizations – and was deeply resented by the Karen leadership.[15]

Nevertheless, it was British rule that provided the vital political framework that enabled the creation of a new cohesion and sense of identity among the Karens. Within this all-important framework, 'Christianity, education and civilization' could together help 're-generate' the Karen community.[16] In the latter part of the nineteenth century, a new Karen social stratum emerged – both male and female – comprising government officials, teachers, pastors and nurses, all Western-educated and imbued, as H.I. Marshall put it, with British ideals of 'justice and fair-play'.[17] Like the Straits Chinese at roughly the same time, the Karen elite underwent a veritable 'revolution of cultural awareness' in the later nineteenth and early twentieth centuries. This was reflected not only in the establishment of missionary institutions and schools, but also in the production of a number of Karen-language books, periodicals and newspapers, published mainly by the American Baptist Mission Press.[18]

The aspirations of the Karen elite, however, went far beyond the consolidation of a privileged loyalist pressure group like the Straits Chinese. The creation in 1881 of the Karen National Association reflected the growing feeling among the Karen leadership that Karen survival and advancement within Burma required above all the con-scious forging of a Karen national identity linking all Karens, whatever their religion and their stage of development. The Karen National Association was specifically designed to help advance Karen education and political representation, forge links between Christian and non-Christian Karens, and to encourage agricultural improvements and access to credit in the Karen villages – in short, in the words of San C. Po, to 'keep the nation together in the march of progress'.[19] As Donald Smeaton – a sympathetic British official – observed in his key book, *The Loyal Karens of Burma* (1887), Christian Karen leadership may have constituted the 'cutting edge of the nation', but the long-term strength of the Karen people ultimately depended on the links between this leadership and 'an intelligent peasantry'.[20]

Given the backward and dispersed situation of the Karen people before British rule, this rapid development of a national identity backed by a solid base of religious, political, cultural and educational institu-tions is most striking. It could be argued that, by asserting and building a strong national identity, the Karen leaders were moving beyond a policy of simple dependence on a loyalist relationship with Britain. But the Karen leaders, and supporters of the Karen cause such as Donald Smeaton, were clearly always anxious that Karen national aspirations should harmonize with British policy in Burma. Smeaton, for example, urged British policy-makers to permit a diversity of political developments in Burma as well as India, in the hope that this would include giving the Karens 'a chance of growing as a nation in their own way'.[21] This would involve, among other things, encouraging the use of the Karen language by local officials, enhancing education, delegating as much self-government as possible to the local level, and permitting the organization of Karen self-defence organizations.[22] Building a self-confident and increasingly self-governing Karen nation would, Smeaton argued, be in the long-term interests of British imperial policy: 'If we succeed we shall not only have achieved a great triumph of administration, but we shall also have raised a living wall of defence against aggression from without and turbulence from within.'[23]

The development of the Burman nationalist movement

The consolidation of this Karen identity was able to proceed peacefully within the safe confines of British-controlled Lower Burma. After the removal of the Burmese monarchy by the British in the mid-1880s, and the manifest failure of the traditional Burmese resistance in Upper Burma, the ethnic-Burman elite went through a modernizing 'revolution' of cultural, religious and national consciousness very similar to that of the Karens. It was through this 'cultural revolution' that the twentieth-century Burman nationalist movement was to take shape. The development of a Karen national consciousness was therefore matched by a parallel development among the historically and demographically dominant community of ethnic-Burmans.

Burma's revolution of national consciousness went through a number of stages. In the first instance, attention was concentrated primarily on a Buddhist reformation: adjusting Buddhism, that is, to the challenges of the modern era and European domination. Thereafter, and particularly after Britain's crucial recognition during the First World War that increasing measures of political participation would have to be conceded to India (of which Burma was at the time a province), political issues came to the fore, and a full-blown nationalist movement emerged.[24]

However, as the British government made more and more significant concessions in the 1920s and 1930s to Burmese demands for self-government, so a detectable gap emerged within the Burman community between the nationalist politics of the elite and the ethnic politics of the grass-roots. While the educated elite – fully versed in the Western idiom of politics – bargained with the British and intrigued among themselves in the jostle for influence at the centre, they became increasingly separated from nationalist activity at the village level. The latter was led largely by local religious or quasi-religious leaders, and emphasized the threat posed to the Buddhist religion and the Burman 'race' by British 'heretic' rule and immigrant (mainly Indian and Chinese) domination of the rural economy.[25] Rural uprisings and urban riots in the 1920s and 1930s were directed quite as much against non-Burmans as against the British colonial authorities.

This gap between elite and grass-roots nationalism reflects a tension that is similar to other nationalist movements of the twentieth century. On the one side, the elite nationalist leadership, influenced as it was by European, secular concepts of the nation, sought to develop what could be called an 'inclusive' *Burmese* idea of national identity: that is, one that included all the peoples of Burma. On the other side, nationalist organizations operating at the local level emphasized 'exclusive' ethnic-*Burman* national symbols: race, religion and the memory of the ousted monarchy. Between these two forms of nationalism, there was an uneasy coexistence. If the Burman nationalist leadership was tempted to lean towards an emphasis on 'exclusive' ethnic-Burman nationalist rhetoric, the growth in its grass-roots support would be counter-balanced by the antagonism of the ethnic minorities in Burma and of the British authorities. Conversely, emphasis on an 'inclusive' national-ist rhetoric would strengthen its hand in negotiations with the British, but ran the risk of losing support among the Burman grass-roots.

In the 1930s, this gap between the traditional populist nationalism of the grass-roots on one side, and elite nationalism on the other, was bridged to some degree by the emergence of a new generation of radical and educated politicians, who in 1930 formed 'Dobama Asiayone' (a movement with a name of somewhat ambiguous meaning, which can be read narrowly as 'We Burmans' Association or more broadly as 'We Burmese' Association).[26] While, however, the left-wing faction of Dobama Asiayone attempted to percolate Western socialist ideas and trade union organizations down to the traditionalist grass-roots, the right-wing faction gave a new sophisticated gloss to traditional ethnic-Burman nationalism.[27] In ideological terms, Burman nationalism tended in the inter-war years to oscillate between socialist and ultra-nationalist rhetoric, and the fateful consequences of this were to become apparent in the war years and the immediate post-war period.

The Karens during the inter-war years

As Burman nationalism increasingly found its strength and its voice, the Karen elite were bound to become more apprehensive about their future, and old historic fears of Burman dominance inevitably re-surfaced. These apprehensions were strengthened by Britain's progres-sive implementation between 1920 and 1940 of a policy designed to give greater and greater self-government to Burma. By the time of the outbreak of the Second World War, Burma was governed by a Burmese prime minister and cabinet, and Burmese nationalist parties dominated the legislative structure, even if ultimate authority lay in the hands of the British governor and the Westminster parliament.

Britain did, in fact, take measures to insulate the less politically and economically advanced minority areas from these rapid constitutional changes. As Burma moved from the so-called 'dyarchy' system – which introduced an elected Legislative Council to Burma as a province of India – to a semi-self-governing 'ministerial' structure separate from India, care was taken to ensure that the border minority regions remained under the direct control of Britain. These 'excluded' areas – comprising the Chin Hills, the Naga Hills, the Kachin Hills, the Federated Shan States and the Karen Salween Hill Region – came under a special chain of command running from the governor to deputy-commissioners, assistant-superintendents and native rulers, known collectively as the Burma Frontier Service.[28]

When the whole question of constitutional change came under consideration towards the end of the First World War, the Karen leaders submitted a 'Memorial' to Britain arguing that Burma was not yet ready for self-government.[29] This in itself indicates the depths of anxiety that the Karens felt, both at the prospect of moves towards even the smallest measures of self-government, and at the certainty that a large number of Karens would willy-nilly be included in any such political development. The problem for the Karens lay in the fact that, unlike the other minorities lying on the periphery of Burma, their communities were widely dispersed. While the Karenni States were treated as native states not strictly speaking within the boundaries of Burma at all, and while the Salween Hill Region on the border was almost exclusively Karen in its population, the remainder of the Karen community lived in areas that were ethnically mixed and stretched into the very heart of Lower Burma.[30]

The British were, however, sensitive to the anxieties of the Karens in this era of political change. The Karen communities within Ministerial Burma were granted special separate constituencies, five in the Legislative Assembly set up under the 1923 Dyarchy Constitution, and twelve in the House of Representatives established in the new constitution of a separate Burma in 1935.[31] However, despite these measures to protect Karen status in the Burmese political system, anxieties remained, and indeed increased over time. Ultimately, the Karen leaders were acutely aware that any increase in self-government for Burma would automatically strengthen Burman control of the future political agenda and so weaken the position of those ethnic minorities who, like the Karens, looked upon Britain as their protection and the focus of their loyalty. At every stage of constitutional consultation that the British undertook in the inter-war years, Karen leaders consistently emphasized, first, the need to maintain British control as the sole guarantee of political stability in Burma and, second, the importance of resolving the relationship between the Burmans and the Karens *before* moving to substantial self-government.[32]

Dr (later Sir) San C. Po's book, *Burma and the Karens*, published in 1928, is a most revealing indication of Karen political thinking in the inter-war years. It not only puts forward constitutional ideas designed to protect Karen interests, but also gives more than a hint of the growing Karen apprehensions of that time. San C. Po reveals the traditional, almost in-built hostility that existed between the Burmans and the Karens – a hostility that was most consistently expressed, during the years of *Pax Britannica*, in competitive sports in which both races were involved, particularly at the school level.[33] But in an era of growing nationalist tension in the rural areas, this hostility occasionally took a far more sinister turn, not least because of the Karen role in the military and the police. The Karens played a major part in suppressing various Burman disturbances in the mid-1920s, and in the Saya San rebellion that seriously threatened British control over parts of lower Burma between 1930 and 1932.[34] As a consequence, even before the outbreak of the Second World War, there was considerable tension between Burman and Karen villages in Lower Burma.[35]

We can easily detect in San C. Po's book an indication of growing concern among the Karen that the special relationship built up between themselves and the British might slowly slip away in the new political climate. In the eyes of the Karens, the Burmans were not only gaining the predominant position in the Legislative Assembly that their numbers undoubtedly warranted, but they were also comprehensively dominating the lower rungs of the administration.[36] San C. Po argued strongly that two essential measures should be taken to ensure the defence of Karen interests. First, he urged that the Karens should be given a separate administrative region that they could themselves dominate and 'call their own'. San C. Po suggested that the Tenasserim region should be designated a Karen-controlled state which should be allowed significant autonomy within a federal Burma.[37] Second, he recommended that a policy of what would now be called 'positive discrimination' be adopted in appointments to government jobs in Tenasserim and other areas where there was locally a large Karen presence. Only this, he argued, could protect Karens against the tendency of Burmans to dominate the lower rungs of the administration.[38]

Above all, the Karen leadership of the inter-war years was clearly worried that the British would 'bend to the prevailing wind' and increasingly develop an exclusive partnership with the Burman political elite. Already, therefore, before the catalyst of the Second World War, the Karen leaders were experiencing what might be called a 'crisis of loyalist identity'.

The impact of the Second World War on the Karens of Burma

These incipient fears were, of course, crystallized during the Second World War and its aftermath. Even before Japan's humiliating removal of the British from Burma in early 1942, Burman nationalist politics had taken a sharply radical turn. Elite politicians like Ba Maw had linked with the younger generation of nationalists – the so-called 'Thakins' (literally 'master') of Dobama Asiayone – to form the Freedom Bloc in October 1939, and demanded outright and immediate independence.[39] When the British authorities responded with emergency measures and arrests, a small number of Thakins fled to Japanese-occupied China, and there formed the nucleus of an anti-British army.[40] Consequently, when the Japanese invaded Burma in early 1942, they brought in their wake the so-called Burma Independence Army (BIA), armed and trained by the Japanese in Bangkok, and led by young Thakin nationalists such as Aung San.[41] In the early months of the Japanese invasion, the Japanese allowed considerable local authority to this quasi-military, quasi-political organization. In the context of the prevailing anarchy in Burma, the vacuum of power, the disintegration of the British army in Burma, and the consequent return of many Karen soldiers to their villages, this was to have disastrous long-term consequences.

As Karen soldiers returned to protect their families and villages, and the ramshackle Burmese Independence Army moved into the Karen areas, it was perhaps inevitable that serious violence would ensue.[42] All the ancient hostilities came to the surface, and were exacerbated by the natural tendencies of an undisciplined army. In areas where responsible leadership existed on both sides – as in the town of Bassein in the Irrawaddy Delta – conflict between the BIA and the Karen community could be averted, at least for a while.[43] In other areas the absence of such restraining influences led to a complete breakdown of law and order, and the emergence of a state of local civil war. In Myaungmya, not far away from Bassein in the Irrawaddy Delta, the Karen community between March and June 1942 endured unremitting persecution, looting and outright murder. Roughly the same thing happened in Papun, the main town of the Salween Hill District. In Myaungmya in particular, only the arrival of regular Japanese troops could put a stop to the cycle of violence.[44] In the history of Karen–Burman relationships in the twentieth century, the importance of these events cannot be overestimated. As the Karen Memorial of September 1945 was to put it: 'this unfortunate, uncalled-for and unprovoked series of bloodshed and persecution has turned the clock back a century in our relationships'.[45]

Despite their encouragement of Asian nationalist rhetoric, the Japanese were primarily interested in maintaining political stability in what was essentially a front-line military zone. To this end, they rapidly removed the BIA administration and encouraged the development of an alliance between older and more experienced Burmese politicians and the Thakins. Accordingly, by mid-1942 a new 'Dobama-Sinyetha Asiayone' was formed linking the Sinyetha Party headed by Dr Ba Maw – a former prime minister of Burma under the British – and the Thakins, dominated by Aung San.[46] There is no doubt that this new administration made serious efforts to repair the damage that had been inflicted during the BIA period of the spring of 1942. Ba Maw took care to appoint Karen administrators in the Karen regions, and co-opted Karens to the institutions of central government.[47] More significantly, perhaps, Aung San, commander of the new Burma Defence Army, which had replaced the Burma Independence Army, incorporated a Karen battalion led by an experienced Karen officer.[48]

All these worthy efforts at ethnic reconciliation and belated nation-building could not, however, overcome the now entrenched suspicions of the Karens. If on the one side the new Burman leaders attempted to address the sensitivities of the minorities, on the other, their rhetoric clearly emphasized ethnic-Burman supremacy, and national unity at the expense of diversity. The principal slogan of the Dobama-Sinyetha Asiayone in 1942 was 'One Party, One Blood, One Voice and One Government'; and when Burma was granted its independence by the Japanese in August 1943, its Declaration of Independence stated:

> The new state of Burma is … established upon the principle of Burmese unity in one blood, one voice, one leader. It was national disintegration which destroyed the Burmese people in the past and they are determined that this shall never happen again.[49]

The impact of the Second World War on British–Karen relations

While the gap between the Karens and the Burmans widened during the war years, ever closer links were being forged between the British and the Karens, and indeed the peripheral ethnic minorities in general. When the Japanese invaded Burma in December 1941, H.N.C. Stevenson of the Burma Frontier Service was allowed to set up an irregular force, the Burma Levies, drawn from the hill peoples that encompassed Burma.[50] Despite the subsequent British defeat in Burma, the Nagas, Chins, Kachins and Muslim Arakanese were to play a major role in the regular and irregular war that was fought along the India-Burma border between 1942 and 1945.[51]

As part of Stevenson's Burma Levies, Major H.P Seagrim set up an irregular Karen force in Papun. When the Japanese army swept over Burma in early 1942, Seagrim's Karen guerrillas found themselves trapped deep inside enemy territory, just managing to keep one step ahead of the Japanese and their informers.[52] By late 1942, the British military authorities in India had developed a plan to parachute in men and supplies to help Seagrim build up a guerrilla network that could provide the British with information and engage in propaganda and sabotage. However, the units that were subsequently flown in during 1943 were quickly located and eliminated by the Japanese, and in 1944 Seagrim himself was captured and eventually executed.[53] Though Seagrim may have achieved little in military terms, what is significant is that he established an exceptional rapport with the Karens and may – unwittingly or not – have led them to expect that the extraordinary sacrifices they made on his and Britain's behalf would be repaid after the war.

Although Seagrim's military efforts may have been in vain, there can be no doubt of the importance of the aid that the Karens gave Britain during the invasion of Burma in 1945. In the race to reach Rangoon before the summer monsoon began in 1945, the British military were particularly anxious to prevent the 15th Japanese Division from moving down from the Shan States to block the British advance at the key town of Toungoo. Accordingly, in early 1945 the army sanctioned the formation and arming of Karen Levies through the Karen hill regions under the code-name 'Operation Character'.[54] The British and Karen units that were subsequently parachuted in were received with huge demonstrations of enthusiasm, and throughout March 1945 these Karen Levies played a key role in blocking the Japanese advance down from the Shan States to Toungoo, and thereafter in harassing the Japanese during their retreat from Burma.[55]

The period of uncertainty in Burma: 1945–46

By the spring of 1945, the fate of Burma was once again in the hands of the British government. So far as the Karens were concerned, their agenda for the future had been more sharply focused by their experiences during the war. The BIA pogroms of early 1942 strengthened their already clear resolve to determine their own future, and to gain solid guarantees against Burman domination of their communities. At the same time, the sacrifices their people had endured on Britain's behalf during the war, coupled with the crucial help they had lent to the British war effort, led them to expect from Britain some form of reciprocal loyalty and support in their political objectives.

The three foci of British decision-making in Burma were, first, the Burma Office in London; second, the British–Burmese government-in-exile in Simla under the leadership of the Governor, Reginald Dorman-Smith; and, third, Southeast Asia Command (SEAC) under Lord Louis Mountbatten, which had responsibility for the Burma theatre of war. In general political terms, both Dorman-Smith and London were convinced during the period 1942–44 that both the devastation inflicted by the war, and what was seen as the corruption and incompetence of the pre-war Burmese governments, meant that moves towards self-government – even at the pre-war level – should be very gradual, and preceded by measures of stabilization and economic rehabilitation.[56] This would inevitably mean that separate British control over the Excluded Areas – including the Karen hill regions – would be retained.

It would be wrong, however, to assume that the British wished to preserve the minority areas in aspic. As early as 1942, a committee of Burma Frontier Officers recommended the formation of a plan to speed up the development of the hill areas as soon as circumstances permitted.[57] In other words, the British authorities were anxious to speed up, not impede, the process of nation-building in Burma, which they saw as a necessary prerequisite for responsible self-government. As Dorman-Smith expressed it in 1943, the minorities in the future Burmese nation should be free 'to practise their own religion, free to maintain their own culture, to converse in their own language' and to have a 'fair deal' in employment. In return, however, 'these minorities are rightly expected to associate themselves intimately with the life of the country in which they live and to look upon themselves as part and parcel of that country'.[58]

Even before the British return to Burma, therefore, new political realities had already begun to intrude, and disturbed any notion of a simple return to the cosy world of pre-war Burma. The need to face military realities was even more pressing. Nineteen forty-four saw a timely shift in the ideological stance of the most important Burmese nationalist leaders under the leadership of Aung San, and the formation of the secret AFO or Anti-Fascist Organization. In essence this meant that the leftist and communist-orientated section of the Burmese nationalist leadership, with its acceptable anti-Fascist credentials, was given greater prominence.[59] This in itself would not have been significant, or have saved those Burmans who had collaborated with the Japanese from retribution, but for the fact that this organization was able to ensure that the Burma National Army (BNA) turned at a crucial moment in April–May 1945 against their Japanese allies and helped the British push to Rangoon.[60]

The ambiguity of Britain's policy towards Burma became apparent after the liberation of Burma in May 1945. On the one hand, government policy, embodied in the White Paper published that month, provided for three years of direct rule by the British governor of Burma under the emergency provisions of the 1935 Government of Burma Act, to be followed by the reintroduction of the 1935 system of limited self-government; only thereafter would there be moves to 'full self-government within the British Commonwealth'.[61] Under this plan, the Excluded Areas were to retain their separate status under direct British rule 'until such time as their inhabitants signify their desire for some suitable form of amalgamation into Burma proper'.[62] Clearly, the integration of Burma proper and the minority areas was seen as a long-term process of 'rehabilitation' and nation-building under British guidance.

On the other hand, the military government that ran Burma from May to October 1945 found itself forced to face certain uncomfortable realities. The first of these was that the British did not have the manpower to guarantee law and order in the very disturbed conditions of post-war Burma. The second was that Aung San, backed as he was by a mass movement – now known as the Anti-Fascist Peoples Freedom League (AFPFL), with a degree of multi-ethnic appeal and participation, but still dominated by the old Burma National Army which had been formed in the Japanese period – was acquiring a growing ability in this vacuum of authority to dictate the political agenda. In other words, Aung San, with the vast grass-roots organization that he had built up during the war, could 'deliver' either chaos or stability to Burma. Inevitably, the pragmatic military administrators increasingly entered into a *de facto* accommodation with Aung San, the most significant fruit of which was the agreement in September 1945 to merge elements of Aung San's army with the regular Burma Army.[63]

When Dorman-Smith resumed his position as governor in October 1945, he found himself faced with the same implacable reality. Aung San had moved from the military to the political arena, and in January 1946 formed a political-cum-paramilitary organization – the Peoples' Volunteer Organization or PVO – out of the remnants of the Burma National Army that had not been merged into the new Burma Army.[64] With this new irregular force, Aung San could make Burma ungovernable, and India, the ultimate guarantor of Britain's position in Burma, was itself moving towards independence. In these circumstances, Dorman-Smith's attempts to exclude Aung San and the AFPFL from power and implement the White Paper policy were doomed to failure. British policy rapidly changed when, in August 1946, Dorman-Smith was replaced by Hubert Rance. Aung San and the AFPFL leadership were appointed to the Governor's Executive Council in September 1946, and henceforth assumed a central role in the process of bargaining for independence.[65] In December 1946 a change of policy was announced by the British government, and in January 1947 it was agreed between Britain and a Burmese delegation in London headed by Aung San that the White Paper policy would be bypassed, and that a Constituent Assembly would be elected almost immediately, with a view to creating the basis for a fully self-governing Burma within one year.[66]

For the Karens, this was a fatal transition. It meant, in effect, that the British, no longer concerned to delay moves to self-government, would now wish to expedite the process as smoothly as possible; and this would mean appeasing the strongest political force in the country – Aung San and his AFPFL – in order to effect that peaceful transition. From the autumn of 1946, the British government and the AFPFL ceased to be adversaries and became partners, conspiring in their joint interest to ensure a peaceful transition of power and good post-independence relations. The British perspective on the minorities and their anxieties – particularly those of the Karens – was bound to be affected.

The Karens: from loyalism to separatism

From the time of the Japanese surrender to the transfer of power from the British to an independent Burma in January 1948, there was a political consensus among leading Karen organizations that the Karen people should be allowed to determine their own future, and that, if they should decide to join with the ethnic-Burmans in a single state, this should be on the basis of partnership, not of Burman domination.

The Karens, however, faced certain inherent difficulties throughout this period in their attempt to pursue a united and effective policy. In the first place, as has already been noted, the Karen community was dispersed, comprising groups settled in the traditional chiefdoms of the Karenni states, in the Salween Hill Tract region in the Excluded Areas, in the hill regions at the edge of Karenni and Salween – so-called 'Part 2' regions which were technically within Ministerial Burma but given an interim separate status – and the Karens outside these defined regions, ranging across the lower Irrawaddy Delta to the Tenasserim peninsula.[67] It was natural that, as the pace of political negotiation became more intense, the different circumstances and concerns of the Karens living in these dispersed areas should create apparent differences of interest and policy. Tied to this question of defining the extent and unity of the Karen community, and hence the Karen nation, was the fundamental problem of demography. It was the contention of the Karen leadership throughout this period that the 1931 census had seriously underestimated the number of Karens in Burma, because the census-takers had tended to lump Buddhist Karens together with Buddhist Burmese.[68] The whole of Britain's policy towards the Karens at this time was based on the assumption of the 1931 census that there were around one million Karens (compared to over nine and a half million Burmans) in Burma, while the Karens argued that their number was nearer three or four million. This was a matter of vital importance in an era of decolonization and its attendant rush to define ethnic and national identities and aspirations. Finally, the basis of Karen policy – at least for a while – depended on Britain's continued presence and support. The years 1945 to 1947 were to reveal the dangers of pursuing this loyalist strategy.

It would, however, be misleading to assume that the Karens were completely locked into a loyalist 'polity'. Looking at the Karen statements made over the whole period 1945–48, it is clear that the Karens had in effect begun pursuing a dual policy even before the end of the war. On the one hand, they continued in their public statements to emphasize the maintenance of the British link as the key to political harmony in Burma, and to remind the British of their close ties and obligations to the Karens. On the other hand, emboldened by their strong position in the new Burma Army, and by the large number of arms held by ex-Karen Levies in the hill areas of east Burma, they were increasingly prepared to defend their national rights with or without British help. As early as August and September 1945, British officials were noting that responsible Karen leaders were talking of the creation of a separate Karen state, or 'Karenistan'.[69] Seven months later H.N.C. Stevenson – who was becoming a key intermediary between the Karens and the government in Rangoon – was to put his finger on the dual policy of the Karens: 'I have come to the regrettable conclusion that the present Karen quiescence means simply that they refuse to quarrel with us. But when we go, if go we do, the war for the Karen state will begin.'[70]

Between 30 June and 5 July 1945, the Karen community in Rangoon held a mass meeting to decide a unified policy for the future. Under the leadership of a new umbrella organization, the Karen Central

Organization (KCO), they outlined a policy that was embodied in a Memorial (see Appendix 2) that was eventually submitted to the British government in September 1945.[71] This document encapsulates the main aspirations and fears of the Karen leaders in the 1945–48 period. Beneath some rather ambivalent wording, the principal point it made was that the Burman-Karen relationship was such that the Karen people could no longer contemplate living within a united Burma, except in the context of overall British protection: 'The Karens ... have come to feel very strongly that they must strike out on a course of their own to preserve their national ideals and develop into a progressive and useful state of Burma in the British Commonwealth of Nations.'[72] In essence, this was an assertion of the Karens' right to self-determination, combined with a reaffirmation of the old policy of loyalism.

As a first step in this affirmation of the right to Karen self-determination, the Memorial requested the creation of a new Karen political entity. This would encompass the Salween Hill Tracts, the whole of the Tenasserim Division, the eastern part of Pegu District, and, at a later date, the Karen regions of Thailand, and would collectively be called 'The United Karen Frontier States'. This Karen political entity would be incorporated as a whole into the British-administered Excluded Areas separate from Ministerial Burma. The fact that it would have access to the sea would ensure its economic viability, while a guarantee that Karens would be given preference for administrative posts in the region would enable the Karens to 'live secure and grow up as one united people'.[73] This regime, the Memorial insisted, should continue until 'our people are willing to accept some form of incorporation' in a wider Burmese state.[74]

This demand for a 'viable' Karen state was to be the most constant feature of Karen policy across the whole political spectrum, even though opinions might differ over its status and its relationship to Burma proper. It is noticeable that even the Karen Youth Organization (KYO), which constituted the Karen branch of Aung San's AFPFL, and contained on the whole younger, more radical and urban-orientated Karens, supported the idea of a clearly defined Karen state.[75]

Between the autumn of 1945 and spring 1946, the Karens moved from using the language of loyalism to asserting their right to self-determination. Against the background of Governor Dorman-Smith's doomed struggle to cope with the hard realities of post-war Burma, it is poignant to note Sir San C. Po's appeals in December 1945 and March 1946 (the last before his death in the same year) for a federated 'United States of Burma' where the Karens would have a 'place in the sun', and where political differences would be resolved by 'real fair

play and sympathies all round'.[76] An entirely different and, for the
British, more menacing tone was subsequently taken at a mass meeting
of Karens held at Toungoo in April 1946. This reiterated the demand
for the creation of the 'United Karen Frontier States', but added that
the 'form of government' given to the Karens should not be 'lower
than that given to Burma'.[77] The meeting firmly emphasized the difference in 'dress, language, culture, custom and especially in moral
character' between the Karens and the Burmans, and asserted that the
Karens were 'unanimous in their desire to be separated from the
Burmese' and wished to develop 'on their own lines ... under the
guardianship of the British'.[78] The language of this meeting amounted
to the demand for a separate Karenistan, though under British tutelage.

It is clear that Karen militancy was growing with their increasing
fears about the evolution of British policy. In fact, there was a fair
degree of unanimity – both in Rangoon and in London – in Britain's
consideration of Karen demands in 1946. In general, the British were
prepared to consider favourably the idea of a consolidated Karen state
within Burma, whose territories could include the Salween Hill Tracts,
the special 'Part 2' areas adjacent to the Karenni States and Salween,
and contiguous areas in Ministerial Burma proper that had a clear
Karen majority. They were prepared to incorporate this newly defined
region into the Excluded Areas under the Frontier Areas Administration, and to leave open the question of its future relationship with
the Karenni States. What they were *not* prepared to contemplate,
however, was any form of 'Karenistan' or ambitious plans to include
chunks of Thailand or areas – like Tenasserim – where the Karens
were clearly in a minority. This amounted to a veto on any idea of a
'viable' Karen state with sea access.[79]

In his comments on the Karen resolution made at their meeting in
April 1946, H.N.C. Stevenson agreed that any 'Karenistan' was out of
the question. It is clear, however, that he was significantly more
sympathetic to Karen aspirations than most other British officials
considering the question: in the first place, he pointed out that the
Karens did not accept the official assessment of their numbers, and,
since this issue was vital for the correct delineation of Karen areas, he
suggested that there should be a new census. He also suggested that
the very mixed races of the Tenasserim region might well prefer an
affiliation with the Karens rather than with Ministerial Burma, and
that at the least their opinions should be considered.[80] For his part,
Dorman-Smith noted, in a letter to the Secretary of State for Burma
in January 1946, that the demand for a Karen state made no provision
for the Karens living in the Irrawaddy Delta region. He thereby put
his finger on the major problem of the Karens: that their dispersed

population made it impossible for a Karen state to be created that would protect the interests of the whole – or even a major part – of the Karen community. Interestingly enough, he went on in his letter at least to suggest that a Karen state *could* include Tenasserim if the non-Karen ethnic groups in the area agreed, and that such a state could secure the whole lower Salween region for British interests in the future. He concluded:

> It is argued that the Burmese have no greater claim to dominance over the Karens than we have to dominance over the Burmese. The case is precisely similar – the Burmese conquered the Karens and we conquered the Burmese. If, therefore, modern internationalism demands that we give the conquered Burmese their freedom, by the same token the Burmans must grant the conquered Karens their freedom.[81]

These were fine words, but the Karens could take no comfort from them. The plain fact was that the whole 'philosophy' of British decolonization after the Second World War went against the idea of encouraging the break-up of existing political units like Burma. The only exceptions were the partitions of India and Palestine, and these were exceptions that proved the rule. There were many reasons for this. The first was that, once the decolonization process started within a particular colonial state, the British entered into a kind of partnership of interest with the dominating political forces of that state – which in turn represented the most powerful ethnic group, or an alliance of ethnic groups whose natural interests were against the break-up of the state concerned. Second, a consensus developed among the new independent states against any tendency to disintegration that might have a knock-on effect. Third, in the wake of the war against Nazism there was a natural revulsion against racially defined small states of the kind that Hitler had created in his Europe. Finally, there was a generally accepted view that small states were not economically 'viable'. This whole line of thinking can be summed up in the view of Pethick-Lawrence, the Secretary of State for Burma, that an independent Karen state 'would be of very dubious viability', and would be 'wholly contrary to [the] general world trend and too retrograde to contemplate'.[82]

There were, however, more immediate and practical reasons for the failure of the Karens to protect their position effectively in 1946. Astonishingly, despite the extensive discussion of Karen demands in Rangoon and London, and despite the general recognition that the Karen issue should be addressed, no concrete measures were taken either by the British government or by the Burmese national leaders to negotiate with the Karens. The British government was completely absorbed by the problem of India, and one gains the impression that

Dorman-Smith and his Executive Council were, by early 1946, simply losing control of events.[83] The result was that, when the Karen leadership followed up their demands by sending a small delegation to London in August 1946, they were under the misapprehension that they were reinforcing a Karen position that was under active and serious consideration by the British government. In fact, neither London nor Rangoon had taken any serious steps to address the Karen problem.[84]

In any case, by the summer and autumn of 1946 the tide of events in Burma was running strongly against the Karens. By this time, Dorman-Smith had already been replaced as governor, and it was apparent that the leisurely political timetable envisaged by the May 1945 White Paper was no longer workable. By January 1947, it was agreed that Burma would become independent within one year, and that an elected Constituent Assembly should decide the structure of the future Burmese state. Although Britain in the meantime was technically in charge of the Excluded Areas, one thing was now clear: all negotiations between the minorities and the Burmese leaders would take place within the framework of the concept of a united Burma. The stated policy which was agreed between the British and the Burmese delegation in January 1947 succinctly balanced Britain's residual obligations to the minorities and the demands of the Burmese nationalists: 'It is the agreed objective of both His Majesty's Government and the Burmese Delegates to achieve the early unification of the Frontier Areas and Ministerial Burma with the free consent of the inhabitants of those areas.'[85]

From January 1947, control of events passed increasingly into the hands of the AFPFL-dominated Executive Council of the Governor of Burma. In February 1947, a conference between Burmese and minority leaders was held at Panglong to determine the future relationship between the Executive Council and the Frontier Areas Administration, which still had responsibility for the Excluded Areas, and to work out the general principles of the future relationship between Burma and the minority regions. On 12 February 1947, the structure of the hill peoples' representation on the Executive Council was agreed, and it was accepted 'in principle' that the Frontier Areas should have 'full autonomy in internal administration'. Based on this agreement, subsequent negotiations outlined the future framework of semi-autonomous Kachin and Shan States.[86] In March and April 1947, a British–Burmese Frontier Areas Commission of Enquiry considered the question of arranging the representation of the Frontier Areas in the Constituent Assembly that was imminently to be elected.

From January 1947 onward, therefore, responsibility for conducting policy with the minorities fell decisively into the hands of Aung San and the AFPFL. Despite Aung San's sincere attempts thereafter to mollify the fears of the minorities, the drift of political events in Burma through 1947 could not have been more calculated to alarm groups – particularly the Karen – that were already intensely suspicious of Burman intentions and political behaviour. Aung San's need to keep the AFPFL juggernaut together in the Constituent Assembly involved a substantial ideological drift to the left, culminating in the decision in June 1947 to form an independent Burmese Republic separate from the British Commonwealth. In the same month, a communist rebellion broke out in Arakan. This was followed in July 1947 by the assassination of Aung San himself, the one man who had held the factions of the AFPFL together and who had the trust of the minority leaders.[87] There then followed a period of political turbulence and a progressive breakdown of law and order, combined with intensified competition between the nationalist factions for support in the ethnic-Burman grass-roots.

During the course of 1947, Karen hopes of British support began to die. At the end of 1946 and the beginning of 1947, British policy towards the minority problem in general and the Karens in particular could be described as one of urging the new Burmese leadership to 'give [the] frontier peoples much of what they want'; otherwise, the consequences 'may be most unfortunate for Burma as a whole'.[88] One thing was clear: the old cosy relationship between the Frontier Areas Administration and the minority regions – the backbone of the 'loyalist' relationship – had come to an end. The consequences of this were clear to H.N.C. Stevenson, who was himself *persona non grata* with the new Burmese leaders:

> knowing the Karens and believing them to be pinning their faith on some mysterious action on the part of HMG to safeguard their interests, I feel it is necessary that it should be made abundantly clear to them that all action rests with them and *nothing* is being done, or can be done, by London.[89]

Stevenson hoped that the Karens would fight their cause in the forthcoming Constituent Assembly but, given the whole trend of Karen–Burman relations at this time, this was a forlorn hope. The immediate reactions of the Karen Central Organization (KCO) leaders to political developments at the beginning of 1947 were to reject the agreement reached between Britain and the Burmese leaders, and to follow a policy of non-participation.[90] The Karens did not in fact abandon negotiations altogether: under the leadership of a new and more militant organization formed in February 1947, the Karen National

Union (KNU), they put forward a series of demands as a precondition for re-entering the political process.[91] These included 'acceptance in principle' of a Karen state with a seaboard; 25 per cent Karen representation on the Executive Council; 25 per cent representation in any future Legislative Assembly; guaranteed quotas in the government service; negotiations over the status and control of the army in a future independent Burma; and, finally, a new census to determine the number of Karens in Burma.[92] Though Aung San was clearly most anxious to respond positively to the Karens, the problem now was that increasing Karen militancy meant that their demands were running far ahead of his capacity to accommodate them. When he demurred at these preconditions, a Karen National Union (KNU) 'Council of Action' met on 3 March 1947, and decided to boycott the forthcoming Constituent Assembly and withdraw its representatives from the Executive Council.[93]

Predictably, as the prospect of Burmese independence loomed, the different Karen communities reacted in different ways to protect their positions. The main worry of the Karens in the Irrawaddy Delta region of Myaungmya, Bassein and Pyapon was that they would once again – as in 1942 – be left isolated and helpless in the face of majority-Burman discrimination or even reprisals. Since they lived far beyond the boundary of even the most ambitiously conceived Karen state, their agenda focused on guarantees of local security; the maintenance of their educational institutions, culture and language; and fair representation in the government services.[94] At the other end of the spectrum – geographically and in terms of development – the Karens of the Toungoo hill region had a different agenda. These Karens, who had played a key role in Major Seagrim's military activities behind the Japanese lines in 1942 and 1943, now demanded that their loyalty be reciprocated by the British. Above all, they wanted their region to be taken out of Ministerial Burma and amalgamated into a Karen state 'where they can have the choice to join or not to join Burma and to be within or without the British Empire'.[95] If the British did not support them, they remarked: 'the Karens should not be blamed if they think of other alternatives to achieve their legitimate objectives'.[96]

Despite this divergence of aims, however, there was no mistaking the underlying unity of the Karens in pursuing their main objective: that of asserting and defending Karen identity and rights. By mid-1947, it was clear that time was running out, and that there was a race on between those advocating Karen separatism on the one side, and those making efforts to achieve a negotiated settlement within Burma on the other. By April 1947, the Karen National Union was talking about preparing 'the Karen masses' for 'their fight for the right to self-determination' and 'living space'. By now the language of loyalism had clearly been abandoned.[97] The new, more radical political rhetoric was repeated in a press release for Reuters in June 1947:

> People of Britain, we solemnly assert to you that we stand today, a strong united people. Our spilt blood in every occasion since our contact with you, has bound us Karens closer and closer together. We have stood by you in your darkest hours, and if you choose to let us stand alone, WE WILL, for we CAN. We take pride in our unity and kinship and we do not bend the knee or bow the head in adversity.[98]

Both the British government and the Burmese leaders were aware of the urgency of the situation. The final rush to settle was, however, complicated by the fact that there were three areas of negotiation that needed to be addressed: there was the question of the relationship between Burma and the constitutionally separate Karenni States; there was the demand that a 'Karen State' should be created in addition to the Karenni States, with the associated problem of delineating its powers and its territorial extent; and, finally, there was the need to consider the anxieties of the Karens in the Irrawaddy Delta, and to establish some kind of institution that could protect their interests.

It became clear by June 1947 that the Burmese leadership was prepared to envisage a Karen State, including the Salween Hill Tracts and the hill regions of the adjoining Yamethin, Toungoo and Thaton districts. The British, too, hoped to see the creation of such a state, and hoped that the Karenni States could be lured into joining it, thereby resolving the issue of the status of the Karenni area. The Burmese, however, refused to contemplate accepting Karen demands that the whole of the Tenasserim Division, or even the whole of Thaton District, be incorporated within this state, and they were reluctant to concede to the Karens the Karen-dominated hill tract region of Amherst District, on the grounds – among others – that they were separated from other Karen areas.[99] It is unlikely, in any event, that a last-minute deal could have been struck on this basis, since the boundaries of this proposed state would not have given the Karens sea access. In any case, negotiations between the Burmese, the British and the Karens were now complicated by confusion over the question of the relationship between this proposed Karen State and the Karens of the Irrawaddy Delta region, who were now demanding a Karen Affairs Council that would defend their interests inside an independent Burma.[100]

With the assassination of Aung San in July 1947, the settlement foundered altogether. Whether the failure to resolve these issues was primarily the responsibility of Burmese deviousness or of Karen obstinacy, the result was that no settlement could be reached before independence. The Karenni States, which had been waiting to see the outcome of the negotiations over the Karen State, now realized that they were about to lose their special protection from Britain, and they rushed at the last minute to settle with the Burmese. With some ingenuity, the Constitution of the Union of Burma, which was adopted in September 1947, provided for a temporary arrangement, by which a separate Karenni State was created, as well as a special Karen region with limited powers of autonomy called Kaw-Thu-Lay, and a Karen Affairs Council, headed by a Minister for Karen Affairs, which would look after the interests of this region and the Karen community in Burma generally. This was to be a temporary arrangement while a special commission would examine the question of creating a Karen State along the lines of the Shan State: with internal self-government, representation in the Burmese legislature and government, and the right to secede after ten years.[101]

Background to the Karen rebellion

The British had, therefore, left Burma with the Karen problem unresolved. In the debate on the Burma Independence Bill in the House of Commons on 5 November 1947, many Conservative members expressed concern for the fate of the minorities, the Karens in particular.[102] Prime Minister Attlee himself conceded in the debate that 'there are still some groups of the Karens who are not wholly satisfied'.[103] Conservatives, on the other side of the House, doubted whether the various forms of 'consultation' with the minorities – formal or otherwise – had been genuinely representative. Their overall view could be summed up in Beverley Baxter's remark that Britain's view of the empire was indeed changing 'when we honour men who fought against us and grow cold towards those who fought on our side'.[104] But the general conservative tone in the debate was resigned rather than combative, containing also a hint of grim satisfaction at the prospect of ruin that faced those who abandoned the empire link.[105]

Because the British had left the Karen question unresolved, they unwittingly facilitated the subsequent Karen rebellion. So long as Britain had been involved in Burma's future, it had the chance to use the loyalist relationship between themselves and the Karens to cajole and persuade the Karens to make a deal with the Burmese leaders. After Britain's 'scuttle' from Burma, the Karen leaders felt they had no alternative but to shake themselves free of the vestiges of a culture of political dependency, and evolve their own strategy for national liberation. This was already apparent in the language used by the

Karen National Union in 1947. More importantly, the KNU set up, in July 1947, a Karen military network called the Karen National Defence Organization (KNDO), which had links with Karen units in the Burmese army.[106] In early October 1947, even as the last details of the Burmese Constitution were being negotiated, the KNU held their own meeting at Moulmein. They rejected the constitutional provisions which had been made for the Karens, and in fact demanded a larger Karen state, including segments of Lower Burma which had never been claimed before.[107]

Clearly, the stage was being set for outright conflict. Why, then, was the Karen rebellion delayed for one year? In the first place, the constitution provided for the creation of a Special Commission to determine the extent of territory to be included within a Karen State that would have substantial autonomy within the Union of Burma, and the ultimate right to secession.[108] In October 1948, a Regional Autonomy Enquiry Commission was set up to examine this issue, and the further question of whether a Karen–Mon State should be established in Tenasserim.[109] There was, in other words, just sufficient political momentum to keep the Karens in check. But the most important guarantee that Karen interests would be respected was the fact that the Karens dominated the new Burmese army. General Smith Dun, the army commander, was himself a Karen. The deal patched up by Southeast Asia Command in September 1945, where selected units of Aung San's army were amalgamated with the Karen-dominated Burma Army created by the British, ensured for the Karens a very strong position in the newly independent Burma.

If ever a reliable and effective army was needed, it was in the Burma of 1948. Immediately after independence, Burma collapsed into a state of semi-civil war. This political turbulence reflected the unleashing of all the political tensions within Burma that had been generated by the nationalist mobilization during and immediately after the war, and only partly held in check during the independence negotiations. A second communist ('White Flag') rebellion in the spring of 1948 was followed by a rebellion in the Karenni States in August 1948 – clearly expressing belated resentment at incorporation within Burma – and this was followed by an outbreak of local rebellions among the vast nationalist militia, the PVO, which had been created by Aung San, but which was now being disbanded after independence.[110]

For a while, these multifarious rebellions served to keep Burman–Karen relations in a state of suspension. In this crucial period, the Burmese government depended heavily – in certain periods of extreme crisis, exclusively – on the loyalty and expertise of the Karen units in the armed forces.[111] Karen–Burman hostility was only postponed, however, not resolved. Indeed, the very role that the Karens in the army played in suppressing local rebellions in ethnic-Burman areas served to rekindle old ethnic hostilities in the Irrawaddy Delta and elsewhere. In late 1948 and early 1949 the unchanging separatist agenda of the KNU and its military wing, the KNDO, was given a final boost by mass defections of Karen units from the army. It only needed some treacherous attacks by Burman police and army units on Karen communities in Tenasserim and Rangoon to stimulate a full-scale Karen rebellion in January 1949, with the aspiration of creating an independent Karen state.[112]

There then followed a complicated, partner-changing dance of ethnic and ideological alliances that was to set the pattern for Burma's more recent history. While Karen troops had remained loyal to the government, a balance could be maintained between the government and the various ethnic-Burman rebel forces. When the Karens as a whole came out in revolt and threatened the heart of government power itself, there was a belated rallying to the government by ethnic-Burman forces. Neither side – the government or the rebel forces ranged against the government – has been able to gain a critical mass sufficient to overwhelm the other side. Burma has remained in this paralysis – what could be called an 'equilibrium of instability' – through the ensuing decades.

A number of factors help to explain the resilience of the long-running Karen rebellion. First, the Karen rebels, despite the scattered location of their population, had a mass base of support within their own community. Second, at least some of the terrain under their control has suited prolonged guerrilla warfare. Third, and perhaps most crucially, they were for a number of decades – between 1949 and 1989 – able to exploit the fact that the whole area of the Burmese border, from the Kachin territory in the far north to the Karen region in the southeast, was the focus of a complex ideological and geo-political conflict. The region became a vital front-line of the Cold War, where conflicts involved not only the Burmese government and the local ethnic minority groups, but also drew in such players as Communist China and the Kuomintang, the anti-government forces of Laos, Thailand and Burma, the pro-American forces of Laos and Thailand, and the United States itself.

Like the other groups, the Karens became involved in the almost impossibly complex kaleidoscope of alliances involving, at one time or another, all the above-mentioned protagonists. In order to survive and further their cause, they have formed alliances of convenience with the Kuomintang remnants that fled into Shan/Wa territory in late 1949; with the Burmese Communist Party, whose principal base became for a time the remote Wa region in the Shan States, but who tried to extend their network of support through the dissident minority areas; with the Thai authorities and their American backers; with other minority groups in Burma, such as the Kachins and Shans, who came out in full rebellion against the Burmese government in the early 1960s; and with Burman students and other dissidents seeking a broad front to overthrow successive Burmese governments. Always, through this confusing period and beyond, the aim of the Karen dissidents has been to coalesce with those forces that could weaken the Burmese government and force it to come to an accommodation with the Karens on the issue of substantial self-government or independence.[113]

It should *pari passu* be noted, however, that the very forces of fragmentation, both in the region and elsewhere in Burma, that the Karens have been able to exploit have affected the fortunes of the Karen rebellion itself. The complex patchwork of local territorial alliances has encouraged an almost ineradicable tendency to warlordism. Further, adoption of communist styles of political and military organization has alienated some and thus created divisions within the Karen rebel forces between the communist-inclined and the convinced anti-communists. The same problems of fragmentation that have affected Burmese governments have also become endemic within the Karen and other minority rebellions. It is for this reason that Burma and its environs continue to suffer an 'equilibrium of instability'.

Conclusion

The objective of this chapter, however, is not to examine the course of the long-running Karen rebellion or its likely outcome, but to consider its roots in the colonial period and the era of nationalist upheavals that culminated in decolonization.

Looking at the background to Burmese independence and the Karen rebellion, it is impossible to escape the conclusion that Britain 'scuttled' from Burma, as it had from India, leaving disastrous short-term consequences in the case of India, and disastrous long-term consequences in the case of Burma. In short, the story of Britain's withdrawal from Burma is one of betrayal, incompetence and ignominy. But ultimate responsibility for the chaos of post-independence Burma must lie in the hands of Burmese politicians themselves – including Aung San – who forced a headlong and irresponsible rush towards independence in 1946 and 1947. The hard fact was that, after the war, the British simply did not have the means to govern Burma if the Burmese nationalists chose to make it ungovernable. As H.P. Seagrim's biographer, Ian Morrison, pointed out in 1947, 'at a certain stage, when peoples have learned to organize, a continuation of foreign rule becomes *physically* impossible'.[114]

The Karen leadership, too, was plainly deficient in the skills of elementary statecraft at this time. Their loyalist relationship with Britain made the Karens at the same time too dependent on Britain and too intransigent towards the Burmese leaders. They had, in effect, so firmly tied themselves to an imperial policy that they were quite unable to adapt and respond flexibly to post-imperial realities. Their only alternative to loyalty to Britain was one of outright resistance to Burma. As General Smith Dun – who never approved of the aspiration to a separate 'Karenistan' – was to put it in his autobiography, 'wishful hopes replaced hard work towards a true settlement.'[115]

At the same time, one overwhelming fact stands out in the modern history of the Karens. Between the period of the arrival of the British in Burma and the end of the Second World War, the Karens became a nation. Any policy that did not take this fact into account was doomed to fail in advance. At the height of the negotiations over independence in June 1947, this was the essential point that was being asserted by the Karen leadership:

> No matter whether a Karen lives in the mountains or in the plains, whether animist, Buddhist, Christian or otherwise, whether from what-soever tribe, Sgaw, or Pwo, Red or Black Karen – A KAREN IS A KAREN: one in blood brotherhood, one in sentiment, one in adversity and one mass of a Karen nationhood. If this war has awakened and aroused nationalism, it has not left the Karens untouched or asleep.[116]

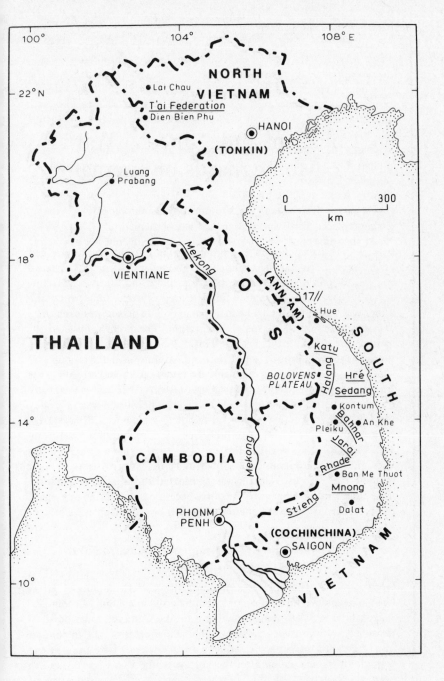

Map 4 Indochina and the Vietnamese Central Highlands

4

Loyalism and 'Special War': the Montagnards of Vietnam

Although British policy in Burma before the Second World War had kept the minority areas administratively separate from Ministerial Burma, Britain's wartime and post-war policy in Burma was consistently based on the notion of a united Burma, into which the minorities would eventually be incorporated. The debate was essentially over the pace and the terms of integration. The French, by contrast, had by the time of the Second World War moved only tentatively towards the creation of a separate administration in the 'Montagnard' ('Hill People') regions of Vietnam. By mid-1946, however, they were framing a policy in the Montagnard regions that was specifically designed to weaken the unity of Vietnam. The differences of policy towards their respective peripheral minority regions can, to a degree, be explained by the different processes of decolonization in Burma and Vietnam. However, the history of France's colonial relationship with the autochthonous minority groups inhabiting the peripheral mountain regions of Vietnam was dominated throughout by paradox. To understand that paradox, it is first necessary to describe in general terms the history of these minority groups or 'Montagnards'.

The French and the Montagnards: background to the special relationship

Geographically, Indochina – containing the modern nations of Laos, Cambodia and Vietnam – is dominated by a spinal column of mountain ranges, hills and plateaux, stretching from the Chinese border down to the northern approaches to Saigon. The major areas of settlement and of the creation of sophisticated states and societies have been at the edge of this spinal column: in the northeast, the Red River Delta has been the heartland of the Vietnamese people; the coastal strip of modern-day central Vietnam was once the locus of the Cham state of

Champa; the Khmer empire dominated the lowlands to the south of
the spinal column of mountains; and the Lao principalities eventually
gained control of the length of the Mekong river that skirted those
mountains on the west. Each of these major civilizations has ethnic
counterparts in the central upland regions: the upland Muong are
ethnically related to the Vietnamese; T'ai minorities – ethnically related
to the Lao – spill across the northern mountains of Indochina from
northeasternmost Vietnam down to the Mekong river in the west;
Cham-related tribes spread back into the mountains from the once
Cham-dominated coast; and the Khmer lowlands are similarly flanked
by related groups in the lower reaches and foothills of these mountains.

The ethno-linguistic distribution of the dispersed inhabitants of the
Indochina mountains reflects, in other words, the dominance of states
and civilizations of a previous era. Up until roughly the fourteenth
century, the southern and central part of Indochina was controlled by
two different peoples: the Mon-Khmer language speakers, who
stretched across the southeast Asian land mass from the Bay of Bengal
to the China Sea; and the Malayo-Polynesians (whose ethno-linguistic
category includes the Chams), who had settled in the maritime regions
south of Taiwan, including the central Indochinese coast.[1] The whole
mountain and upland region of what is now southern Laos, central
Vietnam and northeastern Cambodia was settled by communities
belonging to these two linguistic groups. But from the fourteenth
century onwards, the Cham presence was progressively eliminated by
the southward push of the Vietnamese people, while the Mon-Khmer
groups were squeezed between Lao settlement moving southwards
along the banks of the Mekong river and Vietnamese settlement pushing down along the coast.[2] In their southward expansion, the Lao and
the Vietnamese skirted round the hostile, unhealthy and economically
unattractive mountain regions, following the lowland plains and river
valleys.

From the fourteenth century on, the disparate inhabitants of these
southern mountains (called the Truong Son by the Vietnamese) were
progressively surrounded to east and west by peoples who were
linguistically and culturally alien. The process was one of steady encroachment into the foothills and therefore a squeezing into the interior
of these people, who were collectively and for convenience called the
'Montagnards' by later French colonists. Vietnamese–Montagnard
relations have traditionally been marked by mutual hostility and fear.
Vietnamese encroachment in the past would trigger Montagnard raids,
which would often be followed by harsh reprisals.[3] Up until the
nineteenth century, however, an uneasy equilibrium existed between
the Montagnards and the Vietnamese. Vietnamese settlers were not

interested in moving beyond the foothills into the dangerous and alien territory of the Montagnards. Instead, a trading relationship developed at the margins of Vietnamese-held territory, mediated by Vietnamese semi-officials, semi-traders known as *cac-lai*.[4] The Montagnards were, therefore, able to avoid the fate of the lowland Chams.

The Vietnamese state was, however, anxious to regularize its relationship with the Montagnards. This process involved attempts to establish tributary relations with identifiable tribal chieftains – relations which were uneasily controlled at the local level by the *cac-lai*.[5] But these tributary contacts were intermittent, not only because of the difficulty of establishing political relationships with peoples whose political structures did not generally extend beyond the village level, but also because of the fluctuations in state and dynastic power in Vietnam itself. It was not until the establishment of the Nguyen dynasty in a united Vietnam in 1802 that a more consistent policy of expansion and 'pacification' in the Montagnard region was developed by the Vietnamese. Initially this represented a move to re-establish tributary links that had been lost in the preceding periods of civil war. During the period of the 1820s to the 1850s, however, the policy became more vigorous in response to evidence of the rapid expansion of the influence of the Siamese kingdom across the Mekong river into the western Montagnard region of what is now southern Laos.[6] The Vietnamese state's efforts at 'pacification' were speeded up even more in the 1860s, as the Siamese encroachment was matched by a new and more compelling threat from the French.[7]

Throughout the colonial period, France's relationship with the Montagnards was a by-product of the vicissitudes of its relationship with Vietnam. In the early nineteenth century, the French depended on the special relationship they had established with the Nguyen dynasty in order to build privileged diplomatic and trading links with Vietnam, as well as protected rights of missionary activity. As this relationship deteriorated through the first half of the nineteenth century, religious persecution against Christian missions and their followers intensified. One significant consequence of this was the establishment in 1851 of a Catholic mission in Kontum, situated just north of Jarai territory, and out of direct reach of Vietnamese power.[8]

Between 1858 and 1886, France, by then relying on force rather than partnership with the Nguyen to consolidate its power in the region, first created a colony in Cochinchina, then established a protectorate over Cambodia, and finally imposed a protectorate over the Nguyen dynasty in north and central Vietnam. Unlike the British in Burma, the French did not remove the existing dynasty and administer Vietnam directly – except in the case of the colony of Cochinchina –

but chose instead to work through the Nguyen dynasty and its established administration. In effect, the French created a parallel administration – the *résident* system – that shadowed the Vietnamese administration down to the provincial level, reserving for itself the main policy decisions and matters of security, and inheriting the foreign policy responsibilities of the dynasty.

France's main interest in the Montagnard regions during the early years was to determine the limits of Vietnamese power (which France had now effectively inherited), and to discover the general conditions of the region, the political relationships that existed, and the extent to which other powers (particularly Siam) had penetrated the area. In the 1870s and 1880s, a number of French expeditions worked their way through this area – mainly moving north from Cochinchina – including one by Henri Mayrena, who attempted in 1888 to establish his own 'kingdom' in the Kontum region.[9] Such attempts at individual aggrandizement – à la James Brooke in Sarawak – were discouraged by the French authorities.

The strategic significance of the Montagnard area was, however, fundamentally changed when the French in 1893 gained control of the east bank of the Mekong river from the Siamese, and subsequently set up a French administration in southern Laos.[10] France now had control of both sides of the Indochinese mountain chain, and their Vietnam 'polity' was therefore replaced by an Indochina 'polity'. The implications of this for the Montagnard region were significant, and revealed paradoxes in French policy towards the Montagnards that were to complicate French–Montagnard relations throughout the whole period of colonial rule. Unlike the similar minority regions in Burma, or on the Indochina–China border in the north, the Montagnard region was now no longer at the periphery of the colonial state, and therefore ceased to be strategically important as a frontier region. However, at the same time, it became far more important economically. In a sense, the Montagnard region was a classic colonial peripheral region – ripe for the kind of special relationship that Britain established with the peripheral minorities of Burma – which suddenly found itself at the heart of a colonial polity.

Subsequent French policy in the region reflected this central paradox in French–Montagnard relations. By the end of the nineteenth century, the French administration under Paul Doumer had embarked on an Indochina strategy designed, above everything, to draw Vietnam, Laos and Cambodia together as a political and economic unit, and in particular to detach Cambodia and Laos from their natural links to Siam. Such a strategy depended very largely on the development of an east–west communications network between the three regions. The

Montagnard region – which could now appropriately be called the Central Highlands – was the key to such a network.

The French therefore set out to regularize the administration of the region and delineate clear-cut provincial and national boundaries. In 1898, the *cac-lai* system was ended, and, in those areas that had previously been under Vietnamese control, administrative responsibility was now handed over to Vietnamese provincial governors and their French counterparts, the *résidents*.[11] The same policy was operated in Laos and Cambodia. In those areas, however, where neither Vietnamese, Lao nor Khmer rule had previously been exercised, French administrators relied directly on local village chiefs, who therefore became responsible for taxes and the *corvée*, a system where fixed amounts of labour were made freely available by villagers to the government in lieu of taxes.[12]

The question of the *corvée* – particularly in the building of roads – was to become crucial for the Central Highlands, precisely because of the region's new economic significance for France. The French, however, were not only preparing to embark on a road-building programme in the area, but also began the process of opening up suitable parts of the Central Highlands – mainly the Darlac Plateau – to agricultural development. Land grants were given to French commercial interests and, before long, a plantation economy had begun to take root in parts of the region, bringing in its train, for the first time, a wave of Vietnamese settlement, including Vietnamese petty officials, plantation workers and market gardeners.[13] Of course, this strategy of economic development demanded 'pacification', or the imposition of French authority, over areas that had hitherto been outside Vietnamese, Khmer or Lao control. The tightening of outside administration and the imposition of the *corvée* and other tax demands, however, provoked resistance, which in turn led to demands for ever more energetic and thorough measures of 'pacification.' Although the most coherent and dangerous minority revolts against the French colonial administration occurred outside of the Central Highlands – in the Bolovens Plateau in southern Laos between 1901 and 1902, and among the Hmong/ Meo near the Laos–China–Vietnam border between 1918 and 1921[14] – whole sectors of the Central Highlands remained for decades so-called 'zones of dissidence', and, among the more remote tribes, 'pacification' was barely completed by the early 1940s.[15]

The paradox of French policy towards the Central Highlands in the early to mid-twentieth century lies in the fact that, while on the one hand this region was the hub of a French–Indochinese economic strategy, there was at the same time a clear attempt to insulate the Montagnards from the Vietnamese and to develop a special and exclusive relationship between the Montagnards and the French. The key figure in this strategy was Leopold Sabatier, who administered the Rhadé region of Darlac province from before the First World War to the mid-1920s. During this period, regulations were introduced to consolidate the control of Montagnard village chiefs over the administration of justice; education and health care were made available to the Montagnards; and a beginning was made in the attempt to develop writing systems – particularly for the Rhadé language – and to codify Montagnard law.[16] Despite the economic pressures already mentioned, Sabatier attempted to regulate and restrain encroachment on Montagnard land in the Darlac Plateau.[17] This growing special relationship between the Montagnards and the French was most powerfully symbolized by a special *serment* – or oath ceremony – in 1926, when local Montagnard chieftains in Darlac pledged loyalty directly to the French *résident*.[18] A more practical example of the special relationship was the inclusion of Montagnard units in the Garde Indigène created in 1921, and the formation in 1931 of the Bataillon Montagnard du Sud-Annam.[19]

This attempt to create a special and exclusive relationship between the French and the Montagnards – something akin to that created by the British with the minorities on the periphery of Burma – was, however, continually obstructed by economic pressures. Despite Sabatier's efforts, land encroachments continued, and indeed accelerated after his departure. Land encroachments and intensified *corvée* demands stimulated resistance in the 1930s among, for example, the Mnong inland from Dalat, and the Stieng situated along the Vietnam–Cambodia border.[20] But perhaps the most remarkable manifestation of Montagnard discontent was the general movement of resistance in 1937 to the *corvée* and the alien presence in the Central Highlands, known as the 'Python God Movement'. The stimulus for this movement appears to have been reports of strange events – including that of a woman giving birth to a python – and the spread of prophesies of the imminent departure of both the French and the Vietnamese from the Highlands. The significance of the movement lay not in its effectiveness – it soon died out, and in any event had confined itself largely to non-cooperation rather than active resistance – but in the fact that it spanned a large number of Montagnard groups.[21] It appears that the combined impact of economic and administrative encroachment was helping to create a sense of unity among the Montagnards.

In the broader perspective, France's policies in the Central Highlands were certainly contradictory: on the one side, they were attempting to highlight a separate Montagnard identity by codifying Montagnard laws, entrenching local Montagnard autonomy, and providing writing systems for the languages of the region; on the other, plantations had been set up, Vietnamese communities had established themselves in the Central Highlands, and a whole network of hill stations, schools, medical facilities and a security system had been established throughout the region. Stimulated by both the threats and the opportunities implicit in French policy, a new, educated Montagnard elite was beginning slowly to emerge.[22] In the schools, in the military formations created by the French, and among the more important local rulers, the sense of a common Montagnard identity and interest was beginning to take shape.

The impact of the Second World War on the Central Highlands

The contradictions in French policy towards the Montagnards were not resolved during the course of the Second World War. Initially, the war had little impact; but the sudden defeat of France by Germany in 1940 immediately put the French Indochinese administration on the defensive. In the autumn of 1940, the French were forced to allow the Japanese to place military installations in northern Indochina. Early in 1941, after a brief border war in which the Bataillon Montagnard participated, France was forced to concede territory in Laos and Cambodia to Thailand. By mid-1941, the Japanese had consolidated their military presence in Indochina, and there followed a period of uneasy coexistence between the Vichy French administration and the Japanese military command.

In the Central Highlands, the period between 1941 and 1945 saw a degree of development and prosperity. This was primarily due to the fact that the hill stations in the Central Highlands – particularly Dalat – were expanded during this period in order to cater for the leisure and health demands of a French community that had been cut off from metropolitan France.[23] In March 1945, however, the artificial arrangement between the Japanese and the French administration was finally ruptured when the Japanese dismantled the colonial regime by force. Nominally, the Japanese handed political control over Laos, Cambodia and most of Vietnam back to their respective monarchies. In practice, most areas of Indochina, including the Central Highlands, witnessed a period of uncertainty and near-anarchy.

It was in this context of a vacuum of power that the struggle for control over the Central Highlands began. After the Japanese *coup de force* of March 1945, small units of French troops, trained by the British 'Special Operations Executive' (SOE) in India, were parachuted into selected regions of Indochina – particularly the minority regions – in order to build up networks of resistance to the Japanese and prepare the ground for an eventual French return. One such group established links with the Rhadé in the Central Highlands.[24] These small-scale and generally unsuccessful military adventures were, however, quickly overtaken by events. Immediately after the Japanese surrender to the Allies in August 1945, Ho Chi Minh's Viet-Minh organization – which was in effect a broad patriotic 'front' controlled by the Indochina Communist Party – began its bid to seize power throughout Vietnam. In the months of August and September 1945, the Viet-Minh were able to establish administrative committees in Kontum and Ban Me Thuot in the Central Highlands, and to penetrate certain Montagnard areas in depth, particularly the Hré region above Quang Ngai.[25]

The Free French regime under General de Gaulle was determined to reassert French control over Indochina as quickly as possible at the end of the war. This task was for de Gaulle a matter of extreme urgency, not so much because of the Viet-Minh takeover, but because the United States in particular appeared to be trying to exclude France from the post-surrender arrangements for Indochina, which stipulated that Nationalist China should occupy northern Indochina and Britain's Southeast Asia Command the southern section of Indochina.[26] The French were able to capitalize quickly on British support and connivance in the latter's zone of military control. By October 1945, General Leclerc in Saigon was preparing for the reconquest of south and central Vietnam. By the beginning of December 1945, the French had occupied Ban Me Thuot, and by the end of January 1946 they had expanded their control to Dalat.[27]

The Montagnards in the First Indochina War
1946–1954

After the liberation of France in the summer of 1944, de Gaulle and the Free French were faced with the problem of framing a general policy towards France's colonial empire in the post-war world. France's basic policy centred on the creation of a new concept – the 'Union française' or 'French Union', a political structure in which the entire empire would be represented, but in which dominant control would remain in French hands. It was announced in a government declaration of 24 March 1945 that an 'Indochinese Federation' – under the control of a French governor-general – would operate within the framework of this aforementioned French Union, and that the components of the Indochinese Federation would be allowed a measure of local autonomy with guaranteed rights and opportunities for all inhabitants.[28] Between Japan's *coup de force* in Indochina and its surrender, however, de

Gaulle's objectives became more precise. It is clear that what he wished to create in Indochina was a new partnership between France and the traditional monarchies of Laos, Cambodia and Vietnam, underpinning a gradual evolution to self-government under overall French protection and sovereignty. This is, in essence, what subsequently happened in relation to what de Gaulle called the 'solid dynasties' of Laos and Cambodia.[29] The problem lay with Vietnam: not only because of the fact that French colonial policy had never treated Vietnam as a single political unit, but also because of the Viet-Minh's pre-emptive seizure of power, declaration of an independent and unified Vietnam, and removal of the Nguyen dynasty with Emperor Bao Dai's – forced or willing – acquiescence.

Once again, France's policy towards the Montagnards depended on their policy towards Vietnam. If France decided to negotiate with the forces of Vietnamese nationalism, then its special relationship with the Montagnards would necessarily be sacrificed. If, on the other hand, the French strategy was based on a denial of Vietnamese national unity and an attempt to encourage the political fragmentation of Vietnam, then the special relationship with the Montagnards would become a key part of that strategy. From 1945 to 1954, France dithered between these policies.

By late 1945, the policy of High Commissioner d'Argenlieu was clearly that of first restoring France's military control ('pacification') and then worrying about constitutional structures. By early 1946, however, it was clear that France had reached the limit of its military capacities with the seizure of Cochinchina and parts of Annam. At the same time, both France and the Viet-Minh had a mutual interest in removing Nationalist Chinese troops from North Vietnam, which they were currently occupying in the name of the Allies. Accordingly, an interim agreement was reached on 6 March 1946 between the French and the Viet-Minh, in which France recognized the right of the Viet-Minh state to self-government, and the Viet-Minh, in turn, recognized the overall authority of the French Union in Indochina. The unanswered questions of the constitutional relationship between the Democratic Republic of Vietnam and France, and the definition of Vietnamese unity, were to be matters for future discussion.[30]

In effect, this agreement was nothing more than a temporary stand-off brought about by the fact that neither side had the capacity to impose its will on the other. No sooner was the ink dry on the agreement than France embarked on a strategy of trying to break down the idea of a unified Vietnam by exploiting ethnic, regional and ideological divisions. On 11 March 1946, d'Argenlieu was instructed by the French government to 'examine the possibility of the eventual creation of an autonomous Moi (Montagnard) territory', in order to ensure – as the French put it – the 'sauvegarde et évolution' of the Montagnards.[31] On the other side the Viet-Minh – who still held the Pleiku and Kontum regions in the north of the Central Highlands – now redoubled their efforts to win Montagnard support for a unified Vietnam. In a letter sent by Ho Chi Minh to a 'Congress of Southern National Minorities' held in Pleiku in April 1946, he stressed that all the 'nationalities' of Vietnam should unite against French attempts to exploit dissensions between them.[32]

The Central Highlands had, in fact, become the centre piece of d'Argenlieu's Indochina strategy by the spring of 1946. At the heart of this was the notion that, with the collapse of the Nguyen dynasty and the seizure of power by Vietnamese revolutionaries, France could no longer work with the forces of Vietnamese nationalism. The new objective was, therefore, to insulate those states and regions that could work within the French Indochina framework from the 'virus' of Vietnamese revolution. In geographical terms, this meant consolidating French influence over the Mekong river states – Laos, Cambodia and the colony of Cochinchina – and creating a 'buffer' for the Mekong region along the mountainous spinal cord of Indochina. This would involve detaching all the mountain minorities, from the Chinese border to the Central Highlands, from Vietnamese control, and enabling them to come under direct French protection. 'Cela', noted d'Argenlieu, 'permettrait d'opposer aux vues de Hanoi le barrage des autres Etats.'[33]

In May 1946, d'Argenlieu embarked on his plan to create a separate Montagnard state in the Central Highlands. On 14 May, he received an oath of allegiance from the Montagnard chieftains in Ban Me Thuot, a ceremony that he regarded as the equivalent of a plebiscite![34] On 27 May 1946, d'Argenlieu announced the formation of a special administrative region, the 'Commissariat du Gouvernement Fédéral pour les Populations Montagnardes du Sud Indochinois', or PMSI. This special region comprised five of the Montagnard provinces of the Central Highlands, which were now to be detached from the authority of the regional government of central Vietnam (or Annam), and placed directly under the authority of the High Commissioner for Indochina.[35] This decision to create a separate Montagnard region was followed in June 1946 by the establishment by France of an autonomous 'Cochinchina Republic'.[36] D'Argenlieu's 'Mekong' strategy was further consolidated when, in the same month, the French ousted the Viet-Minh from their strongholds in Pleiku and Kontum in the northern Central Highlands.[37]

It was only in 1948, however, that the French were able to patch together an autonomous 'T'ai Federation' with its centre at Lai Chau in the northwesternmost part of Vietnam.[38] By this time, however, French policy was already in the process of being reversed. Soon after full-scale hostilities broke out between France and the Democratic Republic of Vietnam (DRV) in December 1946, it became apparent to France that their policy of fragmentation, particularly the creation of an autonomous Cochinchina Republic, far from weakening the position of the Viet-Minh, had further alienated Vietnamese political opinion. They therefore reverted, however reluctantly, to a 'nation-building' strategy. In late 1947, the new French High Commissioner announced a plan to incorporate an autonomous Vietnam within the French Union, but affirmed nevertheless that the 'special status' of the Montagnard special region, the PMSI, would be maintained.[39] There then followed a period of tortuous negotiation between the French and Vietnamese non-communist political leaders, particularly the ex-Emperor Bao Dai, in which the key issues in contention were control over defence and foreign policy, and the status of the autonomous regions. In the course of 1949, however, the principle of Vietnamese unity was finally established, and the Cochinchina Republic was incorporated into Vietnam proper. At the beginning of 1950, the new, supposedly independent, 'State of Vietnam' came into being.[40]

Despite France's apparent recognition of Vietnamese independence under Bao Dai as head of state, they still retained real authority through the mechanism of the Indochina Federation controlled by a French High Commissioner, and through the wider French Union. In regard to the Montagnard separate zone, the French and Bao Dai were able to reach a compromise in 1950, by which the region was made into a special administrative division or 'Domaine de la Couronne du Pays Montagnards du Sud' (Crown Domain of the Southern Montagnard Region), or PMS, under the personal jurisdiction of Bao Dai.[41] This special status – which in effect meant that the PMS was under Vietnamese control but not incorporated within the Vietnamese state – was reinforced in 1951 by a so-called 'Statut Particulier'. This guaranteed the special rights and status of the Montagnards in the PMS, and the obligation of the Vietnamese government to protect Montagnard languages in the education system, encourage Montagnard representation in the administration, respect local traditions, and maintain Montagnard law codes in the local courts.[42]

The status of this new PMS 'crown domain' well illustrates the complexity of France's nation-building efforts in Vietnam in the late 1940s and early 1950s. In theory, France was handing over independence to a sovereign, unified Vietnam within the 'partnership' of the French Union; in practice, it still maintained a patchwork of patron–client relationships with groups and regions throughout Vietnam, including the T'ai Federation and the Central Highlands. In the Central Highlands, the special relationship between France and the Montagnards was maintained intact despite the region's change in status. The main officials were still French, and every effort was made to promote Montagnards to the lower rungs of the administration. France's dual policy of simultaneously protecting Montagnard identity from Vietnamese encroachment, and at the same time promoting development, is clearly reflected in economic planning for the Central Highlands in the early 1950s. While, for example, further land development of the Central Highlands – in the form of land grants to settlers – was seen as essential, it was envisaged, even at this late stage, that French, not Vietnamese, settlers should be given privileged access to such land grants.[43]

As in the pre-war days, however, the special relationship between the French and the Montagnards was not invariably harmonious. The demands of Indochina's war economy, and the intensified need to exploit those areas of Vietnam that were still under French control, meant that the need for the *corvée*, or compulsory labour, was greater than ever. In his classic travel book, *A Dragon Apparent*, Norman Lewis presents a vivid description of life in the Central Highlands in 1950, capturing the intense underlying anger felt by the Montagnards at what was in effect their conscription for labour in the neighbouring plantations, and the inability of the local French administrators to protect the Montagnards' interests.[44]

The French also faced the problem of Viet-Minh infiltration of the region. Although the Viet-Minh administrative and propaganda networks had been largely flushed out by the French in 1946, local corners of Viet-Minh influence still remained, particularly in areas adjacent to the coastal lowlands, like the Hré territory near Quang Ngai. One response to this continuing threat was the creation in 1951 of a 'Division Montagnarde' – the 4th Vietnamese Light Infantry Division – in the newly formed Vietnamese armed forces, to cover the southern Central Highlands.[45]

The sudden outbreak of a savage war between the Hré and the local Viet-Minh in 1949 contributed to a quite different military development in the Central Highlands – that of the 'special war'. In the aftermath of the Hré rebellion, the so-called 'Doc Lap Hré' (Hré Independence Movement) was created by the French, and a Hré guerrilla organization was established to fight the Viet-Minh under the leadership of French, not Vietnamese, soldiers.[46] By 1952, a whole network of guerrilla units had been created, from the Central Highlands to the T'ai region in the north. These units, called collectively the 'Groupement de Commandos Mixtes Aéroportés' (GCMA), normally comprised around four hundred men, and were led by French non-commissioned officers.[47] As the war steadily spread into the central mountain region of Indochina in the early 1950s, so the French increasingly relied on these guerrilla units rather than the recently formed regular Vietnamese army.

In 1951 and 1952, the military commander of the Viet-Minh, Vo Nguyen Giap, tried to deliver a *coup de grâce* against the French army in Indochina by launching direct attacks on the Red River Delta. This proved to be a costly failure, and Giap quickly changed his strategy. Giap now directed his attention towards those very areas that d'Argenlieu had identified as the key to the protection of France's interests and position in Indochina: the T'ai autonomous region, northern and central Laos and the Central Highlands. The clear objective of Giap was to force France to defend these regions, and thus disperse and deplete its military resources. The key focus of this strategy was the T'ai autonomous region, where Giap was able, between 1952 and 1954, to entice the French to concentrate their troops in the border plateau of Dien Bien Phu. The Viet-Minh proved to be adept at exploiting the ethnic and clan tensions that lay beneath the surface of the apparent harmony of the T'ai Federation.[48]

Within the Central Highlands the key area was the region of southern Laos stretching roughly from Tchepone to the Bolovens Plateau. Perhaps because of the legacy of the 1901 revolt there, this region became a Viet-Minh stronghold during this First Indochina War.[49] Using this area as a kind of *point d'appui*, the Viet-Minh began a series of increasingly effective probing actions, westwards to the Mekong river, and eastwards to the Vietnamese Central Highlands. While the trap was steadily closing around the French in the T'ai highlands in the China–Vietnam–Laos border zone in 1953, Viet-Minh military operations in the Central Highlands were intensified. By December 1953, the Viet-Minh had begun a concentrated military offensive, first attacking Attopeu in the Bolovens Plateau, and then threatening Kontum province.[50] France was forced to divert troops from the coast, but were unable to hold Kontum, which was evacuated in February 1954.[51] Thereafter the whole An Khe–Kontum–Pleiku–Cheo Reo area came under threat. By the time that the military truce between the Viet-Minh and the French was agreed at the Geneva Conference in 1954, An Khe had fallen to the Viet-Minh, and the French position in Pleiku was perilously close to collapse.[52]

In the Geneva accord, the Viet-Minh agreed to evacuate their troops and cadres from the whole of Vietnam south of the seventeenth parallel. It was then understood that the French-created State of Vietnam would act as the *de facto* political authority to the south of the 17th parallel, and the Democratic Republic of Vietnam to the north, pending elections for a unified Vietnam in the summer of 1956. In theory, this should have removed Viet-Minh influence in the Central Highlands, at least for the time being. In practice, the Viet-Minh bolstered their influence in the region in a number of ways. First, they used Kontum, for a while, as a centre for propaganda and organization; second, and stemming from this, they were able to recruit and train Montagnard cadres and take them north when the time came to evacuate the Central Highlands; finally, they left behind an underground network of supporters both in the Central Highlands and in southern Laos.[53] In the event that the unification of Vietnam could not be brought about peaceably, the Central Highlands and southern Laos would inevitably become the focus of any renewed conflict between north and south Vietnam. The Viet-Minh were clearly preparing for this possibility.

The Montagnards, the Diem regime and the United States

The agreement at Geneva meant the end of French Indochina. The Indochina administration was dismantled, and three independent nations emerged. Two of them, under the royal governments of Cambodia and Laos, had already been given a degree of independence by France. The third, Vietnam, had been temporarily divided between two 'interim *de facto*' states. The Central Highlands, therefore, once again became a peripheral region, as it had been before the arrival of the French. The division of Vietnam into two regimes, both claiming national and ideological legitimacy, however, ensured the region's strategic significance.

The State of Vietnam that now took over responsibility for the whole southern zone of Vietnam was the residue of France's effort to exploit anti-communist and anti-revolutionary fears among a significant section of the Vietnamese nationalists. In June 1954, Head of State Bao Dai appointed Ngo Dinh Diem as prime minister. Georges Condominas, an Indochina-born anthropologist who worked in the Mnong region of the Central Highlands during the First Indochina War, is almost certainly right in his suggestion that Diem's 'hypernationalism' was, first, a natural reaction to French colonial rule, and second, and more particularly, an attempt to compensate for the very weak nationalist credentials of the regime that he led.[54] With increasingly firm American support, Diem set about weakening French influence, eventually ending the residual French presence in Vietnam. This involved prising the Vietnamese army from French control; breaking up the network of exclusive patron–client relationships that France had forged throughout South Vietnam, but particularly with religious sects and regional warlords in Cochinchina; tightening control over the provincial administrations; creating a new political entity – the 'Republic of Vietnam' – untainted by colonial links; and, finally, replacing Bao Dai as head of state.

It was inevitable that the Central Highlands would become an immediate target for this new 'hyper-nationalism'. In 1955, the semi-autonomous status of the 'Crown Domain' of the Pays Montagnards du Sud was ended, the Central Highlands were incorporated into the Republic of Vietnam, and Vietnamese province chiefs replaced the French _résidents_.[55] There then followed an intense period of 'Vietnamization'. Vietnamese settlement in the region was now encouraged; attempts were made to force the Montagnards to end their 'wasteful' slash-and-burn agricultural techniques (thus, incidentally, providing greater access to Montagnard land for settlers); Montagnard languages and, indeed, French were phased out of the schools; local customs were discouraged and disparaged; and official status was removed from the traditional legal systems.[56] In effect, Diem's regime embarked on a forced-pace – and highly insensitive – policy of 'nation-building', in which the key ingredients were Vietnamese settlement in the Montagnard territories and the cultural integration of the Montagnards into Vietnamese society.

Despite Diem's independent nationalist rhetoric, the underlying fact was that the United States had, between (roughly) 1950 and 1955, replaced France as the patron and protector of anti-communist Vietnamese nationalism. The United States was not only steadily inheriting France's position at the national level; it had already developed at least the beginnings of a special relationship with the Montagnards at the local level. As early as 1929, American Protestants had established a Mission in Dalat; and, in the late 1940s, another American Mission – described in very disparaging tones by Norman Lewis in _A Dragon Apparent_ – was set up in Ban Me Thuot.[57] In 1952, in response to an appeal by Bao Dai, a United States medical aid programme was established in the Central Highlands, and the US became involved in other development projects.[58]

After 1955, however, the whole emphasis of American policy in Vietnam was on encouraging 'nation-building'. Teams of American advisers with considerable technical and administrative expertise, but very little knowledge of the country, poured into Vietnam and enthusiastically promoted Diem's plans for rapid national integration. An article by Joseph Buttinger on the 'Ethnic Minorities in the Republic of Vietnam', published in W.L. Fishel's _Problems of Freedom_, gives a taste of this undiscriminating enthusiasm for nation-building.

Buttinger, for example, justified extensive Vietnamese settlement in the Central Highlands as the only way 'of initiating sufficient economic expansion, of instituting effective government quickly in these regions, and of safeguarding national security and of improving tribal existence in the required short time'.[59]

Americans on the ground in the Central Highlands were, however, alarmed and sometimes disgusted at this emphasis on 'national security' above the welfare and rights of the Montagnards.[60] In 1957, Gerald Hickey – an American civilian adviser – made a tour of the Central Highlands, and warned that continued Vietnamese land settlement, and 'Vietnamization' of the educational system, Montagnard culture and law, was creating deep discontent. His warnings were ignored.[61]

Following the dissolution of the semi-autonomous Pays Montagnards du Sud in 1955, Montagnard disaffection had indeed increased, and it was, not unnaturally, intensified by the subsequent policy of Vietnamization. Diem's policy of repression, in fact, helped forge a united Montagnard leadership – in which a particularly prominent role was played by the Rhadé and Bahnar elite – as well as a united programme of action. A number of Montagnard committees and fronts were formed in 1955. It was not, however, until May 1958 that a united organization – Bajaraka – was created by Montagnard leaders with the major objective of gaining autonomy for the Central Highlands.[62] Later in the same year, this movement called for a general strike in the Central Highlands, and its leaders were duly imprisoned.[63]

These developments might have been dismissed by the Americans as just part of the normal trauma of post-colonial nation-building, had it not been for their strategic implications. By 1958–59 it was apparent, first, that the South Vietnamese regime was destabilizing at an alarming rate and, second, that the communist regime of North Vietnam was poised to resume the struggle for Vietnamese reunification. Within South Vietnam itself, Diem's suppression of all manifestations of opposition to the regime, and attempts to assimilate by force all religious sects and ethnic minorities – including the Cao Dai and Hoa Hao sects, and the Khmer, Cham and Montagnard groups – had stimulated movements of resistance in which old Viet-Minh cadres, now called 'Viet Cong' or Vietnamese communists, were playing an increasingly important role. In communist North Vietnam, the leadership had long been aware that unification could be achieved only by force, and they had already made stealthy preparations for the armed struggle. The full-scale civil war which broke out in Laos in 1959 between the American-backed Royal Lao government and the communist Pathet Lao gave the latter undisputed control over the mountainous interior of southern Laos. This presented North Vietnam with the perfect opportunity to reactivate its networks in the Central Highlands and to accelerate the infiltration of cadres into the region. With the formation by North Vietnam of the 'National Liberation Front for South Vietnam' (NLFSVN) in 1960, the stage was set for a communist-orchestrated assault on the Diem regime.

The period between 1959 and 1961, therefore, saw a concerted effort by North Vietnam to win over the Montagnards in order to build a secure base for infiltration into South Vietnam. Montagnard cadres that had supported the Viet-Minh and moved north in 1954–55, were now re-infiltrated back into the Central Highlands in order to build the framework for an insurgency movement in the region.[64] Simultaneously, propaganda broadcasts beamed from Hanoi in Rhadé, Jarai and Bahnar – the main Montagnard languages – advocated Montagnard autonomy and highlighted the North Vietnamese policy of creating autonomous zones for the ethnic minorities of North Vietnam. The fact that these autonomous zones led a precarious existence, and that the Vietnamese Communist Party policy towards minorities combined a limited measure of cultural autonomy with rigid political control, would have been lost on the Montagnard audience. The apparent North Vietnamese respect for Montagnard language and culture, and their promises of regional autonomy, naturally attracted many Montagnards, and the communists therefore presented an effective challenge to the South Vietnamese regime in the Central Highlands.[65]

The Montagnards, the 'special war' and separatism

By 1961, it was becoming clear to the United States that its nation-building efforts in South Vietnam were failing. The regime was threatened from outside and crumbling from within. Since the Americans were determined to maintain South Vietnam as a front-line bastion against the communist threat to the whole of Southeast Asia, they found themselves increasingly constrained to intervene directly in the internal affairs and the defence of the state. Just as the French had, during the First Indochina War of 1946–54, dithered between the policies of, on the one hand, bolstering a strong anti-communist Vietnamese state, and on the other hand, building a patchwork of special relationships with local warlords and ethnic groups, so the United States faced almost exactly the same dilemma. At the root, France and the United States had the same problem: the weakness of Vietnamese anti-communist nationalism.

Faced with the necessity of defending South Vietnam from infiltration, the Americans gradually found themselves building a new special relationship with the Montagnards. A 'Program of Action' for Vietnam put before President Kennedy in May 1961 recommended, among other things, greater American assistance for South Vietnam in protecting the border, including measures to help South Vietnam 'gain the support of nomadic tribes and other border inhabitants'. It was envisaged that this help would be provided indirectly, with United States Special Forces working through South Vietnamese special force counterparts.[66] This general plan formed the basis for the United States policy that was developed thereafter. Beginning in 1961, and under the watchful and suspicious eye of the Diem regime, American Special Forces helped to build up a 'Village Defense Program' in the Central Highlands; later, the resulting 'Village Defense Units' were renamed 'Civilian Irregular Defense Groups', or CIDGs.[67] Fairly quickly, this CIDG programme tended to shift from a defensive to an offensive capacity, with the creation of 'Strike Force' camps given the primary task of detecting and preventing communist infiltration from Laos. As it became increasingly clear that the South Vietnamese Special Forces were neither welcome nor effective, the United States Special Forces developed an almost exclusive control over CIDG units through 1963. Despite American anxiety to 'do everything possible to foster improved Montagnard–Vietnamese relations and to prevent [the] transfer of Montagnard allegiance to [the] US', military imperatives were creating a special patron–client relationship between the Montagnards and the United States.[68] The old Groupements des Commandos Mixtes Aéroportés (GCMAs) of the French 'special war' were re-emerging in a new guise.

In November 1963 the Diem regime was overthrown with indirect help from the United States; but both the political and the security situation, far from improving, continued to deteriorate through 1964. Through the first half of 1964, the United States continued to hover between the policies of working through and by-passing the South Vietnamese government in their relationship with the Montagnards. It was agreed between the Americans and the new regime of General Nguyen Khanh at the beginning of 1964 that the South Vietnamese should have increased command and control over the CIDG programme. By June of that year, however, American officials were becoming increasingly anxious at the consequent deterioration of effectiveness and morale in the CIDG camps, and were considering 'the re-establishment of direct US participation in the Montagnard guerrilla operations'.[69]

In fact, events in the Central Highlands were now moving to a climax. The main source of Montagnard resentment against the South Vietnamese regime was the diminution, and finally the complete elimination, of the autonomous status they had achieved with the creation of the special administrative region of the Populations Montagnardes du Sud-Indochinois (PMSI) in 1946. Although Diem's policy of national integration had stalled in the early 1960s, the outlines of that policy remained intact. The minimum demands of Montagnard leaders were now for the restoration of the semi-autonomous status they had enjoyed under Bao Dai; their maximum demand was for complete autonomy, or even the establishment of a separate state.

Events in the late 1950s and early 1960s had helped to push Montagnard leaders towards this more radical position. During the late 1950s, the Khmer ethnic minority in the Mekong Delta – known as the Khmer Krom – had become more and more restive in response to Diem's policy of 'Vietnamization', as had the Cham communities dotted through south and central Vietnam. On their own, the Cham and the Khmer Krom minorities would not have posed a serious threat to the South Vietnamese. But the neighbouring kingdom of Cambodia harboured a reasonably large Cham community descended from Chams driven out of their homeland by the Vietnamese emperors. In addition, the Cambodians themselves still nurtured a historic resentment against the Vietnamese over their seizure of the Mekong Delta region from the Khmer empire. Old nationalist grudges and irredentist ambitions were linked to new fears among the Cambodian leadership that South Vietnam, manipulated by the United States, was planning to destabilize the Cambodian regime in order to draw Cambodia into the United States' camp in Southeast Asia. The Cambodian regime therefore played a key role in encouraging the formation in 1960 of a Cham irredentist movement – the 'Front Unifié de Lutte de la Race Kam' (FULRK) – and a similar movement among the Khmer Krom.[70] Contacts were developed between these movements and the Bajaraka Montagnard leaders – many of whom had been released from jail by Nguyen Khanh in January 1964 – and plans were laid in the autumn of 1964 for a united separatist rebellion against South Vietnam.[71]

To some extent, the Montagnard leaders were being drawn into a much wider conspiracy in which the Cambodian government and army were playing a shadowy role. But even without this factor, events in 1964 were pushing the Montagnards towards rebellion. The years 1961–63 had witnessed the forging of a patron–client relationship between the Americans and the Montagnards which had been seen by the latter as a vital buffer against Vietnamese encroachment. Whether the American leadership liked it or not, a close link had been developing in the Central Highlands between the US Special Forces and the Montagnard soldiers in the CIDG camps, many of whom had links to the Bajaraka movement.[72] Through 1964, Montagnard leaders saw these links being severed, as the South Vietnamese reasserted their control over the CIDG camps, while at the same time Montagnard officers were being carefully dispersed through the South Vietnamese army. As their grievances accumulated and the Montagnard resistance movement began to take shape, the steady deterioration of political stability in South Vietnam offered the Montagnards a perfect opportunity.[73]

On the evening of 19 September 1964, Montagnard soldiers, some 3,000 in all, seized control of four CIDG camps in Darlac Province, killing up to seventy Vietnamese soldiers in the process.[74] They temporarily gained control of a radio station in Ban Me Thuot, but were soon forced to retreat to the CIDG camps, where they held as hostages a number of Vietnamese soldiers and civilians and US Special Forces personnel.[75] It quickly became apparent, however, that this particular insurgency was confined to troops of Rhadé and Mnong origin, and that the more general uprising that had been planned had failed to ignite.[76] After this false start, the leaders of the rebellion – chief of whom was Y Bham Enoul, a Bajaraka leader who had been imprisoned by Diem, but later released and appointed deputy province chief of Darlac – moved to a secret camp across the border in Cambodia.[77]

The rebellion was spearheaded by a new organization that had been created by Khmer Krom, Cham and Montagnard leaders: the 'Front Unifié de Lutte de la Race Opprimée' (FULRO). The objectives of the rebellion and of this front were, however, obscured by the fact that the leaders of the rebellion had located themselves in a 'liberated area' beyond the Cambodian border, while their subordinates, holed up in the CIDG camps, were facing the problem of immediate negotiations with the South Vietnamese government. The 'Declaration' produced on 20 September 1964 (see Appendix 3) by the 'Haut Comité' of FULRO outlined the unity of the oppressed Cham, Khmer Krom and Montagnard peoples; claimed that the South Vietnamese Government had embarked on a 'genocidal' policy against the ethnic minorities; and concluded: 'Notre but est de défendre notre survie et notre patrimoine culturel, spirituel et racial, et ainsi l'Indépendance de nos Pays.'[78]

The declaration was couched in very general terms, and the above phrase could be interpreted as anything from a general desire to vindicate ethnic minority rights, to an irredentist claim for a return of the whole of Cochinchina to the Khmers, and the whole of ancient Champa to the Chams and Montagnards. This broad irredentist objective was confirmed by the maps produced by FULRO in 1965. On top of the fact that the demands of FULRO were vague but potentially extreme, the language of the 'Declaration' – with its violently anti-American, anti-SEATO rhetoric – clearly reflected the influence of Cambodia, where Prince Sihanouk's policy was at this time swinging decisively against the Americans and towards the communist bloc.[79]

Set against these generalized maximum demands were the practical concessions that the Montagnard leaders hoped to wrest from the South Vietnamese. Looking at the lengthy negotiations that continued through 1964 and 1965, it could be said that their demands boiled down to, first, a return to the semi-autonomous status that had been guaranteed to them by Bao Dai's 'Statut Particulier' in May 1951, including the rights to have Montagnard administrators in the Montagnard region, to use their own law-courts and systems of law, to use their own languages in the schools, and to have control over the disposal and use of their land.[80] Second, in the specifically military sphere, they wanted Montagnard CIDG units to be kept strictly for regional defence, and Montagnard officers and American advisers to be put in charge of these units, with Vietnamese advisers to be removed.[81]

Initially, although the South Vietnamese regional commander refrained from using force against the rebels, the South Vietnamese were reluctant to make concessions. They were intensely suspicious of what they saw as American 'interference' in the Montagnard region, and felt that some of the US Special Forces may have connived at the rebellion. This sensitivity was hardly surprising, particularly in the light of French policy in the Central Highlands a decade earlier, and of the clear evidence that the rebels wished to remove Vietnamese influence in the Central Highlands and at the same time strengthen patron–client links with the Americans. American Ambassador Maxwell Taylor had to go out of his way to reassure the Saigon government that the United States' only interest in the area was to bolster the defence of the region against communist insurgency and infiltration.[82] It is interesting to note, incidentally, the gap between the anti-imperialist, anti-US rhetoric of the FULRO declaration, and the reality, particularly at the Special Forces level, of close Montagnard–American ties.

On 27 September 1964, with the help of American mediation and guarantees, the rebel leaders released their hostages, and a period of negotiation over Montagnard demands began. From the outset, the South Vietnamese made it clear that they would not agree to anything that weakened the 'indivisibility' of Vietnam.[83] They therefore avoided making any concession that gave any kind of autonomous status to the Montagnards, and dismissed out of hand anything that might help encourage an exclusive relationship between the Montagnards and the United States: for example, the provision of direct US aid to the Central Highlands.[84] What they *were* prepared to contemplate were measures designed to protect Montagnard interests and give them a greater say in government, within the framework of a united South Vietnam. In the course of a conference between Montagnard and South Vietnamese leaders in Pleiku on 15–17 October 1964, the outline of a new agreement was reached. Montagnard landownership rights – which had been severely restricted by a decree of Diem in 1959 – were to be restored; local languages were to be used in primary schools along with Vietnamese; Montagnards were to have greater access to higher administrative and military positions; the status of the traditional Montagnard law-courts was to be respected; a measure of 'positive discrimination' was to be exercised on behalf of Montagnards, for whom scholarships would be made available; a special Montagnard 'Directorate' was to be established at central government level, which might eventually acquire the status of a ministry; and the Montagnard CIDGs were to remain separate from the army of Vietnam, or ARVN, proper.[85]

The reaction of the United States – the embassy, the military and Washington – to these developments is interesting. In the short term, their main anxiety was to make it clear both to the Montagnard rebels and to the South Vietnamese government that they did not in any way condone the rebellion. The anti-imperialist, anti-SEATO and anti-American rhetoric of the FULRO declaration made this task easier for them, particularly since such rhetoric suggested at least a measure of Vietnamese communist influence in the rebellion.[86] A clear-cut warning issued a few days after the outbreak of the rebellion by General West-moreland, head of Military Assistance Command Vietnam (MACV), that 'disloyal' CIDG units would get no support and – more to the point – no pay, undoubtedly helped bring about a quick accommodation.[87]

In their general appraisal, however, the US authorities were pessimistic about the future of Vietnamese–Montagnard relations. Despite the interim agreement reached in October 1964 – an agreement which was a statement of intent rather than a hard-and-fast undertaking – the American Embassy in Saigon believed that large numbers of Montagnards, particularly those in the CIDG camps, had sympathized with the aims of the September rebellion. At the root, they believed that the 'average Montagnards in both cities and hamlets would like to rid [the Central] Highlands of Vietnamese settlers and government', and ultimately would settle for nothing less than complete autonomy. The United States was anxious, therefore, to steer a delicate course of, on the one side, nudging the South Vietnamese government to make substantial concessions to the Montagnards, while, on the other, 'making it clear, as it was in the past, to Montagnard CIDG that [the] US stands with [the] Vietnamese Government and will assist it in suppressing rebellious acts which would only benefit [the] Viet Cong in the long run'.[88] It is clear that the United States saw its relationships with the South Vietnamese government and the Montagnards through the prism of the ultimate priority: that of building an effective bastion against communism in Southeast Asia. By early 1965 events in the Central Highlands had provided further confirmation of the view that only direct American military intervention could maintain that bastion.

In the aftermath of the Montagnard rebellion, there was a fatal split in the Montagnard leadership between those who were prepared to negotiate with the South Vietnamese government and those who moved to outright confrontation.[89] On the former side, intermittent negotiations continued between some FULRO leaders and the Saigon government between 1965 and 1968. Although Saigon stood firm against any concessions of real autonomy, they were prepared to expand Montagnard rights and representation in the Central Highlands and in the government: in 1967, for instance, a Ministry for Ethnic Minority Development was set up under Paul Nur, a Montagnard.[90] FULRO 'young Turks', on the other hand, rejected negotiations with the Saigon government and continued their liberation struggle from the Cambodia–Vietnam border. As early as October 1964 a shadowy 'Provisional Government of the High Plateaux of Champa' was set up to form the nucleus for this resistance.[91] The emphasis on 'Champa' rather than the 'Pays Montagnardes' illustrates one important aspect of the FULRO movement from this point on: that it had come increasingly under the influence of more politically sophisticated and better-connected Cham and Khmer Krom leaders, and that it was – via these leaders – being manipulated by Cambodian military leaders and politicians.[92]

Montagnard–Vietnamese relations were, however, overtaken by events in the mid-1960s. Montagnard society was to pay a terrible penalty for its peripheral status and its position on the front line in the confrontation between communism and the West. The reactivation of North Vietnamese infiltration in the late 1950s had stimulated the American–South Vietnamese response outlined above; this in turn had prompted full-scale North Vietnamese infiltration into the Central Highlands by 1965. By that year, the North Vietnamese and the Viet Cong had built up a solid base of support among the Mon-Khmer Montagnard groups in the northern sector of the Central Highlands from the seventeenth parallel south to Kontum and stretching down to the coastal regions; in the southern Montagnard region, they particularly targeted the Stieng people on the Cambodia–Vietnam border, poised to the north of Saigon.[93] In the same year, the Americans effectively took over the conduct of the war from the South Vietnamese, and tried to establish a 'shield' in the Central Highlands, behind which, it was hoped, South Vietnam could stabilize and strengthen in the main populated regions.

Rapidly, what had hitherto been a small-unit war in the Central

Highlands became a full-scale military conflict. It is, in the end, rather academic to debate whether the subsequent wholesale upheaval of the Montagnards was primarily caused by fear of the North Vietnamese or by American bombing. The result was the same: the disruption of an entire society. There is no doubt, however, that the flight from the Central Highlands caused by the communist offensives – and American–South Vietnamese counter-offensives – of Tet 1968 and Easter 1972 had a particularly devastating effect.[94]

Conclusion

The Montagnards of the Central Highlands of Vietnam are a classic – and an exceptionally tragic – example of a backward people in a peripheral region in the pre-colonial order of things who were ruthlessly exploited in the era of decolonization and the subsequent era of Cold War confrontation. With the utmost deliberation, the French created a Montagnard autonomous region as part of their strategy to weaken and contain Vietnamese nationalism; then they rapidly ditched Montagnard autonomy when they decided to switch strategies. The North Vietnamese, in order to win support from the Montagnards in their war against the Americans and the South Vietnamese, projected the image of a regime that would respect minority rights and cultures, and allow the creation of autonomous zones; these promises were not fulfilled after the unification of Vietnam in 1975–76, and the new socialist authorities were themselves soon fighting against FULRO guerrilla units in the Central Highlands.[95]

For their part, the Americans reproduced the strategy that France had followed in the First Indochina War. Faced with the inability of either Lao or Vietnamese pro-Western nationalism to build an effective bastion against communism in the region, they built up a *de facto* military alliance with minority groups from the Hmong in the Plain of Jars to the Khmer Krom in western Cochinchina, including the CIDG units of the Central Highlands. But the 'special relationship' built up by Americans with the Montagnards was strictly subordinated to wider strategic considerations.

Even the FULRO organization set up in 1964 – the clearest of all expressions of the Montagnards' political aspirations – was manipulated from the outset by non-Montagnard elements: in particular, Khmer Krom leaders, Cham officers in the Royal Cambodian Army, and Sihanouk himself. Before and after 1975, the FULRO guerrillas became involved in a complex network of regional geopolitical alliances, very much at the expense of the movement's original practical goal of promoting Montagnard autonomy.[96]

From the beginning, French colonial policy in the Central Highlands had been paradoxical. A peripheral region in the pre-colonial dispensation, the Central Highlands became the core of the French concept of a united Indochina economy. Anxious as they were to draw the Montagnards out of their primitive conditions, at the same time the French sought to protect Montagnard culture, customs and self-government. But while they tried to insulate the Montagnard culture from Vietnamese encroachment, it was during the period of French rule that an entire Vietnamese settler society was able to establish itself in the Central Highlands.

It could be argued that these alternating threats and encouragements helped to create a united Montagnard elite out of what had been a bewildering diversity of language groups and tribes in a region where traditional political organization had rarely extended beyond the village level. From this, it is possible to imagine the evolution of a common Montagnard identity transcending barriers of language and custom; indeed, the French creation of PMSI and the later Montagnard formation of FULRO are landmarks along the path to the development of such an identity. This process, however, was never completed, and it was soon drowned by larger conflicts: the struggle for Vietnamese independence and unity, and, beyond that, the global Cold War.

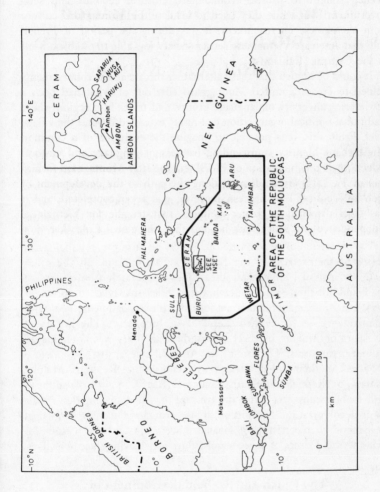

Map 5 Eastern Indonesia and the Republic of the South Moluccas

5

Defining 'Self-Determination': the Republic of Indonesia vs. the South Moluccan Republic

As colonial powers in Southeast Asia, Britain, France and the Netherlands tended – with the exception of Britain's interests in Malaya and Borneo – to create large political units. In the eastern mainland region, the French created the super-state of French Indochina; further west, the British incorporated Burma into another colonial super-state, British India. In both cases, however, these super-states disintegrated during the period of decolonization, largely because pre-colonial states reasserted themselves. In the East Indian archipelago, on the other hand, the colonial super-state created by the Dutch from scores of small and medium-sized pre-colonial polities managed to forge for itself, over time, a single national identity; it eventually emerged, with independence, as the unified 'Republic of Indonesia'. The history of the island of Ambon, however, shows that this unity was not achieved without great stress. The fate of the Ambonese separatist movement – embodied in their failed attempt to establish the 'Republik Maluku Selatan', or 'Republic of South Moluccas' (RMS), in 1950 – also raises fundamental questions about the concept of self-determination in the era of decolonization. In addition, it also provides a useful exemplar of the general characteristics of loyalist movements, and the reasons for their varying degrees of success and failure in achieving their objectives.

The Dutch and Ambon: development of a loyalist relationship

Between the fifteenth and the seventeenth centuries, Ambon and neighbouring islands of the Moluccan group, in what is now eastern Indonesia, experienced succeeding waves of outside intervention that were to transform the nature of their societies. In the fifteenth century

Islam came to Ambon via the expanding political power of the north Moluccan states of Ternate and Tidore; in the early sixteenth century, the Portuguese gained a foothold in Ambon, and thence expanded both their trading network and the Christian religion into the south Moluccan region; then, in the early to mid-seventeenth century, the Dutch gradually ousted the Portuguese.[1] Thereafter, the Dutch were able to consolidate their control over Ambon and the Moluccan islands in general, and to establish a monopoly over the valuable exports of cloves and nutmeg from these islands. Ambon and the other 'spice islands' of the Moluccas became a vital link in a Dutch trading chain stretching along the East Indian archipelago and up to northern Asia.

During these centuries, therefore, Ambon was located at the intersection of imperial competition and religious confrontation. Out of this emerged what has been described as a 'Creole Moluccan' culture.[2] The traditional pre-Islamic and pre-Christian culture and *adat* (customary law) of Ambon and the neighbouring islands of Haruku and Saparua was not eliminated, but it was buried under new Christian and Islamic cultures, particularly in the major settlements. In both the Christian and the Islamic villages, there was a natural tension between traditional *adat* sources of authority and the new religious leadership provided by the church and the mosque.[3] Not only was there implicit tension between traditional *adat* and the new religions, but Ambon was also divided between distinct Christian and Muslim communities. The 1930 census shows that roughly two-thirds of the population were Christian (mainly Protestant) and one-third was Muslim.[4] Over the centuries, in fact, Ambon became a classic example of the kind of mixed society, in terms both of racial intermarriage and the coexistence of separate cultures, that so often emerges in regions that lie at the crossroads of colonial empires.

During the course of the eighteenth and nineteenth centuries, however, the value of the spice trade declined, a trend that was confirmed in the mid-nineteenth century when the clove monopoly was officially ended.[5] As the spice trade lost its significance, the centre of gravity of the Netherlands' eastern empire shifted decisively to Java and Sumatra, where plantation economies were developing. Ambon, which had previously lain at the crossroads of a complex imperial trading network, now became a peripheral region both in political and economic terms. This sense of 'peripherality' – which intensified during the nationalist period – was to have a profound effect on the subsequent political development of Ambon.

Although the Ambonese had, by the mid-nineteenth century, been part of the Dutch empire for roughly two hundred years, the special relationship of loyalty between the Dutch and the Ambonese Christians only developed gradually. Until the nineteenth century, the relationship could be described as one of mutual suspicion tempered by mutual dependence. The fact that the Dutch had to face a revolt in Saparua island – the 'Pattimura' revolt of 1817 – when they returned to Ambon and the neighbouring islands after an interval of British rule in the Napoleonic War period, gives some indication of the ambiguity of the relationship.[6] As late as the mid-nineteenth century, Alfred Wallace was to describe the Christian Ambonese as a 'strange, half-civilized, half-savage, lazy people', certainly not as the trusted partners in empire later portrayed by Dutch imperial enthusiasts.[7]

As a consequence of the evolution of Dutch colonial policy, however, a special relationship between the Christian Ambonese and the Dutch was consolidated in the course of the nineteenth century. In 1800, the Dutch state imposed direct colonial rule over the East Indies, replacing the impoverished and sometimes hand-to-mouth government that had been exercised by the Dutch East Indies Company, the VOC.[8] Long-term consequences of this change in government included administrative rationalization, an increase in missionary activity and, so far as Ambon was concerned, a strengthening of the status and role of the Dutch and native clergy at the expense of the traditional adat chieftains in the villages.[9] Another consequence was the rapid expansion and consolidation of Dutch power throughout the East Indies in the mid- to late-nineteenth century. One of the key instruments of this process of consolidation and pacification was the Netherlands Indies colonial army, or KNIL, in which the Ambonese Christians came to play an essential role. The importance of the Ambonese Christian soldiers lay not so much in their numbers – though these increased greatly between 1805 and 1896 – as in the fact that they filled a special non-commissioned officer niche within the army.[10] The importance of the Christian Ambonese for the Dutch is best shown by the decisive part they played in the 'Marechaussée' Corps in the most bitter and pro-longed of all the colonial wars that the Dutch had to fight in the East Indies: the war to conquer Aceh, which began in 1873, and did not really end until the beginning of the twentieth century.[11]

In effect, the Christian Ambonese became a special caste or pangkat (literally rank, position) within the Dutch colonial system, providing low-ranking administrators and separate (and reliable) military units for the administration and pacification of the whole of the Dutch East Indies. The sense of this special role under the Dutch was reinforced by the fact that the Christian Ambonese were treated, in theory at least, as 'Europeans' for legal purposes, and were given equal rates of pay to the Dutch in the colonial army.[12] The Christian villages of Ambon became a regular source of recruitment for the army and

administration, and small Ambonese communities established themselves throughout the archipelago – always retaining, however, an
umbilical link with Ambon itself. If Ambon itself now lay on the
periphery of the Dutch East Indies, this separate Christian Ambonese
'caste' had acquired a central role as intermediaries in the colonial
administration. One inevitable consequence of this was a deepening
divide in terms of role and status between the Christian and Muslim
communities in Ambon.[13]

The creation of the Indonesian nation

During the course of the nineteenth and twentieth centuries, the Dutch
East Indies was transformed from a rambling and disparate empire
into a coherent state. As they consolidated their power, the Dutch co-
opted a multiplicity of local rulers into their administrative structure,
creating a kind of semi-hereditary caste of local 'regents'. These regents
or *bupati* formed the basis of the local administration, and along with
the colonial army, the field-police and a highly efficient network of
communications between the scattered islands, formed the essential
pillars of the new colonial state.[14]

There were a number of factors apart from the Dutch administrative
framework which helped bind the Indies together. The majority of the
inhabitants were Muslims, and the languages and laws (*adat*) of the
separate regions, although different, did share many general characteristics. Above all, the Malay language had gradually acquired an
informal status as the general language of commercial intercourse
between the islands, and as the language of religious communication.[15]

On the other hand, it is also clear that there was no common sense
of identity or of unifying historical memory throughout the Dutch-
controlled Indies. For example, none of the pre-colonial states had
exercised authority over anything more than a fraction of the region;
and, although Islam was the dominant religion of the region, there
were some considerable differences in the interpretations of Islam that
had taken root in the different states. Moreover, although there had
been resistance to the consolidation of Dutch power throughout the
Indies, these revolts – whether the Pattimura revolt in Saparua (1817),
the Diponegoro revolt in Central Java (1825–30), the Banten revolt of
1888, or any of a number of others – can only retrospectively be
described as manifestations of *Indonesian* nationalism.[16] These were, in
fact, *regional* resistance movements defending the rights of local states
and the indigenous religion. Even when the Dutch introduced a programme of native reform at the beginning of the twentieth century –
the so-called 'Ethical Policy' – and encouraged, among other things,

an expansion of education and a greater exposure to Western culture and ideas among the indigenous population, the immediate response was regional or sectional rather than 'Indonesian'. The mass of native organizations that were formed in the years before the First World War reflected a burgeoning cultural, religious, and even political awareness, but they were all essentially pre-nationalist.[17]

Gradually, however, a sense of a common identity *did* emerge, particularly in the decades after the First World War. In part, this was an unconscious process, a consequence of the Ethical Policy of the Dutch. As the children of the native elite of the whole East Indies – including Ambon – met at the new schools and colleges of Batavia (Jakarta), Bandung and Surabaya, links were inevitably developed, and there emerged a sense of a common struggle against outdated regional customs and the restrictions of Dutch rule. In part, however, this *was* a conscious process, as the new political leadership of the 1920s became aware that a common – 'Indonesian' – identity would have to be shaped if the various impulses of anti-colonialism were to be united, and if the competing anti-colonial political parties were ever to be effective.[18]

The Dutch and the Ambonese: vicissitudes of the special relationship in the inter-war years and during the Second World War

There is a clear connection between these developments and that of the special relationship between the Dutch and the Christian Ambonese. The rapid emergence of an Indonesian national identity and an Indonesian nationalist movement – with its natural emphasis on anti-colonialism and Islam, and its base in the big cities of Java – increasingly marginalized the Christian Ambonese, in both territorial and ideological terms. It is possible that even the Dutch authorities were inclined to place less emphasis on the special relationship with the Ambonese, as a new, apparently Western-oriented native elite began to emerge in the early years of the twentieth century.[19] During the First World War, however, and especially in the 1920s, the Dutch became seriously alarmed at the growth of violent anti-colonial activity and the emergence of a new nationalist political agenda. As the nationalist threat increased, the Dutch once again turned to the old special relationship. By 1930, something like a tenth of the Ambonese population was scattered through the East Indies, working as soldiers and administrators, and living in separate communities with their families.[20]

The growth of Indonesian nationalism also had an effect on the island of Ambon itself. The large number of Christian schools active on the island meant that its population was one of the most highly educated in the East Indies. One unforeseen consequence of this, however, was that a number of the children of the Ambonese elite were able to take advantage of the higher education opportunities that had opened up in Java. Here they mingled with the sons and daughters of the elite from the other islands of the Indies, and, even if they did not become nationalists, they tended inevitably to develop a more 'Indonesian' outlook. In May 1920 a 'Sarekat Ambon' (Ambonese Association) was formed in Semarang, in Java. Although this was primarily an educational and welfare organization, it definitely formed part of the new 'cultural revolution' that was beginning to sweep through the Indies, challenging not only the grip of local *adat* and the status of the traditional regents, but also, eventually, the legitimacy of Dutch rule itself.[21] In other words, a new, radical, Javanese-educated and 'Indonesian'-oriented group was emerging from within the ranks of the Christian Ambonese elite.[22]

Ambon, therefore, entered the era of the Second World War with a divided society. The traditional village chiefs who had been supported by the Dutch administration clung to their colonial links in this era of growing political change and upheaval.[23] Christian Ambonese villages continued to provide the Dutch with a specialized military and administrative caste, at what might be called the 'NCO' level. As the Indonesian nationalist threat grew, this community clearly identified itself – and was identified by others – with the Dutch. On the other hand, the Muslim villages of Ambon were excluded from this privileged relationship, and did not identify themselves with the Dutch. At the same time, a growing number of urban, educated Ambonese – both Christian and Muslim – were tending to adopt what might be called an 'Indonesian' perspective.

The Japanese military conquest of the region early in 1942 isolated Ambon from the western islands for some time. Eastern Indonesia was administered by the Japanese separately from the islands of Java and Sumatra, which themselves had separate administrations. In addition, economic and communication links between the islands were all but severed during the period of Japanese occupation. An important consequence of Japanese rule was the disruption of the interrelationship which had been growing – with all of its attendant political and cultural implications – between different parts of the archipelago in the pre-war period. Thus, while Java experienced massive political and cultural upheaval during the war years, Ambon remained a backwater.[24]

This is not to say that there were no political developments on Ambon during the period of the Japanese occupation. Here, as in other parts of the Indonesian archipelago, the Japanese encouraged pan-Asiatic, anti-Western propaganda, and forbade the use of the

Dutch language, thereby stimulating the official use of the Indonesian language (developed by nationalist leaders and writers before the war and based on a Sumatran variant of Malay). Equally, as in other parts of Indonesia, those who opposed the regime in any way were harshly treated. In more specific terms, this meant that Indonesian-oriented members of Sarekat Ambon were allowed to play a leading role in the regional administration; the Christian community was regarded with a considerable degree of suspicion by the Japanese; and, conversely, the Muslim community found itself relatively favoured and privileged. On the other hand, the Japanese naval administration kept the traditional village chiefs in their positions and, in line with their general policy, kept the lid on political activity. Although communal tensions on Ambon increased during the war, they did not, on the whole, break out into the open.[25]

More significant for the future of Ambon was the fate during the war of the Christian Ambonese communities stranded in Java. When the Dutch colonial army (KNIL) surrendered to the Japanese, the Ambonese troops in some regions were simply sent home; in other areas, however, they became prisoners of war, and shared the same hardships as their Dutch comrades-in-arms. The whole Ambonese community left stranded on Java, however – including members of Sarekat Ambon – were regarded with great suspicion by the Japanese military authorities and the local Indonesian nationalists.[26] Throughout the whole period 1942–45, the Japanese mobilized the different sections of the Javanese population behind their war effort, creating militias and building up a whole network of 'loyalty' organizations. In the middle of the accompanying blitz of anti-Western, anti-colonial and pan-Asiatic propaganda, the isolated Ambonese communities in Java found themselves vulnerable and threatened.

This sense of vulnerability was dramatically sharpened when, in August 1945, the Japanese surrendered and the Indonesian nationalist leaders in Jakarta seized the opportunity to declare, on the 17th of that month, the independence of a unified 'Republic of Indonesia'. Although the nationalist leadership, headed by Sukarno, Mohammed Hatta and Sutan Syahrir, sought to establish their authority in an orderly manner and reassure all regions and sections of the community, they were quickly overwhelmed by events. All of the accumulated political and sectional tensions that had built up before and during the war now burst out into the open, in both Java and Sumatra, during the autumn of 1945. During this period of political turmoil, tensions on these islands escalated between the multitude of local revolutionary nationalist groups and stranded Ambonese communities; in some cases, these tensions exploded into serious violence.[27]

Given these circumstances, it was natural that the Christian Ambonese – both in Java and in Ambon itself – should have welcomed the return of the Dutch to the East Indies. The different experiences of Java and Ambon in the crucial 1945–46 period provides a key to understanding future developments in relation to the Ambonese. On the island of Java, the returning Dutch were only able to gain control only of tenuous bridgeheads – including Jakarta – during the months after the Japanese surrender. Although they were subsequently able to reconquer Java in the period 1947–49, their authority in large areas was never more than nominal. On Ambon, on the other hand, there was no interregnum between the Japanese surrender and the arrival of Allied troops and Dutch administrators. In late September 1945, Australian troops, accompanied by Dutch civilian administrators, took control from the Japanese without fuss.[28] The Dutch immediately set about restoring their authority, and, in July 1946, they resumed full control over the whole of eastern Indonesia.[29]

The return of the Dutch: Ambon and the formulation of Dutch policy

The Dutch had formulated the outlines of a new colonial policy during the war, based on a statement made by Queen Wilhelmina in December 1942. This envisaged the creation of a Dutch 'Commonwealth', including the Netherlands, Indonesia, Surinam and Curaçao, in which each of the component territories would have internal self-government, but would amalgamate in a democratic partnership under ultimate Dutch sovereignty.[30] H.J. van Mook, the Dutch lieutenant governor-general of Netherlands Indies and head of the returning Dutch colonial government, tried initially to implement this policy, which involved as a first step the restoration of Dutch authority throughout the Indies.[31] It soon became apparent, however, that Indonesian nationalism was too firmly entrenched in Java and Sumatra, and the Dutch too weak, for the latter to impose their plan of 'democratic partnership'.[32] The Dutch faced a situation early in 1946 in which they had only a foothold in Java and Sumatra, but had re-established their authority in eastern Indonesia. During the course of 1946, van Mook faced some pressure to create a 'Moluccan Commonwealth' – including the north and south Moluccas and Dutch New Guinea – as a separate component of the Dutch Commonwealth.[33] Van Mook, however, resisted the temptation to follow a separatist strategy as a counter to the threat of Indonesian nationalism. When he called delegates from eastern Indonesia to a conference in Malino (Sulawesi) in July 1946, he was surprised to discover a groundswell of opinion, even among the more conservative delegates, in favour of a unified and independent, but strictly federal, Indonesia.[34] Accordingly, van Mook worked thereafter to reach a settlement with the leaders of the Indonesian Republic (which principally controlled the islands of Java and Sumatra) that would involve the incorporation of the Republic as a unit in a wider federal state. Following negotiations between November 1946 and March 1947, an agreement was eventually reached – the Linggajati agreement – in which the Dutch and the Republican authorities agreed to form a federal 'United States of Indonesia' (the components of which were to be the 'Republic of Indonesia, Borneo and the Great East, *without prejudice to the rights of the population of any territory to decide by democratic process that its position in the United States of Indonesia shall be arranged otherwise*'.[35] It was understood, by the Dutch at least, that within this federal framework, and under interim Dutch sovereignty, moves towards self-determination would be gradually negotiated with the full participation of all parties.

These developments had an important impact on the politics of Ambon between 1946 and 1948. In the wake of the Japanese defeat and the re-establishment of Dutch power, there was, not unexpectedly, a considerable degree of tension between what could generally be described as the 'loyalist' and the 'nationalist' communities, the former comprising the traditional village leaders and the Christian Ambonese who had formed close links with the Dutch, the latter comprising the Muslim community and that section of the educated elite who had been linked to Sarekat Ambon. In August 1946 a new Ambonese party, the 'Partai Indonesia Merdeka' (PIM) was formed, headed largely by former Sarekat Ambon leaders, and supported by Muslims. In November 1946, this party was able to gain a majority of seats for Ambon in the assembly (*dewan*) of the newly formed administrative unit of 'Maluku Selatan', or the 'South Moluccas', which comprised Ambon and the surrounding islands (see Map 5).[36]

It seems clear, however, that through 1947 and 1948 some kind of political consensus developed in Ambon. The key to this consensus was van Mook's policy of working towards a federal, independent Indonesia. In December 1946, it was agreed at a meeting of east Indonesian delegates – including Ambonese – that a new political entity, the 'Negara Indonesia Timor' (NIT), (or 'State of East Indonesia', should be created as a component state of federal Indonesia.[37] Subsequently the *daërah*, or region, of the South Moluccas provisionally joined this new state as a subordinate administrative unit.[38] From early 1947, therefore, policy appeared to be moving towards a federal solution in which nationalist aspirations for self-government would be satisfied, but in which the Ambonese – under the aegis of the *negara* (state) of East Indonesia and *daerah* of the South Moluccas – would be protected from the revolutionary instability of Java.)

Unfortunately for this Ambonese consensus, the federal policy built up by van Mook proved to be unworkable. (The primary reason for this was the fact that the Republic of Indonesia was never prepared to accept the idea of even temporary Dutch sovereignty. In July 1947, the Dutch resorted to force in order to impose their policy on the Republic, and the subsequent Renville Agreement of January 1948 emphasized the Netherlands' sovereign status during the period of forming the federal United States of Indonesia.[39] Buoyed up by the apparent success of their policy of force and their seizure of large chunks of territory in Java and Sumatra, the Dutch broke up the territory they had captured into three *negara*: East Sumatra, Madura and West Java.[40] Exasperated as they were by their failure to achieve any kind of consensus with the Republic of Indonesia, the Dutch were clearly moving from a policy of trying to create a federal state comprising two major units – the Republic and East Indonesia – (to one of simply using the federal system to squeeze the Republic out of existence. (This policy reached its natural conclusion in December 1948, when the Dutch again used their military power to take over the rest of the Republic and arrest its leaders.[41])

(The consequences of this policy were fatal for Dutch colonial power in the Indies. In the first place, an international consensus, headed by the United States of America, put irresistible pressure on the Netherlands to negotiate a political settlement with the Republican leaders.) (Second, the very success of the Dutch policy of force meant that they now had to hold down large areas of Java and Sumatra that had been free of Dutch rule since 1942, and had undergone a thoroughgoing nationalist revolutionary upheaval in the interval. (Finally, the Dutch elimination of the Republic upset the delicate political balance in the State of East Indonesia that had been held together by the plan to create an independent – but federal – Indonesia.)

(All these factors combined to force the Dutch to return to negotiations.) (After agreement on a ceasefire, the Round Table Conference was opened in the Netherlands in August 1949, with the participation of the Dutch, the Indonesian Republic, and representatives of the various *negara* and *daerah* of the areas of Indonesia outside the Republic. After complex negotiations, a new entity, the 'Republic of the United States of Indonesia' (RUSI), or 'Republik Indonesia Serikat' (RIS) was formed in December 1949.[42] (At first sight, this new state would seem to have been a culmination of the federal strategy projected by the Dutch since 1946, and the rights – even the ultimate right of secession – of the various component states (*negara*) were firmly entrenched in the Provisional Constitution and the 'agreement on transitional measures'.[43] In practice, the whole edifice created by the Round Table Agreements was vitiated by the fact that the Dutch ceded sovereignty in late December 1949 *before* the details of the structure of the new state had been agreed.[44] The new Republic of the United States of Indonesia emerged into independence as a federation without a federal administration, without a federal army, and without the means of enforcing the constitutional measures that had been painstakingly agreed at the Round Table Conference.[45]

The plan, essentially, was that, from the beginning of 1950, the Republican and *negara* leaders would negotiate a federal constitutional and administrative structure along the lines of the 'agreement on transitional measures' reached in the Netherlands. At the same time, a merger was to be negotiated between the armed forces of the Republic and those of the Dutch colonial army (KNIL) to form the basis for a new federal army. The reality was that the various *negara*, lacking their own armed forces and deprived of Dutch protection, immediately came under pressure – through a combination of inducements and threats – to be absorbed into the unitary structure of the Republic.

The declaration of Ambonese/Moluccan independence

In these unpromising circumstances, the political situation in Ambon and in the whole East Indonesian State (*negara*) deteriorated rapidly. The first source of tension in Ambon was the gradual return there of Ambonese troops in the colonial army and units of the colonial 'special forces' (KST or 'Korps Speciale Troepen') after the ceasefire agreed in summer 1949. By early 1950, some 2,000 Christian Ambonese soldiers had quartered themselves in Ambon, anxious about their future and bitter at what they saw as the increasing disengagement of the Dutch from the responsibilities they had incurred.[46] At this point it is possible that the peaceable integration of Ambon into an independent Indonesia could still have been achieved, but only in the context of the maintenance of the East Indonesian *negara* and full adherence to the measures agreed in the Round Table Conference – in particular, the guarantees for a federal structure and for a right of democratic free choice on the issue of joining or staying out of the federation. As it became increasingly apparent in the early months of 1950 that the Republic of Indonesia was working to dismantle the whole federal structure, and that the Dutch were not prepared to exert themselves to prevent this from happening, even erstwhile nationalist sympathizers in Ambon became alarmed at this violation of regional rights.[47]

The decisive moment came in April 1950, when the government of the East Indonesian *negara*, based in Makassar, effectively collapsed in the face of a campaign of threats and blandishments orchestrated by the Republican government.[48] With the liquidation of the *negara* of East Indonesia, nothing now stood between Ambon and the unitary Republic of Indonesia. Under these circumstances, it was inevitable that separatist sentiments, which had to a great degree been held in check during the period of the federal experiment, should resurface. The forces in favour of breaking away from Indonesia, backed as they were by a large number of troops that had fought on the side of the Dutch against Indonesian nationalism, now gained a decisive upper hand. At an informal public gathering in the Ambonese capital on 25 April 1950, the independence of the South Moluccas was declared, and the former *daerah* (region) of South Moluccas renamed itself the 'Republic of South Moluccas' or 'Republik Maluku Selatan' (RMS). The declaration itself (see Appendix 4) stipulated that the right to do this was based, first, upon the fact that the *daerah* of South Moluccas had only incorporated itself into the East Indonesian *negara* on a provisional basis; second, that the Republic of Indonesia had breached the Round Table agreements; and, finally, as a consequence of the latter, that the East Indonesian *negara* had ceased to exist. Accordingly, the *daerah* of South Moluccas had the freedom to dissolve its relationship with the now non-existent East Indonesia *negara*, and take upon itself the right, enshrined in the Round Table agreements, of each component part of the Republic of the United States of Indonesia to secede from the federation.[49]

The declaration of South Moluccan independence and the subsequent formation of a government were daring moves, a combination of *coup de force* and a genuine expression of popular feeling.[50] It is possible that, for some of the South Moluccan leaders, the declaration was primarily designed to force the Indonesian Republic into negotiations and jolt the Dutch into some kind of action; in other words, a classic *pronunciamento*.[51] If so, the move failed in both its objectives. The Dutch conspicuously failed to take decisive action; the Republic of Indonesia, however, moved rapidly – if not in the first instance effectively – to quell this separatist threat. By the end of 1950, the Republic of Indonesia had finally managed to gain control of Ambon, and the leaders of the rebellion were forced to continue the struggle on the neighbouring island of Ceram.[52] Although the Moluccan/ Ambonese secessionist movement continued to wage a guerrilla war in the inaccessible interior of Ceram through the 1950s, most traces of resistance were finally snuffed out by the early 1960s.[53] More significant in many ways was the fate of the large number of Christian Ambonese troops of the Dutch colonial army – along with their families – who had been stranded in scattered positions throughout Indonesia at the conclusion of the conflict between the Dutch and the Republic in 1949. Many of them were shipped to the Netherlands in 1951, and have there, ever since that date, maintained their aspiration to create an independent South Moluccan state.[54]

⌁ Separatism and self-determination: the Ambonese example

The impulse to national self-determination is clearly the key to the whole decolonization era. But the very term 'national self-determination' stimulates two questions: how is the national entity to be defined, and how is self-determination to be defined?

In 1957 Roeslan Abdulgani, the main theoretician of what was to become 'Guided Democracy' in Indonesia, defined the impulse to national unity in the following terms, which were based on Ernest Renan's famous essay, *What is a Nation?*:

> Modern times confront us with a historical necessity, the necessity of having a unifying bond in the form of a desire and will to live together, of the existence of a great sense of solidarity to be welded further day by day, which comes into existence because of a common historic destiny, a common historic suffering, a common historic victory, in short, a common historic sharing of joys and sorrows.[55]

Using this definition as a foundation, could it be argued that Ambon experienced with the rest of Indonesia 'a common historic sharing of joys and sorrows' and thus a common national identity? This is, of course, precisely what the Ambonese separatists of the RMS sought to deny. They argued that the historical experience of Ambonese relations with the Dutch was entirely different from the experience of other parts of Indonesia, and that, even when the Dutch forged the territory of the East Indies into one united state, a sense of a united 'Indonesian' identity did not really begin to take shape until the mid-1920s.[56] By this time, far from sharing a common 'historic destiny' or 'suffering', the interests of Indonesian nationalism and of the loyalist Ambonese community were, in fact, diametrically opposed. This sense of difference was intensified during the war years – when eastern Indonesia was administered separately from the rest of Indonesia – and sharpened during the revolutionary period, when the Ambonese as a whole found themselves isolated from, and threatened by, the prevailing political turmoil.[57]

The Ambonese separatists argued that this difference had implications in international law as well. At the time that the independence of the Republic of Indonesia was declared in August 1945, (Ambon was under the interim control of the Japanese navy. There was no subsequent vacuum of power, since the Allied military authorities took over directly from the Japanese in Ambon, and the Dutch resumed full authority in the spring of 1946.)Ambon then became part of the State (*negara*) of East Indonesia. (This state was in the process of forming, in collaboration with the Republic of Indonesia, a united federal state of Indonesia, when the Republic illegally seized overall power) The Republic of South Moluccas had been formed in April 1950, several months before the Republic of Indonesia finally eliminated the structure of the Republic of the United States of Indonesia, in August of that year. The Ambonese separatists thus argued that Ambon had never been part of the Republic of Indonesia, and that the latter's crushing of the RMS was, therefore, a clear violation of international law.[58]

This argument, however, overlooks the ambiguity and complexity of Ambonese affiliations and loyalties. The history of modern Ambon reveals a divided society whose members reacted in very different ways to Dutch rule.(These divisions reflected not only the gulf between the Christian and Muslim communities, but also that between the traditional political elite and those who had come into contact with, and were influenced by, the ideas of the Indonesian nationalist movement.) The fact that there was a significant section of Ambonese society that supported Indonesian nationalism – even if it also supported a federal structure – cannot be overlooked, particularly when we consider the fact that this section dominated the Council (*dewan*) of South Moluccas after the war.[59]

The Republic of Indonesia's claim to Ambon and other sections of the former Dutch East Indies – including Dutch New Guinea – was not, however, based ultimately on historical detail of this kind. Certainly, the leaders of the Republic were not prepared to test the issue of self-determination on the basis of regional plebiscites. Rather, they took what might be described as the 'primordial' line: that Indonesia was an 'already existing', indivisible political entity. From this position, it was asserted that the declaration of the Republic of Indonesia on 17 August 1945 automatically included all of the former regions of the Dutch East Indies, including Ambon.[60] Seen from this perspective, all of the complex federal arrangements negotiated with the Dutch between 1946 and 1950 were so many *de facto* prevarications brought about by temporary weakness.

This intransigent assertion of a 'primordial' Indonesian unity was, in fact, a reflection of the inherent weakness, not strength, of

Indonesian national identity. (In reality, Indonesian identity had been forged not by any indigenous historical process, but simply by the consolidation of the Dutch Empire. (It was precisely because of this weakness of what might be called historic national legitimacy that the Indonesian nationalists could not afford to compromise on the issue of national unity)

The key argument of the supporters of the Republic of South Moluccas was that this emphasis on 'primordial' Indonesian national unity denied the basic right to Ambonese self-determination.[61] If, they asserted, 'the colony that has won independence is inhabited by different population groups which have not grown into one nation in the course of time', the distinct regions and communities must have the intrinsic right to indicate by democratic means the political unit within which they wish to live. (Otherwise, old colonialism was merely being replaced by a new form of colonialism – a common problem in the newly independent states, 'which in spite of the fact that they acquired their independence and liberty in virtue of the universally and internationally acknowledged right of self-determination, refuse to grant this same right to their own minorities'.[62]

(Whatever the merits of the argument that the Ambonese had completely different aspirations from the population of the Indonesian Republic, the question of the definition of self-determination during the period of decolonization is a matter of general importance) In the overwhelming majority of cases of state formation during the period of decolonization in the decades following the Second World War, the concept of 'national' identity in a colonial region was assumed to follow the contours that had been created by the colonial state. Thus, the exercise of the right to self-determination was constricted in advance by this predetermined notion of what 'the nation' was. Under these circumstances, minority regions within the colonial states – including Ambon – were denied the opportunity to exercise their right to self-determination. In fact, the denial of this right to regional self-determination in the process of decolonization was actually enshrined in the United Nations' General Assembly resolution 1514 of December 1960, passed with eighty-nine nations in favour, and only nine abstentions. After an interminable preamble that culminated in a declaration of the right to national self-determination, the following clause was slipped in: 'Any attempt at the partial or total disruption of the national unity and the territorial integrity of a country is incompatible with the purposes and principles of the United Nations.'[63]

The reason for the consensus behind this rather unedifying document can easily be explained. Whatever their other conflicts, it was manifestly in the interest of all the nation-state successors to the former colonial states to prevent the principle of self-determination from being applied to their own internal regions. Equally, each state, conscious of its own vulnerability to separatist assertions, has tended to hesitate before encouraging separatist aspirations in neighbouring states. There was, and is, a general fear that the success of one separatist movement could create a chain reaction that could affect all of the states in a particular region. This has certainly been a prevailing attitude in Africa and Southeast Asia, although it could be argued that this law of mutual preservation has frequently been breached in the Indian sub-continent. In general, however, it is remarkable – given that so many states in the post-colonial world were created by the arbitrary boundaries of Western imperialism – that so few separatist movements have succeeded.

Of course, it was a persistent fear of anti-colonial nationalist movements and the post-colonial states that the West would seek to exploit separatist sentiments, first in order to delay independence itself, and then in order to weaken – and thus ensure the compliance of – the post-colonial states. This fear explains the wording of the aforementioned United Nations resolution 1514. In practice, however, the former colonial powers tended not to encourage separatist movements, even during the process of decolonization. It is worthwhile reiterating why this was so.

During the later stages of a nationalist struggle, it is often true that a colonial power wishing to maintain its position will emphasize the divisions – ethnic, religious or regional – within the particular colonial state. The clear intention here is to weaken the legitimacy of the nationalist movement, and provide a justification for the continuance of colonial rule. As can be seen from the history of France in Vietnam, this tendency to encourage division may intensify as the power of the nationalist movement increases. However, there comes in most processes of decolonization – however bitter – a moment when it is recognized by the colonial power that the process cannot be halted. At this stage, there will tend to be a reversal of policy. Anxious to avoid further conflict, to expedite the transition of power smoothly, and to establish good relations with the successor nation-state, the colonial power will now tend to put their weight behind the most powerful elements in the nationalist movement. At this point, those elements that had previously been encouraged by the colonial power to resist the main nationalist movement will suddenly find themselves isolated and betrayed.

The above process could be described almost as a 'law' of decolonization, and we can certainly see its operation in Indonesia in 1949 and 1950. In 1949, having built a federal edifice ultimately designed ·to weaken and even destroy the Republic of Indonesia, the Dutch were, in the end, forced to cede sovereignty to a political entity that was only half-formed: namely, the Republic of the United States of Indonesia. The success of this complex federal structure depended entirely on the willingness of the Dutch to play an active and forceful role. The events of 1950 – including the collapse of the East Indonesian State (*negara*), the subsequent collapse of the RUSI, and the creation of the Republic of South Moluccas – showed that they were unwilling to do this. Overriding considerations of policy, particularly the need to protect Dutch economic interests throughout Indonesia, had by now forced the Dutch into compliance with the political objectives of the Republic of Indonesia. By the end of 1950, the Republic of South Moluccas had been abandoned to its fate.

Separatism and post-war global politics: the Indonesian example

If the new nation-states had little to fear from the machinations of the old colonial powers, once those powers had recognized that the 'game was up' there was still an acute danger that international competition – the Cold War in particular – could affect their fragile unity. Through the 1950s and early 1960s, the Cold War competition between the West and the Soviet Union became increasingly global, as both sides sought ideological or geopolitical allies in the 'Third World'. There was an evident danger that, if a particular country fell into one or the other ideological camp, the other camp would seek to destabilize that country. One of the easiest methods of destabilizing a new nation-state was the encouragement of separatist activity.

The South Moluccan rebels were certainly alert to this opportunity. Through the course of the 1950s and in the early 1960s, the Indonesian Republic slowly shifted from a global stance that was 'non-aligned' to an ever more anti-Western position. Though Indonesia did not move fully into the communist camp, the Indonesian Communist Party (PKI) had in the early 1960s become by far the most powerful political party in Java, and Indonesian links with the Soviet Union and the Peoples' Republic of China were growing closer by the day. Given these circumstances, supporters of the Republic of South Moluccas – both in the Netherlands and in the jungles of Ceram – hoped to win American support for their cause. In a revealing article written by H.J. Kruls in 1960, it was pointed out that Indonesia was likely to 'go communist' and that, if this were to happen, the whole of Southeast Asia would be destabilized. A strong South Moluccan state could in this event provide a reliable bastion against communism in the region, and would moreover 'plug the gap' in the Western defensive 'archipelago' between Japan and Australia.[64]

Quite apart from the fact of the actual weakness of the South Moluccan resistance movement, there were several reasons why the Americans were reluctant to resort to a strategy of fragmentation in the Third World in general, and Indonesia in particular. The Americans were acutely aware of the general sensitivity of all Third World countries to any threat to their national unity. A policy of destabilizing 'unfriendly' regimes in the Third World by encouraging separatism would not only create the very conditions of political chaos in which, it was believed, communism thrived, but it would have the effect of uniting most Third World states against the West. The general strategy of the United States, therefore, was to work for a change of regime and ideological affiliation in hostile states, rather than encourage a break-up of the state itself.

This becomes very evident when we consider the relationship between the United States and Indonesia in the period 1948–75. By 1948, the United States was convinced of the anti-communist credentials of the Republic of Indonesia, and American influence was decisive in forcing the Dutch to cede independence to Indonesia in 1949, which in turn ensured the victory of the political agenda of the Republic. By the late 1950s, however, the Americans were clearly alarmed at political developments in Indonesia, and were at least toying with the idea of supporting such pro-Western rebellions in Indonesia as the Sumatran rebellions of 1956–58.[65] It is important to note, however, that these rebellions were ideological in character rather than separatist. In any case, it became apparent early in the 1960s that there was a growing rift developing between the leadership of the armed forces on one side, and Sukarno and the Indonesian Communist Party (PKI) on the other. The United States was therefore particularly anxious to avoid any policy that would tilt the delicate balance of power towards the communists in Indonesia. Accordingly, they not only desisted from encouraging separatist movements in Indonesia, they actually played a significant role – via the United Nations – in enabling Sukarno to take over Dutch New Guinea/West Irian from the Dutch. Given that the Americans, and indeed the world, were prepared to stand aside and allow the Indonesians to swallow up West Irian on the basis of the flimsiest pretences of national legitimacy, it was hardly likely that the South Moluccans' plea for international support would be heard.

The US strategy bore fruit when, in 1965, the armed forces of Indonesia crushed the Indonesian communists and effectively overthrew Sukarno. It is interesting to note that Indonesia was able to exploit another period of international tension during their takeover of

East Timor in 1975.[66] In the mid-1970s, the United States and the West in general became increasingly alarmed at what they saw as spectacular communist advances in the Third World. Ethiopia, Angola, Portuguese Guinea, Mozambique and Afghanistan had either already 'gone communist', or were sliding towards a communist takeover. In Southeast Asia itself, communists in 1975 gained power in Vietnam, Laos and Cambodia. It was in this apparently threatening international context that the Americans allowed the Indonesian army to violate international law, crush the communist-orientated government of East Timor, and absorb East Timor into Indonesia.

This history of the relationship between the United States and Indonesia illustrates one vital point in relation to the new nation-states: that the global Cold War, far from threatening them, actually helped to sustain the national unity of these successor states to colonialism. A glance at the Third World between 1945 and 1990 will show that very few separatist movements have succeeded in their objectives. This had much more to do with the unfavourable international climate prevailing during that period than with the intrinsic strength or weakness of separatist sentiment in the Third World.

PART II

National Identity: Decolonization and Separatism in the Muslim Regions of Southeast Asia

6

Islam, Ethnicity and Separatism in Southeast Asia

Introduction

Thus far, the separatist movements that have been considered have all been non-Muslim. Indeed, in the case of the Penang secession movement and of the South Moluccan Republic, the intention was to secede from a state whose population was predominantly Muslim. It is now necessary, however, to consider Muslim revolts which occurred during or immediately after the decolonization process in Southeast Asia, and which were located at the periphery of the colonial states that were in the process of moving to independence. The most significant of these occurred in Aceh, the Arakanese region of Burma, and – a special case – the Patani region between Thailand and Malaya.

It is difficult, however, exactly to match the dominating characteristics of the above revolts with those that have already been considered. In the case of the Patani revolt, although the objectives of that revolt were ultimately separatist, the essential difference lay in the fact that the Thai state against which the Malay Muslims of Patani were rebelling had never come under Western colonial control. In the case of the Muslim Arakanese, the objectives of the rebellion were mixed, and the post-war disturbances in the Arakan region were as much the result of a sectarian conflict within Arakan as a challenge to the central Burmese state. The case of the Acehnese rebellion is even more complex. In the first place, although Aceh's position was peripheral in the sense that it found itself at the edge of the Dutch-created colonial state of the East Indies, it did not lie at the periphery of the Islamic world. Secondly, the Acehnese rebellion that began in 1953 was not separatist, in the sense of aspiring to break Aceh away from the Indonesian nation. What these rebellions *did* have in common with the separatist movements of Part I of this book was, first, timing – the fact that the rebellions all occurred during the immediate period of decolonization – and second, a common condition of peripherality in relation to the new independent states that were emerging in Southeast Asia.

In considering these Muslim separatist movements, however, it is first necessary to discuss the role of Islam, from the point of view of its historical impact in Southeast Asia, and then from the point of view of its influence in shaping the objectives of the separatist or semi-separatist movements concerned. The key to any such discussion is to understand the symbiotic relationship between Islam as a system of belief and Islam as a focus of identity; the relationship, in other words, between *believing* and *belonging*.

The impact of Islam in Southeast Asia

Islamic expansion into Southeast Asia preceded that of Christianity. Indeed, one of the stated aims of initial European expansion into the region was the crusading desire to outflank and check Islam at a global level. Well before the arrival of the Europeans in Southeast Asia, Islam had steadily spread along the maritime trading routes connecting West Asia and India to East Asia. By the fifteenth century, maritime Southeast Asia was itself linked by a chain of Muslim trading states. The process of 'Islamization' at that time and thereafter consisted of a very uneven and incomplete consolidation through conversion and conquest of intervening islands and the island interiors, and expansion of the 'Islamic periphery' along existing trade routes. On the mainland of Southeast Asia, by the seventeenth century, Islam had gained a foothold in the maritime state of Champa and in the ports of the kingdom of Ayuthia, had spread via Bengal into the kingdom of Arakan at the edge of modern Burma, and had taken root in the Malay region.

This process of Islamic expansion was partially checked by European colonialism in maritime Southeast Asia in the course of the sixteenth, seventeenth and eighteenth centuries, and by the consolidation of powerful non-Islamic states in mainland Southeast Asia, particularly during the eighteenth century. In Arakan, in the northernmost Malay states, at the edge of the Philippine Islands seized by Spain in the late sixteenth century, and in the easternmost part of the Dutch trading network, the boundaries of what could be called the 'Islamic periphery' were being defined. Certain segments of the Islamic periphery were in fact absorbed within non-Muslim states – the Moro region of the Philippines, the Muslim area in northern Arakan, and the Muslim region in the north of the Malay world are obvious examples – and have, ever since, found themselves trapped outside the Islamic global community, the *umma Islam*. The consolidation of the borders of the European colonial states in Southeast Asia in the nineteenth and early twentieth centuries did not alter this state of affairs. Rather, the Western colonial period ensured that pre-colonial borders congealed into the hard and fast international frontiers of modern nation-states.

Generally speaking, conversion to Islam in Southeast Asia took place at the community or state, rather than individual, level. The result is that the delineation of the boundary between the Islamic and non-Islamic world is not haphazard, but follows the contours of clear-cut communities and political systems. This is why the need to understand the historically created link between believing and belonging in Islam is so vitally important. The boundaries of modern Southeast Asia have not only cut off sections of the Islamic periphery from the Muslim world conceived as a whole; they have also often had the effect of dividing local communities and severing local links of affiliation that had developed in the era of Islamic expansion.

During the high period of European expansion, when most of the Muslim world was subject to colonial rule, the fate of the Southeast Asian Islamic periphery was just part of a much wider misfortune for Islam. The revolution of cultural, religious and political awareness at the beginning of the twentieth century affected Islam in Southeast Asia quite as much as the other religions, and helped to regenerate a sense of pan-Islamic unity.[1] This was countered, however, by the revolution in national awareness and assertiveness in the inter-war period, which had the effect of isolating and threatening the sense of identity of those Muslim groups at the peripheries of the non-Muslim colonial states. It was not until the upheavals of the Second World War and its immediate aftermath, however, that we see a clear-cut interlinking of ethnic and Islamic irredentism in the peripheral Muslim regions of Southeast Asia.

Islam, nationalism, ethnicity and resistance

It should be reiterated at this stage that the Muslim separatist movements, even if they did have this extra 'Islamic' ingredient, did nevertheless share many common characteristics with the separatist movements we have already examined. The most obvious common feature is a growing awareness of marginality and a sense of alienation from the prevailing nationalist idiom of the particular state they inhabited. It could also be argued that some of the non-Muslim separatist movements had irredentist objectives. If we define irredentism as the desire to reconstitute or 'redeem' the unity and integrity of a particular ethnic group, historic entity or community, then, clearly, the Penang Secession Movement was 'irredentist' in the sense that it wished to recreate the Straits Settlements and reunite the Straits Chinese; equally, the Karen dream of a 'Karenistan' embraced Karen regions across the

Thai border as well as those in Burma itself; and, even if we exclude the more extravagant claims of FULRO and the Chams for the reconstitution of the pre-Vietnamese 'Champa', the ultimate plan of the *montagnard* separatists of the Central Highlands of Vietnam was to unite the mountain minorities across the borders of Laos, Cambodia and Vietnam into one political entity. In each of these cases, the separatist aspiration was combined with a desire for new forms of unity.

It could also be argued that many of the non-Muslim separatist movements had a religious dimension to their political programme. In all of the cases examined a sense of religious as well as ethnic difference served to heighten the distance between the peripheral communities concerned and the mainstream identity of the people of the state they inhabited.[2] As for the matter of 'loyalism', it will be seen in the ensuing pages that a direct loyalist relationship was created between the British and the Arakanese Muslims, which played a crucial role in stimulating the subsequent Muslim revolt; and that the Malay Muslims of Patani tried to develop a loyalist relationship with Britain after the Second World War.

It must, nevertheless, be conceded that Islam itself as an autonomous religious and political force does add an extra, if unpredictable, dynamic to the Muslim separatist movements. Islam had far deeper pre-colonial roots than Christianity in the Southeast Asian region. The most important point about Islam, however, is its relationship with other forms of identity, particularly ethnic and national identity.

It is a fundamental tenet of Islam that religious imperatives, ultimately embodied in the Qur'an,[3] should govern society and politics. Although there is much dispute in the Muslim world as to how these religious imperatives should actually operate in the state and society, there can be no doubt that religious principles pervade the Islamic world to a degree that is inconceivable in the more secular societies of the modern Western world. Two Islamic principles are of particular importance in our understanding of the outlook of Muslim societies. First, there is the ideal of one universal Islamic community, uniting all Muslims and overriding all differences of race, nation and clan.[4] In practice, the Islamic world has since its early years been divided into separate states. But the concept of a united Islamic *umma* (community/nation), where religious affiliation ultimately supersedes other forms of national and ethnic affiliation, remains an unchanging ideal. Linked to this is the ideal of the Islamic state, where sovereignty lies in the hands of God, whose will is revealed in the Qur'an, made known to Muhammad, and elaborated in detail by the actions and sayings of Muhammad embodied in the *sunna*. Even in those areas of social and political life that are not explicitly covered by the Qur'an and the *sunna*, the Islamic state can take no initiatives that offend Islamic principles. It is clear, therefore, that the Islamic concept of the *umma* challenges the Western secular concept of national sovereignty; and that the concept of the Islamic state must ultimately conflict with the Western notion of popular sovereignty or democracy. The divine constitution of the ideal Islamic state places absolute limitations on the freedom of action of human government, whether that government is tyrannical or democratic in form.[5]

At the heart of Islam, therefore, is the idea of *tauhid* or unity, linking the key notion of the 'one-ness' of God with the unity of the *umma*.[6] But the concept of *tauhid* had a further dimension, that of universality. Muhammad's mission as the last of the prophets of God was not directed to one particular people – as was the case with many of the earlier prophets – but to all mankind. Because of the unity in Islam between religion, society and politics, this missionary imperative was necessarily linked to the political expansion of the *umma*. In Islamic terms, humanity is divided, therefore, between the *Daru'l-Islam* (the house or abode of Islam) and the *Daru'l-Harb* (the house/abode of conflict, that is, the non-Islamic regions). Following from this, it is the basic obligation of all Muslims to help expand the *Daru'l-Islam* by missionary effort and conversion, and to protect the *Daru'l-Islam* from any threat by the *Daru'l-Harb*.[7]

The principles governing Muslim behaviour in this state of constant tension between the world of belief and the world of unbelief can best be understood from Quranic references relating to immediate dilemmas faced by Muhammad during his mission. It is important to remember that the Meccans initially rejected Muhammad's prophetic message and that, until Muhammad's final takeover of Mecca in 630 AD, the religious community of Islam was a persecuted minority within the Arab world. A major response of Muhammad to the persecution and rejection of Islam in Mecca was the promulgation, via the Qur'an, of the principle of *hijra* or 'emigration'. In order to save and sustain Islam, the *umma* was enjoined to withdraw or migrate 'in the cause of God' to the friendly sanctuary of Medina. Two fundamental principles emerged from the concept of *hijra*: first, that an Islamic community should withdraw from persecution if that persecution endangers the very survival of the community;[8] second, there is a strong implication in the term *hijra* of the replacing of the old ties of blood and kin by a new community and new bonds under Islam.[9]

The other major guidance for Muslim behavior, both in adversity and in the task of missionary work, revealed in the Qur'an to Muhammad was that of *jihad* or endeavour 'in the cause of God'. In

Muhammad's life, the precise implications of *jihad* varied according to the historical context. In the early period of the persecution and rejection of the small Islamic community in Mecca, *jihad* involved steadfastness and the maintenance of religious unity and principles in a time of difficulty.[10] In the next period, beginning with the flight of Muhammad to Medina and the plot of the Quraishi clan of Mecca to kill Muhammad, *jihad* meant fighting, and even killing, until victory was achieved by the Muslims over the Meccans.[11] In the final stage of Muhammad's life, when Islam dominated Mecca and the Arab world, the concept of *jihad* reflected the imperative of realizing Islam's destiny as a universal creed and the *umma* as a universal community – not by the instrumentality of war, but through missionary work and 'invitation' (*da'a*).[12]

It is important to note that the injunctions concerning *jihad* and *hijra* were formulated during a period of unprecedented and unsurpassed religious expansion. *Jihad* and *hijra*, therefore, were seen in dynamic terms that were less easily applicable to subsequent, more static eras in the history of Islam. Gradually, codes of behaviour for Muslims living within or on the 'front-line' of the *Daru'l-Harb* were elaborated by Muslim scholars interpreting the general spirit of the Qur'an and the *sunna*. Though there were variations of emphasis between the different law schools, two major points did emerge. The first was that Muslim individuals and communities – normally merchants – sojourning or living within the *Daru'l-Harb* of their free choice should respect the laws of the state in which they lived, so long as they were allowed to practise their religion freely, and so long as they engaged in no activity that would harm the *Daru'l-Islam*. On the other hand, retreat (*hijra*) into the *Daru'l-Islam* or resistance (*jihad*) – depending on practical circumstances – was expected of those Muslim communities within the *Daru'l-Harb* that were unable to practise their religion freely. This was especially true of areas on the Islamic periphery that had been conquered by force.[13]

It was, however, still difficult to apply these general rules concerning the relationship between the *Daru'l-Islam* and the *Daru'l-Harb* to that nadir of the Muslim experience, the era of Western colonial rule. By the end of the First World War, practically all parts of the Muslim world were under some form of *kafir* (unbeliever) rule or tutelage; this was the culmination of a long, agonizing period of decline and retreat that had accelerated in the eighteenth century.

In many ways, the reaction of the Muslim world to the fact of subjection to Europe was similar to the reaction of other colonized areas, but expressed in a specifically Islamic idiom. In Vietnam, for example, the reaction of the indigenous leadership to the French take-

over in the late nineteenth century could be divided – always allowing
for nuances – into four categories. There were those who resisted the
French; those who 'submitted', feeling that a continuation of the fight
against France would be futile and damaging to the interests of the
people; those who committed suicide or retreated into a private world;
and those who saw French rule as an opportunity to change Vietnamese
society, and adjust to the modern world.[14]

In the Islamic world, there was ample evidence of resistance (*jihad*)
to the imposition of colonial rule, including the revolt of the self-
proclaimed *Mahdi* in the Sudan during the 1880s and the Indian
Mutiny of 1857. As far as Southeast Asia was concerned, there were
many local examples of *jihad*, the most significant of which was the
Acehnese war against the Dutch which began in 1873. But Islam has
always been guided by the fundamental principle that God does not
impose upon human beings an obligation beyond their capacity.[15] While
the Qur'an enjoins believers to strive to the uttermost 'in the path of
God' (*fi sabilillah*), it recognizes that there can be impossible odds,
limits to human endurance, and financial or physical constraints that
may restrict a community's ability to resist or remove itself from the
Daru'l-Harb.[16] In such extreme circumstances, *taslim*, or acceptance of
the unavoidable, may be contemplated, as long as it is submission to a
kafir power that only intends to impose its rule, and not to destroy
Islam itself.[17]

When the Muslim world entered into this reluctant state of
submission, one consequence was a marked tendency for the *Daru'l-
Islam* to withdraw into itself, both physically and spiritually. Snouck
Hurgronje noted in his observations on Mecca in the late 1880s that
the Hijaz had become ever more important for Muslims, not just as a
place of pilgrimage, but as a haven from the pervasive *kafir* presence.[18]
This natural instinct to retreat, however, also had the inevitable effect
of shutting Islam off from the outside world, stultifying its educational
institutions, and emphasizing tradition and ritual: a general condition
known as *taqlid*.[19] At the same time, the plight of the *Daru'l-Islam* also
stimulated a more positive reaction. The Qur'an and the *Hadith* (reports
of the words and deeds of Muhammad) indicated that the relationship
between believers and unbelievers need not be implacably hostile, and
could in fact be friendly, so long as Muslims were not oppressed and
had freedom of religion.[20] It was in this spirit that many significant
leaders of the Muslim community in India, for instance, were prepared
to accept British rule in the late nineteenth century, and to exploit the
prevailing conditions of peace and prosperity in order to initiate wholesale educational and religious reform.[21]

In the late nineteenth and early twentieth centuries, in fact, a wave of Islamic reform swept through the Muslim world, including South-east Asia. In many senses, it was an Islamic version of the 'revolution of cultural awareness' that affected large parts of the colonized world at this time. In part, it was an attempt to rejuvenate Islamic education, and reinterpret Islamic doctrine in a way that would enable Islam to engage positively with the revolution in ideas that had, so it seemed, enabled Europe to dominate the world. In part, it was an attempt – via the concept of 'pan-Islamic' unity – to rebuild the notion of the international mission of the Islamic *umma*. The retreat of Islam in the colonial period had had the inevitable effect of driving Islam back into ethnic roots and the defence of local cultures. The primary task of the Islamic reformers was therefore to re-create an outward-looking, modernizing Islam, that would cut itself free from local practices and accretions to the pure doctrine, and reaffirm the central notion that Islam was a universal mission that transcended the links of family, clan and tribe.[22]

It was inevitable that, in the course of the early decades of the twentieth century, the Islamic reform movement should confront the parallel revolutions in national and ethnic awareness. To an extent greater than any other of the main world religions, Islam challenges the primary concepts of nationalism. It is true that practical con-siderations led Muhammad to take into account and respect the complexity of clan loyalties and the inter-connections between clans; this is clearly shown in that ideal model of the Islamic state, the Medina constitution.[23] But the primacy of the unity and the goal of the *umma* is always paramount in Islamic doctrine. In a sense, Islam is a culmina-tion in the progression of the relationship between belonging and believing in the monotheistic tradition of the Middle East. Judaism affirmed the unity of God, but ascribed a special divine role to a particular people and to a particular land; Christianity created the concept of a universal spiritual community but did not link this to any notion of a universal political entity;[24] Islam, however, inextricably linked the spiritual and the political community in the *umma*, and gave this community a universal goal. The relationship between Islam and nationalism, therefore, is always likely to be problematic.

In Indonesia, the confrontation between Islam and nationalism in the inter-war years was manifested both in debate and in the realm of political action. The dispute was focused not so much on the question of whether or not to resist Western colonialism, but on whether that resistance should primarily be seen as a national/Pan-Asian struggle against European rule, or as an Islamic struggle against *kafir* rule. For many Islamic leaders in Indonesia, an emphasis on nationalism (*kebangsaan*) would break up the dynamic unity of Islam and endanger the chances of attaining Islam's spiritual goals; in religious terms, the nationalists were seen to be guilty of the sin of *shirk*, or of highlighting a merely human creation – the nation – at the expense of a divine creation, the *umma*.[25] For nationalists like Sukarno, on the other hand, too great an emphasis on Islamic goals and loyalties would not only alienate non-Muslims in Indonesia, but also the large number of Indonesian Muslims who were not strict in the practice of their faith. This would create fundamental ideological divisions that could irreparably split the anti-colonial movement.[26]

The complexity of the relationship between Islamic identity on the one side, and ethnic, regional and national identity on the other, can be seen in the history of modern Aceh. It also helps to explain the background to the Acehnese revolt of 1953, and the ambiguous interaction of Islamic loyalties, nationalist objectives and regional affiliations that underlay that revolt.

Glossary of terms

Da'a   'Invitation' to the Islamic faith.

Daru'l Harb   'House/Abode of Warfare/Conflict'. Area where non-Muslim political power is exercised, and/or where Muslims do not have the free exercise of their religion.

Daru'l Islam 'House/Abode of Islam'. Area where the edicts of Islam are fully promulgated.

Hadith   Record of divinely inspired declarations and actions of the Prophet Muhammad.

Hijra   Emigration or separation 'in the cause of God'.

Islam   From the root verb *aslama*, meaning to submit or resign oneself. The basis of the religion of Islam is 'submission' to God through acceptance of the Qur'an and the prophethood of Muhammad.

Jihad   Striving or effort 'in the cause of God' to promote and protect Islam.

Kafir   'Unbelievers'. Those who deny any of the main principles of Islam.

Mujahidin   Those who wage *Jihad*.

Muslim   Derived from the root *aslama*, it refers to 'one who submits'. Therefore means an 'adherent to the religion of Islam'. In practice, may be used as a noun or an adjective.

Qur'an   The word of God revealed gradually to the prophet Muhammad in the course of his mission.

Shirk   'Idolatry'. Seeking to weaken the concept of *Tauhid* (see below).

Sunna   Deeds, utterances and recorded instances of unspoken approval by Muhammad, constituting the basis, along with the Qur'an, of the Islamic law or *Sharia*.

Taqlid   Those who follow existing customs and authorities without exercising individual judgement.

Taslim   Usually, benediction at the end of Islamic prayers. By extension, an act of submission 'where it is appropriate'.

Tauhid   The basic principle of Islam, asserting the 'one-ness' of God.

Ulama   From the Arabic word for knowledge or wisdom. By extension, religious scholar and teacher.

Umma   A community, particularly a community united for a religious purpose. From this, the concept of the whole world community of Islam.

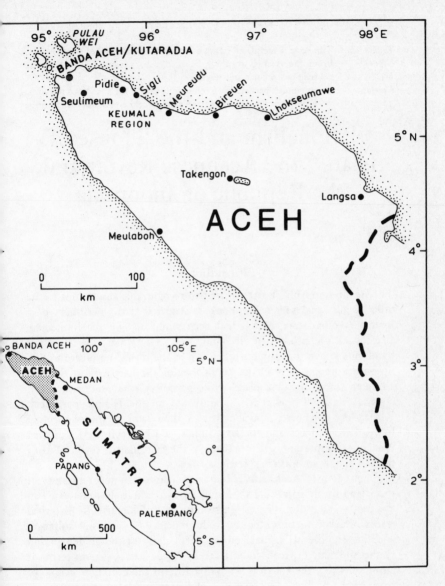

Map 6 Aceh and Sumatra

7

Nationalism and the 'House of Islam': the Acehnese Revolt and the Republic of Indonesia

Introduction

The Acehnese revolt of 1953 bears two recognizable similarities to the other revolts analysed in this book: it occurred at the periphery of a former colonial state, and it had been stimulated by the immediate stresses of the process of decolonization. There was, on the other hand, no element of ethnic irredentism in the revolt, no desire to link up with a people beyond the boundaries of the new nation. Equally, although the revolt took place at the periphery of a Southeast Asian state, Aceh itself was most certainly not on the Islamic periphery. Rather, the Acehnese traditionally saw their land as the connecting link between Mecca and the East Indies, and between West and East Asia. Most important of all, perhaps, is the fact that the revolt of 1953 had no stated separatist aspirations.

The region of Aceh, situated at the northwesternmost extremity of the island of Sumatra and of Indonesia as a whole, has possessed in the past – and still possesses – a strong sense of identity. In historical terms, the key to this identity is the memory of a strong sultanate wielding significant regional power, particularly in the golden period of the Sultanate of Aceh under Iskandar Muda (1607–36).[1] In terms of ethnic identity, the roughly two and a half to three million people of Aceh have a distinctive language which has many Malay characteristics, but also some linguistic links to the Cham languages of Indochina.[2] Acehnese is still spoken widely in Aceh as the first language, although publications in the language are scarce and the public media are dominated by Indonesian.[3]

Although it is clear from the language and society of Aceh that the Acehnese share many cultural characteristics with their Sumatran neighbours, and indeed with the Malay world as a whole, it is the self-identity of a people that is all-important in determining their outlook, not the 'scientific' distinctions made by outside ethnographers. In this context, it is significant that the Acehnese make great play, anecdotally, of the notion that the name 'Aceh' reflects the Arabic, Chinese, European and Indian ('Hindia') origins of its inhabitants. At the very least, this suggests that the Acehnese have an inclination to link their identity and their history with the Asian world beyond the Malay archipelago, and to look west and north as well as eastwards towards the Malay world.

The key to this non-parochial perspective of the Acehnese is Islam. Acehnese historians see Aceh not merely as a bridge between the Islamic centre and the Malay periphery, but as one of the great Islamic sultanates in its own right.[5] This tendency to highlight Aceh as a centre of Islamic power and scholarship is given credibility by, above all, the remarkable flowering of Islamic learning and debate in Aceh in the golden age of the late sixteenth and seventeenth centuries; the era of Hamzah Fansuri, Syamsuddin Samathrani, Syekh Nuruddin ar-Raniri and Syekh Abdur-Rauf of Singkel.[6] It is noticeable, however, that while modern Acehnese writers like Ali Hasjmy draw attention to this overwhelming evidence of Aceh's historical credentials as a centre of Islamic learning, they tend to downplay the testimony that that era also provides of strong tendencies to Sufi unorthodoxy in Acehnese religious thought.[7] It is also significant that the impressive body of literature produced in Aceh at this time was written in Malay; indeed, the mystical religious poetry of Hamzah Fansuri has been cited as an outstanding model of classical Malay literature.[8] Aceh, in fact, was an intrinsic part of the Malay world, not only in terms of trading relations, customs and traditions, and politico-dynastic contacts, but also – and crucially – in terms of Islamic scholarship.

The tradition that Sultan Iskandar Muda harmonized local customs (*adat*) with Islamic Law during his reign sums up, perhaps, the inextricable relationship in Acehnese self-identity between the Sultanate, Acehnese society and Islam, coupled with the historic memory of Acehnese greatness.[9] By the nineteenth century, however, the actual power of the Sultanate had shrunk, and this decline was matched by the growing local power of the regional chieftains, or *ulebalang*. It was virtually inevitable by this time that Aceh would eventually have to confront the Dutch, who were, in the early to mid-nineteenth century, steadily consolidating their power in the interior and along the coasts of Sumatra. By the 1850s and 1860s, Dutch control was creeping up the north Sumatra coast towards Aceh itself.[10] The ensuing war between Aceh and the Dutch was stimulated by growing Dutch involvement in and interference with internal Acehnese affairs –

particularly matters of trade.[11] Behind this, however, was the implacable determination of the Dutch to ensure that no potentially hostile power should gain a foothold in Aceh via an alliance with the Sultanate, and the fact that Britain was prepared to sanction the extension of Dutch power throughout Sumatra.[12]

There then followed a long and costly war between the Dutch and the Acehnese, lasting officially from 1873 to 1903. After an initial disastrous failure to seize the Sultan's capital of Kutaraja, the Dutch were eventually able to take the town in November 1873. With the death of the Sultan in early 1874, the Dutch announced the annexation of Aceh, and thereafter refused to contemplate anything less than the complete subordination of the region to Dutch rule.[13] However, the Acehnese leaders retreated southwards, and the new Sultan established a new military base in the Pidie–Keumala–Seulimeum region. Since the Dutch in the first phase of the war confined themselves to limited military actions and a blockade designed to strangle the rebels into surrender, the Sultan and his followers were able to build up a powerful resistance network with relative impunity.[14]

From the mid-1870s onwards, the Aceh war had all the characteristics of a classic guerrilla struggle, with local and intermittent military activity, small-scale attacks and reprisals, along with a Dutch effort to win over regional military leaders and gradually weaken the revolt by piecemeal submissions.[15] As the nature of the war became more decentralized, so conduct of the resistance movement fell increasingly into the hands of local 'charismatic' leaders, either regional warlords – like Teuku Umar of West Aceh – or the religious scholars (*ulama*).[16] In 1881, the religious leadership in Aceh declared the war a *jihad*, or *perang sabil*, and this undoubtedly gave a new lease of life to the struggle and strengthened the local influence of the *ulama*s. This rejuvenation of the Acehnese war effort was also helped by the Dutch 'concentration' policy, which involved an attempt to encircle and stifle the rebel regions rather than directly pacify them. This gave precious space for the rebels to organize and mobilize.[17]

The revolt began to collapse, however, when the Dutch at length launched full-scale assaults on the rebel strongholds. Between 1896 and 1899, the Dutch gained control of the crucial rebel regions of Seulimeum, Pidie and the interior of Keumala, and the Sultan and his military leadership were forced to regroup in the region stretching from Bireuen on the coast to Takengon deep in the interior.[18] The Dutch continued their pressure and, in 1903, the Sultan finally surrendered to the Dutch. This – along with a brutal pacification 'sweep' across the interior of southern Aceh in 1904 – ensured the end of all but spasmodic resistance.[19]

The Acehnese war against the Dutch assumed an enormous symbolic significance in the later history of Aceh. The fact that the Sultanate was able to prolong the war for thirty years made it the primary example of enduring resistance to the imposition of colonial rule in the East Indies. On a wider scale, the anti-colonial war of Aceh had also explicitly been declared a *jihad* or *perang sabil*.[20] As such, it confirmed Aceh's status as one of the principal centres of the struggle against the imposition of *kafir* colonial rule in the Muslim world as a whole.[21] The implantation among the Acehnese of the ideal of the *perang sabil* had been a major propaganda success, a result of the diffusion at the local level of epic poetry giving examples of acts of martyrdom, heroism and divine intervention in the early history of Islam.[22] These examples – along with appropriate references from the Qur'an – were designed to appeal to a spirit of endurance as well as sacrifice; the *hikayats* (stories) emphasized the duty of the faithful to contribute their wealth to the cause of the *perang sabil* quite as much as the dedication of lives in the field of battle.[23]

Aceh in the era of colonial rule

With the defeat of the Acehnese Sultanate, the region was incorporated into the administrative system of the Dutch East Indies. Following the general lines of Dutch colonial policy, the local hereditary or semi-hereditary leaders were integrated into the regional administration, while local religious leaders were permitted freedom of activity on the condition that they did not become involved in politics. In Aceh itself, the institution of the Sultanate – the apparent focus of resistance – had already been removed, and the Sultan himself was exiled.[24] The local chieftains or *ulebalang*, on the other hand, had their status and salaries regularized as part of the administrative structure.[25] (Despite the fact that many members of this *ulebalang* elite had played a key role in the resistance war, and were to play an equally important role in the Indonesian nationalist movement, it was inevitable that the *ulebalang* as a class would be associated with the Dutch, and with all the impositions of the Dutch administration.[26]) The sense of resentment this generated, and the widespread perception of the alienation of the *ulebalang* from the Acehnese people as a whole, was deepened by their tendency to exploit their legal and administrative power in order to expand their land holdings, and by the fact that their children were often educated outside Aceh in elite Dutch-language institutions.[27])

In spite of the Dutch co-option of the *ulebalang* elite, outbreaks of resistance continued throughout Aceh in the 1910s, 1920s and 1930s.[28] It is because of this continued resistance that the assertion was made

that 'Aceh never surrendered its sovereignty to the Dutch'.[29] A picture
of endless outright resistance to the Dutch in the 1900–1940 period
would, however, give a very distorted impression of the history of
Aceh. In fact, just as the Dutch were anxious to steer Acehnese Islam
away from what they saw as its tendencies to backward 'fanaticism', a
new generation of Islamic scholars in Aceh were just as anxious –
though for different reasons – to bring Islamic reform to the region.
The period 1900–1940 – particularly the decade of the 1930s – saw a
revolution in Islamic education in Aceh, with the creation of new
madrasah (Islamic schools) and a serious effort by the younger generation of *ulama*s to purify Islamic practices and improve educational
standards.[30]

It is interesting to note the extent to which this phase of Islamic
reform linked Aceh to general developments in Indonesia as a whole.
(In the first place, non-Acehnese Islamic organizations like 'Sarekat
Islam' and 'Muhammadiyah' established a foothold in Aceh during
this period, and, conversely, the Acehnese *ulama*s often gained their
religious education outside Aceh and played a key role in the above
organizations.[31]) Second, the new Islamic educational institutions that
were set up, far from entrenching themselves in an exclusive Acehnese
identity, tended to use the Indonesian language.[32] (The whole inter-war
movement for Islamic reform involved, in fact, a process of looking
beyond the constraints of traditional Acehnese society – in terms of
both customary Islam and government – and linking it with the intellectual and political trends of the new nationalist era.)

This crucial development, however, can be understood in specifically
Acehnese terms. (The struggle for Islamic reform, for example, could
be seen as a continuation of the efforts of the Acehnese *ulama*s during
the war against the Dutch to encourage the ordinary people to look
beyond their local communities to the wider world of Islam.[33]) In a
similar sense, Ali Hasjmy has characterized the period of Islamic
reform as an extension of the war against the Dutch, waged by other
means, and as a modern version of the campaign against ignorance and
illiteracy that the *ulama*s had fought throughout Acehnese history.[34] (In
a more precise sense, the reforming *ulama*s of the inter-war years had
an agenda that was specific to Acehnese society: the removal of
ulebalang control over the Acehnese legal system.[35]) The formation of
PUSA ('Persatuan Ulama Seluruh Aceh', or All-Aceh Religious
Scholars' Association) in 1939 reflects this link between Islamic reform
as a pan-Islamic objective, and the pursuit of a specific programme for
Aceh itself.[36]

Aceh during the Second World War and
revolutionary period

From 1939 on, PUSA was able to expand its influence considerably, particularly in northern Aceh.[37] With the Japanese invasion of Southeast Asia in late 1941, PUSA seized the opportunity to move directly into the political sphere and challenge Dutch rule. As the Japanese moved through Malaya, PUSA members established contact with them and, in early 1942, carried out acts of sabotage in Aceh itself.[38] This was but part, however, of a general uprising against the Dutch in Aceh and northern Sumatra, in which all sections of the nationalist movement participated, including dissidents among the *ulebalang* elite.[39]

In general, it could be argued that PUSA, under the leadership of Daud Beureueh, had as their primary objective not only the removal of Dutch colonial rule, but also the replacement of the traditional government of Aceh by a new radical and reforming Islamic leadership. As in many parts of Indonesia and Southeast Asia in general, however, the Japanese preferred to rely initially on the existing administrative stratum, the *ulebalang*, that had collaborated with the Dutch.[40] In the long run, this served only to heighten the political tensions within Aceh; the *ulebalang* were now associated, not only with Dutch *kafir* rule, but also with the hardships and excesses of Japanese *kafir* rule.[41] At the same time, however, the Japanese discovered that *ulama*-led organizations had a far greater capacity to mobilize popular support for the war effort.[42] As a consequence, PUSA-based organizations gained increasing influence in Aceh during the war years; by 1944, for example, the administration of religious law in Aceh was placed in the hands of the *ulama*s, and the legal powers of the *ulebalang* were severely reduced.[43]

The Japanese surrender of 1945, therefore, had the immediate effect of releasing political tensions in Aceh that had been building up for decades, but which had been greatly intensified during the war. The Indonesian Declaration of Independence on 17 August 1945 and the subsequent revolutionary period had a confusing impact. On the one hand, the new leaders of Indonesia wished above all things to preserve unity – political, regional and social – in the face of the likely return of the Dutch. They accordingly appointed as chief administrator of Aceh an established nationalist figure from an *ulebalang* background, Teuku Nya' Arif, who himself opted for continuity and kept many local *ulebalang* in their posts.[44] On the other hand, as in many other parts of Indonesia, the local pressure for radical change developed an irresistible momentum in the later months of 1945 and the beginning of 1946. As in other regions of Indonesia, militarized revolutionary youth organizations proliferated in Aceh in the course of 1945, and an unbridgeable gap was fast developing between the official local leaders of the Indonesian independence movement – headed by Nya' Arif – and unofficial radical forces organizing at the grass-roots level.[45]

What was special in Aceh was the link between the radical aspirations of the *pemuda* youth organizations and the more established PUSA-influenced Islamic organizations. In October 1945, four of the leading *ulama*s of Aceh – including Daud Beureueh – put a firm Islamic imprint on the Indonesian war of independence when they issued a proclamation declaring the struggle against the Dutch to be a holy war, or *perang sabil.* After warning that a return of the Dutch would not only mean the end of Indonesian freedom but also a threat to Islam itself, the proclamation called on all Indonesians to unite behind Sukarno to protect the nation and Islam. A significant Acehnese touch was added when the *ulama*s declared the independence war to be a 'continuation' (*sambungan*) of the Aceh war of the late nineteenth century.[46] In Indonesian terms, this was a clear reaffirmation of loyalty to the cause of independence; in Acehnese terms, it implied a reassertion of Islamic values and Islamic leadership in the revolutionary process.

Matters came to a head in Aceh at the end of 1945 when open warfare broke out in the Pidie–Sigli region between the local *ulebalang* forces on one side, and youth and Islamic organizations on the other. In the course of December 1945 and January 1946, PUSA-dominated militias (the *mujahidin*) gained control of the Pidie region and established their own administration.[47] By this time, the challenge to Teuku Nya' Arif's authority and the whole edifice of government in Aceh had become irresistible. In the spring of 1946, the *mujahidin* and a newly formed militia dominated by *ulama*s, the *Tentara Perjuangan Rakyat* (Army of the Struggle of the People), combined to force Nya' Arif to surrender power in Banda Aceh.[48] This revolutionary period saw a growing vacuum of authority in Aceh, where old scores were paid off – particularly against unpopular *ulebalang* families – and land was seized and redistributed by *ad hoc* local administrations.

From 1946 onwards, the central government of the Republic of Indonesia could exercise little influence in Aceh, for the simple reason that from this time on it was struggling to ensure its own survival in the face of increasing Dutch encroachment. Since the Dutch made no attempt to reoccupy Aceh – with the exception of Pulau Wei, an island off the north coast of Aceh – the region was in effect increasingly left to its own devices.

The whole period from August 1945 to the outbreak of the Acehnese revolt in 1953 was marked, in fact, by a growing divergence between the central government's view of Aceh's status within the Republic and the views of the Acehnese leaders. The overall intention of the central government was to create provincial units that were sufficiently large to encompass different regions and ethnic groupings – thus preventing tendencies to regional and ethnic exclusivity, and so encouraging sentiments of national unity. It was in accordance with this general line of policy that the Republic of Indonesia tried to establish a sub-province of North Sumatra, linking the Batak and Acehnese regions, with its capital in Medan.[49]

The problem for the central government lay in the fact that its inherent weakness meant that, far from dominating the regions, it was often forced to work through the local power-structures that had been established in the revolutionary period of 1945–46. This is shown in the history of Aceh at this time. In the aftermath of the first Dutch 'Police Action' in July 1947, Aceh was made into a special 'Military Region' and Daud Beureueh was appointed 'Military Governor'; in effect, Aceh had been given, even if only provisionally, an autonomous status.[50] As the political and military situation stabilized in early 1948, an attempt was made to reconstitute the administrative unit of North Sumatra, including the regions of Aceh, Tapanuli and East Sumatra. The old military regions were re-established, however, after the second Dutch 'Police Action' in December 1948.[51] By this time, in fact, most of the Republican leadership had been taken into custody by the Dutch, and Aceh was one of the last areas of the Republic that had not been captured by Dutch troops.

Increasingly through this period, but particularly after the second Dutch 'Police Action', Aceh became a *de facto* autonomous zone beyond the control of the central government. This led to a paradoxical situation. From one perspective, Aceh, far from cutting loose from the Republic, became the last redoubt of its resistance to Dutch rule. Aceh could not only provide the 'sinews of war' in military and economic terms, but could, in diplomatic terms, give credibility to the notion that the Indonesian Republic still had a legitimate existence. In this sense, the service that Aceh gave to the Republic in this time of crisis was of incalculable importance; certainly the Acehnese were – and are – proud of the role that they played.[52] Not only this, but Daud Beureueh resisted all blandishments enticing him to link Aceh with the federal *negara* structure that the Dutch were trying to establish at this time as a way of discrediting and weakening the Republic.[53] It could reasonably be argued, therefore, that Aceh's loyalty and constancy in the resistance struggle had in this period of extreme national crisis been more firm than in any other part of Indonesia.

However, even if Aceh had no separatist intentions, the fact remains that Acehnese autonomy was greatly strengthened during this period.

As a military region, Aceh had its own military force under the command of Daud Beureueh; equally, it had its own trading links – developed in the chaotic revolutionary period – that were independent of central government control.[54] Just as important was the fact that Daud Beureueh and the PUSA leadership were now free to impose measures of Islamic reform, and take steps to suppress what were seen as 'impure' or un-Islamic accretions that had become ingrained in the customary religious practices of Aceh.[55] By the time that the Dutch and the Indonesian Republic were eventually able to agree an independence settlement in December 1949, Aceh had become accustomed to a situation where it had considerable scope for autonomous action] Aceh felt in addition that the Republic owed it a debt of gratitude.

In December 1949, the interim government of the Republic of Indonesia, based in Sumatra, which was sympathetic to Acehnese aspirations, established a new province of Aceh in place of the old military region.[56] This arrangement – seemingly the culmination of Aceh's autonomous ambitions – came at the precise time that the Republic of Indonesia, having finally negotiated its independence from the Netherlands, was to set about the task of retrieving and consolidating its central authority. (In the early months of 1950, the newly established Republican government refused to confirm Aceh's provincial status or Daud Beureueh's position as governor.[57] Instead, they made it clear that they intended to create a province of North Sumatra and absorb Aceh within that province. Despite furious protests from the Acehnese administration and provincial assembly, and direct warnings from Daud Beureueh in December 1950 that the ending of Aceh's 'autonomy' would lead to widespread disaffection in Aceh, the government pressed ahead with its plan.[58] By early 1951, Aceh's separate provincial status had effectively come to an end.

The moves to rebellion in Aceh

(As Daud Beureueh had warned, there then followed a steady breakdown of Acehnese-central government relations] The incorporation of Aceh within North Sumatra not only offended Aceh's *amour propre*, but also destroyed the *de facto* network of self-government that had been operating in the late 1940s. The bulk of the administration was shifted south to Medan; control over trade was taken out of the hands of local interests, and now came under the regulation of the provincial government; and Acehnese military forces were gradually integrated into a wider command structure, while at the same time Acehnese troops were stealthily removed from Aceh and replaced by non-Acehnese.[59]

Not only was Acehnese integrity – as it seemed – under assault from the outside, but it was also seriously affected by internal tensions. The revolutionary upheavals of 1945 and 1946 had left a legacy of resentment and bitterness among the sections of the community that had suffered. The chaos of the revolutionary period had led to arbitrary arrests and confiscations, and these in their wake encouraged extensive corruption.[60] On top of the accusations of incompetence, tyranny and corruption that were made against the regime by its opponents was the fact that Daud Beureueh's programme of Islamic reform had seriously offended the more traditional *ulama*s. A significant section of the population, in other words, opposed the Acehnese government, and it was natural that they should seek help from the central government, and that the central government, in turn, should try to exploit divisions among the Acehnese political and religious elite.[61]

Far from bringing Aceh to heel, these internal dissensions merely served to raise the political temperature and strengthen the forces in Aceh that were inclined to resist the central government. What brought matters to a head, however, was not simply the issue of Aceh's autonomy. If that had been the sole issue, then the subsequent revolt would have been confined to an Acehnese agenda pure and simple. The Acehnese leaders, however, did not merely limit themselves to the issue of Acehnese provincial rights; indeed, as we have seen, they prided themselves on the central role that they had played in the general Indonesian struggle against the Dutch. What they particularly resented now was the fact that not only had Aceh been slighted and marginalized, but that Islam – for them the central dynamo of the revolution – had also apparently been sidelined. From the time of the foundation of the Indonesian Republic, in fact, strict Muslims had had to accept the fact that religion was only to be one among the five ideological foundations, or *pancasila*, of the new state.[62] By the early 1950s, it seemed that the Islamic leadership in Jakarta had not only lost the ideological battle in 1945, but that it was steadily losing political influence to the secular-nationalists of the PNI (Partai Nasional Indonesia), and even – worst of all – the rejuvenated PKI (Partai Komunis Indonesia) that had only recently failed in a conspiracy to seize power within the Republic.

The anxiety of the Acehnese leaders at this trend of events was shared in other strongly Islamic regions of Indonesia. Already, in 1948, an Islamic rebellion against the Republic had begun in the mountainous region of West Java, mainly east of Bandung. The stimulus for this defiance was the first Dutch 'Police Action' in July 1947 and the subsequent agreement between the Dutch and the Republic of Indonesia that Republican troops should withdraw from large parts of West Java, including the Bandung region. Local Muslim leaders – *ulama*s and militia chieftains – refused to comply with this agreement, established an independent Islamic assembly and army, and continued the war against the Dutch.[63] This would have been written off as one of the many 'incidents' of a confused period, had it not been for the fact that this movement subsequently not only refused to submit to the authority of the Republic, but in August 1949 declared the creation of an Islamic State of Indonesia (Negara Islam Indonesia, or NII).[64]

While the Acehnese leaders had given an Islamic gloss to the war against the Dutch, the West Javanese Muslim leaders had gone a step further and challenged the legitimacy of the Republic itself. The aim of the rebels was to replace the 'Pancasila' Republic by an Islamic state, and thereby reclaim Indonesia for the *Daru'l Islam*, or global 'abode of Islam'.

As Acehnese disenchantment with the central government came to a head in the early 1950s, it was perhaps inevitable that the region should attach itself to this so-called 'Darul Islam' rebellion. Between 1951 and 1953, an atmosphere of conspiracy and anxious anticipation enveloped Aceh. On the one side, the central government tightened its control by pre-emptive arrests of potential or actual anti-government plotters; on the other side, Daud Beureueh warned that the Acehnese, although patient, would be ready to resist if pushed too far.[65] By 1953, there were open demands in Aceh for the creation of an Islamic state; in addition, paramilitary organizations were being set up, and Daud Beureueh established contact with Kartosuwiryo, the leader of the Darul Islam movement in West Java. By now, the slide to war had become irresistible, and on 21 September 1953, Daud Beureueh and his followers formally linked Aceh to the NII and joined the Darul Islam rebellion.[66]

The Darul Islam rebellion in Aceh

In looking at the course of the rebellion and its objectives, it is first of all necessary to distinguish between its regional and its Islamic dimensions, though these were to a very great degree intertwined. The regional grievances were based on a sense that Aceh, the hero of the revolutionary period, had been marginalized. Beyond this, there was the sense that Sumatra as a whole – and the main Sumatran-based party, the Masyumi – was losing its influence at the centre of power. This went hand-in-hand with a fear that Java was increasingly dominating the administration of the Republic and its general policies at the expense of the outlying islands. This was linked to growing alarm at the steady resurgence of the mainly Java-based 'Partai Komunis Indonesia', or PKI.[67]

If these, mainly regional, fears provided the immediate *motivation* for the Acehnese insurgency, the *objective* of that rebellion was clearly Islamic. By joining Darul Islam and becoming a part of the Negara Islam Indonesia, Aceh was linking itself to an Indonesia-wide project – which also included parts of Sulawesi and Kalimantan – to replace the Republic of Indonesia by an Islamic state. As the manifesto issued by the Acehnese rebels to justify their insurgency (see Appendix 5) made clear, the defining of this objective of an Islamic state was not a matter of detail but of overall, fundamental principle. For the Darul Islam rebels of Aceh, the key point was that Islam was indivisible. They therefore rejected the notion, embodied in the *pancasila* principles of the Indonesian Republic, that 'Belief in one God' should constitute a mere aspect of the state ideology:

> Belief in the One God is for us the very source of social life, and every single one of its directives must apply here on Indonesian soil. It is not possible for only some of these directives to apply while others do not, be this in criminal or civil affairs, in the question of religious worship, or in matters of everyday life. If the Law of God does not apply, this means we are deviating from Belief in the One God.[68]

Islam, in other words, cannot be restricted to a limited role within the state and society: it must encompass all aspects of public and private life.

Although Muslims would point out that Islam is a matter of faith, not ideology, it is nevertheless useful to see the programme of the Darul Islam rebels of Aceh in the context of a conflict of ideologies. What the rebels objected to in Sukarno's *pancasila* principles – and, indeed, in the *pancasila* state itself – was the fact that nationalism had been elevated from an instinct into an ideology. They were particularly outraged by Sukarno's view, expressed in 1953, that too great an emphasis on Islam in the state ideology would only divide the people, while nationalism alone could provide a focus of unity.[69] Like the Islamic reformers of the 1920s and 1930s, the Darul Islam movement condemned this elevation of nationalism above Islam as the fundamental pillar of the *pancasila* state as the worst form of idolatry, or *shirk*.

In a curious way, the Darul Islam attitude to *pancasila* nationalism mirrored the perspective on the national-liberation process of Asian communist parties of that time. Like Marxism-Leninism, Darul Islam saw the nationalist phase of gaining independence as just part – though a vital part – of a much more profound process. While, therefore, they could accept the prevailing nationalist rhetoric of the period of the anti-colonial struggle, what they could not accept was that that rhetoric had been hardened into a state ideology. What they were rebelling against, therefore, was not Indonesia as such, nor the ideal of Indonesian unity, but the ideological forces of *pancasila* that had gained control of the Indonesian state. This is made clear in the manifesto of the Acehnese rebels:

> If we now establish a state, this does not mean that we shall be setting up a state within a state, because in our hearts and souls we have always regarded the state of the Republic of Indonesia as but a golden bridge leading to the state for which we have long been yearning. But this golden bridge no longer appears as a means of getting where we want but as an obstacle, especially since our sense of loyalty to a Republic based upon nationalism no longer exists.[70]

In his book *Revolusi Islam di Indonesia*, Hasan Saleh, one of Daud Beureueh's main supporters in the early period of the Acehnese rebellion, virtually echoed the communist 'two-stage' theory of national liberation. Like the communists, he argued that the first stage was that of the struggle for national independence, in which all sections of the people and points of view should ideally be united. Once that stage had been reached with the gaining of independence, however, the struggle of ideology for the soul of the nation would begin. Hasan Saleh argues in his book that, in the context of Indonesia, this second phase began after the Dutch–Indonesian independence agreement of December 1949.[71] After this, the battle of ideologies started, with the supporters of a *negara Islam* confronting the *pancasila* ideology of the Republic of Indonesia and the ultimate ideological enemy, atheistic communism.[72] At the heart of Hasan Saleh's argument is the view that the final confrontation was between the *negara Islam* and communism; far from offering a 'golden bridge' to the Islamic state, the confused, quasi-secular ideology of the *pancasila* state would merely pave the way for the victory of a *negara komunis* (communist state).[73]

Hasan Saleh pursued this theme by using the image of two hills that had to be climbed by the faithful Indonesian Muslims. The first hill was the *negara merdeka*, the attainment of an independent Indonesia. The danger was that Muslims would stop and rest at this first hill, not realizing that there was another, more formidable, hill to be climbed – the *negara Islam*.[74] This image clearly indicates what Hasan Saleh – and, indeed, other Darul Islam leaders – felt to be the main danger facing Islam in this ideological struggle: namely, complacency. The huge numerical strength of Islam in Indonesia masked the fact that a large section of the Muslim community was either apathetic or consisted of outright *munafiqin*, pretend Muslims. How else, argued Hasan Saleh, could the communists win so much support in elections?[75]

The sense that the real, underlying struggle of Darul Islam was against communism is heightened in *Revolusi Islam di Indonesia* by the use of the language of 'People's War'. Just as a communist revolution would be led by the party, spearheaded by a 'people's army' and supported by 'the masses', so the Islamic revolution should be led by the *ulama*s, spearheaded by Islamic youth in the militias, and supported by the population as a whole.[76] This notion of a popular struggle echoed the old heroic literature of the Dutch–Acehnese war, as did the emphasis on sacrifice – financial and personal – and the need to place loyalty to God above ties of affiliation to locality, family and friends.[77] It is noticeable, however, that Hasan Saleh gives no indication of any Acehnese separatist agenda; on the contrary, the main objective of *Revolusi Islam di Indonesia* was to win the support of the faithful Muslim community *outside* the strongholds of Darul Islam.[78]

Whatever the stated aims of the Darul Islam movement, however, everything ultimately depended on the military outcome of the revolt. Although in the initial stages the rebels were able to gain control of substantial areas of northern Aceh, forces loyal to the Republic of Indonesia held on to Kutaraja/Banda Aceh and the crucial southeastern coastal town of Langsa. Supplemented by troops brought up from Medan, the troops in Langsa were then able to push their way up Aceh's main communications route, the coastal road leading to Banda Aceh. By the end of 1953, a pattern had been established, with troops loyal to the Republic maintaining a tenuous control over the main towns and connecting roads of Aceh, while the rebels controlled the countryside beyond. It soon became apparent that the main rebel strongholds were the regions of Aceh Besar that surrounded the capital, Banda Aceh; the Pidie–Sigli region on the coast to the southeast of Banda Aceh; the Aceh Utara region down the coast from Pidie; and the central Aceh region around Takengon and Lake Tawar.[79] Not surprisingly, these were the traditional rebel regions that had held out against the Dutch in the *perang sabil* and had played a key role in the revolutionary events of 1945–46. It was here that PUSA had always had its main strength. The evident PUSA–Darul Islam link now enabled the rebels effectively to build an alternative government in the countryside, exercising powers of administration, taxation and justice. Indeed, this network of support and information extended deep into the towns that were nominally under the control of the central government.[80]

Hasan Saleh, one of the key commanders of the revolt, argued that the various Darul Islam rebellions had a better chance of success than, in particular, the South Moluccan revolt, for two main reasons – one practical, one ideological. The ideological reason he cited was that, while the South Moluccans were merely fighting for selfish interests, Darul Islam was fighting selflessly for an ideal.[81] The practical reason was that the Darul Islam revolt in Aceh, like that in West Java, was able to take advantage of an extensive and rugged interior – in other words, had strategic depth – while at the same time maintaining lines of communication with the population as a whole.[82]

It is certainly true that by the mid-1950s, the war in Aceh had settled down into the kind of stalemate where the forces of resistance often have an inherent advantage. The central government forces found themselves defending fixed positions, while the rebels had a relative freedom of initiative. As is frequently the case in these circumstances, the response of government troops to rebel actions tended to be clumsy and brutal. Since the security forces of the central government came mainly from outside Aceh, this had the inevitable effect of increasing sympathy and support for the rebels.[83]

There were, on the other hand, factors which worked against the rebels, and cast doubt on Hasan Saleh's view that this was a united people's war. In the first place, it was regionally circumscribed, in two important senses. From the local perspective, there were large areas of western, southern and eastern Aceh that effectively did not participate in the revolt and which had, in fact, never been PUSA strongholds.[84] From the broader perspective of the Darul Islam revolt in Indonesia as a whole, the regions of West Java, Kalimantan, South Sulawesi and Aceh were strategically isolated, and there was no way they could help each other in military terms or build up a credible alternative government to the Republic of Indonesia. Indeed, the central government structure of the Negara Islam Indonesia steadily loosened and disintegrated through the mid and late 1950s.[85]

Furthermore, even in the centres of revolt in Aceh, ancient grudges and hostilities within the Acehnese elite meant that important elements in the population actively – if on occasion secretly – opposed the Darul Islam revolt. In many ways, the history of Aceh in the 1940s and 1950s is that of a slow-burning civil war quite as much as a confrontation between Aceh and Jakarta. Most important of all, however, is the fact that there were divided counsels among the rebels themselves. In very broad terms, a three-way division can be identified. First, there were those who sympathized with the rebellion but who did not participate, or only participated marginally – the people, as it were, at the edge of the rebellion – whose main concern was the loss of Aceh's regional autonomy.[86] Then there were those who supported Darul Islam's objectives, but who were prepared to reach an accommodation with the Republic if the position of Islam was enhanced and guaranteed, both locally and nationally. Finally, there were those, like

Daud Beureueh, who tended to favour vigorous resistance to the *pancasila* Republic, and who – having acquired a taste for autonomy in the loosely structured Negara Islam Indonesia – ultimately wanted to hold out for a more federalized system of government in a reconstructed Indonesian state.[87]

These divisions were matched by divisions within Jakarta. Despite the fact that there were powerful elements in Java – including the PKI – who were reluctant to support concessions to Aceh, there were significant political forces that had from the outset of the rebellion been inclined to seek some form of accommodation with the Acehnese rebels. These included the leaders of the main Islamic party, Masyumi, whose power base lay in Sumatra and the outer islands, and who sympathized with Darul Islam's desire to create an Islamic state, though not with its outright challenge to the legitimacy of the Indonesian Republic.[88] Politicians, administrators and military leaders in Sumatra itself were also anxious to look for a settlement through establishing contact with moderate Acehnese intermediaries.[89]

Although the political power balance fluctuated sharply in Jakarta in the mid-1950s – and along with it the fortunes of Masyumi – certain general trends were emerging that were to work in favour of a settlement of the Acehnese rebellion. Principal among these was a growing concern in the armed forces leadership – Javanese as well as Sumatran – at the decline in political stability in Indonesia as a whole and the accumulation of grass-roots power in Java by the communists. There was, in other words, a search for political and religious forces that could form a bulwark against the PKI.[90]

It is in this context that we see a slow and immensely complex process of negotiation develop between the central government and the Acehnese rebels in the period between 1955 and 1962. The principal objective of the central government was to make just enough concessions to weaken the rebellion piecemeal, and thereby eventually bring it to an end, without in any way compromising the unity and ideological integrity of the Indonesian Republic. Indeed, as concessions were gradually squeezed out of Jakarta, so more and more individuals and groups *did* peel away from the rebellion and subsequently use their influence to put pressure on the remaining insurgents.[91] The crucial steps in this tortuous progression to peace were, first, the granting of provincial status to Aceh in 1956, and, second, the decision in 1959 to confer on Aceh the status of 'Special Region' (*daerah istimewa*), with significant autonomous rights in the areas of religion, culture and education.[92] These concessions weakened but did not end the rebellion, not least because of the fact that Daud Beureueh tried to exploit a flurry of Sumatran rebellions at this time to squeeze more concessions – mainly in the area of regional autonomy – from the central government. By 1962, however, the honourable surrender of Daud Beureueh brought the rebellion to an end.

Aceh since the Darul Islam rebellion

It is noticeable that the concessions made by the central government to Aceh were made to Aceh as a province, not to Aceh as part of the Darul Islam movement. In other words, Aceh had gradually been detached, and indeed had detached itself, from the Negara Islam Indonesia, which had in any case disintegrated as a coherent political entity long before Aceh was given Special Region status in 1959. Although, therefore, Daud Beureueh's Darul Islam revolt was not separatist in terms of its objectives, the outcome of that revolt had been a series of concessions to Aceh's 'special' status. Indeed, as the revolt continued, so Daud Beureueh concentrated more and more on the question of Aceh's autonomy at the expense of the general question of the status of Islam in Indonesia as a whole.

Aceh's Special Region status boiled down in the end mainly to concessions for the special position of Islam in Aceh. In this context the Council of Religious Scholars (*majelis ulama*) has played a crucial role.[93] Up to the present day, its pronouncements have covered a wide range of issues – dancing in nightclubs, logging in southern Aceh, the use of drugs – which undoubtedly help maintain the sense of the absolute dominance of Islamic principles in all aspects of Acehnese life. It has, in addition, made decisions on what is acceptable and unacceptable in the teaching of Islam in Aceh, and has provided 'guidance' to religious leaders and organizations which have, it is felt, strayed from the orthodox path.[94] Not only does it police the teaching of Islam, but it also defines and legitimizes the scope of traditional cultural activity in Aceh; thus, in effect, controlling important aspects of Acehnese *adat*.[95] It has also played a major part in encouraging the creation of, and watching over, educational institutions in Aceh.[96] In this context, the establishment in 1963 of a higher education 'Islamic Institute' in Banda Aceh was seen as a vital step in the recovery of Aceh's status as a centre of religious learning.[97]

In so far as the central government has made any special concessions to Aceh, they have been primarily in the field of Islam. In the wider perspective, however, the hope of the Acehnese leaders that the *pancasila* principles of the state would either be replaced or, at least, modified by fully Islamic principles, was not realized. In the early 1960s, the line-up of the military, Islamic groups and conservative elements generally against the growing threat of the Left, in particular the PKI, must have fuelled the expectation that victory over the PKI would decisively help the Islamic cause in Indonesia. This hope almost certainly eased the way to the settlement of the Acehnese rebellion. The destruction of the PKI, when it finally came in 1965, was hailed in Aceh as a *jihad*, a final liberation of Indonesia from the forces of *jahilia*, or ignorance and unbelief.[98] It was, however, the armed forces rather than Islam that had gained control of the state. Like Sukarno, the armed forces leaders were determined to maintain unity; unlike Sukarno they were determined to give an absolute priority to political and economic stability. They were, therefore, resolved to subordinate all political forces – including that of Islam – to the three objectives of unity, stability and development. *Pancasila* – now interpreted in non-radical terms – remained, indeed was strengthened, as the state philosophy. While, therefore, the Acehnese leaders more or less gained their Islamic goals at the provincial level, they were forced at the national level to accept and to adjust to the absolute priority of *pancasila* principles.[99]

Beyond the sphere of Islam, the scope of Aceh's regional autonomy is in fact rather limited. This is as much a result of broad economic and cultural developments as it is of a deliberate policy by the central government. Although Acehnese is predominantly the language of the street and the home, Indonesian language absolutely dominates the media, and is the key to any form of educational advancement. In economic terms, Aceh has substantial natural resources – particularly natural gas in the Lhokseumawe region; but the structure of investment, profit, employment and communications all help give the impression that Aceh has no real control over these resources.[100] This, it should be said, is not simply a matter of an exploitative policy at the centre, but also a reflection of the overwhelming influence of the city of Medan as a regional magnet. This is apparent in terms both of economic activity and of educational and employment opportunities.

In general, it is evident that in the thirty-odd years since the granting of Special Region status, resentment against the 'Javanese' central government has remained high at all levels of Acehnese society. Periodically – particularly in the periods 1976–79 and 1989–91 – resentment has spilled over into conspiracy and open rebellion, and the heavy-handed reactions of the government, though they have effectively quelled the disturbances, have only increased the sense of alienation.[101] It is surely significant that the framework for this new resistance is provided by an organization calling itself the Gerakan Aceh Merdeka (Movement for Acehnese Independence) or GAM, founded in 1976. Its objectives are overtly separatist, since it seeks to detach Aceh from the Republic of Indonesia. Given the indivisibility in Acehnese eyes of the link between Aceh and Islam, this movement also has clearly Islamic objectives; unlike the Darul Islam movement, however, it seeks to create not a 'Negara Islam Indonesia', but a 'Negara Islam Aceh'.[102] And, whereas the Darul Islam leadership argued that the transfer of sovereignty from the Dutch to the Indonesians in December 1949 opened the door to an ideological struggle within a united Indonesia, the new generation of Acehnese insurgents has argued that, since Aceh never participated in the 1949 agreement, their link to the Indonesian Republic since that date has been maintained by force, not consent.[103]

It is impossible to calculate whether general discontent in Aceh against Jakarta implies overall support for the Acehnese secessionists. The connection is probably highly volatile, and will depend ultimately on the evolution of central government policy over the next decades, and of general events in the region.

Conclusion

It will be evident from the above that the connection in modern Acehnese history between attachment to Islam, to regional patriotism, and to Indonesian nationalism is virtually impossible to disentangle. If these attachments could be seen as the three main pillars guiding the Acehnese generation of the era of decolonization, then the aspirations of Darul Islam can be seen as an attempt to link these pillars together. In the eyes of the Darul Islam leaders, if Indonesia became an Islamic state, then the relationship between the centre and the regions of Indonesia would automatically be harmonized. However, there has been a consensus among all the regimes that have dominated independent Indonesia – whether constitutional democracy, Guided Democracy or the military-dominated New Order – that too great an emphasis on Islam in the state ideology would have a divisive effect on the nation. While the centre has, therefore, made limited concessions to Acehnese autonomy and the right of Islam to play a special role in the province, it has forced Acehnese leaders to abandon any hope of changing the *pancasila* basis of the state. It is perhaps inevitable, therefore, that the post-independence, post-Darul Islam generation should see its grievances against the centre in provincial terms. This has formed the basis for an overtly separatist agenda in Aceh.

There are, nevertheless, strong ties that link Aceh to Indonesia. The first of these is the shared historical experience of the anti-colonial struggle. It is certainly true that the original struggle – the *perang sabil* against the Dutch – was fought on purely Acehnese and Islamic terms, and that this has helped to generate what might be called a sense of regional particularity.[104] But when we consider events in Aceh in the first half of the twentieth century, what stands out is the extent to which political and educational developments in Aceh mirrored those in Indonesia as a whole. The most clear examples of this are the educational revolution in Aceh in the 1920s and 1930s, and the revolutionary upheavals of the late 1945 and early 1946 period. These events may have been expressed in a special Islamic idiom in Aceh, but they were part of a general Indonesian trend.

Then there is the fact that Indonesia is a Muslim country, even if it is not an Islamic state. Even though Islamic Law is not the central basis of the state, it is possible for Muslims to lead an unhindered religious life; indeed, given the huge majority of Muslims in Indonesia, the government could and would do nothing to offend the basic principles of Islam. Indonesia could, therefore, be reasonably described as part of the *Daru'l-Islam* (Abode of Islam), particularly since the PKI has been outlawed, and *pancasila* implicitly discourages atheism. In this sense, the condition of Aceh is very different from that of a Muslim region within a non-Muslim state. In the latter case, regional and religious identity are absolutely intertwined, and reinforce each other in the confrontation with the central state. Although it *is* true to say that Acehnese and Islamic identity are very closely linked, the history of PUSA – and indeed of Darul Islam – has shown that Acehnese religious leaders have never regarded Islam as simply an exclusive badge of regional identity. It is probable that one of the reasons why the Darul Islam revolt petered out in Aceh was a sheer sense of disgust – on both sides – at the sight of Muslim killing Muslim.

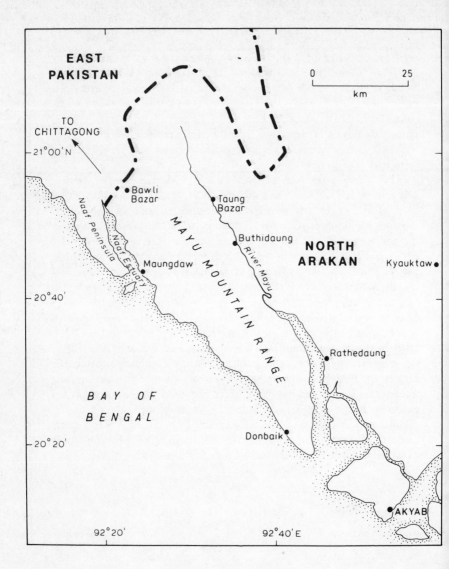

Map 7 Northern Arakan

8

At the Frontier of the Islamic World: the Arakanese Muslims

Dissidence and rebellion at the Islamic periphery

Roughly speaking, the Islamic periphery of Southeast Asia comprises the northern section of Arakan in Burma, the Patani and Satun regions of southern Thailand, the islands between Borneo and the Philippines, and the scattered islands of eastern Indonesia. These areas are the meeting-ground between the Islamic and the non-Islamic worlds, between the *Daru'l-Islam* and the *Daru'l-Harb*. In the course of the untidy evolution of modern history, many communities in these regions have found themselves 'trapped' on the 'wrong' side of the nation-state frontiers that have been created. In insular Southeast Asia, these frontiers have principally been determined by European colonialism. In mainland Southeast Asia, on the other hand, the frontiers between Burma and British India, and between Siam and Malaya, also reflect pre-colonial patterns of political power. Already, before the imposition of European colonialism, Burmese and Thai control had consolidated in the respective Muslim regions of northern Arakan and Patani.

It was the era of national consciousness, nationalist organization and decolonization that highlighted the plight of these marginal communities. Since the Southeast Asian nationalist movements of the twentieth century tended to define their respective identities in terms of the already existing boundaries of the colonial states, the peripheral Muslim areas faced the danger of being definitively cut off from their historical links of religious affiliation. The period of decolonization, therefore, saw protest and resistance in the Muslim-majority regions of Burma, southern Thailand and the Philippines. In the case of Burma and Thailand, this resistance came to a head during the war years 1941–45 and the period immediately after the war, and therefore falls within the general time-frame of this study. Because the process of the United States' decolonization effectively began earlier in the Philippines

– in the course of the 1920s and 1930s – the protests of the Moros (as the Filipino Muslims of the southern and western Philippines collectively came to be known) took place in a rather different political environment.[1]

In each of these cases, the sense of difference from the prevailing national identity of the state in which the respective Muslim communities were situated was connected to some form of irredentism: the desire, that is, not merely to separate from the existing state, but also to link up with another unit of identity outside that state. In the broadest sense, the main irredentist magnet was that of Islam and the desire to reunite with the Muslim *umma*. But, precisely because, as we have already noted, allegiance to Islam normally involves coherent communities rather than *ad hoc* individuals, Islam itself has been historically linked to specific ethnic groups and to traditional political entities. Islamic irredentism, therefore, has normally been intertwined with other affiliations. The case of the Moros of the Philippines is particularly instructive in this respect, since they are geographically dispersed and linguistically divided. The memory of the Sulu and Mindanao sultanates that stretched from eastern Borneo to the Philippine islands helped to re-create the sense of a traditional strength and coherence that had been broken up by the Western colonial era.[2] But evocation of the Sulu and Mindanao sultanates is inextricably linked to the feeling of belonging to the Islamic world, and it is the idea of adherence to Islam and the Islamic world that has been the primary unifying factor among the Moro separatists.[3] In this case, irredentism can be defined not so much as the expression of a direct political aspiration, but as the conjuring up of interconnected sources of religious and historical legitimacy that pre-date and override the legitimacy of the Filipino nation-state. In the case of the Arakanese Muslims, the question of links across the Bengal border was extremely complex, as will be shown. With the Patani separatists, however – particularly in the crucial period during and immediately after the Second World War – we have a much more clear-cut example of ethnic cross-border connection, and a much more specific and practical irredentist programme.

Unlike the case of Aceh, where, as we have seen, the rebellion was directed against a Muslim state, the revolts of the Muslims of Arakan and Patani had more substantial credentials in terms of *jihad*. In both circumstances, the nation-states that they confronted were non-Muslim, and the core national identity was closely linked to the Buddhist religion. In consequence, any repression of Muslim communities rapidly acquired a religious dimension. In the broader Islamic perspective, the Muslims of Arakan and Patani – and, indeed, the Moros of the

Philippines – were not Muslim communities that had moved into the non-Muslim world. Rather, they were slices of the *Daru'l-Islam* that had been forced to submit to *kafir* rule. The traditional Islamic view was that, while such communities were not expected to engage in *jihad* unless they were directly repressed and prevented from practising their religion, at the same time they were expected only to submit to, not to accept the legitimacy of, the state and its laws.[4] Their situation was anomalous in Islamic terms, and the appropriate response was withdrawal into their own community; in other words, a spiritual rather than a territorial *hijra*.

'Forgotten in the rush of government': the Arakanese Muslims

It has been the unfortunate fate of the Arakan region in the modern historical era to be squeezed between two religions and two distinct regions; between the Islamic world and the Buddhist world, and between the Indian sub-continent and Burma. The consequent tension is reflected both in Arakan's relations with the outside world and in its internal circumstances. In ethno-linguistic terms, the majority of its population is closely related to the ethnic Burmans of Burma proper; and the separate Arakanese kingdom was, like Burma, predominantly Buddhist, although it was more closely linked to Buddhist communities in Bengal. Influences from the south and east were thus matched by pressures from the north and west. From the mid-fifteenth century, a process of Islamicization spread into northern Arakan from the now Muslim Bengal, and, even if Buddhism remained the main religion of the Arakanese kingdom, Islamic influence – both at the political and cultural level – became more and more evident.[5] One consequence of this process was the formation of a distinct Arakanese Muslim community in the north of the kingdom, who called themselves 'Rohinga'.[6]

In the course of the seventeenth century, the Arakanese kingdom fell into what turned out to be a terminal state of decline. In 1666, the Mughal Viceroy of Bengal gained control of the town of Chittagong in the north.[7] Thereafter, while the threat from India receded, the power of the Burmese state grew. In 1785, Burma absorbed the rest of Arakan and the kingdom was finally dissolved. The expansion of Burma into the region, however, almost inevitably brought it into conflict with the British, who had by this time gained control of Bengal. Accumulating tension along the Burma–British India border finally culminated in war in 1824–26, and the Burmese monarchy was forced to cede Arakan to Britain.[8] In the ensuing decades the rest of Burma was absorbed into the British Empire.

Not only had Burma lost its independence and its monarchy, but it now became a province of British India. The pre-colonial territorial integrity of Burma was, however, maintained, including the Arakanese region. But the fact that British rule spanned Bengal and Burma meant that, while poor communications created an almost impermeable barrier between Arakan and the rest of Burma, there were no equivalent restraints to the cross-border contacts between Chittagong and Arakan.[9] In these circumstances, there was a considerable degree of Bengali Muslim settlement in northern Arakan, and in the main towns throughout Arakan, particularly Akyab.[10] In northern Arakan, these Bengali Muslims or 'Chittagongs', as they were called, tended over time to merge into the local Rohinga community. In addition, although on the whole the Rohinga were distinguished from the Bengali-speaking Chittagongs, this distinction tended to be blurred in northern Arakan by the constant interaction across the border. The 1931 census identified approximately 130,000 Muslims in Arakan, mostly in the northwestern area next to Bengal.[11]

The porous border between Bengal and Arakan, both during the period of British rule and in previous centuries, had created, in fact, a considerable degree of ethnic inter-mixing in what could be described as a classic 'multi-cultural' region. Arakanese Buddhist settlers in Bengal – known colloquially as 'Maughs' or 'Muggs' – were able, for example, to gain a significant reputation as cooks throughout British India.[12] But the years of British rule in Burma saw increasing resentment against unhindered Indian settlement, particularly in Arakan, Tenasserim and Lower Burma. The issue became a focus for grass-roots Burmese nationalism, and in the years 1930–31 there were serious anti-Indian disturbances in Lower Burma, while 1938 saw riots specifically directed against the Indian Muslim community.[13] As Burmese nationalism increasingly asserted itself before the Second World War, the 'alien' Indian presence inevitably came under attack, along with the religion that the Indian Muslims imported. The Muslims of northern Arakan were to be caught in the crossfire of this conflict.

Arakan during and after the Second World War

As in so many other of the regions examined so far in this book, tensions that were building up in Arakan before the war boiled over during the Japanese invasion of Southeast Asia. Arakan was the furthest extremity of Japan's push through Burma towards India and, as such, it became a frontline in the conflict in early 1942 and remained so until the British finally managed to push the Japanese out of Arakan in early

1945. During these three years, Arakan experienced all the horrors that are the fate of any region trapped between two opposing armies. These included a complete breakdown in the civil administration, and a consequent development of the habits of lawlessness that were greatly exacerbated by the easy availability of modern arms: exploitation – and thereby aggravation – by both armies of feuds and resentments within the local population in order to enlist support for their respective military goals, and, of course, sheer physical devastation. On top of this, the long years of war were to have the effect of cutting Arakan off from the world in general and the rest of Burma in particular; a fact that was to have serious long-term consequences for the region.[14]

One of the major effects of the war in Arakan was the development of a 'loyalty' relationship between Britain and the Arakanese Muslims. The Japanese advance into Arakan in 1942 triggered an inter-communal conflict – amounting to a virtual civil war – between the Buddhist and Muslim communities. In the Japanese-controlled, Buddhist-majority regions, the Muslims were driven out, and fled northwards to the refuge of the remaining British enclave in northern, Muslim-dominated Arakan. This stimulated a reverse 'ethnic cleansing' in the British-controlled areas, particularly around the town of Maungdaw.[15] Between December 1942 and April 1943, an attempted counter-offensive by the British failed, with the result that the Japanese were able to consolidate their hold on the bulk of the Muslim region of Arakan, including Maungdaw.[16] One consequence of this British military fiasco was the abandonment of even more of the Muslim population, and an intensification of the cycle of inter-communal violence.[17]

In April 1942, the British had built up a guerrilla force – the so-called 'V' force – which operated along the whole front line between the British and Japanese armies. Arakanese Muslims were recruited into this force in September 1942. In the period of relative military stalemate after spring 1943, these Arakanese Muslims of 'V' force began to play an important role on the Arakan front. From launching-pads in the northernmost part of Arakan, and across the mouth of the Naaf River dividing Bengal and Arakan, this 'V' Force operated in no man's land and behind enemy lines, gaining information, guiding troops, rescuing pilots who had been shot down, and punishing known 'traitors' working for the Japanese.[18] There can be no doubt that the officers in charge of these 'V' force groups were able to establish a firm rapport with the Arakanese Muslim villagers, and to depend on their loyalty and support to a remarkable degree.[19] As Anthony Irwin describes in his memoir, *Burmese Outpost*, the British leaders of 'V' Force initiated a 'hearts and minds' campaign among the villagers, helping to build schools and provide medical care, even in the depths of 'no man's land'.[20] The *moulvi*, or Muslim religious leaders, were the key to the support that the British were able to enlist in the villages; it should be noted, however, that a few of the *moulvi* (Irwin describes them as 'the rotters') worked with the Japanese, and accordingly became targets for punishment as 'traitors'.[21]

At the end of 1943 and the beginning of 1944, the British military began a new offensive in Arakan, designed in the first instance to gain control of key points in north Arakan, and thence to push southwards to Akyab. In January 1944, the British took Maungdaw, with 'V' Force playing an important supporting role.[22] Thereafter British plans were seriously delayed by a Japanese offensive launched from Buthidaung with the purpose of pushing the British back into Bengal. After a prolonged and sometimes desperate struggle, in which air-power proved to be crucial, the British eventually checked the Japanese offensive, and gradually gained control of the mountain road connecting Maungdaw to Buthidaung.[23] It was not until December 1944, however, that British forces finally took Buthidaung. However, once this stronghold had been captured the Japanese position rapidly collapsed, and by early January 1945 most of Arakan was in British hands.[24]

It is not at all clear whether unofficial but specific undertakings had been made to the Arakanese Muslims concerning their status after the war. Undoubtedly, the Muslim leaders themselves were under the impression that the British had promised them a 'Muslim National Area' in Maungdaw sub-division.[25] What is certain is that 'V' Force officers like Anthony Irwin were most anxious that the Arakanese Muslims, along with other minorities along the edge of Burma that had lent such important help to the British, should be rewarded for their loyalty. As Irwin himself put it:

> it is these minorities that have most helped us throughout the three years of constant fighting and occupation and it is these minorities who are most likely to be forgotten in the rush of Government. They must not be. It is the duty of all of us, for whom they fought, to see to this.[26]

Whatever the long-term future, however, in immediate terms the Arakanese Muslims were able to consolidate their position throughout northern Arakan. The British authorities appointed them to the main posts in local government; from this secure position, old scores were paid off against those – particularly Buddhists – who had collaborated with the Japanese. Arakanese Muslim refugees who had fled into Bengal during the war now returned to their villages. In addition, a new wave of land-hungry immigrants from the Chittagong area – the so-called 'Chittagongs' – took advantage of the changed situation to move into northern Arakan.[27]

As the British consolidated their hold in Burma through 1945, however, their main preoccupation turned from the issue of warfare to that of reestablishing a stable administration. Arakan gave the British an early example of the inevitable consequences of the wartime policy of creating and arming local militias.[28] It became apparent through the spring of 1945 that Arakan as a whole was awash with arms and dominated by local warlords – armed by either the British or the Japanese – over whom the British military administration had little control.[29] So far as Muslim-dominated northern Arakan was concerned, the principal fear of the administration was that the inflow of refugees (and immigrants) from Bengal would exacerbate racial and religious tensions and make a very bad situation worse.[30]

Arakan, in fact, was a classic example of an area in which the Burmese nationalist leaders could demonstrate to the British that Burma was 'ungovernable' without their consent. Right through 1946, and particularly towards the latter end of that year, a situation of increasing anarchy, coupled with growing communist influence, was being reported from the province.[31] Unfortunately – as in so many other parts of Burma – Aung San and his AFPFL were unable to retrieve the situation in Arakan when they gained control of the political agenda in Burma and increasingly began to assume responsibility for government from late 1946 onwards. The power of local warlords and communist factions, and the sheer habits of lawlessness, had become embedded in the region. It is in this bleak context that the unravelling of events in northern Arakan between 1946 and 1948 should be understood.

The conflict in northern Arakan after the Second World War should be seen as operating at two levels. At the local level, the state of virtual civil war between Buddhists and Muslims, which had effectively begun in 1942, continued through the pre- and post-independence period. At the national level, Arakanese Muslim leaders were increasingly apprehensive as it became apparent that the British were pulling out of Burma, and would inevitably be replaced – whatever the rhetoric of national unity – by a Buddhist, Burman-dominated independent state. In these circumstances, developments across the border in Bengal offered an increasing attraction to many Rohinga (Arakanese Muslims) as well as the 'Chittagongs'. As India moved towards independence between 1945 and 1947, the demand by Jinnah and his Muslim League for the creation of a separate Pakistan in the Muslim-majority areas of India became irresistible. As it became clear that the overwhelmingly Muslim area of East Bengal – including Chittagong – would be included in Pakistan, so irredentist aspirations emerged in northern Arakan. By May 1946, there were open calls for the inclusion of the

Muslim-majority areas of Arakan in Pakistan, and in July 1946 an explicitly irredentist North Arakan Muslim League was established.[32] The impulse behind this latter movement, however, came largely from 'Chittagongs' rather than from Rohinga as a whole. In any case, Jinnah was most anxious not to add to his already massive problems by antagonizing the Burmese political leadership, and he firmly discouraged these irredentist ambitions.[33] This provides an early example in post-war Southeast Asia of national leaders favouring good state-to-state relations over the pull of ethnic and religious loyalties.

Arakan and independence: the Mujahidin revolt

After Burma gained its independence in January 1948, the state of chaos in Arakan deepened. The Arakanese Muslims immediately discovered the disadvantages of their peripheral status in a non-Muslim nation, when Muslim officials were replaced by Buddhists, and Buddhist refugees in the south of Arakan were allowed to return to their houses and villages from which they had been removed in the preceding years.[34] Tension rapidly built up, and after a series of 'incidents' and riots, a full-scale rebellion – describing itself as a *jihad* – ignited in April 1948. Within a year, the *mujahidin* rebels had gained control of a large section of northern Arakan and, given Rangoon's total preoccupation at the time with the virtual collapse of the state itself, the government was not in a position to begin to take serious counter-measures until 1951.[35]

Given the fact that the irredentist objective of linking with what had now become East Pakistan was no longer feasible, the rebellion was principally defensive in its objectives. In the run-up to the outbreak of rebellion, many *moulvis* had been preaching the defence of Islam, or *jihad*, against what was seen as a concerted attack on Muslim rights and Muslim land. In more specific terms, what the rebels, and indeed many Arakanese Muslims who did not directly support the rebellion, wanted was the creation of a special Muslim region – a 'Frontier State', as a Muslim meeting in Maungdaw in April 1947 called it – not necessarily separate from Burma itself, but separate from the rest of Buddhist-dominated Arakan.[36]

The situation in Arakan at this time was enormously complicated by the fact that there was turmoil in the whole of Arakan, not just in the Muslim-dominated northern enclave. As has been seen, the war years isolated Arakan from the rest of Burma, and this sense of separateness was made, if anything, more acute in the post-war period. Arakan's infrastructure, already inadequate, had been destroyed in the war years, and it seemed to many Arakanese that Burma's politicians were putting a low priority on the region's economic rehabilitation. This feeling of neglect also stimulated separatist sentiments, and the demand for an Arakanese State as a 'separate autonomous unit' within the Union of Burma, among the Buddhist Arakanese.[37] Agitation for Arakanese statehood persisted throughout this period. More serious for the Burmese nationalist leaders was the fact that Arakan was a stronghold of the Red Flag communist faction, which began a rebellion in 1947. After independence the condition of Arakan deteriorated rather than improved, with communist and separatist rebellions posing a general threat to the authority of Rangoon.[38]

In this condition of virtual anarchy, Arakan was in effect dominated by regional warlords, whose number included the *mujahidin* leaders of the Muslim revolt. Since there was a degree of practical interdependence on the ground between these rebellions, there was inevitably some collusion – particularly in the matter of arms and rice-smuggling – between the *mujahidin* and the rebel groups in the rest of Arakan.[39] But the general relationship between the Arakanese Muslim rebels and the Arakanese separatists was one of mutual suspicion and hostility, occasionally degenerating into open conflict.[40] For this reason, the *mujahidin* revolt was as much, if not principally, the symptom of an intra-Arakan conflict as it was a challenge to the central government. The last thing that the Arakanese Muslims wanted was the creation of a semi-autonomous Arakanese State where they would be at the mercy of an Arakanese Buddhist-dominated government centred in Akyab.[41] The *mujahidin* rebellion was, in many senses, a separatist movement within a separatist movement. The complexity of this relationship between the Arakanese Muslims, the Arakanese Buddhists and the central government gave Rangoon the opportunity to exploit regional and communal differences; at the same time, it made it enormously difficult to reach a political settlement that would satisfy all the rebellions. Rather the reverse: concessions made to one rebel group would merely antagonize rival rebellions. Arakan, therefore, is a perfect example of that 'equilibrium of instability' that has afflicted other peripheral regions of Burma in the decades since independence.

Between 1951 and 1954, however, the Burmese army was able to turn more of its attention to Arakan. A series of small-scale campaigns against the *mujahidin* culminated in November 1954 with 'Operation Monsoon', which was directed at the main rebel areas.[42] The overall effect of these military operations was to break up the coherence of the Muslim revolt. From that point onwards, *mujahidin* action was mainly confined to cross-border smuggling – of rice into Pakistan, and arms and illegal immigrants in Arakan – from safe havens across the border. The revolt degenerated into semi-banditry, in which the general population became victims rather than supporters.

The Arakanese Muslims since 1954: a question of identity and survival

From the 1950s onwards, the Muslim-dominated area of Arakan has remained what could be described as a zone of 'dissidence' rather than one of outright rebellion. The border with East Pakistan (later Bangladesh) has remained a centre of smuggling and illegal immigration, which – because of the terrain – it has proved impossible to control effectively. Political instability, inter-ethnic conflict and land-hunger have contributed to a permanent condition of lawlessness and disturbance on both sides of the border, and indeed in the whole region of the India–Burma–Pakistan/Bangladesh border.[43]

From the time of independence to the present, the Arakanese Muslims have found themselves engaged in a continuous struggle to preserve their rights as a distinct people. In the period of the late 1950s and the early 1960s, this primarily involved resistance to their inclusion in an Arakanese state. As it became evident in 1960 that the Burmese government of the day was committed to granting semi-autonomous statehood to Arakan, the Arakanese Muslims demanded that they should either be excluded from this state, or given very extensive guarantees for autonomy within its structure. Paradoxically, Arakanese Muslim fears coincided by chance with growing alarm in the armed forces at what was seen as a progressive threat to the unity and stability of Burma. In May 1961, the so-called Mayu Frontier Administration was set up under direct military control. This zone covered precisely the main Muslim-majority border regions of Maungdaw, Buthidaung and Rathedaung.[44] After the military *coup d'état* of 1962, the idea of a separate Arakanese state was scrapped, but the Mayu military region remained in existence.[45] In a curious way, the old war-time ideal of a 'Muslim National Area' separate from the rest of Buddhist-dominated Arakan had been realized, but only in the highly unpropitious circumstances of permanent military rule.

Far from benefiting from their new special status, the Arakanese Muslims discovered in the ensuing years that their very right to residence in Burma came under periodic threat. Since the outbreak of the *mujahidin* rebellion, the Burmese government and army have tended to blame the insurgency on 'Chittagongs' operating across the frontier, possibly in collusion with friendly Pakistani/Bangladeshi authorities.[46] Linked to this perception has been the notion that there was a plan among the 'Chittagongs' to bring about the eventual inclusion of the northern Arakan region within Pakistan/Bangladesh by a combination of exploiting Arakanese Muslim discontent, and a stealthy process of illegal immigration. In consequence, the history of northern Arakan has been punctuated, ever since the *mujahidin* rebellion, by a series of military 'sweeps' and the forced deportation of illegal immigrants. The principal 'sweeps' have taken place in 1959, 1975, 1978 and, recently, in 1991–92.[47] Given the tendency of the Burmese army to regard *all* Muslims in the area as a potential security threat and as 'aliens', many Arakanese Muslims have been caught up in these sweeps. The undiscriminating brutality of these actions has given rise to the suspicion that a *de facto* process of ethnic cleansing is taking place.[48]

Conclusion

The Muslim-majority region of Arakan surely provides a classic example of peripherality. It lies at the frontier between the Muslim and the non-Muslim world: between what can broadly be described as the South Asian and East Asian cultural blocs, and between the two modern nation-states of Burma and Pakistan/Bangladesh. But this condition of peripherality was made many times worse by the fact that the area also had the misfortune to find itself on the front line in the Second World War. Guns and divided loyalties in a bitter conflict added fatally to the tensions and tendencies to lawlessness that are the natural feature of an unstable border region. As in the case of the conflict between the Karens and Burmans in Lower Burma in 1942, or the racial disturbances that took place in Malaya in August and September 1945, the cycle of ethnic violence that broke out in Arakan in 1942 is yet another example of how events of the Second World War were to have a profound and decisive effect on the subsequent history of Southeast Asia.

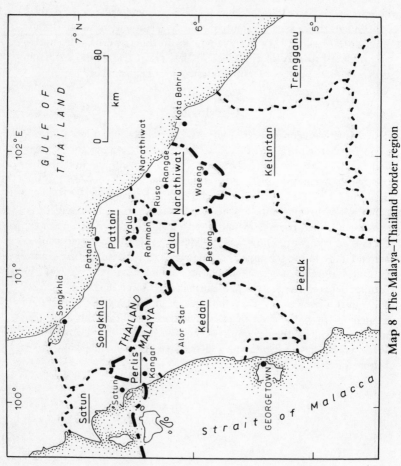

Map 8 The Malaya–Thailand border region

9

Ethnicity, Islam and Irredentism: the Malays of Patani

Introduction

The region of Patani in southeasternmost Thailand[1] provides a very clear-cut example of the almost inextricable link that can occur between an ethnic and a religious identity. At the height of their campaign of resistance to the Thai government in early 1948, the Patani Malay leaders appealed to the outside world in the following terms: 'Give us back our race as Malays and our religion as Islam.'[2] As in the rest of the Malay world, for the Malays of Patani, 'Malayness' and Islam are virtually indistinguishable. It is this fact above everything else that has stymied the consistent attempt of successive Thai governments to detach Islam from Malay ethnic identity in Patani, and encourage the inhabitants of the region to see themselves as 'Thai Muslims'.

Since the border between Thailand and Malaysia cuts Patani off from the rest of the Malay world and from the *Daru'l-Islam*, it follows that irredentism – the desire to reconnect with their Malay brethren and with the world of Islam – has played an important part in the political ambitions of the Patani Malays. For the most part, these irredentist hopes have taken the form of a broad and unspecified aspiration. But for a short time – in the period during and after the Second World War – irredentism hardened into a specific political goal.

The Malays of Patani: ethnicity and religion in the colonial era

Patani is an undisputed part of the *tanah Melayu* (the Malay land). The heartland of the traditional Patani area comprises the three modern-day provinces of Pattani, Yala and Narathiwat. Although the Malay-Muslim population of Patani – estimated to be between 700,000 and over a million people – only constitutes a tiny proportion of the total population of Thailand, it forms the substantial majority of these three provinces.[3]

The three main pillars of Patani-Malay identity are the former Kingdom of Patani (*negri* Patani Darussalam), the Malay race and Islam. These three ingredients are woven together in the *Hikayat Patani*, the traditional history of the origins and the achievements of the Patani kingdom – a history that was composed 'cumulatively' at the end of the seventeenth and the beginning of the eighteenth century.[4] The first section of the *Hikayat Patani* describes in fabulous terms the process of Malay settlement in the coastal region of modern-day Patani, and the subsequent establishment of the town of Patani and of the kingdom, these last events probably occurring in the fourteenth century. The second section explains – in terms that are scarcely complimentary to the religious zeal of the *raja* – how the kingdom as a whole became one of the earliest states in the region to be converted to Islam.[5] The history particularly concentrates on Patani's era of greatness in the seventeenth century, and has helped thereby to contribute to Patani's pervading sense of nostalgia for a golden past.[6] Also a source of nostalgic pride is Patani's traditional status in the Malay world as a centre of Islamic scholarship worthy of comparison to the Sultanate of Aceh itself.[7]

These records of past glory have only served to remind the Patani Malays of their relative decline and peripheral status in the modern historical era. Throughout the seventeenth and eighteenth centuries, Patani faced intermittent threats to its independence from Thai Buddhist kingdoms in the north. It was not until the late eighteenth century, however, that the newly formed Chakkri dynasty was able to impose a permanent control over Patani.[8] Thereafter, the history of the relationship between Patani and the Siamese/Thai state was one of periodic but intense resistance on one side, and a process of ever-tightening central control on the other.[9]

In the initial stages of their rule, the Chakkris officially included Patani within the Kingdom of Siam, but exercised a kind of protectorate over an intact Patani state. In the early nineteenth century, however, central control was strengthened when Patani was broken up into seven statelets, governed by nominated Malay *rajas* under the overall authority of a Siamese administrator. A similar process was begun by the Siamese in the Sultanate of Kedah: Satun, the northern-most region under the authority of Kedah, was later to find itself – like Patani – on the 'wrong' side of the Malaya–Siam border.[10]

The major factor determining the evolution of Siamese policy towards Patani was the steady expansion of British colonial influence throughout the Malay peninsula in the late eighteenth and early nineteenth centuries. It became increasingly apparent through the nine-teenth century that one of the keys to the expansion of Western colonial power in Southeast Asia was the apparent lack of a clear definition by the traditional political structures of the boundaries of authority between states. The power of the traditional Southeast Asian states diminished as it radiated out from the centre; weak state control over peripheral communities thus left abundant room for exploitation and misunderstanding in their relations with Western powers. For example, in the case of Vietnam's relations with France, the dynasty found itself unable to control the independent actions that its peripheral popula-tions took against the French; and in Aceh, the Sultanate could not prevent the Dutch from establishing direct relations with areas that were under traditional but shadowy Acehnese control. In both these cases and in many others, a failure to delineate the scope of central authority, and thereafter exercise that authority firmly, provided a stimulus for colonial expansion.

One of the keys to the maintenance of Siam's independence through-out the colonial period was the ability of the Chakkri dynasty to understand this threat. From the 1890s onwards, a uniform, centralized administrative structure was introduced in Siam. Accordingly, the chieftains in the Patani rajadoms were absorbed into the salaried administration, and effectively became Siamese civil servants.[11] Unlike the British administration of its protectorate system in the Malay States to the south, therefore, the Siamese government policy was one of centralization. This involved not only the creation of a direct adminis-trative system, but also, in 1902, the incorporation of the administration of Islamic law within the Siamese legal system, and a reduction in the range of issues that could be dealt with by the Islamic judges.[12]

Siam, however, could not safeguard its position in its more remote Malay tributaries and, in 1909, the Siamese government was forced to cede the outlying Malay States of Kelantan, Trengganu, Kedah and Perlis to Britain in a border adjustment. But Patani and the south-western Malay region of Satun remained on the Siamese side of the border. This division provides a classic example of an *ad hoc* colonial arrangement that has since hardened into a permanent international frontier. The British takeover of the four Malay states undoubtedly had the effect of triggering irredentist ambitions in Patani itself – particularly in view of the close links that existed between the Patani and Kelantan royal families – and the period between 1909 and the Siamese revolution of 1932 saw a series of uprisings in the Patani area.[13] Siamese suspicions of the links between the Kelantan and Patani royal families encouraged policies of greater centralization – particu-larly in the areas of taxation, education and the imposition of the

Siamese language – and this, in turn, stimulated such violent responses as the Patani revolt of February–March 1923.[14]

Even before the 1932 revolution in Siam, therefore, the irredentist aspirations of the Patani Malays were being clearly expressed. Nevertheless, the 1932 revolution had a fundamental impact on Patani. In part, the events of 1932 in Siam were – however imperfectly realized – a democratic revolution; in part, they were the culmination of a revolution in national awareness – Siam's equivalent, in fact, of the nationalist phase in the colonized countries of Southeast Asia. In so far as the revolution brought a new era of democratic opportunity, the Patani Malays were able after 1932 to gain representation in the National Assembly and in the Senate.[15] But – as in France following the 1789 revolution – in Siam the new concept of popular sovereignty brought in its wake a redefinition of the relationship between the state and the people. Under the authoritarian monarchy, the state had merely required the obedience of its subjects. In the new Thai *nation* that was to emerge in the course of the 1930s, the relationship was no longer that of state/subject but of nation/citizen. Normally, the key definition of citizenship is the right – often, indeed, obligation – of democratic participation; in the context of Siam in the 1930s, where the army and the bureaucracy were anxious to concentrate power in their hands, citizenship was primarily seen in terms of national integration.[16] The results of this national revolution were an emphasis on Thai racial identity, for which the Buddhist religion and the monarchy now served as central symbols; an acceleration in the process of assimilation of outlying ethnic groups; and ever more state centralization.

The Patani Malays soon felt the effects of this new nationalist fervour. The new constitution emphasized the absolute unity and indivisibility of the nation.[17] At the local level in Patani this meant that the old local government structure, through which Patani Malay appointees had been incorporated into a complex administrative hierarchy, was replaced by a simpler and more centralized system. Three provincial units carved from the old Patani region – Pattani, Narathiwat and Yala – were, along with Satun on the west coast, placed under the direct control of the Ministry of the Interior, and Thai administrators were sent out from Bangkok to administer these new provinces.[18] The process of national assimilation was then intensified. Up to 1932, the monarchy had steadily increased its control over the Patani Malays in the areas of administration, education and language. In the context of the imposition of the new nationalist ideology, this process was now greatly accelerated.[19]

The climax of this nationalist revolution came after 1938, when Marshal Phibun and the armed forces consolidated their power. Under the auspices of an authoritarian military regime, a political programme was pushed through that shared many ideological characteristics with other 'national revolutions' of the inter-war period, particularly that of Kemal Ataturk. In essence, the policy of Phibun's government combined an emphasis on Thai racial identity and unity, with forced-pace modernization. In 1939, Siam was renamed *Thailand*, thereby highlighting the one-ness of Thai ethnic and national identity. Pan-Thai rhetoric encouraged the irredentist dream of bringing the whole Thai (or *T'ai*) family – including the Shans and the Lao – within one state.[20] This went hand in hand with a modernization programme designed to break down 'backward' customs and 'dialects', and enforce uniformity in language and social behaviour. The policy was embodied in the notorious 'Royal Decree prescribing customs for the Thai people' of 1941. Like Ataturk's reforms in Turkey, these contained elements of Westernization – cutlery to replace customary methods of eating; Western-style hats, trousers and dresses to replace traditional clothing; and a prohibition on betel-chewing – along with an emphasis on national pride and unity. In Muslim areas, for example, the Friday holiday was banned, and steps were begun for the phasing out of the use of Islamic law.[21]

Although this policy was not aimed solely at the Muslim Malays of South Thailand, it clearly constituted a direct threat to the very foundation of their ethnic and religious identity. In Islamic terms, there could not be a clearer justification for *jihad*; and, although there had always been resistance to Siamese rule, it is from this time that the modern Patani separatist and irredentist movements began.

The Patani region during and after the Second World War: the irredentist phase

When the Japanese invaded Southeast Asia late in 1941, the Thais felt they had no choice – if they wished to keep a vestige of their independence – but to enter the war on the side of Japan. It is clear, however, that there was already a considerable ideological affinity between Japan and the authoritarian, ultra-nationalist military regime of Phibun. Moreover, Japan's conquests in Southeast Asia gave its Thai ally the golden opportunity to fulfil its pan-Thai irredentist dream and, as an additional bonus, regain non-Thai as well as 'Thai' territories that had been detached from Siam by neighbouring colonial powers before the First World War. Accordingly, Thailand was able to re-acquire slices of territory in Laos, Cambodia, Burma and, in 1943, the four Malay states of Kedah, Kelantan, Trengganu and Perlis.[22]

This brought Thailand into direct confrontation with Great Britain, and thereby laid the foundations for a short-lived, one-sided but never-theless significant 'loyalty' relationship between Britain and key figures among the Patani Malays. Undoubtedly the most important of these figures was Tengku Mahmud Mahyiddeen, second son of Tengku Abdul Kadir, the last *raja* of Patani, who had been exiled by the Thais earlier in the century. From 1933 to the Second World War, Tengku Mahmud Mahyiddeen had worked in the Kelantan civil service.[23] During the Second World War, he joined the Kelantan Volunteer Force and, when the Japanese invaded Malaya, he was able to escape with the British Army to India. There he played a leading role in recruiting Malay volunteers for Force 136, the organization that was coordinating guerrilla activity in Malaya against the Japanese.[24] Although there were some British–Malay operations in north and central Malaya against the Japanese, Tengku Mahmud Mahyiddeen's main task was to prepare the ground – particularly in the strongly anti-Thai northern Malay states and Patani – for the eventual British invasion of Malaya.[25]

While Mahmud Mahyiddeen was directly helping the British war effort in India, Malay resistance to Thai policy was building up in Patani itself. Leadership of this opposition came from Islamic leaders and the traditional Patani elite. Tengku Abdul Jalal, MP for Narathiwat and son of the former *raja* of Saiburi, protested to the Thai govern-ment about the cultural and religious repression of the Malay Muslims, and an Islamic reformist scholar called Haji Sulong formed a movement for the defence of Islam and Islamic Law in Patani.[26]

Indeed, despite a timely change of regime in July 1944, and a belated attempt by the new Thai government to dissociate itself from the former military regime and – covertly – from the Japanese war effort, a convergence of interest did seem to be developing between the irredentist aspirations of the Patani Malays and Britain's long-term political and strategic objectives.

In security terms, Britain's wartime planners for the post-war period were mindful of the fact that Japan's attack on Malaya in 1941 had initially been launched from the Songkhla–Patani coastline, and that it had moved through the Patani region before the British had been able to respond effectively.[27] Britain's objective in 1944, therefore, was the creation of some kind of unspecified 'strategic arrangement ... within the framework of an international security system' that would cover the whole of the southernmost part of Thailand from the Kra Isthmus down to the Malayan border.[28] Clearly any such 'arrangement', however vaguely conceived, would have involved at the very least an abridge-ment of Thai sovereignty in the specified region, which included Patani.

In connection with this proposed strategic arrangement, Britain undertook during the later stages of the war a major assessment of the whole future of the Malayan region. Given the fact that Thailand had taken advantage of Japan's victories to reassert control over Perlis, Kelantan, Kedah and Trengganu, the whole question of the siting of the Thailand–Malaya border was included in the assessment. As an irreducible minimum, the British were determined to recover the Malay states that Thailand had gained.[29] But beyond this, there was serious consideration of the question of Patani's status, and whether the inclusion of Patani in a post-war Malaya would not only make sense in ethnic terms, but also help safeguard Britain's security interests.[30] Moreover, a territorial adjustment in favour of Malaya would be welcomed by the Patani Malays, and would serve as a suitable 'punishment' for Thailand's behaviour in the war. As in the case of other small states that had sided with Germany or Japan, Britain was determined that the Thais should, as the phrase went, 'work their passage home'.[31]

This indication that, at the very least, the question of the Thai border and of Patani's future status was on the agenda was mooted at a time of burgeoning Malay nationalism in Malaya itself during 1945 and 1946. This rise in nationalist feeling was stimulated partly by the general nationalist rhetoric of Southeast Asia during the period of Japanese occupation; partly by the savage inter-ethnic conflict that broke out in Malaya after the Japanese surrender; and particularly by Britain's attempt to create a new political structure in post-war Malaya, based on the removal of the sovereignty of the separate Malay States and on the concept of an equal citizenship status for all the races of Malaya. This last development provoked a mass reaction among the Malays of Malaya in defence of the *tanah Melayu* and Malay rights. It was natural that the question of Patani, and the perceived right of the Patani Malays to rejoin their brethren in the *tanah Melayu*, should become a major issue in this new environment of heightened ethnic consciousness.[32]

With the sudden surrender of Japan in August 1945, Britain's Southeast Asia Command assumed responsibility for post-surrender tasks in Thailand, Malaya, southern Indochina, Sumatra and Java. The ensuing period of interim British military control offered the Patani Malay leadership an opportunity to push their irredentist demands. This they did in November 1945, when they sent to the British Secretary of State for the Colonies a petition (see Appendix 6), outlining their grievances against the Thai government and their request 'that the British Government may have the kindness to release our country and ourselves from the pressure of Siam, because we do not wish to remain any longer under the Siamese Government'.[33]

The petition, which was signed by seven high-ranking members of the traditional governing elite of Patani, outlined both the cumulative and the more recent grievances of the Patani Malays against the Thai state. In the first part, it presented recent examples of arbitrary arrest and murder by the Thai authorities – acts of terror that had taken place *after* the collapse of the Thai military regime. The next section outlined complaints concerning the systematic suppression of the Malay language, which not only constituted an assault on Malay iden-tity, but also meant that the Malay population was denied access to jobs and forced into a position of permanent backwardness. It then cited the attempts of the Thai government to abolish Malay customs, force the Malays to wear Thai or Westernized clothing, and prevent Muslims from using their own religious courts. Finally, it pointed out that the Thai government had neglected the region; as the petition put it: 'In developing the country, the Siamese have done nothing, leaving the country overgrown with bushes and in [an] insanitary condition having no comparison with conditions in the Malay States in Malaya.'[34] The clear implication of this last complaint – one that has often been made since that time by the Patani Malays – was that Patani would have been far better off economically if it had been included in British Malaya.

After citing these grievances, the petition ended by appealing to the international principles of human rights and self-determination that were being shaped by the new United Nations in the wake of the Allied victory:

> It is said that according to the decisions of the San Francisco Conference, all dependent States should be given freedom and the nations or people of such States should be allowed to administer their countries in the ways most suitable to them. Patani is really a Malay country, formerly ruled by Malay Rajas for generations, but has been Siam's dependency only since about fifty years ago. Now the Allied Nations ought to help the return of this country to the Malays, so that they can have it united with other Malay countries in the peninsula.
>
> We therefore hope that the Allied Nations who are just, may help us in our desire, and release us from the hand of Siam. (See Appendix 6.)

'If the Allied nations delay or are late to give [a] peaceful settlement in Patani and its districts', the petition warned in conclusion, 'surely there will be an intense feeling of dissatisfaction and future danger to all the Malay population (*ra'yat Melayu*) there'.[35]

The explicit irredentist hopes expressed in this petition were not, however, to be realized. Noting in passing that the petition was the work of the 'pre-war governing class' of Patani, and that it had possibly been masterminded by Tengku Mahmud Mahyiddeen – by then returned to Kelantan from India – both the Foreign Office and the Colonial Office were clear that the British government could not respond to a petition presented by the inhabitants of a foreign country.[36] In the treaty concluded between Britain and Thailand in January 1946, the British territories of Malaya and Burma that had been seized by Thailand during the war were duly returned, but no further territorial concessions were extracted from the Thais.[37] The British, in other words, did not take advantage of Thailand's weak position in 1945–46 to 'rationalize' the border between Malaya and Thailand, and thereby realize the Patani Malays' irredentist ambitions.

It is interesting to consider the reasons for this. In the first place, it is quite possible that the history of the region would have been different if Britain had had to fight its way back into Malaya and Thailand with the help of the Malays of the northern Malay States and Patani. As it was, Britain suddenly found itself overwhelmed after the Japanese surrender by administrative responsibilities, and with inadequate resources to meet these responsibilities. In such circumstances, the immediate British priority was stability; this involved working with, not against, existing governments and political forces, including the Thai government. Above all, the war-ravaged regions of Burma and Malaya desperately needed rice supplied from Thailand, and this necessitated a degree of cooperation between the Malayan and Thai governments.

The key to the maintenance of the independence and territorial integrity of Thailand, however, was probably the attitude of the United States. Despite the fact that Britain and the United States were allies in the war against Japan, the Americans were intensely suspicious of what they saw as Britain's innate imperialist attitudes and ambitions in Asia as a whole, and in Thailand in particular. Through 1944 and 1945, they were alarmed at Britain's talk of making the Thais 'work their passage home' in the post-war settlement, particularly when it was connected with the suggestion that Britain's security needs required the creation of a 'special strategic area' under international supervision in the southern Thai isthmus.[38] For the United States, independent Thailand served as a kind of model of the post-war world of free nations that they wished to see created in Asia.[39] Accordingly, they made it abundantly clear to Britain that they were not prepared to accept any post-war arrangement that would impair Thai sovereignty.[40] Paradoxically, therefore, Patani's demand for the right to self-determination was at least in part stymied by the United States' anti-colonial suspicions.

However, although Patani's status was not changed at the end of the war, the very *threat* that Britain might annex Patani probably contributed to the mollification of Thailand's policy towards the Patani Malays in 1945 and 1946. The old danger that Thai misrule could serve as an excuse for the expansion of British power in the Malayan peninsula had re-emerged at this delicate moment in Thailand's history. So, by 1946, the Friday religious holiday was restored for Muslim areas, and new regulations permitted the application of Islamic law within the legal system in the areas of marriage, the family and inheritance.[41] In 1945, the 'Patronage of Islam Act' created a state-sanctioned (and state-controlled) Islamic hierarchy, with a crown-appointed national head of Islam (*chularajmontri*), a National Council for Islamic Affairs, and Provincial Councils for Islamic Affairs 'in every province where there are a substantial number of Thai Muslims'.[42] In 1947, this process of trying to integrate Islam into the state structure was deepened, when regulations were made governing the registering of mosques, the election of local mosque councils and the appointment of mosque officials.[43]

Clearly, these reforms were a significant reversal of the Thai policy towards Thai Muslims as a whole, and the Malays of Patani in particular, that had been in force before and during the Second World War. Equally, however, while state sanction was now given to Islam, it was the obvious intention of the Thai authorities that the institutions of Islam should be kept firmly under the state's patronage and control. It was at this stage that the first clear signs became evident of the Thai state's long-term post-war strategy of widening the concept of Thai citizenship and identity to include the Muslim community, while at the same time trying to sever the link in Patani between a Muslim identity and a Malay identity – the creation, in other words, of the new categories of *Thai Muslims* and *Thai Islam*.

So far as the Patani Malays were concerned, this new Islamic hierarchy – particularly the Provincial Councils for Islamic Affairs – did have the effect of laying the basis for a new leadership within the community that, over time, gradually replaced the old Patani aristocracy. But in immediate terms, the reforms did not overcome the deep mistrust of the Patani Malays, or help to blunt their separatist and irredentist aspirations. In fact, political turbulence in Patani and a sense of Thai misrule if anything deepened during the immediate post-war period. Although the Patani region had not suffered the devastation that had been endured by the Arakanese during the war, the Thailand–Malaya border became a centre for smuggling, particularly rice-smuggling into Malaya.[44] Circumstances that would naturally encourage lawlessness and corruption were exacerbated by the fact that political stability in Thailand as a whole had seriously eroded since the succession of the Thai civilian government. From his home in Kelantan – to which he had returned from India at the end of the war – Tengku Mahmud Mahyiddeen aroused public opinion in Malaya in early 1947 with his warnings that atrocities and repression directed against the Malays in Patani were if anything intensifying, and that local Thai officials, far from suppressing, were often linked to the banditry and anarchy that afflicted the region.[45]

In these unpromising circumstances, the volume of protest increased in Patani and, indeed, in Satun through 1947. The most famous and clear statement of Patani Malay objectives at this time was the list of seven demands presented to the Thai government in April 1947 by Haji Sulong, head of the Islamic Council of Pattani Province.[46] Unlike the unsuccessful petition given to Britain in November 1945, this document was not overtly separatist in intent. This reticence reflected a simple recognition of political realities. But it did put forward an unambiguous claim for the political autonomy of the Patani Malay region. It demanded that a single Patani Malay Governor be appointed for the four existing Malay-dominated provinces, including Satun; that at least eighty per cent of the officials in this designated region be Muslim; that Malay be given equal status with Thai as an official language there, and that it be introduced into primary schools; that Islamic law be administered in separate Islamic courts, not from within the Thai legal system; and, finally, that revenues raised in the region be kept for the welfare and development of the region.[47] Though the irredentist dream of joining the Malay States had been sidelined, the realization of these above demands would have amounted to the creation of a self-governing Patani Malay and Satun Malay region, with direct control over its language, its culture and its finances.

These demands went far beyond anything that any Thai government could have possibly accepted. The immediate post-war administrative changes demonstrated that Thailand was prepared, in theory at least, to make concessions on the issue of religious freedom, and to accept the idea that Muslims in Thailand could become part of the Thai national family as 'Thai-Muslims'. What Thai governments could not accept was any weakening of national unity, any recognition of separate rights for separate ethnic groupings, or any demands for regional autonomy on the basis of such separate ethnic rights. Acceptance of any of these ideas would have meant the undermining of the central philosophical basis of the Thai state.

In any case, even if the Thai government had been disposed to make serious concessions to Haji Sulong, it appeared to have very little control over local events in the Patani region in 1947. In late October 1947, the *Straits Times* published a report of a recent journey

through Patani by Barbara Whittingham-Jones, a freelance journalist
who had close contact with Tengku Mahmud Mahyiddeen in Kelantan
and who sympathized strongly with the Patani Malay cause. Even
though the report was clearly biased, it painted a convincingly bleak
picture of lawlessness in Patani, and of arbitrary oppression of the
Malays in the region by the Thai authorities.[48]

By late 1947, in fact, it was clear that the Thai military – manipulated behind the scenes by Marshal Phibun himself – was poised to
seize power and end what was seen as the chaos of civilian rule. In
November 1947 a military coup shifted the balance of political power
decisively towards the Thai conservative and authoritarian elements,
including Phibun. These events naturally had a drastic impact on
opinion in Patani, where it was assumed that the stealthy return of
Phibun to the centre of power would mean a resumption of the
assimilation policy of the late 1930s and early 1940s.[49] Events thereafter
moved rapidly towards a climax in Patani. After the Thai military
coup, Haji Sulong and other Patani leaders urgently requested that
Tengku Mahmud Mahyiddeen in Kelantan head a Patani resistance
movement and appeal for support from the outside world.[50] As a
consequence of what were seen by the Thai authorities as these
treacherous intrigues, Haji Sulong himself was arrested in January
1948.[51]

After Haji Sulong's arrest, local disturbances inside Patani itself
multiplied.[52] From a base in Kelantan, refugees from Patani, along
with local Malay sympathizers, attempted to build up support for the
Patani cause throughout Malaya and the Muslim world, as well as in
the United Nations. In December 1947, Tengku Mahmud Mahyiddeen
had already considered trying to force the pace of events by simply
declaring the independence of Patani. The British authorities, however,
had heavily discouraged him from making any such move.[53] So early in
1948, under the aegis of an organization with the acronym GAMPAR
('Gabungan Melayu Patani Raya', or 'League of Malays of Greater
Patani'), an attempt was made in Malaya to publicize to the outside
world the plight of the Patani Malays, and to push for realistic political
objectives.[54] These boiled down to: first, an assertion that under Article
3 of the Atlantic Charter, Patani had a right to self-determination by
plebiscite; and second that, on the basis of any such plebiscite, a united
Patani – 'Patani Raya' or 'Greater Patani' – should have the right to
'internal self-government', within either Thailand *or* Malaya.[55]

While this international campaign was being mounted from Malaya,
in Patani itself tension steadily escalated in the early months of 1948.
By the time that Phibun finally returned to power in April 1948, a
widespread if uncoordinated state of insurrection existed in Patani,

with full-scale clashes occurring between rebel bands and Thai security forces.[56] However, despite the fact that these events, and the evidence of Thai repression, were given full publicity in Malaya and a reasonable degree of publicity in Britain, there was no international reaction, and certainly no move for international or even local intervention.[57]

The Malay leadership of UMNO were sympathetic to the cause of the Patani Malays, but during 1947 and 1948 they were fully absorbed in issues relating to Malaya itself. In the process of post-war inter-ethnic bargaining in Malaya, a crucial stage had been reached in 1948 with the creation of the Malayan Federation and the beginning of serious discussions on the shape of a future self-governing Malaya; in these delicate circumstances, involvement in Patani, though tempting, would have been a potentially dangerous distraction. As far as Britain was concerned, although it clearly disliked the idea of the return to power of its old wartime adversary Marshal Phibun, there was no serious inclination to 'rock the boat' over the issue of Patani. Elsewhere in Southeast and East Asia, radical nationalism had infected the Indonesian archipelago; communist revolts were breaking out by 1948 throughout Southeast Asia; the French were bogged down in a war against communism in Indochina; and in China the balance in the civil war between the Kuomintang and the Chinese Communist Party was shifting, by 1948, decisively to the communists. Under these circumstances, although there was some sympathy at what might be called the 'Malaya level' for the Malay cause in Patani, from the overall regional point of view Thailand appeared to be a rock of relative stability in an increasingly unstable world.

Of even more immediate importance to Britain was the fact that the communist insurgency in Malaya – which had broken out in 1948 – began to spill over into the Malaya–Thailand border region by late 1948. Thereafter, alarming reports were being received of communist appearances along the sensitive Kelantan border, raising the real possibility that the Narathiwat, Yala and Songkhla regions could be used as a *point d'appui* for communist attacks and infiltration in the whole of northern Malaya.[58] It thus became absolutely vital for the British authorities in Malaya to secure the cooperation of Thailand for the effective policing of the border. These agreements on border security were reached between 1948 and early 1949. By the end of 1948, this policy of accommodation with Thailand was accompanied by a firm clamp-down on pro-Patani irredentist activity in Kelantan.[59]

However, in concluding this brief review of the failure of the Patani irredentist movement after the Second World War, it is important to stress the decisive influence of wider geopolitical factors on relations between Malaya and Thailand at this time. While British diplomatic representatives in Bangkok saw relations with Thailand from the perspective of Britain's global interests, the Colonial Office and colonial civil servants in Malaya were naturally acutely aware of the local Malay dimension to the problem. Even before the war, the Colonial Office had been conscious of the close relationship between Patani and the Malay state of Kelantan in particular; and after 1945 local British officials tended to feel that oppressive Thai rule in Patani had made a major contribution to the disturbances there.[60] In 1946, while the Colonial Office concurred with the general view that Britain could not respond to the Patani petition, it made it clear that Malaya had a special interest in events in Patani; and in 1948, when the issue of providing arms for the Thai government for the fight against communism was being discussed, both the Colonial Office and the Malayan government were anxious to ensure that the arms should not be used to repress the Patani Malays.[61] It is true that when, in 1949, the War Office informally put forward the suggestion that Malaya's regional security would best be protected by an enforced transfer of Patani from Thailand to British Malaya, the idea was briskly rejected by the Colonial Office as well as the Foreign Office. However, if the situation in mainland Southeast Asia had been more desperate – particularly in Thailand itself – the response might have been different.[62] In the early 1950s, in fact, Britain did draw up contingency plans for the military occupation of Southern Thailand in the event that Thailand should 'fall' to communism.

Patani since the 1940s

Mahmud Mahyiddeen believed in early 1948 that the global upheaval of the Second World War and the particular political situation of Southeast Asia at the end of the war offered the Patani Malays a 'once-and-for-all' chance to break away from Thailand and reintegrate themselves into the Malay world. 'If we miss the boat this time', he wrote to Barbara Whittingham-Jones, 'we [have] had it'.[63] Subsequent events have shown his assessment to be correct. In fact, the moment of opportunity had probably passed by 1944. By that time Britain, in the face of American pressure and the new prevailing anti-colonial ethos, no longer had the power to adjust borders at will.

Throughout the post-war period, the principal aim of successive Thai governments in their dealings with Patani has been to integrate – but not necessarily assimilate – the Patani Malays. At the root, this has involved severing the link between Islam and 'Malay-ness'. In its purest form, Thai policy has been aimed at the creation of a Thai-speaking population that uses Arabic in the mosques and in the pursuit of Islamic studies, with Malay withering away as a quaint local dialect. Certainly the Thai authorities have discouraged the import of Malay-language reading materials from across the border. The fact that the main Malay publications in Patani itself are still written in the *Jawi* (Arabic) script has also helped to insulate Patani Malay culture from the mainstream Malay culture of modern Malaysia.[64] In addition, attempts have been made to translate the key religious texts into Thai, and even gradually to 'Thai-ize' Malay by using the Thai script for the Malay language.[65]

The key to the success of this underlying strategy of drawing a distinction between Thai national identity and Islam on one side, and Malay 'custom', 'tradition' and 'dialect' on the other is, of course, the education system.[66] Just as the Thai government sought to integrate the whole Islamic hierarchy down to the mosque level into the government structure in the late 1940s, so Thai governments have since the 1960s tried to draw traditional Malay-Muslim education into the national education system.[67] Once again, the main victim of this policy has been the Malay language.[68]

A crucial part of this integration process has been the attempt to improve the administration and the economy of the Patani region. This has involved trying to entice Malay Muslims into the administration by providing them with privileged access to education, and at the same time ensuring that Thai Buddhist officials are of high quality and well versed in the unfamiliar characteristics and sensitivities of the Muslim community.[69] From the 1960s on, there has also been a concerted effort to improve and diversify the economy of Patani, and to build a road network that would connect the region with the rest of Thailand.[70]

Generally speaking, it could be said that these efforts to draw the Malay Muslims into the national family have not succeeded, except in the special case of Satun.[71] From the 1950s until quite recently, Patani remained a 'zone of dissidence', with intermittent outbreaks of guerrilla activity and, at best, only a sullen submission to Thai rule. The reason for this failure of integration has undoubtedly been the determination of the populace to maintain their Malay identity: a determination that has been repeatedly strengthened by cross-border contacts. For the Malay Muslims of Patani, the relationship between Islam and 'Malay-ness' has been, and to a great degree still is, inextricable. All the integrative efforts of Thai governments – including, for example, road-building programmes – have therefore been interpreted as attempts to weaken Malay identity and strengthen the control of the central government. In addition, well-meaning policies devised at the centre have rarely been implemented effectively on the ground. Maladministration, neglect, corruption and arbitrary repression have persisted since the 1940s – a situation that has been made worse by the fact that this is a border region with an difficult terrain perfectly suited to warlord and guerrilla alike.

In the 1960s and 1970s, a variety of resistance movements emerged in Patani with diverse objectives, from the reconstitution of the old kingdom of Patani to the formation of an Islamic republic. What these guerrilla organizations have all had in common, however, is a separatist agenda, and a plan of creating, in one form or another, an independent Patani state.[72] Military action against the Thai authorities has normally fallen into the classic pattern of 'low-intensity warfare': ambushes, assassinations, kidnapping, extortion, sabotage and bomb attacks.[73] Significantly, the main 'soft targets' of these intermittent terrorist campaigns have been what could be seen as the front line of the Thai threat to Malay identity: schools, teachers, local administrators and Thai Buddhist settlers in the region.[74] Inevitably, inept and brutal government responses to these activities, based on inadequate intelligence, merely stimulated and justified intensified resistance and alienated the population as a whole.[75]

However, although there have been 'high points' in this violence – particularly in the late 1960s, the mid-1970s, and again in the period 1979–1981 – guerrilla activity has never reached a 'critical mass' where it would have seriously threatened the central government. The only time that popular resistance and protest reached a stage where it required immediate attention and prompt remedial action was in 1975, when the whole of Thailand was passing through a period of political turmoil.[76]

Two major reasons why these guerrilla campaigns have never come near to achieving their goals are, first, the lack of international awareness and support and, second, the lack of sufficient assistance across the border from Malaysia. It is true, however, that Malay nationalism has frequently been tempted to come to the aid of its Malay brethren trapped across the Thai border, and that the main Malay opposition party, PAS (Partai Islam), has used this issue as an example of the failure of the Malay governing party, UMNO, to support Malay and Islamic causes. The fact that the traditional stronghold of PAS is Kelantan, and that Kelantan has the strongest links with Patani, illustrates another point: that good government-to-government relations between Thailand and Malaysia may often be vitiated by poor relations and mutual suspicions on the ground.[77] Ever since the Second World War, the Thais have suspected that Patani Malay guerrilla activity has been sustained by Malay support from across the border, particularly from Kelantan; in return, Malaysian governments and the Malaysian army have been periodically infuriated at the apparently lackadaisical Thai attitude to the Malayan communist guerrillas ensconced in Thai territory.[78]

These mutual suspicions have, in fact, helped to maintain a 'balance of threat' that has, in the end, forced both sides to desist from irredentist or destabilizing adventures. However, the failure of Malaysia to support rebellion in Patani cannot be explained solely on the basis of this local 'balance of threat'.[79] From the end of the Second World War right through the period of the Cold War, Malaya/Malaysia and Thailand had a mutual interest in maintaining regional stability against the communist menace. Both sides have shared, and continue to share, the consensus view in Southeast Asia that their common interests must prevail over their local differences, and that any threat to existing border arrangements in particular could upset the delicate balance of the whole region. It is in this context of *realpolitik* that colonial borders have hardened into mutually accepted inter-state frontiers.

Conclusion

The failure of what might be called the 'Malay strategy' of irredentism has naturally led to a greater emphasis within the Patani resistance forces on the concept of *jihad*, or Islamic irredentism. The propaganda issued by Patani resistance movements has certainly abounded in scriptural justifications for the waging of *jihad*.[80] In more practical terms, the Patani resistance has since the 1960s greatly relied on support from the Islamic world as a whole, and radical regimes in the Middle East in particular.[81] Although aid from the outside Islamic world is said to have been intermittent and largely ineffective, the leadership of Patani resistance has increasingly been provided by Patani Malays who have received a religious education in the Middle East or in South Asia.[82]

The continuing failure of Patani Malay resistance to achieve its separatist goals does not, however, mean that Thai rule has been accepted in the region. In fact, the history of twentieth-century Patani is that of a classic region of internal *hijra*, or withdrawal from and non-recognition of *kafir* authority. The Patani Malays have – ever since the Thais began their policies of administrative, political, religious and educational integration – attempted to live within their own world as if the Thai state did not exist. Many observers have noted that the Patani Malays have generally striven to minimize their contacts with the Thai authorities.[83] In local disputes and in the administration of justice, for example, Malay village elders have always tried to ensure that Thai administrators have been given no occasion to interfere.[84] It is, moreover, a notable feature of Patani that the Thai Buddhist and Malay Muslim communities have barely any contact with each other.[85]

This internal *hijra* has therefore contributed to the relative failure until recently of Thai policies of integration – particularly in the Patani countryside – and Malay Muslim culture has remained intact. This is true even in the towns, where a kind of Malay 'counter-culture' exists side by side with the predominant Thai and Chinese presence. But the price that has had to be paid for this successful *hijra* has been a continuing condition of backwardness, given the fact that the Thai language remains the only avenue for educational and economic advancement.[86]

In this condition of *impasse*, a more sophisticated effort has been made by the Thai government and armed forces in recent years to build a programme for the south that would combine development with a recognition of the strength and legitimacy of Malay culture in the region.[87] It remains to be seen if such a combined policy can lead to a genuine process of integration by consent. Always hovering in the wings, however, is the possibility that the creation of an Islamic state in Malaysia or a triumph of Islamic radicalism in the wider Islamic world might again open up the joint issues of Malay and Islamic irredentism in Patani.

10

Conclusion

Factors in the creation and survival of separatist movements in Southeast Asia

In the era of decolonization which followed the Second World War, parallel events in Southeast Asia encouraged the formation of a number of separatist or semi-separatist movements directed against the new independent nation-states that were emerging in the region. The patterns followed by these separatist movements were not, however, the same. The Patani Malays, for example, sought to break away from a state – Thailand – that had never been colonized and to join Malaya, which had. On the other hand, an attempt has been made in the preceding pages to show that the history of Patani separatism in the 1940s was fundamentally affected, first, by the process of defining Thai nationalism; second, by the emergence of Malay nationalism in the neighbouring state of British Malaya; and, finally, by the general process of decolonization. Equally, it could be argued that the Acehnese Darul Islam revolt of 1953 was not separatist in its aim. It is clear, however, that the Acehnese rebels explicitly wished to *secede* on ideological grounds from the existing Republic of Indonesia, and that the Darul Islam rebellion that lasted in Aceh from 1953 to the early 1960s was sustained by the desire to regain Aceh's *autonomy*. The argument of this book is, therefore, that while there are many obvious differences between the separatist or semi-separatist movements of Arakan, the Karen region, Penang, Patani, the Montagnard region, Aceh and the South Moluccas, they are all part of a general historical process that simultaneously affected the whole of Southeast Asia.

At the root of the issue of separatism lies the issue of identity. In political terms, identities are defined not by categories devised by ethnologists or linguists, but by shared or divisive historical experiences. The key historical experiences that gave shape to the separatist movements of Southeast Asia in the era of decolonization were, first, the consolidation modern nationalist movements in the inter-war years and,

second, the rapid process of nationalist struggle and subsequent decolonization that began with the Japanese invasion of Southeast Asia.
The nationalist movements had perforce to define what the nation *was*.
Although Southeast Asian nationalist movements of the 1920s, 1930s
and 1940s generally made strenuous efforts to draw all communities,
cultures and religions within the existing colonial states into the
concept of the national family, it was inevitable that even the most
generous definitions of national identity would fail to be wholly
inclusive. Some communities and regions inevitably felt themselves to
be excluded from the new national identities, and therefore resisted
integration into the new nation-states that were being forged. These
included loyalist groups that saw themselves as inextricably linked to
the colonial presence; communities, like the Karen, that also had a
deeply embedded memory of pre-colonial persecution by a dominant
ethnic group; or communities whose religion would naturally exclude
them from the mainstream national identity.

The era of nationalism and decolonization, therefore, helped create
and define 'counter-identities', and the whole process was sharpened
in the two decades of national and ideological turmoil in Southeast
Asia between 1940 and 1960.

Separatist movements were stimulated by a sense of 'marginality'.
For a separatist movement to hope to succeed, however, it was necessary
that this 'marginality' should be not merely conceptual, but physical.
Dispersed Eurasian communities in Southeast Asia, for example, may
have felt alienated from and threatened by the new independent nation-
states. They lacked, however, the physical means – the essential condition of *peripherality* – to convert their fears into concrete political
goals. Geographical peripherality was the vital first condition for the
viability of any separatist movement and for the success of any separatist
resistance.

Another vital condition for the strength and endurance of a separatist
movement was a sense of territorial legitimacy. As Ruth McVey has
pointed out in her important analysis of the phenomenon of nationalism, 'Separatism and the Paradoxes of the Nation-State in Perspective',
the modern nation-state tends to value its peripheral territory above its
peripheral population.[1] While, therefore, it is virtually unheard of for
a nation-state voluntarily to cede sections of its territory, the removal
of populations, or 'ethnic cleansing', is all too common. One of the
main causes of hostility between the Thai-majority population and the
Patani Malays has been the tendency of Thais to refer to the latter as
khaek, or 'foreigners'. The implication is that the Patani Malays have
only a conditional, not an absolute, right to inhabit what is inherently
'Thai' soil. In similar fashion, there has been a consistent inclination

in Burma to confuse the native Arakanese Muslims or Rohinga with 'Chittagong' illegal immigrants. Given the relatively recent immigrant character of much of the population of Penang, Malays were able with more credibility to counter the Penang secession movement with assertions that the island of Penang was an intrinsic part of the *tanah Melayu*. In each case, however, an attempt was being made to detach the issue of the rights of the population from the issue of rights over the land they inhabited. The strength of a separatist movement, therefore, depended to a great degree on its ability to link the rights of a people to the rights of that people over their territory.

Connected with this is Ruth McVey's argument that a separatist movement will be greatly strengthened if the separate identity of the movement can be linked to the memory of a historical state.[2] There can be no doubt, for example, that memories of the Aceh sultanate and the kingdom of Patani have helped to sustain the identities of Aceh and Patani respectively. In this sense, those separatist movements that can invoke a pre-colonial identity of this kind have a great advantage over loyalist communities, like the Straits Chinese of Penang or the Christian Ambonese, whose identity was fundamentally defined by the colonial presence.

It is obvious that a sense of religious difference has acted as a powerful dynamo in some of the separatist movements. It is equally clear that Islam, especially, cannot merely be pigeon-holed within the overall identity of a particular people, but that it can act as an important autonomous force. We may, for example, detect the forces of Acehnese separatism lurking within the Darul Islam rebellion; it would be quite wrong, however, to dismiss the broad *Islamic* priorities of that movement. Likewise, the grass-roots *hijra* of the Patani Malays directed against the Thai presence was more than just a manifestation of petty local disgruntlement; it was a reflection of the fact that the Patani Malay community lived within the all-embracing world of Islam, and was unable as well as unwilling to adjust to the completely alien world that began to envelop it in the twentieth century.

It would also be inadequate to dismiss the ideas underlying loyalism as merely the defence of sectional interests. It is certainly true that established job opportunities – indeed, a secure niche in the colonial administration – were at stake for some groups when the process of decolonization began. But the Straits Chinese and Karen leaders and opinion-formers, for instance, had a concept of empire that was not ignoble, particularly since it insisted on a greater degree of racial equality and partnership within the empire. Loyalism was sustained by an idea, and decolonization was seen by loyalists not merely as the betrayal of a people, but also as a betrayal of that idea.

For a separatist movement to survive, however, it needed grass-roots support and a mass organization. This was, first, because the colonial powers were, after the Second World War, no longer susceptible to the kind of elite lobbying that had worked in pre-war days. The Straits Chinese and other Penang leaders – as well as Tengku Mahmud Mahyiddeen and members of the Patani elite – discovered this to their cost. Second, it soon became apparent that the survival of a separatist movement would depend ultimately on its capacity to threaten, and ultimately use, force. The fact that the Karen leadership had built up a mass organization and that they could rely on a reasonably efficient military formation – the Karen National Defence Organization (KNDO) – helps explain why Karen resistance to Burmese rule has survived for so long.

In addition to this, the relative success or failure of a separatist movement depended to a great extent on the level of outside support that it could muster. In this context, geographical and geopolitical circumstances were, and are, of great significance. While the Arakanese Muslim and Patani separatist movements, for example, were able to rely on a sufficient trickle of support to keep their resistance efforts afloat, the geographical position of the Christian Ambonese doomed their rebellion from the outset. But it was the intrusion of the Cold War into mainland Southeast Asia that particularly affected the fate of some of the separatist movements. The fluid relationships between big-power manipulation, ideological confrontations and the traditional state and ethnic hostilities of an already volatile region could be exploited by separatist movements that were situated in strategically important areas, like 'Karenistan' or the Central Highlands. Exploiting the Cold War and its attendant geopolitical consequences was, however, a dangerous game that required above all things tactical agility and ideological adaptability on the part of the leadership of separatist movements.

Factors militating against the success of the separatist movements in Southeast Asia

Some of the key weaknesses of the Southeast Asian separatist movements can be stated by simply reversing the points made above. For example, ethnic loyalty based on a common historical memory and shared sufferings can provide a rock-like foundation for a separatist movement; on the other hand, ethnic loyalty is in its very nature self-limiting, unless the separatist movement concerned can rely on a powerful diaspora.[3] The main problem, however, is that the very things that help strengthen separatist identities – religious, political or social

– are inherently static, conservative, hierarchical and resistant to change.[4] To some extent, separatist movements in Southeast Asia of the 1960s and 1970s were able to overcome this difficulty by adopting the idiom of 'revolution' and 'nation-liberation'; this is particularly true of the Karen, Patani and Moro separatists. Ultimately, however, there has always been the problem that central government concessions on matters such as development, communications, educational availability and access to government jobs will all have the effect of threatening to dilute the separatist identity concerned. Separatist movements, therefore, have naturally tended to regard such 'intermediate' concessions with extreme suspicion and even resistance. Such a reaction, however, can trap separatist movements in a position where they appear simply to be perpetuating and defending vested interests.

Even access to outside aid brings with it as many liabilities as it presents opportunities. A separatist movement may be able to exploit the opportunities offered by a historical event like the Cold War; it may equally – as in the case of FULRO in the Central Highlands of Vietnam – become helplessly enmeshed in its ramifications. Furthermore, a separatist movement that comes to rely on networks of outside support will be exceptionally vulnerable to changed international circumstances. Self-reliance may be self-limiting, but reliance on others can be equally dangerous in the long run. More important still, a drip-feed of outside support may simply have the effect of perpetuating a conflict, and inhibiting moves to a negotiated settlement.

The crucial reason, however, why these separatist movements failed in their objectives and never reached a 'critical mass' was the general priority given by the states of Southeast Asia to regional stability. Despite certain hiccups – particularly the period of 'Confrontation' in the early 1960s – a consensus has generally been maintained in the region against exploiting the separatist problems of neighbouring states. The solid reasoning behind this consensus has been an awareness that most if not all the states of Southeast Asia are vulnerable to regional discontents and separatist impulses, and that a policy of tit-for-tat provocations could rapidly lead to the unravelling of the stability of the whole region. In this respect, the history of Southeast Asia since the Second World War has been very different from that of South Asia, where the states of the region have rarely hesitated to exploit the separatist difficulties of their neighbours.

It might be argued that Indochina provides an exception to this general rule. It should be noted, however, that the confrontation between North and South Vietnam was ideological; if the two sides agreed on one thing, it was on the need to maintain the unity and territorial integrity of Vietnam. Likewise, those who in the early 1970s predicted that either Laos or Cambodia – or both – would disintegrate under the strain of war, or be swallowed up by their more powerful neighbours, have yet to be proved right. Even the American 'Special War' strategy of relying on an assortment of minority and mercenary forces in Indochina had strict limits, as the Montagnards were to discover. Somehow, despite all the pressures of war and revolution, the post-1945 boundaries of Indochina have survived.

The signal failure of the post-Second World War separatist movements raises the question of the extent of support that these movements have actually enjoyed. This is a very difficult question to discuss with any confidence. It is easy for academics, journalists or other observers to suggest that these movements were – or are – of little importance, and that they have maintained their profile largely by misleading propaganda. It would be equally easy to ask how, in such an extremely sensitive area of investigation, levels of support for separatist movements could possibly be measured. Proof of intimidation or extortion does not necessarily rule out the possibility of widespread support for a movement; on the other hand, widespread and successful guerrilla activity does not necessarily mean that a majority of the population supports that activity. Probably the most that can be said is that, wherever a serious separatist movement has emerged, a 'fault-line' exists in that particular state. So long as the security consensus of the region concerned and the overall stability of that state is maintained, the fault-line will lie dormant. If for any reason the regional security consensus or the stability of the state breaks down, it is very likely that the fault-line will become a fissure.

The issue of separatism and identity needs to be seen in the global as well as the regional context. It is possible to identify in the twentieth century key periods of imperial disintegration. These have been followed by phases of what might be called 'primary' and then 'secondary' separatism; the first phase being when the most powerful political forces of a region are able to carve out nation-states; the second phase, when separatist tensions begin to develop within these nation-states. The first key period of imperial disintegration stretched very roughly from the beginning of the century to 1919, when first the Ottoman and then the Austro-Hungarian Empires broke up. This resulted in the creation of new nation-states in Europe and the Middle East, many of which had to cope with separatist pressures that subsequently exploded into the open in the 1930s and 1940s. The second period encompassed the vast process of global decolonization, as the old colonial empires began to break up. This began in 1945 and stretched over the ensuing decades. The final period of disintegration, from 1990, has seen the break-up of the Russian Empire – where Bolshevik had inherited Tsarist power – coupled with the re-emergence of separatist tensions in the nation-states of the Balkans and Eastern Europe that had been 'frozen' in the aftermath of Hitler's defeat and during the Cold War.

The experience within Europe during this century has been that the second phase of the break-up of empire – that in which separatist tensions are encouraged to explode within states formed in the wake of imperial fragmentation, due to unresolved economic or political grievances – is by far the messiest and most dangerous. As far as the world beyond Europe is concerned, the important point to make is that the process of separatism after 1945 stopped at the 'primary' phase. With a few exceptions – India, Palestine, or, ultimately, Cyprus – nation-states were created that followed the sometimes rather artificial borders of existing colonial territorial units. But on the whole, and precisely for the reasons that have been cited in the case of Southeast Asia, separatist pressures within these states have been contained. The 'secondary' phase of separatism in Asia and Africa has not yet reached the stage – with the exception of one or two special cases like Somalia – of seriously threatening the integrity of the states that achieved independence in the decolonization period. Indeed, the example presented to the world by the break-up of the Soviet Union and Yugoslavia has made Asian and African governments all the more determined to maintain the consensus against separatist pressures.

Separatism and self-determination

At the end of his book on the Moros of the Philippines and the Malays of Southern Thailand, W.T. Che Man comments:

> The Moros and the Malays regard the concept of 'national self-determination' as a fundamental right of every people, believing, with Woodrow Wilson, that 'every people has a right to choose the sovereignty under which they shall live'.[5]

In more general terms, the same point has been made by Gerard Chaliand in his introduction to *Minority Peoples in an Age of Nation-States*. Chaliand has pointed out, however, that the concept of 'self-determination', as it has been elucidated in the decisions of the United Nations, has tended to ignore the rights of groups demanding separation from existing nation-states. The definition of 'self-determination', in other words, was framed for the convenience of nationalist movements and nation-states in the age of decolonization. Chaliand has enlarged on this point to show the consequent gap that exists in the international concept of 'rights' between the rights to sovereignty of nation-states, and the 'human rights' of individuals.[6] The whole question of rights of minority communities within nation-states – including the right of those communities to self-determination – remains a grey area.

Of course, it has to be recognized that care must be used in defining minority communities within the nation-state. There is a vast difference, for example, between indigenous or long-established communities that have become territorially linked to a particular region, and non-indigenous minority communities that are the result of recent immigration, and that have tended to disperse throughout the nation-state. This is the difference, for example, between the Karens of Burma and the Chinese or Indians of Malaysia. There is a vital need to make a distinction between these two types of minority communities, not least because the right to self-determination cannot begin to operate in a dispersed community, as opposed to one whose origins are rooted in a particular part of a state. There is a great danger that the loose rhetoric of 'multi-culturalism' and the consequent undifferentiated claim for the rights of *all* minorities will obscure this essential distinction.

So far as the rights of non-indigenous and dispersed minorities are concerned, the British Malayan Union plan offered a model that was not, in the end, implemented, but had interesting possibilities. All would have the equal right to Malayan citizenship, the plan stated, who lived in Malaya and who, 'irrespective of race ... regarded Malaya as their true home and the object of their loyalty'.[7] This formula offers a simple reciprocal balance of right and duty on which it would be difficult to improve. The question of the rights of indigenous or long-settled minorities, and particularly the right to self-determination of these minorities, is far harder to resolve. In the post-imperial world, the sovereignty of nation-states is enshrined in the international system. There have been attempts to break down this absolute supremacy of the nation-state, and create sources of authority above and below the level of the sovereign nation – as, for example, the European Union experiment, with its supra-national structure and its plans to emphasize regional or 'sub-national' levels of decision-making. It is in such a context only that one can envisage even the beginning of a peaceful solution to the problems of separatism in many parts of the world. But the European Union experiment is in its infancy, and its outcome uncertain. There is, moreover, very little chance that this model will spread rapidly to the world beyond Europe. In Asia and Africa the sovereign nation-state is generally seen not as a threat to, but as the best available guarantee of stability in an uncertain world.

Ethnicity, democracy and stability: Southeast Asia
since the 1960s

How stability was maintained in Southeast Asia during and after the crucial decade of the 1960s is instructive. In the late 1950s and early 1960s, the United States became more and more deeply involved in the Indochina region. This intervention was not only designed to protect the Royal Lao Government (RLG) and the Republic of Vietnam (South Vietnam) from what was seen to be an imminent communist threat; it was also intended, in the broader sense, to be a means of creating a 'bastion' against communism, behind which the rest of Southeast Asia could stabilize in political and economic terms, and develop forms of collective security that would enable the region to defend itself from internal subversion and external threats.

Perversely, at the very time – in 1965 – that the United States found itself taking over military responsibility for the war against communism in South Vietnam, the rest of Southeast Asia had already entered a period of dramatic economic growth and was, moreover, on the point of achieving regional stability.[8] The key to this turnaround was the failure of the communist-supported coup in Indonesia on 30 September 1965, the subsequent removal of Sukarno from power, the military take-over, and the annihilation of the Indonesian Communist Party (PKI). By this time, a whole plethora of regional or Islamic revolts had been either quelled or resolved in Indonesia; the 'Emergency' had come to an end in Malaya in 1960, and the Malayan communist guerrilla remnants were largely confined to bases in southern Thailand; and the newly independent Singapore government was in the process of rooting out communist organizations in that city. After the armed forces take-over in Indonesia, the military 'Confrontation' (Konfrontasi) between Indonesia and Malaysia – which had been triggered by Sukarno's claim that the Federation of Malaysia, formed in 1963 and linking Malaya, Singapore, Sarawak and Sabah, was a 'neo-colonial' and therefore illegitimate political entity – was rapidly resolved. The stage had now been set for political stability, regional cooperation and unhampered economic development. This new political climate was consolidated in August 1967 with the formation of the Association of Southeast Asian Nations (ASEAN), comprising Indonesia, Malaysia, the Philippines, Singapore and Thailand, which was designed to enhance regional cooperation in the economic and foreign policy spheres.

In an article in *Foreign Affairs* in October 1967, Richard Nixon argued that it was precisely the American military commitment in Vietnam that provided the basis for this Southeast Asian stability and prosperity. The Vietnam war, he implied, had worked as a kind of lightning-rod, concentrating the energies and the threat of Asian communism on the Indochina theatre, and thereby preventing the diffusion of the revolutionary virus through the region.[9] In subsequent years, this became one of the main *ex post facto* justifications for what otherwise appeared to be a wholly disastrous national adventure.

Leaving aside what might be called the 'lightning-rod' thesis, there is no doubt that American attempts to bolster anti-communist regimes in Southeast and East Asia *did* help build the basis for long-term regional stability and prosperity. The 'front-line' states in the struggle to contain communism – South Korea, Taiwan, South Vietnam, Laos and Thailand – were all boosted in the 1950s and 1960s by massive amounts of United States aid. This aid not only provided a useful dynamo for economic growth but also relieved these states of what would otherwise have been the crippling costs of paying for their own defence. In political terms, although the United States made gestures towards the ideal of encouraging the establishment of democratically based regimes, the reality was that the armed forces increasingly formed the hub of the United States' strategies in these states. Thailand and (after 1963) South Vietnam are classic examples of these American-backed, military-dominated, so-called 'national security states'.

However, it is not just the United States' presence and influence that helps explain the stabilization of Southeast Asia in the 1960s. Throughout the region this period witnessed the collapse of the political systems that had been instituted after independence, and their replacement by more authoritarian structures. In the cases of Burma and Indonesia, army rule replaced what might be described as the charismatic, populist regimes of U Nu and Sukarno respectively. Although in the case of Burma this brought only a brief respite from chaos, rebellion and economic decline, the military-dominated 'New Order' regime in Indonesia set about effectively 'depoliticizing' Indo-nesian society and creating a new national ethos emphasizing stability, unity and development. In Singapore, the threat of communist subversion undoubtedly helped cement what could be called an 'author-itarian democracy'. In Malaysia, the near breakdown in the 1969 elections of the fragile political consensus created by the Malay-Chinese elite at the time of independence led to the re-forging of a modified democratic structure.

In all of these cases, what was in effect occurring was a reclaiming of power by central military and political elites from the institutions that had been formed in the era of mass political mobilization during the period of the Second World War and the subsequent independence struggles.

Political and regional stability – guaranteed by various defence arrangements with the West – formed an essential precondition for economic growth. Although the prevailing development policies of the time emphasized what were on the whole protectionist and *dirigiste* national economic strategies, it is interesting to note in this context the key role played by Chinese private enterprise in the creation of a strong economic foundation in Southeast Asia. This is evident in Thailand, South Vietnam, the Philippines, Singapore and Indonesia. These economies also benefited from the Chinese links – greatly bolstered by the flight of Chinese entrepreneurs from mainland China after the communist take-over – with Hong Kong and Taiwan. In the special case of Malaysia, the issue of economic development was intertwined with ethnic politics. In very general terms, it could be said that there existed an understanding between the Malay and Chinese elites that the state would specifically protect and advance the interests of the Malays, but that, as a *quid pro quo*, the Chinese-dominated private sector should be given a free rein. This understanding – which was modified but not abandoned as a result of the renegotiated ethnic elite consensus of the early 1970s – contributed substantially to the spectacular economic growth of Malaysia after independence.

In the early 1970s, however, Southeast Asia entered into a new period of turbulence. It is nevertheless significant that the source of these new threats to stability came from outside, or at least from the fringes of the region. By the late 1960s, it had become clear that the United States would be unable to sustain their military commitment to Vietnam indefinitely. They therefore embarked under President Nixon on an emergency 'nation-building' programme, designed ultimately to enable South Vietnam to develop sufficient military strength, economic resilience and political stability to defend itself. The experience of South Vietnam between 1970 and 1975 – and, indeed, of Laos and Cambodia – demonstrated, however, that 'nation-building' depended on something more than massive aid and the creation of war-generated, modern urban-enclave economies.[10] What was missing in South Vietnam – and what had been missing since its inception – was that vital but intangible ingredient of 'nationalist legitimacy'.

Wider developments than the collapse of non-communist Indochina, however, helped to destabilize the Southeast Asian region. Primary among these was the oil crisis of the mid-1970s, in which, in the aftermath of the Arab–Israeli war of 1973, the oil-producing countries of OPEC engineered a dramatic increase in the global price of oil. This had a drastic – if unintended – effect on the rapidly industrializing economies of Thailand and the Philippines in particular, and also incidentally played a major role in weakening South Vietnam in the last years of its existence. The combined impact of economic uncertainty and the withdrawal of the American commitment to Indochina contributed significantly to the destabilization of Thailand during this period. In the decade of the 1970s, the military-dominated 'national security' structure of Thailand began to break down, but was not replaced by a stable democratic alternative. Partly as a consequence, a revived communist insurgency posed a serious problem, and the separatist movement of the Malay-Muslims of Patani was given a new lease of life. Instability, therefore, hit at the very heart of mainland Southeast Asia.

The most potent general threat to the region at this time, therefore, appeared to be that of the expansion of communism into the Third World. It is tempting in retrospect, and in the light of subsequent events in the late 1980s, to play down the importance of this threat in the mid-1970s. This is to overlook what appeared to be the spectacular gains of international communism, with the establishment in the mid to late-1970s of Marxist-Leninist regimes in South Vietnam, Laos, Cambodia, Ethiopia, Angola, Portuguese Guinea, Mozambique, Afghanistan and even, briefly, in East Timor. The rhetoric coming out of Hanoi and Moscow left no room for doubt that these gains were seen as bridgeheads for further advances in the Asian and African continents.[11] Furthermore, global and regional events in the late 1970s seemed beyond any reasonable doubt to confirm, for Southeast Asian states, the aggressive intentions of international communism. In central Asia the Soviet Union intervened, first politically and then militarily, to bolster the gains of communism in Afghanistan. In Southeast Asia itself, the Vietnamese Communist Party, following its victory in 1975, moved rapidly thereafter to unify the country, embark on a forced-pace socialist programme in the South, link itself economically and militarily to the Soviet Union, and, finally, use its massive army to invade Cambodia in late 1978 in order to consolidate its ideological and political control over the whole Indochina region.

In the light of these ominous events, it is hardly surprising that the Southeast Asian countries outside Indochina reacted with vigour and unity to the immediate danger that they faced. The fact that they could no longer depend on the protection of the United States in itself stimulated a discipline of mutual reliance (largely reflected in the key role played at this time by ASEAN) and an imperative sense of reciprocal interest that helped bind the region together. This era of Southeast Asian resistance to what were seen as the twin dangers of Vietnamese power and communist penetration had some unpalatable side-effects: in particular, the Indonesian occupation of East Timor, and the bolstering of the Khmer Rouge regime on the Thai–Cambodian border. But the fact remains that the ASEAN states were able to ride out this period of turbulence with their security strengthened, their stability intact and their prosperity enhanced.

In reality, of course, the apparent 'victories' of Soviet-influenced communism in the mid- to late-1970s actually hastened the collapse of its entire international network. The rapid advances of communism in the Third World, the 'crisis of capitalism' ignited by the spectacular rise in the price of oil, and the concurrent political weakness of the United States seemed to vindicate the ambition for global victory that had driven Marxism-Leninism since its inception. But the burden of carrying forward the momentum of this 'victory determined by the Marxist laws of history' rested on an archipelago of vulnerable, desperately poor and war-torn nations, and a state – the Soviet Union – that was sunk in economic and political stagnation and did not possess the mechanisms to reform itself. The Soviet Union's attempts at this time to sustain and advance its global ideological role may not have been the primary cause of its eventual collapse in 1991, but it was an important contributory factor.

With the collapse of international communism and, thereby, the ending of the global Cold War, the question of Southeast Asia's regional security had to be redefined. For Southeast Asian states in the immediate post Cold War era, the key question was: will the end of communist and associated revolutionary threats eventually lead to the resurfacing of ethnic, religious, regional and political tensions that had effectively been submerged in the period 1945–90? In order to address this question, it is first of all necessary to assess the nature and extent of the external and internal threats that the region potentially faces.

Among the most unpredictable issues facing Southeast Asia is its relationship with China. In the late 1970s and through the 1980s, Southeast Asia was able to benefit from the global competition between the two communist super-powers of the Soviet Union and China. For reasons of geopolitical calculation, but also for ideological reasons which may now seem obscure but should never be discounted, China joined the United States and the ASEAN countries of Southeast Asia in a *de facto* alliance of mutual interest to block what were seen as Soviet and Vietnamese ambitions in the region. In the aftermath of the collapse of the Soviet Union, this alliance of interest no longer exists. Instead, the Southeast Asian nations are witnessing with varying degrees of apprehension the unshackling and the redefinition of communist China as a dynamic giant with huge economic potential and ever-increasing military strength. The Chinese Communist Party has taken on a new role as guarantor of stability and unity in this dangerous period of transition, but the guiding ideology of Marxism-Leninism has been replaced by a reassertion of Chinese nationalism pure and simple.

This new reality affects Southeast Asia in a number of ways. The withdrawal of direct European, American and Soviet involvement in the region – a process that stretched from 1945 to 1990 – has inevitably left China as the predominant regional power. Historically, China has cast the shadow of its influence and power over mainland Southeast Asia; that shadow has tended to lengthen during periods of dynastic renewal. Throughout the modern historical era, however – certainly in the nineteenth and twentieth centuries – China's influence has been restricted by civil war, political instability and, in the Maoist period, self-inflicted economic weakness. It was not until very recently that the Chinese leadership has been able to match economic recovery with growing military strength – and reach.

The new power and reach of China has potential implications for the ethnic situation in Southeast Asia. In Malaysia and Singapore in particular, the problems raised by the sheer size of the ethnic Chinese presence and the extent of its influence always underlies the politics of the region. Even in other countries – where they form a smaller or less visible proportion of the population – the Chinese play a disproportionate role in the respective economies. Up till now, the relative weakness of Communist China, and its ambiguous attitude to the Chinese capitalist diaspora, helped to maintain a barrier between the homeland and the Overseas Chinese of Southeast Asia. This barrier now no longer exists.

China's power, its traditional interest in Southeast Asia, and its inextricable ethnic links will inevitably have implications for the region. The role that China will play in the future, however, is utterly unpredictable, and will ultimately depend on the evolution of events in China itself. Whether China sustains its unity and economic dynamism, or breaks up under the stresses of political and economic change, there will almost certainly be repercussions in Southeast Asia. The future relationship between China and the Overseas Chinese in Southeast Asia is likely to be complex, not least because of the fact that the Chinese presence is spread throughout the region, rather than – with the exception of Singapore – concentrated in a defined area. It might be tempting to talk of the imminence of a new era of Pax Sinensis in Southeast Asia; it is not yet certain, however, whether 'pax' would be the appropriate term.

Returning to the threat of separatism in Southeast Asia, however, it would seem at first sight that this has been considerably reduced. Post-Cold War readjustments have enabled the Burmese armed forces to deal more effectively with Burma's separatist problems – including that of the Karens – than had hitherto been the case. Similarly, the Thai government seems to have stabilized the situation in South

Thailand, and Indonesia has silenced the recent stirrings of revolt in Aceh.[12] These and other potential regional-separatist problems – the question of the ethnic Lao in northeast Thailand, the Vietnamese in Cambodia, the Moros of the Philippines, and the non-Malay populations of Sarawak and Sabah – still lurk beneath the surface. But these tensions do not appear to threaten the integrity of existing states for the foreseeable future.

The most serious separatist threat in the region comes from a conflict that should not properly be described as a separatist issue at all. Those East Timorese who are resisting the Indonesian presence would argue that their aims are not separatist, for the simple reason that they were never legally incorporated into the Indonesian Republic. They would, rather, equate their struggle with that of the Poles against Germany in 1939, or that of the Kuwaitis against the Iraqi invasion of 1990; the East Timorese resistance sees itself as the victim of an act of international aggression, not internal suppression.

Even if we accept this interpretation – which obviously has its merits, despite the ambiguous political situation in East Timor in 1975, along with its ideological ramifications – the fact remains that the situation in East Timor has separatist *implications*. The manifest failure of Indonesia to absorb East Timor into the Indonesian Republic – in the manner, say, that India was able to absorb Portuguese Goa after a similar violation of international law – has trapped the Indonesian government in an extremely dangerous situation. Pushing ahead with the forced assimilation of the East Timorese – with all its brutal implications – is causing increasingly serious international repercussions. On the other hand, any attempt to make serious concessions to East Timorese aspirations might not only fail to satisfy the East Timorese, but might at the same time run the risk of unravelling Indonesia's position in other regions where separatist sentiments lie dormant. The same dilemma – though in a less acute fashion – faces Indonesia in West Irian, where it confronts a Papuan resistance movement.

In many ways, Indonesia's problems in East Timor underline the crucial point that the Indonesian nation was defined by the shared experience of Dutch rule. Moreover, Indonesia's attempt to annex and integrate a region that has fundamental cultural, religious and historical differences – an act that would have been a commonplace of the colonial period – presents   huge long-term difficulties in an era dominated by the ideology of the right to national self-determination.

Another threat to the stability of the region has been the resurgence of populism, this time in a religious guise. 'Populism' here means a process of mass mobilization on the basis of ideas, or one fundamental idea, designed to appeal to the prejudices of as large a section of the population as possible. Populist prejudices normally identify and isolate a common enemy, and at the same time try to transcend the different interests of the broad population it is attempting to mobilize. As such, they have the quality of an overall simplicity of appeal, an inherent 'anti-elite' bias, and, quite often, a lack of intellectual coherence. Nationalism (mass mobilization against an outside enemy), racism (mass mobilization against an internal enemy), and certain forms of socialism based on hostility to the wealthy, coupled with state patronage for the urban poor, naturally lend themselves to populist programmes. The ideologies underpinning the post-1945 nationalist movements of Southeast Asia all had a strong populist tinge, with their concentration on a common enemy, their rhetoric of mass mobilization and their vague linkage between nationalism and socialism. Sukarno's Guided Democracy regime – underpinned as it was by an almost classic populist programme – showed that populism and democracy were not necessarily the same thing; populism is, nevertheless, emphatically a phenomenon – even if in a debased form – of the era of democracy.

As has been argued above, the decade of the 1960s in Southeast Asia saw the end – or at least the severe curtailing – of the populist politics of the era of decolonization, and the reclaiming of power by political and military elites. In the 1970s, however, populist politics re-emerged in Southeast Asia in different, mainly non-nationalist, forms. In mainland Southeast Asia, new populist movements often adopted the language of a modified peasant-based Marxism; this is especially true of the rejuvenated communist parties of Burma and Thailand in the 1970s. In Malaysia and insular Southeast Asia, populist dissidence was expressed in Islamic terms. In part, this 'Islamic resurgence', as Chandra Muzzafar describes it,[13] was merely an echo of the Islamic resurgence in the Middle East, which had emerged in the wake of the manifest failure of Nasser-style Arab nationalism either to stabilize or democratize Arab politics, or to strengthen the Arab world against the West in general and Israel in particular. Mainly, however, Islamic radicalism appealed – and continues to appeal – to the urban dispossessed: not the economically, so much as the culturally and spiritually dispossessed, uprooted by economic change from their traditional rural life, and searching for new forms of affiliation in the threatening and alien world of the city.

It is important to note the interaction of these threats that have been outlined above. Normally, modern Islamic radicalism explicitly rejects an emphasis on race and nation; in Malaysia, however, non-Muslims have tended to see the Islamic resurgence as a new and more virulent expression of Malay chauvinism. Equally, the Chinese 'shadow' over Southeast Asia is not merely a matter of dealing with a powerful neighbour: it has vital implications for the future of ethnic relations within Southeast Asia itself. Finally, Indonesia's war in Timor may be seen regionally as a turbulent whirlpool in what is otherwise a lake of tranquillity, but the way that Indonesia resolves – or fails to resolve – the question of East Timor could have a serious knock-on effect for the whole region.

Southeast Asian governments, in other words, must sustain a continuous, delicate balancing act. The imperatives of stability and prosperity have to be balanced against the assertion of ethnic rights, human rights (which could be defined as rights against the state), regional rights, and religious aspirations.

The problems of maintaining this 'balancing act' can best be illustrated by examining the issue of democracy and human rights. From one point of view, the entrenching of human rights and the expanding of democratic structures can be seen as a means – maybe an essential means – of stabilizing a nation. If we understand democracy not merely as a mechanical and intermittent system of soliciting votes from the population, but more as a process of expanding the base of political participation and gradually entrenching the notion of the responsible and well-educated citizen as the essential ballast of the state, then its stabilizing role is evident. From the point of view of political stability, the real advantage of democracy lies not in its ideological foundations but in its role as a *mechanism*. For all its inherent faults, democracy is a necessary machinery for ensuring peaceful political change. The catastrophic failure of Leninism can be explained by this simple point.

On the other hand, the *dangers* of democracy are all too apparent. There is always a volatile link between democracy, populism and ethnic politics. In a democratic political structure, ethnic politics provides a perfect means of mobilizing popular support, because of its ability to tap those visceral feelings of affiliation and hatred found at the heart of rooted identities. As we can see from the case of Northern Ireland, where ethnic politics dominates the political system, the operation of democracy in such circumstances merely entrenches ethnic differences, and thereby perpetuates a kind of institutionalized instability. The same problem faces those Southeast Asian states, such as Malaysia, where ethnic politics plays a key role. As in the case of Northern Ireland, the situation is made worse in Malaysia by the link between religious and ethnic identity.

Though there are wide variations of political systems in Southeast Asia, two general strategies for the maintenance of stability can be observed.[14] The first is that of encouraging and maintaining the momentum of economic growth. This is based on the perception that, so long as all sections of society find that their standard of living is improving and believe that it will continue to improve, they will have a stake in the continuance of political stability. In countries such as Malaysia, it could be argued that ethnic stability depends on this economic strategy of encouraging rising expectations: experience has shown that a downturn, or even a faltering, in the economy leads to the heightening of ethnic tensions. On the other hand, spectacular economic progress can also have ethnic repercussions, particularly if that progress leads to ever greater disparities of wealth which seem disproportionately to benefit certain ethnic groups. This has often, for example, been a danger for the Chinese community in Indonesia.

The other major strategy for the maintenance of stability is the entrenching of what could be described as 'authoritarian democracy', 'modified democracy' or perhaps 'guaranteed democracy'. Broadly speaking, in such a system the democratic process operates, but it does not in the end control the state. In each Southeast Asian case a political or quasi-political organization – normally one that played a key role in decolonization and the forming of the independent state – acts as a final arbiter and guarantor of political stability. In the case of Indonesia – at least until very recently – this role has been openly played by the armed forces. In the case of Malaysia and Singapore, the 'guarantor' roles of UMNO and the PAP (Peoples' Action Party) respectively have been implicit. In Thailand, the 'guarantor' role of the armed forces – a role that is historically legitimized by the revolution of 1932 – has been exercised more intermittently, but would still undoubtedly come into play in a real crisis. In the case of Vietnam and Laos, of course, the guiding role of the Marxist-Leninist party in all aspects of political life forms the very basis of the regime, and is not hampered by the inconvenience of democratic structures.

If we consider the 'core' nations of Southeast Asia, and for the moment leave aside Burma and Indochina, it is possible to envisage a steady, controlled movement from a regulated to a complete democratic system, where power could be transferred between parties without disturbance to the essential structure of the state. But it is difficult to see how this process could be easy. We need only refer back to Northern Ireland to understand the difficulties of operating democracy in a country, like Malaysia, with significant ethnic divisions.

In fact, the whole political culture of Southeast Asia since the 1960s has been based on a determination not to gamble with stability. There is, paradoxically, a danger that this concern for stability will encourage sclerosis; that regulated democracy will stagnate and that the 'guarantor' institutions could transform effectively into a permanent ruling class controlling the levers of state power, using the threat of destabilization as an excuse for entrenching their position. In such a situation, the essential mechanisms of democracy would atrophy, and the avenues for political change would be blocked. Long-term stability would be sacrificed for the temptations of short-term gains.

But an intelligent appraisal of the political systems of Southeast Asia cannot begin until the immensity of the dangers facing these states is fully appreciated. In the end, Southeast Asian statecraft is driven not so much by the nostrums of social and political science, but by what might be called the 'discipline of the alternative'.

In the history of the formative years after independence, there were all too many instances in the decolonized world of tragic failures of statecraft, where elites gambled with stability. These all serve as glaring examples for Southeast Asian leaders, though the lessons they provide are varied. Lebanon in the 1970s showed how easy it was for a delicately constructed inter-communal consensus to break down, how vulnerable such a consensus could be to outside interference and how rapid could be the descent into complete anarchy – and how dreadful the consequences of that anarchy. Sri Lanka in the early 1980s showed the dangers of allowing the populist exploitation of ethnic politics to spin out of control. The succession of crises in the peripheral regions of India, and then in Hindu–Muslim relations, provided a sharp lesson on the dangers of an institutional party trying to manipulate ethnic, religious and regional differences for its own perceived short-term benefit. India's experience in Kashmir since 1947 provides a perfect example of a state overreaching itself, and then putting itself in ever greater danger by trying to cling to an inherently untenable position. More recently, Algeria has demonstrated the dangerous relationship between religion, populism and democracy.

Beyond the colonized world, the history of the Soviet Union has shown how a sclerotic political system, lacking the mechanisms for change, will in the end not only itself break down, but also involve the whole state in its ruin. As a consequence, separatist forces and ethnic aspirations that had apparently been consigned once and for all to the 'dustbin of history' have once again reasserted themselves: 'losers' have become 'winners'. The bleak recent history of Bosnia has reinforced the lesson of Lebanon. The West in general, and the English-speaking democracies in particular, have demonstrated the fatal consequences for social cohesion – what traditional Islamic historiography has called 'asabîyah'[15] – of allowing permissive and 'rights-oriented' social and educational ideas to take root; of encouraging cultural 'diversity' and, at the same time, a dogmatically-imposed free market philosophy, both of which have helped to fragment any sense of social unity; and of failing to stem the decline in traditional cultural and religious values.

Facilis descensus Averno ... [16] The manifest failures of European civilization, as well as those of the decolonized world, instruct not only the political leaders of Southeast Asia, but also an increasingly sophisticated, wealthy and well-educated civil society. The persistent tendency of the electorates of 'core' Southeast Asian countries to vote for establishment parties probably reflects not so much enthusiasm for their political programmes, but a natural bias towards stability. In a region where there have been remarkable achievements in stability and prosperity, but where that stability is built on fragile foundations, there is a general, inbuilt reluctance to take risks with the political system. If the penalty for this bias towards stability is a lack of vibrancy, a certain sterility in intellectual, political and cultural life, Southeast Asia can hardly be blamed for being prepared to pay that price.

Appendix 1

Straits Chinese Memorandum

Memorandum submitted to the British Secretary of State for the Colonies by the Penang Chinese Chamberof Commerce on 30 May 1950. (This memorandum, submitted on the occasion of the Secretary of State's visit to Penang, recapitulates the main grievances of the Straits Chinese and the Penang elite.)

1. According to Article 2 of the Atlantic Charter, it is specifically stated that no territorial changes shall be effected if they do not accord with the freely expressed wishes of the inhabitants of the territories concerned. Part of Article 3 states that the right of all peoples to choose the form of Government under which they live, shall be respected.

The Settlement of Penang was included in the Federation of Malaya in violation of the spirit of the above declarations.

2. The Penang Chinese Chamber of Commerce in conjunction with the Chinese Town Hall and the Straits Chinese British Association, representing the Chinese public opinion of the Settlement, protested against the Constitutional Proposals, particularly those relating to citizenship and unequal privileges.

A Petition dated 9.3.47 was forwarded to the Right Honourable Arthur Creech Jones, His Majesty's Secretary of State for the Colonies, praying that he would advise His Majesty to appoint a Royal Commission to make enquiries regarding provisions in the said Constitutional Proposals for Malaya and matters connected therewith.

Nothing was heard further about the matter, when we suddenly found ourselves included in the Federation as a pawn in the political chessboard, very much against our will.

In the new Constitution which came into force on the 1st. of February, 1948 it was found to have minor changes here and there but the points disputed practically remained the same as originally proposed.

3. We were asked to have patience and give the new Constitution a fair trial.

The result after the expiration of one year was a public meeting called on the 31st [*sic* – 13th] of December, 1948 of British subjects of all races to discuss the vital question of Secession of the Settlement of Penang from the Federation and by an overwhelming majority it was decided to secede on economic and political grounds.

4. Local as well as China-born Chinese want amity and [not] enmity, harmony instead of animosity and in order to avoid distrust by Malays with their insistence on the special privileges and unequal rights which have been extended to them, we feel it would be in the best interests of all if we can revert to our former status, where we can at least be on a par with all other races as envisaged in the Bill of Human Rights.

5. It is felt that, to have a unified country, there must be no racial, religious or communal discrimination.

We were put in the Federation on the basis of equal partnership and we naturally feel frustrated when the so-called equal partnership turned out to be a one-sided affair.

6. While Singapore which is out of the Federation has advanced by leaps and bounds politically, Penang has remained stagnant, tied down to a Constitution which renders us impotent even in the deciding of our own fate.

7. We have no wish to embarrass the Home Government if what has been done cannot for the present be undone, but we wish to stress that we must at least be given consideration as enumerated below:

(a) All local-born irrespective of race or creed should acquire full citizenship (*vide* Nationality in International Law) and have equal rights, freedom and privileges, the same as we enjoyed when under British rule.

(b) Every local-born whether the subject of His Majesty or of a Ruler is entitled to serve in the Government service without distinction of race, sex or religion.

(c) In high appointments there should be no discrimination, the choice should be made on merit or after competitive examination so that our very best may be selected for our administrative services.

8. The claim of the Malays that they are the sons of the soil is not in accord with historical facts.

The indigenous inhabitants of the Malay Peninsula are not the Malays but the Sakais, Jakuns and Semangs, a race of negritos said to have emigrated from Yunnan province of China, over 2,000 years ago.

Many of them still inhabit the jungle fastnesses of the country after being driven by force by the Malays from time to time. Compared for example with the Arabs who have been in Palestine, the Malays are comparatively newcomers to the Peninsula having migrated from Sumatra, Acheen and the Celebes from the 13th century onwards.

9. The next comers were the Chinese who emigrated from China in the early part of the 14th century. Then came the Portuguese who took Malacca by force of arms and then the Dutch in the 18th century.

10. Francis Light took possession of Penang on the 11th of August, 1786 which was then practically uninhabited with the exception of a few temporary fishing huts. He negotiated with the Rajah of Kedah and obtained a lease of the island in perpetuity.

From 1786 until the present day Penang and Province Wellesley have been developed by the British with the help of Chinese immigrants from Siam, Kedah and Malacca, and later on from China and also Indians from India.

11. The local-born Chinese who have been British subjects for some generations, are educated in English and bred in [the] British tradition, and have proved themselves at all times loyal subjects of His Majesty the King.

They are afraid that in the future they may be handed over to the tender mercies of non-British subjects who are already showing signs of fostering that narrow type of nationalism which invariably carries with it discrimination against those who are not of their religion or race.

12. Economically Penang has lost a good deal of her mainland trade since she was linked with the Federation.

From a financial point of view the Settlement is sound but its revenue is being sent to the Federation, and we are allotted a budget which we find inadequate for the development of this Settlement which is far in advance of the Malay States.

13. It is only natural that the merchants and traders in the Settlement do not feel satisfied with the present order of things.

14. In conclusion, we would refer to a recent editorial in the 'Economist' in which it was suggested that the Chinese should be given a position of influence commensurate with their commercial importance.

Signed   Lee Boon Jim,
          Secretary, Penang Chinese Chamber of Commerce.

Source: Colonial Office records in the Public Record Office (London), CO 717/ 204/52928/15/50.

Appendix 2

The Karen Memorial

The Humble Memorial of the Karens of Burma to His Britannic
Majesty's Secretary of State for Burma, Rangoon, 26 September 1945.

May it please Your Honour that your Memorialists, the Karens of
Burma, at this momentous time, have great cause to be very much
concerned about the future of the Karens in this transitional stage of
the much promised Constitutional Progress pledged to the Burmese
people to full Self-Government as soon as may prove possible. Our
National Identity, jealously preserved as the Karens of Burma, and our
National Virtue and National Morals, anxiously nurtured during the
long trying centuries, appear at last to be recognised, though formerly
we felt that only the baby who cried the most got the most attention.
The Karens have faithfully and loyally followed the flag they vowed to
fight for, to distant lands, and not merely as evacuees. We realise that
many of our interests have in the past been overlooked, because we
failed to make adequate representation of our needs; but now, if the
Majority could possibly merit Constitutional Progress to full Self-
Government, we the Karens of Burma do deserve a 'double claim to
British consideration'.

The Karens are known to have lived in Burma long before the
advent of the Tibeto-Burmans into Burma. The Tibeto-Burmans in
their advent pressed out the Karens southward to the Delta Areas, and
eastward to the mountainous fringes bordering on Thailand, yes, even
into Thailand and Indo-China. However much they were pressed
during these long centuries, they, unlike the Pyus, the Thet, the Kan-
yans and the Mons, did never succumb as a race to the evil influence
of their neighbours. They kept aloof as a race, jealously preserved
their National Identity, and anxiously nurtured their National Virtue
and National Morals, untarnished and unsoiled by contamination with
their neighbours. There is a story current among the Burmese themselves that when a Buddhist monk was preaching to a crowd of Shans
about the abode of Spiritual Beings called in Burmese 'Nat-Pye', an
old Shan among the crowd asked the monk whether there was any
Burmese in 'Nat-Pye'. The Spiritual Divine replied, 'Certainly, the

Burmese would be there also.' Then the old Shan murmured, 'Alack! Nat-Pye also will eventually be ruined by the Burmese.' Likewise, the Karen attitude towards Burmese, for similar reason, is such that a whole village community would rather move away than live side by side with Burmese who have immigrated into their area. In this way they keep up their National Identity, which may be taken for Clannishness. Even in the field of education, they successfully establish and smoothly maintain their own system of co-education.

Geographically and socially, there should be no reason why the Karens and the Burmese living on the same soil for so many centuries could not live harmoniously, and be united and treated as one race. Naturally, the by-stander cannot realise or appreciate the situation as those who have to suffer, and live under circumstances of great strain both mental and physical. Over a hundred years ago, before the British ever set foot in Burma, the Burmese Kings and the Burmese people literally made slaves of the Karens, and persecuted them generally. Ko Tha Byu, who later earned the epithet of 'The Apostle of Burma', was a Karen slave redeemed both body and soul by Dr. A. Judson just a century ago. The Karens, the Hill tribes, therefore, had to flee or evade the Burmese whenever possible. Under such circumstances, the Karens underwent both mental and physical torture. Then came the British, not only as a Liberator, but also as a Guardian Angel, maintaining Law and Order, and preserving Peace and giving Protection. Under such a benign Government, the Karens began to thrive, but still with great difficulty. There was no more physical torture; but the mental tortures still had to be endured. The Burmese still treated the Karens with contempt socially. They still imposed on the Karens in business. They crowded out the minority races in official posts. In every sphere of life the Burmese took the best. Such was the situation. But in 1942, no sooner was the back of the British turned, no sooner was the Liberator and the Guardian Angel taken away, than reoccurred both the mental and the physical torture in a manner unequalled in the whole history of Burma. This unfortunate, uncalled-for and unprovoked series of bloodshed and persecution has turned the clock back a century in our relationships. The Karens, therefore, have come to feel very strongly that they must strike out on a course of their own to preserve their National Ideals and develop into a progressive and useful State of Burma in the British Commonwealth of Nations.

The Karens have unreservedly rendered military aid to the British Crown and the Empire in all the crises ever since the British annexation of Lower Burma. In the early stages of the British occupation, crime, plunder and risings were very rampant in the country; and the Karens under the leadership of pioneer Missionaries helped considerably in suppressing crime and petty revolutions. Later on when the Karens were given opportunities to serve in the Burma Military Police, the Burma Sappers and Miners and the Burma Rifles, they readily responded; and from time to time helped considerably in maintaining Law and Order, and suppressing risings such as the Chin Hills rising, the Shwebo rising, the San Pe rising, the crime waves of 1925–27, and the Burma Rebellion of 1930–32, in which not only Karens of the Regular Services, but also Leaders, Elders and the Karen Irregulars played prominent parts. Again in the Great World War I, the Burma Sappers and Miners, the Burma Mechanical Transport, and the Burma Rifles, and in the Moplah rising the Burma Rifles acquitted themselves with credit. Here again in this Great World War II the Karens occupy no second place in Burma both in numbers, integrity and daring achievement. There are no less than one Lieut. Colonel, seven Majors, over twelve Captains, fifteen Lieutenants, and more than sixty VCOs of the Burma Rifles in addition to hundreds of Karens in the ranks. There are also over one hundred young Karens holding the status of British Other Ranks in the BAF, and BIC, add to this the young Karens of the Burma Army Signals and GPT, the Burma Navy and the Burma Hospital Company. These are the young men who neither hesitated nor looked back in a struggle for Freedom and Justice. Then again the world-renowned Wingate Expeditions, which paved the way for the successful re-occupation of Burma, and which consisted mainly of picked young Karens who gladly sacrificed their noble lives in the Valley of Death for their King and Country. Last but never least our Karen Levies, numbering well over ten thousand who are no fair weather friends to the Allies.

Every crisis in our history of the past century convinces us more and more strongly that the time has now come for definite and determined effort to secure due recognition of our merit and an adequate consideration of our just cause by the British, whom we have faithfully and conscientiously served and suffered for especially in this present war. May we, therefore, quote a few instances how the Karens left behind in Burma suffered at the hands of opportunists? While Burma was under the Military Administration of the Burma Independent Army (the Burmese Army under the Japanese General Minami, known in Burmese as Boh Mogyo, during the transitional stage) they branded the Karens as rebels, and persecuted and tortured them in all possible ways and in certain Districts resorted to wholesale massacre, not even leaving babies, and set the Karen villages on fire. In Myaungmya District alone, the Official Report reveals that about 400 villages were set on fire in this way, and more than 1800 Karens were slaughtered, including a Karen Judicial Minister of the British Burma Government and his whole family. Karens of the Salween Hill District, Papun, fared worse. All the leading men were slaughtered, and their wives and daughters before being massacred, were subjected to immoral degradation in the presence of their husbands and fathers. Others of our fair womenhood were forced to live in shameful submission to the BIA soldiers. Their Mission Stations were looted and set on fire. Two of their missionaries, Father Calmon and Father Loizot, were arrested, and their fate up to now is unknown. Taking advantage of the Military Administration, the Burmese did all in their craftiness to brand the Karens with a bad name, and caused them thus to be put to death. Many died the death of Christian martyrs under horrible conditions. At that time no influential Burmese Leader raised his hands and called a halt to such a senseless massacre. Were it not for the timely intervention of the Nippon Imperial Armies, we could not imagine how far the matter would have gone.

The National Policies of the Karens are all broadly based on holding high British Honour and Prestige, and to imbibe all that is finest in British Ideals. The events of this war, both at home and abroad, have made us stronger in these beliefs, and the Karens are, therefore, more determined to achieve their National Ideals; for these again affect our future security as a Nation. The pressing problem before us is to secure for ourselves a future security and safeguards in order that we may peacefully develop as a separate Individual people in our Home Land, Burma. We were given to understand that the new Bulgarian Government has liberated the Macedonians to do what they like with themselves, to form an Independent State by uniting the Macedonians in Bulgaria, Yugoslavia and Greece, and join up with Federated Yugoslavia. Likewise, the Benes Government has declared that the new Czechoslovak State will consist of the three Autonomous States: Czech, Slovak and Ruthenia with freedom for the Carpatho-Ukranians of Ruthenia to vote themselves out if they like, and join up with their blood-brother Ukranians in USSR. If such a magnanimous spirit could possibly be expressed in the Balkan States, we believe and trust that the British Government could do as much and more still for the Loyal Minorities in Her Dominions, so that they could live secure and grow up unhindered as Progressive Nations under the Guardianship of the British Government.

With the hope of realising our just and national aspiration at this momentous juncture, when Constitutional Progress is being pledged to the Burmese by His Britannic Majesty's Government, a Mass Meeting of the Liberated Karens of Burma was convened from 30th June to 5th July 1945, in Rangoon, where leading Karens from all the Karen Liberated Areas were fully represented. The past history of the Karens, since they came in contact with the British, was reviewed from one historical crisis to another, where the Karen interests were invariably ignored, when each crisis had been over. Though we were second to none in Burma in loyalty, integrity and daring achievement in this World War, yet the Karens were not invited to express their views on Burma Reconstruction activities formed in India. In our Home Land too, we Karens were almost obliterated from existence through deliberate wholesale persecution, torture and massacre, as could be clearly seen by the proof of documentary evidence in our possession, and by the systematic propaganda that was circulated against us in 1942. Taking all these facts into serious consideration and having in view our future security, and facility to develop freely and quickly in our own way, under the guiding hands of the British Government, the following well considered and well balanced Resolution was unanimously passed:

> That this Mass Meeting of the Liberated Karens of Burma considered and unanimously resolved to ask the British Government and the Conference of the United Nations of the world to
> (a) Extend the Excluded Area in Schedule II of the 1935 Act in Tenasserim Division mentioned in the last paragraph of the White Paper, to include the remainder of the Tenasserim Division and Nyaunglebin Sub-Division of Pegu District in Pegu Division, and to add to it later adjacent Karen Areas in Thailand, and designate the whole as the United Frontier Karen States to be administered by the Karens directly under a Governor.

We beg to submit that the Resolution fully supported the Act of 1935 in providing the Administration of the 'Scheduled Areas' enumerated in Part I of the Second Schedule to the Act. These Excluded Areas are in fact in the mountainous tracts of the East, North and West of Burma proper, which are inhabited by the Karens, the Shans, the Kachins and the Chins, differing in language, social customs and degrees of political development from the Burmese inhabiting the Central Areas. The Karens of the Excluded Areas in the East, together with their blood-brothers in the small protected Karenni States, fully agree to remain subject to a special Regime under the direct Authority of the Governor and a specially selected Administrative Staff of Karens (and when Karens are not available, only those selected by a Karen Advisory Board on the advice of the Governor) until our people are willing to accept some form of incorporation. The reason for a selected staff is that experience has proved that only those who understand the people can be sympathetic and could help to develop the country. We are firmly determined to avoid association with undesirable influences.

The Scheduled Areas in question are Karen Areas inhabited mainly by the Karens; and there is no reason why they should not, therefore, be given a name and christened 'The United Frontier Karen States', while there already existed the protected Karenni States. This terminology shall be applicable to Excluded Karen Areas, and not to the Shan, the Kachin and the Chin Areas. The Area of the present-day Thailand between the Salween River and Chieng-Mai, the northern capital of Thailand, is inhabited mainly by the Karens; and likewise, the Mesod Area between the Thoungyin River and Raheng Hills, and the old Prathuwun State called Kyaukkhoung. Our humble suggestion is that the Karen Areas in Thailand bordering on Burma, and the Karen Areas in Burma, i.e., Tenasserim Division and Nyaunglebin Sub-Division in Pegu Division be amalgamated under one Special Regime for uniform development socially, economically and politically.

In 1927, that is seventeen years ago, our accredited Leader Sir San Crombie Po, Kt, CBE, MD, in his book *Burma and the Karens* advocated the self-same Tenasserim Division for the Karen Country to be administered by the Karens directly under British Supervision. Mr. Donald MacKenzie Smeaton of the Bengal Civil Service, of middle 19th Century, in his book *The Loyal Karens of Burma* pleaded the same thing for the Karens even in those trying days; and in support of our humble claim, your Memorialists beg to quote Mr. Smeaton's words in giving his reason for such a Karen State:

> Why should we not try – if only as a political experiment – to give to the Karens a chance of growing as a nation in their own way? Why should we not try and bring their wild growth under cultivation, grafting on the ancient roots as time and experience improve our perception and increase our skill? We have here a people – probably under a million in all – who aspire to keep their own nationality intact. Why should we not allow them and encourage them to do so. The result may be of the highest interest in the future, and cannot fail to be fraught with great benefit to the people themselves; and it will strengthen British Rule and safeguard it in the times of trouble which may yet be in store for us in Burma.

Surely, those British Officials who have given the subject a thought, and have carefully looked into the matter, could not but be convinced of the reasonableness and potential significance of Mr Smeaton's comment.

We believe the British Government realise the necessity of developing the Hill tribes and the soil they live in; but under the present conditions, the Scheduled Areas are wholly comprised of Mountainous fringes with no out-let to the sea and the world outside. It would, therefore, be a great disadvantage, amounting to an impossibility, to develop a cramped-in little state without any modern means of inter-communication with the outside world. We, therefore, plead that the Excluded Karen Areas be extended so as to include the remaining Tenasserim Division and Nyaunglebin Sub-Division in Pegu Division with a good prospect of having a considerable import and export by sea.

Our blood-brothers, the Karens in Thailand, are more backward than we are in many ways. They are either severely left alone, or made to adopt the Thai culture, which is foreign to them. They are not encouraged to study, and do not receive the education that we have received in Burma. We therefore submit that they and the Areas they inhabit be put under the Special Regime so that we may together live secure and grow up as one united people.

The Mass Meeting referred to above unanimously resolved to send a deputation to England headed by Saw Ba U Gyi, Bar-at-Law and two others (under the Supervision of their Guardian Angel Sir San Crombie Po, Kt, CBE, MD) to support this humble Memorial in all fair and possible means, with implicit trust in 'British consideration' to which we are given to understand we have 'a double claim'.

Wherefore your Memorialists pray with all confidence, faith and hope that we cherish within us, that His Majesty's Government may be pleased to grant the above mentioned Resolution, after due delibera-tion, patient and sympathetic consideration, and facilitate the meeting of our elected delegates with His Majesty's Secretary of State for Burma.

Signed: Saw Tha Din, President of the Karen National Association
          Mahn Ba Kin, General Secretary of the Karen National
              Association
          Saw Mya Thein, ex-Member of the House of Representatives
          Saw Johnson Kan Gyi, Lecturer, Judson College
          Saw Ba U Gyi, Vice-President, Karen Social and Service
              Club
          (The Executive Members of the Karen Central Organisation)

Copy to HE the Governor, Major General H.E. Rance, Chief Civil
              Affairs Officer

Source: IOR: M/4/3023. Hugh Tinker (ed.) (1983), *Burma: The Struggle for Independence 1944-1948*, (London, HMSO) Vol. I, pp. 492-7.

Appendix 3

The Montagnard Declaration

Declaration du Haut Comité du Front Unifié de Luttede la Race Opprimée; 20 Septembre 1964.

Nos peuples Cham, Rhadé, Jarai, Churu, Raglai, Chauma, Bih, Hruê, Bahnar, Sédang, Hrê, Kabuan, Hadrung, Mnông, Stiêng, Khmer-Krom ... sont happés de force dans la comminauté [sic] expansionniste sud-vietnamienne. Une politique systématique de négocide [sic: genocide] s'est acharnée à détruire notre civilisation, notre culture, notre religion, notre nationalité et notre langue. Nos chefs religieux ont été fusillés, nos mouvements [sic: monuments] historiques et nos temples bombardés, nos écoles fermées, les éléments valides de notres jeunesse enrôlés dans l'Armée des impérialistes Sud-Vietnamiens pour servir de chair à canon dans leur guerre civile contre les communistes Viêt-congs. Ces souffrances immenses, nous les avons subies depuis 10 ans et elles ne font qu'augmenter encore l'ampleur.

L'élimination totale de notre grand race du Centre et du Sud-Viêtnam serait inévitable, si nous ne réagissions pas contre les crimes des Sud-Viêtnamiens perpétrés pour notre perte. C'est ainsi que toutes les minorités représentant de nos an[c]êtres communs, habitants originels des Pays de nos pères du Centre et du Sud, qui étaient des parties intégrandes [sic] des Royaumes du Campa et du Kamboj-bas, ont décidé de constituer un front UNIFIE DE LUTTE appelé: FRONT UNIFIE DE LUTTE DE LA RACE OPPRIMEE. Notre but est de défendre notre survie et notre patrimoine culturel, spirituel et racial, et ainsi l'Indépendance de nos Pays.

Il ne serait pas superflu de souligner à tous les Pays épris de paix, la vie très dure que nous avons menée, face aux impérialistes Sud-Viêtnamiens appuyés par les Impérialistes américains qui ne cherchent qu'à entrainer par tous les moyens les Pays du Sud-Est Asiatiques dans leur bloc de guerre, le SEATO, et ne reculent devant aucun crime, si odieux soit-il, pour atteindre leur objectif.

La liste de leurs crimes est déjà longue et bien connue du monde entier, et il n'est pas de notre intention d'en dire de plus.

Nous signalons solennellement aujourd'hui, à tous les membres des Nations Unies, les Pays membres du Comité de Décolonisation, l'existance de notre Front Unifié de Lutte, et aussi notre détermination de lutter jusqu'au bout pour sauvegarder notre Race de l'extermination par les Impérialistes Viêtnamiens et leurs patrons Américains.

Et nous avons la conviction que tous les peuples du mond épris de paix ne manqueront pas d'apporter leur aide efficace pour nous libérer du joug des Colonialistes Sud-Viêtnamiens.

Fait au Campa, le 20 Septembre 1964

Le Haut Comité du Front Unifie de Lutte de la race Opprimée

Source: Front Unifié de Lutte de la Race Opprimée (FULRO) (1965), *Historique* (Phnom-Penh), p. 18.

Map outlining the territorial claims of FULRO and
the Front de Libération des Hauts Plateaux du Champa
(original map accompanying Montagnard Declaration)

Appendix 4

Declaration of Independence of the South Moluccas:
25 April 1950

The original English-language transcript of the Proclamation broadcast by the Ambon Broadcasting Corporation.

To grant the real will, wishes and demand of the people of the South Moluccas, we hereby proclaim the independence of the South Moluccas, de facto and de jure, with the political structure of a republic, free from any political connection with the Negara Indonesia Timur and the Republic of the United States of Indonesia, on account of the fact that the Negara Indonesia Timur is unable to maintain her position as part of the United States of Indonesia, in accordance with the 'denpasar-regeling', which is still valid now and concerning to [*sic*] the resolution of the Council of South Moluccas of march eleventh 1947, while the Republic of the United States of Indonesia has acted incompatible [*sic*] with the resolutions taken at the Round Table Conference and its own constitution.

Ambon, April 25th 1950

The Government of South-Moluccas
The President, J.H. Manuhutu
The Prime Minister, A. Wairisal

Source: Dr Gunter Decker (1957), *Republik Maluku Selatan; Die Republik der Sud-Molukken* (Gottingen, Otto Schwartz and Co.), p. 111.

Appendix 5

Manifesto of the Atjeh Rebels (1953)
(selections)

In the name of ALLAH, we the people of Atjeh have made new history for we wish to set up an Islamic State here on our native soil.

We are tired of watching developments in the State of the Republic of Indonesia. And no wonder! For many years we have been hoping and yearning for a state based upon Islam, but, far from these dreams of ours being realised, it has become increasingly evident with each passing day that some Indonesian leaders are trying to steer us onto the wrong path.

We are conscious that the basic principles of the Republican State do not guarantee freedom of religion, freedom to have a religion in the real sense of the word. To put it plainly, the Islamic religion which makes the life of society complete cannot be split up. For us, the mention of the principle of Belief in One God in the Constitution of the State of the Republic of Indonesia represents nothing more than a political maneuvre. Belief in the One God is for us the very source of social life, and every single one of its directives must apply here on Indonesian soil. It is not possible for only some of these directives to apply while others do not, be this in criminal or civil affairs, in the question of religious worship, or in matters of everyday life.

If the Law of God does not apply, this means that we are deviating from Belief in the One God.

If the Constitution of the Republic of Indonesia guaranteed freedom of religion, that is to say, Islam, religious law would long have been able to operate in Atjeh, whose people are 100 per cent Muslim.

[Part excluded here, relating to some specific grievances.]

It was with bitterness that we heard the remarks of Sukarno, President of the Republic of Indonesia, calling in essence for the establishment of a State based solely on nationalism. Sukarno declared he is afraid that if the State is based upon religion, those who do not want religion to be the basis of the State will secede from it. Very well: then we shall therefore be the ones to secede from a state that is based upon nationalism. We understand the meaning of nationalism and religion. Some people may think that religious people have no sense of devotion to the Indonesian nation and motherland. Such thoughts are only possible among people who do not understand the meaning of the Islamic religion.

These feelings of bitterness and dissatisfaction have nurtured our desire to set up an Islamic State. Some people may blame us for this, but the blame should in the first place be placed on the shoulders of Sukarno himself.

Our God has said: 'Any one who does not practise the laws established by God is an infidel ...'

If we now establish a State, this does not mean that we shall be setting up a state within a state, because in our hearts and souls we have always regarded the State of the Republic of Indonesia as but a golden bridge leading to the creation of the state for which we have long been yearning. But this golden bridge no longer appears as a means of getting where we want but as an obstacle, especially since our sense of loyalty to a Republic based upon nationalism no longer exists. Yet loyalty is the very pillar of a state; and moreover our unity within the Republic of Indonesia is not bound by any universally valid law. Their State experts believe that the laws in force in the Republic should be the laws of the state itself, laws enacted according to certain processes, even though these laws may differ from the laws of our religion; but in our opinion it is the laws of Islam that should apply.

If some people maintain that the establishment of an Islamic State in Atjeh is a violation of the law and will bring chaos in its train, then our answer is that what we do is the natural result of chaotic laws or of chaos in legal affairs. Chaos which results from chaotic laws cannot be remedied unless we first correct the basic cause.

We regard action to set up an Islamic State as being better than living under chaotic laws, and if the Republican Government understands this, it will appreciate that the only way to solve the problem is by improving the basic principles of the state and its policies. The path of violence will be quite useless for we can well imagine how many victims would fall in the armed conflict. This is why we urge the Indonesian Government not to use arms in dealing with our problem. If they do, then we shall certainly resist with whatever arms we have.

Source: Herbert Feith and Lance Castles (eds) (1970), *Indonesian Political Thinking 1945–1965* (Ithaca, NY, Cornell University Press), pp. 211–13. Used by permission of the publisher.

Appendix 6

Patani Petition

To the Secretary of State for the Colonies, through the Commander in-Chief, British Forces, Malaya1 November 1945. (English version, in Barbara Whittingham-Jones Collection.)

Sir,

We the undersigned, representatives of the Malays of the State of Patani and its districts (i.e. Patani, Yala and Naradhivas) have the honour to inform you that we Malays feel happy that the Allied Nations have come to administer the state of affairs in Siam. We take this opportunity to request that the British Government may have the kindness to release our Country and ourselves from the pressure of Siam, because we all do not wish to remain any longer under the Siamese Government, our reasons being as follows:

1. The Siamese Government are oppresively [sic] cruel and unjust on the Malays without any consideration whatever, always pressing the Malays under their rule in all matters. Some of the policemen kill the Malays without investigation as to their crimes, in fact whenever they wish to kill any Malay they simply arrest him, make him walk in front of them, and having gone some distance and arriving at a certain suitable spot, shoot him dead, just the same as what was done to Pa' Da Serendah of Kampong Jenerih, Jajahan Kota Bharu Reman, Yala, which was committed by policemen at a place called Pasar Minggu, Pohon Jerai, Mukim Belukar Samak, Jajahan Bachok in Naradhivas in July, 1945. Many people have become victims in this way. Further, in connection with other crimes such as robberies and thefts are terrorizing the inhabitants, including head officers of the Government themselves who are leaders of the perpetrators.

2. If the people happen to mention in praise of the British administration the Siamese officials will be angry and have inflicted various punishments but the people have to remain silent.

3. The Siamese Government do not open Malay Schools in the Country. They force people to learn the Siamese language only, their object being to wipe off Malay Nationalism and language and also like to see the Malays remain in ignorance. When the Malays learn Siamese

which is not their mother tongue, they naturally find it difficult to be proficient, especially when they are denied of higher education facilities in their States and therefore they cannot be employed in any high post in the Government service. This is why although Siam has ruled this country (Patani) directly more than fifty years and yet there are no Malays holding any high post in Government Service.

4. In addition to the above reasons, the Government have given secret instructions to heads of departments not to engage any person who is not of the Budhist [sic] faith, in any high post, except those who have already worked a long time in Government Service, but of course there are only very few of them.

5. The Siamese are trying their best to put the Islamic religion out of existence in the State, trying to force the Malays to believe in Budhism instead. They order the Malays to pay homage to, or worship idols, and order the Malays to dress like Siamese – men to wear pants, and no matter 'Hajis' or 'Lebais' must wear helmets or European hats in place of turbans; while women must put on skirts or gowns. People failing to obey these orders are punished in many ways; they are humiliated with kicks etc., the women are subjected to have their Malay dress pulled off and are forbidden to report to any office for redress but must dress themselves as ordered.

6. Formerly there were Kadzhis to hear and decide cases in connection with Mohamedan religion in their courts, but now such cases are tried by Siamese magistrates who pass all judgements as they think fit.

7. In developing the country, the Siamese have done nothing, leaving the country overgrown with bushes and in insanitary condition having no comparison with conditions in the Malay States in Malaya.

8. It is said that according to the decisions of the San Francisco Conference, all dependent States should be given freedom and the nations or people of such States are allowed to administer their countries in the ways most suitable to them. Patani is really a Malay country, formerly ruled by Malay Rajas for generations, but has been Siam's dependency only since about fifty years ago. Now the Allied Nations ought to help the return of this country to the Malays, so that they can have it united with other Malay countries in the peninsula.

We therefore hope that the Allied Nations who are just, may help us in our desire, and release us from the hand of Siam. If the Allied Nations delay or are late to give peaceful settlement in Patani and its districts surely there will be an intense feelings [sic] of dissatisfaction and future danger to all the Malay population there.

We have the honour to be, Sir, yours obediently.

Signed: Tengku Abdulkadir Bin Raja Saiburi

Tengku Mohamed Bin Raja Saiburi
Tengku Abduljalal Bin Raja Saiburi
Wan Leh Bin Abas
Wan Ahmad Bin Wan Abdullah
Tengku Ismail Bin Tengku Ahmad
Tengku Hussin Bin Tengku Yusoff

Original version in Malay

Ada-lah kami sekelian yang bertanda tangan di-bawah ini ialah menjadi wakil bagi sekelian ra'yat2 Melayu di-dalam Negri Pattani serta jajahan-nya (i.e. Pattani, Yala dan Naradhivas) dengan hormatnya di-perma'-lomkan kehazarat Tuan bahawasa-nya kami sekelian umat Melayu sangat sukachita di-atas kedatangan Pehak Berikat pada membicharakan hal ehwal dalam Negri Siam, peluang ini kami umat Melayu Pattani sekelian berharap dengan kemurahan hati tuan mudah-mudahan tulong menyampaikan surat kami ini pada pengtahwan Kerajaan British yang maha 'adil supaya melepaskan kami serta tanah ayer kami daripada tindehan Kerajaan Siam kerana kami sekelian tidak suka dudok di-bawah perintah-nya lagi yaitu oleh sebab-nya seperti di-bawah ini:

1. Ada-lah pemerintahan Kerajaan Siam ini sangat-lah membuat dzalim di-atas umat Melayu dengan tidak ada timbang rasa dan selalu di-tindeh, di-pijak pada orang2 Melayu dalam hal serba serbi setengah daripada-nya yang buleh di-sebutkan Mata2 (Policemen) Siam selalu membunoh orang2 Melayu dengan tidak ada pereksa lagi bila sahaja ia hendak bunoh siapa2 di-tangkap dan di-suroh berjalan kehadapan-nya bila sampai separoh jalan terus di-tembak-nya seperti berlaku pada Pa'Da Serendah, Kampong Jenerih, Jajahan Kota Bharu Reman, Negri Yala, maka berlaku perbunohan ini uleh Mata2 (Policemen) ia-lah di-tempat Pasar Minggu di-Pohon Jerai, Mukim Belukar Samak, Jajahan Bachok, Negri Naradhivas pada bulan July tahun 1945, demekian-lah telah di-perbuat beberapa orang sudah. Dan lagi di-dalam perkara kejahatan seperti penyamun atau penchuri di-dalam jajahan itu yang akan memberi mudzarat pada ra'yat2 itu ia-lah datang-nya daripada ketua2 pegawai Kerajaan sendiri menjadi kepala-nya.

2. Jikalau ra'yat2 negri menyebut mereka bersetuju atas Kerajaan British atau pembesar2–nya neschaya di-marah dan di-gera macham2 jenis kelakuan kepada ra'yat2 sahingga berdiam diri masing2.

3. Kerajaan Siam tidak membenarkan membuka sekolah2 Melayu dan di-paksa belajar bahasa Siam sahaja. Maka tujuan-nya ia-lah hendak menghapuskan Bangsa dan Bahasa dan membudohkan umat2 Melayu kerana menakala di-suroh belajar bahasa Siam neschaya susah-lah mendapat pengtahwan-nya kerana bukan daripada bahasa sendiri akhir-

nya tertinggal dengan kebudohan, uleh sebab itu-lah selama lima puloh tahun (50) ia memerintah Negri Pattani tidak ada anak2 Negri Pattani yang ada berpengtahwan tinggi dan memegang jawatan Kerajaan-nya.

4. Tambahan pula dalam masa ini Kerajaan telah berpesan dengan sulit kepada ketua2 pegawai-nya tidak di-benarkan menerima orang2 tidak berugama Bhudha memegang jawatan tinggi melainkan mana yang telah bekerja dahulu beberapa orang sahaja.

5. Di-dalam Ugama Islam ialah memang berikhtiar hendak meng-hapuskan dengan daya-upaya serta bersunggoh2 hendak memasokan ugama Bhudha kepada umat2 Melayu seperti di-suroh orang2 Melayu menghormat-kan BERHALA dan memaksakan orang2 Melayu memakai pakaian sechara Siam seperti orang2 laki2 di-suroh berseluar tidak bichara Haji atau Lebai di-suroh memakai topi ganti serban dan song-kok dan orang perempuan di-suroh memakai skirt dan gown, maka siapa yang melanggar-nya di-seksa dan di-hinakan dengan berbagai2 ragam seperti di-sepat, di-terajam dengan kaki di-rabut pakaian perem-puan dan di-larang tidak di-beri apa2 perhubongan-nya kepada tiap2 pejabat melainkan hendak-lah memakai separti yang di-suroh-nya.

6. Pada masa dahulu di-adakan juga Kadzi2 buat membicharakan undang2 ugama di-Mahkamah-nya sekarang telah di-buangkan mana perkara yang bersangkut dengan ugama tidak di-pakai Kadzi lagi di-bicharakan ikut patut-nya sahaja.

7. Dalam hal membenarkan negri ia tiadak ambil bichara tiap2 tempat itu di-biarkan semak dan kotor tidak buleh hendak di-band-ingkan dengan Negri2 Melayu yang lain2.

8. Keputusan Meshuarat San Francisco kata-nya ada-lah Negri dan Bangsa masing2 itu akan di-kembalikan kepada semua bangsa memileh sendiri bagimana negri-nya patut di-perintah. Maka Negri Pattani ini ia-lah hak Melayu sejati, di-perintah uleh Raja2 Melayu dari turun temurun beberapa lama-nya, orang Siam baharu sahaja mena'lok-kan-nya yaitu lebeh kurang lima puloh tahun. Sekarang maka patut-lah Kerajaan pehak Berikat menulong-kan balik kepada Bangsa Melayu seperti sedia kala supaya buleh bersekutu dangan Negri2 Melayu Sem-ananjong ini.

Uleh yang demikian kami sekelian berharap-lah bahwa Kerajaan Pehak Berikat yang maha 'adil ini buleh menulongkan bagimana chita2 dan hajat kami supaya buleh melepas kami daripada tangan Siam. Dan jikalau sekira-nya Kerajaan Pehak Berikat lambat memberi keamanan kepada Negri Pattani dan jajahan-nya itu neschaya akan mendapat kepanasan atau mudzarat kepada sekelian ra'yat Melayu kelak.

Source: The Barbara Whittingham-Jones Collection of Manuscripts in SOAS Library, *MS 145 982*.

Notes

1 Introduction

1. In the Bible, the Greek word *ethné* is used to convey the sense of the Hebrew word *goyim*. In this use it distinguishes between the community of the faithful and those communities living outside the faith. This sense of *ethnics* as *heathens* was retained as late as the seventeenth century in England. See Robert Burton (1978), *The Anatomy of Melancholy* (London, J.M. Dent), p. 319. In Latin and Greek, *patris* or *patria* normally implied 'place of origin' or birthplace. Ovid's *patria*, for example, was not Rome, but his birthplace of Sulmo; see Ovid's *Tristia*, Book 4, elegy 10, line 3.

2. See Niccolo Machiavelli (1950), *Discourses On The First Ten Books of Titus Livius* (New York, Random House).

3. See Elie Kedourie (1974), *Nationalism* (London, Hutchinson Library).

4. Charles Darwin (1913), *The Descent of Man* (London, John Murray), especially Chapter VII; Arthur de Gobineau (1915), *Essay on the Inequality of Human Races* (London, Heinemann).

5. Both 'race' and 'ethnicity' are notoriously slippery terms. For purposes of convenience and consistency, 'race' is defined here as comprising the broader definitions such as white/black or Caucasian/Semitic/Mongolian; 'ethnicity' is used to define sub-groups within these wider definitions, such as French/German, Jew/Arab or Japanese/Chinese. While 'ethnicity' clearly comes from the Greek word *ethnos* or *ethné* (see note 1), the etymology of 'race' remains uncertain.

6. J.S. Mill (1948), *On Liberty, and Considerations of Representative Government* (Oxford, Blackwell), p. 292.

7. In this discussion, the history of the US rule in the Philippines will only be seen in marginal terms. The primary reasons for this are, first, that the American theory and policy of colonialism was markedly different from that of the European powers; secondly and more importantly, despite the fact that the Philippines is linked geographically and ethnically to insular Southeast Asia, its social and economic structures differed – and continue to differ – significantly from the rest of the region. In many senses, it resembles far more closely – in political, economic and cultural terms – the plantation economies of central America.

8. The main edict of the *can vuong* or 'royalist' rebellion in Vietnam, for example, did not refer to Vietnam's history of resistance to China in order to stimulate support for the war against the French. Rather, it used examples of dynastic loyalty from *China's* history: see Truong Buu Lam (1967), *Patterns of Vietnamese Response to Foreign Intervention 1858–1900* (New Haven, CT, Yale University, Southeast Asia Monographs), pp. 116–20.

9. Ssu-yu Teng and John K. Fairbank (eds) (1969), *China's Response to the West: A Documentary Survey 1839–1923* (New York, Atheneum), p. 267.

10. Albert Hourani (1970), *Arabic Thought in the Liberal Age 1798–1939* (London, Oxford University Press), Chapters 4, 5 and 6; Trevor Ling (1979), *Buddhism, Imperialism and War* (London, George Allen and Unwin), pp. 78–83.

11. Maurice M. Durand and Nguyen Tran Huan (1985), *An Introduction to Vietnamese Literature* (New York, Columbia University Press), pp. 109–11; J.-B. Petrus Truong Vinh Ky (1910), *Dictionnaire Franco-Annamite* (Paris, Librairie Larousse).

12. See Sutan Takdir Alisjahbana (1966), *Indonesia: Social and Cultural Revolution* (Kuala Lumpur, Oxford University Press).

13. Islamic scholars may reasonably object that Islam, as a religion based on divine principles, cannot be described as an 'ideology'. I am describing Islam as an ideological force here only in relation to its engagement in the political sphere.

14. See R.H. Bruce-Lockhart (1936), *Return to Malaya* (London, Putnam), p. 327. Bruce-Lockhart gives a personal view of the difference between the political atmosphere in Java and Malaya in the period just before the Second World War.

15. For evidence of British concern over this matter, see the memorandum written by the Political Intelligence Office of the Foreign Office on 'Japanese Pan-Asiaticism and Siberia', 16 September 1918, *Cabinet Office Papers*, CAB 24/64.

16. See Point Fourteen of President Woodrow Wilson's 'Fourteen Points', announced to the United States Senate on 8 January 1918. Oscar Theodore Buck (ed.) (1961), *America in the World* (Cleveland, OH, Meridian Books), p. 169.

17. B.N. Pandey (ed.) (1979), *The Indian Nationalist Movement 1885–1947: Select Documents* (London, Macmillan), p. 41.

18. V.I. Lenin, 'Preliminary Draft of Theses on the National and Colonial Questions', for the Second Congress of the Communist International, in V.I. Lenin (1947), *Selected Works* (Moscow, Foreign Languages Publishing House), Vol. 2, pp. 654–8.

19. I. Milton Sacks, 'Marxism in Vietnam', in Frank N. Trager (ed.) (1960), *Marxism in Southeast Asia: A Study of Four Countries* (Stanford, CA, Stanford University Press), pp. 127–32. On the weaknesses and mistakes of the Indonesian communist revolts of 1926–27, see Harry J. Benda and Ruth T. McVey (eds) (1960), *The Communist Uprisings of 1926–1927 in Indonesia; Key Documents* (Ithaca, NY, Cornell University Modern Indonesia Project), especially pp. 153–8.

20. See Alberta Joy Freidus (1977), *Sumatran Contributions to the Development of Indonesian Literature 1920–1942* (Hawaii, University Press of Hawaii).

21. Mohammad Hatta (1972), 'Indonesia Free', in *Portrait of a Patriot: Selected Writings by Mohammad Hatta* (The Hague, Mouton Publishers), pp. 277–8; R.T. McVey (ed.) (1969), *Sukarno's Nationalism, Islam and Marxism* (Ithaca, NY, Cornell University Press).

22. Joyce C. Lebra (1977), *Japanese-Trained Armies in Southeast Asia: Independence and Volunteer Forces in World War II* (London, Heinemann), Chapter 4.

23. Concerning French contacts with the Hmong people of Laos during the Second World War, see Michel Caply (1966), *Guerilla au Laos* (Paris, Presses de la Cité), Chapter 7.

24. Robert H. Taylor (1987), *The State in Burma* (London, C. Hurst and Co.), pp. 234–5; Josef Silverstein (1980), *Burmese Politics: The Dilemma of National Unity* (New Brunswick, NJ, Rutgers University Press), p. 61.

25. See British government statement of policy, cmd.6635, in Hugh Tinker (ed.) (1983), *Burma: The Struggle for Independence 1944–1948* (London, HMSO), Vol. 1, pp. 262–4.

26. J. de V. Allen, A.J. Stockwell and L.R. Wright (eds) (1981), *A Collection of Treaties and other Documents affecting the States of Malaysia 1761–1963* (London, Oceana Publications), Vol. 2, pp. 94–5.

27. See extracts from radio broadcast by Queen Wilhelmina on 6 December 1942, in H.J. Van Mook (1950), *The Stakes of Democracy in South-East Asia* (London, George Allen and Unwin), p. 181.

28. See text of the March 1946 agreement in Jean Sainteny (1967), *Histoire d'une paix manquée: Indochine 1945–1947* (Paris, Fayard), pp. 199–201.

29. Colonial Office (1949), *British Dependencies in the Far East: 1945–1949* (London, HMSO), p. 52.

30. See Chapter 4.

31. See Chapter 4.

32. See Chapter 2.

33. See Ho Chi Minh's 'Political Report read at the Second National Congress of the Viet-Nam Workers' Party', February 1951, in Bernard B. Fall (ed.) (1968), *Ho Chi Minh on Revolution: Selected Writings, 1920–1966* (New York, New American Library), pp. 188–208.

34. Clive J. Christie (1979), 'Marxism and the History of the Nationalist Movements in Laos', *Journal of Southeast Asian Studies*, 10(1): 146–58.

35. See Chapter 4.

2. Stranded by the Tide

1. The 1948 Census gave the total population of the Penang Straits Settlement as 446,222 inhabitants. Of these, 247,715 were Chinese and 57,477 were Indians. The majority of the rest were Malays (*Glasgow Herald*, 22 January 1949).

2. See Colonial Office Records *CO 717/183/1/52928/15*, 23 November 1949.

3. *CO 717/183/1/52928/15/49*, 10 February 1949, 16 February 1949.

4. Clive J. Christie (1971), *The Problem of China in British Foreign Policy 1917–1921* (Ph.D. thesis, Cambridge University), p. 259. The British commercial community in Shanghai dominated the Shanghai Municipal Council, and the British Consul-General in Shanghai also played a key role in the government of the Shanghai Treaty Port in pre-communist China.

5. Diana Ooi (1967), *A Study of the English-speaking Chinese of Penang* (MA thesis, University of Malaya), pp. 101–3.

6. Leng Hin-seak (1969), *Political Leadership in a Plural Society: Penang in the 1960s* (Ph.D. thesis, Australian National University), pp. 122–4.

7. Ooi 1967: pp. 156–8, Leng 1969: pp. 116–18.

8. John Clammer (1980), *Straits Chinese Society: Studies in the Sociology of the Baba Communities of Malaysia and Singapore* (Singapore, Singapore University Press), p. 138.

9. Ooi 1967: 71, 94.

10. For example, see Syed Abdul Vahid (ed.) (1964), *Thoughts and Reflections of Iqbal* (Lahore, Ashraf Press), and Albert Hourani (1991), *A History of the Arab Peoples* (Cambridge, MA, Harvard University Press), pp. 299–308.

11. Donald E. Smith (1965), *Religion and Politics in Burma* (Princeton, NJ, Princeton University Press), pp. 86–7.

12. M.C. Ricklefs (1990), *A History of Modern Indonesia* (London, Macmillan), p. 149 and Chapter 14.

13. *Straits Chinese Magazine*, June 1900, 4(14): 88; December 1902, 6(24): 166–7.

14. *Straits Chinese Magazine*, June 1899, 3(10): 61–7.

15. *Straits Chinese Magazine*, September 1903, 7(3): 109.

16. *Straits Chinese Magazine*, June 1898, 2(6): 35; March 1904; 8(1): 2.

17. *Straits Chinese Magazine*, March 1897, 1(1): 3–8.

18. *Straits Chinese Magazine*, December 1902, 6(24): 168–9; March 1904, 8(1): 30.

19. *Straits Chinese Magazine*, March 1901, 5(17): 36.

20. *Straits Chinese Magazine* (no date); 1(2): 72.

21. Lily Lim (1960), *The Municipal Government of Georgetown, Penang, 1946–1957* (Singapore, University of Malaya), p. 1.

22. *Straits Echo*, 16 November to 8 December 1920. It is interesting to note that a Penang Eurasian Association was formed slightly earlier, in November 1919. See Bernard Sta. Maria (1982), *My People, My Country* (Malacca).

23. Ooi 1967: 102–3.

24. Ibid.: 117–58; Yeap Joo Kim (1975), *The Patriarch* (Singapore), pp. 53–60.

25. *Malayan Chinese Review*, 16 July 1932, 1(6): 4; 3 December 1932, 1(18): 1; 17 December 1932, 1(17): 1.

26. Rupert Emerson (1964), *Malaysia: A Study in Direct and Indirect Rule* (Kuala Lumpur, University of Malaya Press), pp. 312–15; G.P. Means (1970), *Malaysian Politics* (London, University of London), pp. 32–44.

27. *Malayan Chinese Review*, 7 May 1932, 1(1) : 1; 21 May 1932, 1(2): 1.

28. *Malayan Chinese Review*, 2 July 1932, 1(5): 1; 16 July 1932, 1(6): 1; *Straits Times*, 3 May 1929, p. 8; *Hu Yew Seah Magazine*, September 1932 v(1): 15–16.

29. Speech by Tan Cheng Lock in the Legislative Council, Straits Settlements, 1 November 1926, in Tan Cheng Lock (1947), *Malayan Problems from a Chinese Point of View* (Singapore, Tannsco).

30. *Malayan Chinese Review*, 1933, 1(23): 3; *Hu Yew Seah Magazine*, January 1937, IX(1): 25–7.

31. *Malayan Chinese Review*, 22 October 1932, 1(13): 1; 19 November 1932, 1(15): 2; 14 January 1933, 1(19): 11–12.

32. *Malayan Chinese Review*, 4 June 1932, 1(3): 1; 5 November 1932, 1(14): 1.

33. Report of speech by the president of the Straits Chinese British Association (Penang) to the Committee of the Penang SCBA, 31 December 1938, Microfilm 233.1:13 in the Library of Universiti Sains Malaysia, Penang.

34. Yeap Joo Kim (1975), *The Patriarch* (Singapore), pp. 60, 87–8.

35. Felix Chia (1980), *The Babas* (Singapore, Times Books International), pp. 175–6.

36. Lim Beng Kooi (1973–4), *The Japanese occupation of Penang, 1941–1945* (BA thesis, University of Singapore), pp. 15–16. In the collection of the Library of Universiti Sains Malaysia, Penang.

37. Lim 1973–4: 20.

38. *Sunday Gazette*, 17 March 1946, p. 1.

39. Tan Cheng Lock 1947: 4–7, 8–9, 11–42.

40. T.H. Silcock and Ungku Abdul Aziz (1950), *Nationalism in Malaya* (New York, Institute of Pacific Relations), pp. 23–7.

41. A.J. Stockwell (1979), *British Policy and Malay Politics during the Malayan Union Experiment 1945–1948* (Kuala Lumpur: Malaysian Branch of the Royal Asiatic Society), pp. 25–7.

42. Colonial Office White Paper (1949), *British Dependencies in the Far East 1945–1949*, Cmd.7709 (London, HMSO), p. 52.

43. Stockwell 1979: 25.

44. Means 1970: 53–4.

45. Lim 1973–4: 48–9.

46. Penang Indian Chamber of Commerce/Penang Chinese Chamber of Commerce Petition, 16 February 1946; Secretary of Muslim Chamber of Commerce (Penang) to Colonial Office, 15 March 1946, *CO 537/1556/50823/34/10/1946*.

47. *Penang Chinese Chamber of Commerce Annual Report for 1946*, p. 2; Colonial Office to Malaya, 19 March 1946, *CO 537/1556/50823/34/10/1946*.

48. B. Simandjuntak (1969), *Malayan Federalism 1945–1963* (Kuala Lumpur, Oxford University Press), pp. 42–5.

49. Simandjuntak 1969: 42–5.

50. Colonial Office White Paper 1949: 53.

51. R.K. Vasil (1980), *Ethnic Politics in Malaya* (New Delhi, Radiant Publishers), pp. 24–6.

52. Colonial Office White Paper 1949: 53.

53. Tan Cheng Lock 1947: 163–4.

54. Ibid.: 165–6.

55. Tan Cheng Lock (20 December 1946), *Memorandum on the future of the Chinese in Malaya* (Malacca), Microfilm 240.3: 7, Library of Universiti Sains Malaysia, Penang.

56. *Penang Chinese Chamber of Commerce Annual Report for 1948*, p. 1.

57. Mohamed Noordin Sopiee (1974), *From Malayan Union to Singapore Separatism: Political Unification in the Malaysian Region 1945–1965* (Kuala Lumpur, University of Malaya), pp. 61–4.

58. Malayan Govt. to Colonial Office, 10 June 1950, *CO 717/204/4/52928/15/50*; Md. Salleh bin Mhd. Gaus (1984), *Politik Melayu Pulau Pinang 1945–1965* (Kuala Lumpur, Dewan Bahasa dan Pustaka), pp. 154–5.

59. Md. Salleh bin Mhd. Gaus 1984: 158.

60. *Penang Chinese Chamber of Commerce Annual Report for 1946*, p. 3; *Penang Chinese Chamber of Commerce Annual Report for 1947*, p. 4.

61. *Penang Chinese Chamber of Commerce Annual Report for 1947*, p. 8; Memorandum by Penang Chinese Chamber of Commerce to Colonial Office, 30 May 1950, *CO 717/204/4/52928/15/50*, see Appendix 1.

62. *Straits Times*, 26 February 1948, p. 4.

63. *Straits Times*, 16 March 1948, p. 6.

64. M.R. Stenson (1974), 'The ethnic and urban bases of communist revolt in Malaya', in J.W. Lewis (ed.), *Peasant Rebellion and Communist Revolution in Asia* (Stanford, CA, Stanford University Press), p. 150.

65. *Malay Mail*, 20 November 1948, p. 5; *Penang Gazette and Straits Chronicle*, 15 December 1948; *CO 717/204/5/52928/15/51*.

66. *Malay Mail*, 11 November 1948, pp. 1–2.

67. Mohamed Noordin Sopiee 1974: 60.

68. *Penang Chinese Chamber of Commerce Annual Report for 1948*, p. 4.

69. Ibid.

70. *Malay Mail*, 11 December 1948, p. 5; 14 December 1948, p. 5; *Times* (London) 14 December 1948: enclosure in *CO 537/3761/55400/15/1948*.

71. *Times of Malaya and Straits Echo*, 14 December 1948: enclosure in *CO 717/*

183/1/52928/15. G. Shelley, later to become a senator in independent Malaya, played the leading role for the Eurasian community of Penang. In terms of exerting political influence, the Eurasians of Malaya were disadvantaged not only by their geographical dispersal, but also by the fundamental divide between the Eurasian community in general and the Portuguese–Eurasian community of Malacca. See Sta. Maria 1982: 191–3.

72. 'Press summary', 22 January 1949, in *CO 717/183/1/52928/15*.

73. *Penang Gazette and Straits Chronicle*, 20 December 1948.

74. Secretary, Muslim Chamber of Commerce (Penang) to Colonial Office, 15 March 1946, *CO 537/1556/1946/50823/34/10*.

75. *Straits Budget*, 27 January 1949, *CO 717/183/1/52928/15*.

76. M. MacDonald to Colonial Office, 15 February 1949, *CO 717/183/1/52929/17*; *Malay Mail*, 11 February 1949, p. 5; 12 February 1949, p. 4.

77. *Financial Times*, 17 February 1949, *CO 717/183/1/52928/15*.

78. Gurney to Colonial Office, 20 October 1949; Gurney to Colonial Office, 23 November 1949, *CO 717/183/1/52928/15/49*.

79. Gurney to Colonial Office, 10 June 1950, *CO 717/204/4/52928/15/50*.

80. Gurney to Colonial Office, 23 November 1949, *CO 717/183/1/52928/15*.

81. Ibid.

82. Memorandum of Penang Chinese Chamber of Commerce to Colonial Office, 30 May 1950, *CO 717/204/4/52928/15*.

83. Gurney to Colonial Office, 23 November 1949, *CO 717/183/1/52928/15*.

84. Ibid.

85. *Penang Gazette and Straits Chronicle*, 14 December 1948, p. 2.

86. Gurney to Colonial Office, 12 January 1950, *CO 717/204/4/52928/15/50*.

87. Memorandum of the Penang Chinese Chamber of Commerce to Colonial Office, 30 May 1950, *CO 717/204/4/52928/15/50*.

88. Press reaction report, 21–2 December 1948, *CO 717/183/1/52928/15*; Gurney to Colonial Office, 15 January 1949, *CO 717/183/1/52928/15*.

89. Memorandum by D.R. Rees-Williams (Colonial Office), 20 October 1949, *CO 717/183/1/52928/15*.

90. Mhd. Salleh bin Mhd. Gaus 1984: 173.

91. *Penang Chinese Chamber of Commerce Annual Report for 1948*, p. 1.

92. Gurney to Colonial Office, 12 January 1950, *CO 717/204/4/52928/15/50*.

93. Press reaction report, 21–2 December 1948, *CO 717/183/1/52928/15*.

94. Gurney to Colonial Office, 12 January 1950, *CO 717/204/4/52928/15/50*.

95. Report of a press conference given by the Chief Secretary to the Federation of Malaya, 17 December 1948, *CO 717/183/1/52928/15*; memorandum by J.D. Higham (Colonial Office), 20 May 1950, *CO 717/204/4/52928/15/50*.

96. Report of a press conference given by the Chief Secretary to the Federation of Malaya, 17 December 1948, *CO 717/183/1/52928/15*; memorandum by J.D. Higham, 20 May 1950, *CO 717/204/4/52928/15/50*.

97. Tan Cheng Lock, *Memorandum on the future of the Chinese in Malaya*, 20 December 1946 (Malacca): USM microfilm 240.3.

98. *Malay Mail*, 7 December 1948, p. 5.

99. M. MacDonald to Colonial Office, 30 January 1949, *CO 717/183/2/52928/17*.

100. M. MacDonald to Colonial Office, 15 February 1949, *CO 717/183/2/52928/17*.

101.   *Straits Times*, 28 February 1949.

102.   Heng Pek Koon (1988); *Chinese Politics in Malaysia: A History of the Malaysian Chinese Association* (Singapore, Oxford University Press), pp. 139–40.

103.   Tan Cheng Lock, 'Memorandum on the Future of Malaya', 1 November 1943, in Tan Cheng Lock 1947: 11–42.

104.   Mohamed Noordin Sopiee 1974: 73.

105.   J.D. Higham (Colonial Office), memorandum to Secretary of State for the Colonies, 19 May 1950, *CO 717/204/4/52928/15/50*.

3. Anatomy of a Betrayal

1.   Frank Lebar, Gerald C. Hickey and John K. Musgrave (eds) (1964), *Ethnic Groups in Mainland Southeast Asia* (New Haven, CT, Human Relations Area Files), p. 58; see also Map 3.

2.   Harry Ignatius Marshall (1922), *The Karen People of Burma: A Study in Anthropology and Ethnology* (Ohio, Ohio State University Press), pp. 127–9.

3.   Hugh Tinker (ed.) (1983), *Burma: The Struggle for Independence 1944–1948* (London, HMSO), Vol. I, p. 492.

4.   Tinker 1983: I, 493.

5.   Donald M. Smeaton (1887), *The Loyal Karens of Burma* (London, Kegan, Paul, Trench and Co.), pp. 6–12, 32–5 et passim.

6.   These three Karenni statelets were called Bawlake, Kantarawadi, and Kyebogyi; each had a British 'adviser'. See H.N.C. Stevenson (1944), *The Hill Peoples of Burma* (Calcutta, Longmans, Green and Co.), Burma Pamphlets no. 6, pp. 19–20.

7.   Marshall 1922: 309.

8.   Smeaton 1887: 6–12, 32–5; Marshall 1922: 313.

9.   Andrew Selth (1986), 'Race and Resistance in Burma 1942–1945', *Modern Asian Studies*, 20(3): 483–95. Until 1937, Burma was administered by Britain as a province of British India.

10.   Ian Morrison (1947), *Grandfather Longlegs: the life and gallant death of Major Seagrim* (London, Faber and Faber), pp. 30–31.

11.   Tinker 1983: I, 493.

12.   Marshall 1922: 296–7, 300–1.

13.   Memorandum by H.N.C. Stevenson, 15 June 1946. Tinker 1983: I, 849. The census identified approximately 1,200,000 Karens in Burma, a figure that Karen nationalists subsequently condemned as a gross underestimate. See also Lebar, Hickey and Musgrave 1964: 59.

14.   Dr. San C. Po (1928), *Burma and the Karens* (London, Elliot Stock), p. 58.

15.   Smeaton 1887: 29–32, 48–53; Marshall 1922: 313.

16.   Smeaton 1887: 194.

17.   Marshall 1922: 304; Smeaton 1887: 194.

18.   Ibid.: 310.

19.   San C. Po 1928: 62.

20.   Smeaton 1887: 201–3.

21.   Ibid.: 220.

22.   Ibid.: 229–33.

23.   Ibid.: 237.

24.   J.S. Furnivall (1956), *Colonial Policy and Practice* (New York, New York University Press), p. 142.

25. E. Sarkisyanz (1965), *Buddhist Backgrounds of the Burmese Revolution* (The Hague, Martinus Nijhoff), p. 134.

26. Khun Yi (1988), *The Dobama Movement in Burma 1930–1938* (Ithaca, NY, Cornell University Press), pp. ix, 4.

27. Ibid.: 84.

28. Stevenson 1944: 24.

29. San C. Po 1928: 66; Josef Silverstein (1980), *Burmese Politics: The Dilemma of National Unity* (New Brunswick, NJ, Rutgers University Press), p. 45.

30. See Map 3.

31. Martin Smith (1991), *Burma: Insurgency and the Politics of Ethnicity* (London, Zed Books), p. 50; Silverstein 1980: 46.

32. San C. Po 1928: 67–8.

33. Ibid.: 73.

34. General Smith Dun (1980), *Memoirs of the Four-Foot Colonel* (Ithaca, NY, Cornell University, Department of Asian Studies, Southeast Asia Program Data Paper 113), p. 104.

35. San C. Po 1928: 70–2, 75–6.

36. Ibid.: 83–4.

37. Ibid.: 73–4, 77–9.

38. Ibid.: 80–3.

39. Ba Maw (1968), *Breakthrough in Burma* (New Haven, CT, Yale University Press), pp. 68–75.

40. W.Z. Yoon (1973), *Japan's Scheme for the Liberation of Burma: the role of the Minami Kikan and the 'Thirty Comrades'* (Ohio, Ohio University Papers in Southeast Asian Studies 27), p. 37.

41. Frank N. Trager (ed.) (1971), *Burma: Japanese Military Administration; Selected Documents 1941–1945* (Philadelphia, University of Pennsylvania Press), p. 16.

42. Smith Dun 1980: 25–6.

43. Morrison 1947: 183–6.

44. Ibid.: 61–72, 186–90.

45. Tinker 1983: I, 493.

46. Ba Maw 1968: 279–82.

47. Morrison 1947: 90–5; Trager 1971: 184.

48. Trager 1971: 19.

49. Ibid.: 132, 167.

50. Charles Cruickshank (1983), *SOE in the Far East* (London, Oxford University Press), p. 69.

51. Selth 1986: 496–9.

52. Morrison 1947: 44–7.

53. Ibid.: 100–55.

54. Report by HQ, 14th Army (Southeast Asia Command), 5 March 1945, in *WO 203/58*.

55. Cruickshank 1983: 186–90; Colonel T. Cromarty-Tulloch (1946), 'The Karens in the War in Burma', *Asiatic Review*, 42(151): 248–9. Subsequently, Colonel Cromarty-Tulloch became involved in the Karen guerrilla war against the independent Burmese government. See Leslie Glass (1985), *The Changing of Kings: Memories of Burma 1934–1949* (London, Peter Owen), pp. 217–19.

56. Tinker 1983: I, 13, 38.

57. Stevenson 1944: 50.

58. Sir Reginald Dorman-Smith (1945), *Some Public Utterances 1942–1945* (Rangoon, Government Printing and Stationery), p. 26.

59. Smith 1991: 60–63.

60. J.F. Cady (1958). *A History of Modern Burma* (Ithaca, NY, Cornell University Press), pp. 499–504.

61. Tinker 1983: I, 234–5.

62. Ibid.: I, 231.

63. Ibid.: I, 396, 468.

64. Smith 1991: 65–71.

65. Hugh Tinker (ed.) (1986), *Burma: The Struggle for Independence* (London, HMSO), Vol. II, pp. xiv–xv.

66. Tinker 1986: II, xviii–xix.

67. The Part 2 areas were the more developed minority areas which were included within Ministerial Burma but were areas where the Governor had a special oversight and responsibility. HMG (1947), *Burma: Report of Frontier Areas Committee of Enquiry 1947* (London, HMSO), pp. 11–12.

68. Memorandum by H.N.C. Stevenson, 15 June 1946, Tinker 1982: I, 849.

69. Tinker 1982: I, 398, 468.

70. Memorandum by H.N.C. Stevenson, 15 June 1946, Tinker 1982: I, 850.

71. 'The Humble Memorial of the Karens of Burma to His Britannic Majesty's Secretary of State for Burma', presented by the Karen Central Organization, 26 September 1945, *IOR M/4/3023/pt. 4.*

72. Tinker 1982: I, 493.

73. Ibid.: I, 496.

74. Ibid.: I, 495.

75. Ibid.: I, 617, 642.

76. Sir San C. Po to Dorman-Smith, received 19 December 1945, Tinker 1982: I, 573–4; Sir San C. Po to Dorman-Smith, 11 March 1946, Tinker 1982: I, 681–2.

77. Tinker 1982: I, 740–1.

78. Ibid.

79. Tinker 1982: I, 735–6; Tinker 1986: II, 73–4, 83, 87–8.

80. 'Observations by H.N.C. Stevenson on Karen Resolution adopted 25 April 1946', 15 June 1946, Tinker 1982: I, 849–51.

81. Dorman-Smith to Secretary of State for Burma, 31 January 1946, Tinker 1982: I, 634–8.

82. Pethwick-Lawrence to Dorman-Smith, 17 April 1946, Tinker 1982: I, 735.

83. Tinker 1986: II, 452–3.

84. Smith 1991: 72–3.

85. Tinker 1986: II, 381.

86. Ibid.: II, 405, 411.

87. Cady 1956: 554–9.

88. L.B. Walsh (Burma Office in Burma) to J.P. Gibson (Foreign and Frontier Areas Department, Burma Office), 10 December 1946, Tinker 1986: II, 184.

89. H.N.C. Stevenson to P.G.E. Nash, 15 February 1947, Tinker 1986: II, 413.

90. Tinker 1986: II, 406–7.

91. Smith 1991: 77.

92. The Karen National Union to the Prime Minister, 12 February 1947, Tinker 1986: II, 417–19; 'Resolutions of the Karen Council of Action,' 22 February 1947, Tinker 1986: II, 435.

93. Tinker 1986: II, 449–50.

94. Ibid.: II, 437–8.

95. Ibid.: II, 590.

96. Ibid.: II, 456–7.

97. H. Rance (Governor of Burma) to Secretary of State for Burma, 26 April 1947, Tinker 1986: II, 494.

98. Karen National Union press release for Reuters, 25 June 1947, Tinker 1986: II, 612.

99. For Britain's position, see memorandum by W.B.J. Ledwidge (Burma Office), 21 August 1947, for Secretary of State's visit to Burma. *IOR/M/4/3023, pt 1:* 1–206.

100. For evidence of the growing militancy of the Karen leaders, and at the same time the increasing confusion and division within that leadership over the question of the extent and power of the proposed Karen State, and the relationship between this state and the 'Karen Affairs Council', see 'Daily Intelligence Summaries', Rangoon Town Police, June 1947 to September 1947, *FO/643/66/6/51/GSO.*

101. Tinker 1986: II, 759–65.

102. House of Commons Parliamentary Debates (1947), *Hansard*, Vol. 443, First Volume of Session 1947–1948 (London, HMSO), columns 1850, 1868–1869, 1908, 1922–1923, 1942.

103. *Hansard* (1947) Vol. 443: c. 1840.

104. Ibid.: c. 1888.

105. Ibid.: c. 1852.

106. 'Daily Intelligence Summary', Rangoon Town Police, 6 June 1947, *FO 643/6/51/GSO.*

107. Smith Dun 1980: 81–5; 'Daily Intelligence Summary', Rangoon Town Police, 19 September 1947, *FO/643/6/51/GSO.*

108. Tinker 1986: II, 762.

109. U Ba U (1959), *My Burma* (New York, Taplinger), p. 200.

110. Cady 1958: 595–9.

111. Smith Dun 1980: 51–3.

112. Ibid.: 53, 59.

113. This complex tale is best told in Martin Smith's (1991) book.

114. Morrison 1947: 232.

115. Smith Dun 1980: 67.

116. Press Release, Karen Union for Reuters, 25 June 1947, Tinker 1986: II, 612.

4. Loyalism and 'Special War'

1. Georges Condominas (1965), *L'exotique est quotidien* (Paris, Plon), pp. 117–18.

2. Georges Condominas (1971), 'Vietnamiens et Montagnards du centre et sud-Vietnam', in Jean Chesneaux, Georges Boudarel et Daniel Hemery (eds), *Tradition et révolution au Vietnam* (Paris, Editions Anthropos), pp. 135–7.

3. Condominas 1965: 114.

4. Ibid. *Cac-lai* is short for *Cac-lai buon*, meaning 'all traders' in Vietnamese.

5. Nghiem-Tham (1959), 'Seeking to understand the highland people', in *Que-Hong*, no. 31, pp. 130–40.

6. G.C. Hickey (1982a), *Sons of the Mountains: Ethnohistory of the Vietnamese Central Highlands to 1954* (New Haven, Yale University Press), pp. 164–8, 178–82.

7. Joanne L. Schrock (1966), *Minority Groups in the Republic of Vietnam* (Washington, HQ, Department of the Army), Department of the Army Pamphlet no. 550-105, pp. 164-6.

8. Hickey 1982a: 197.

9. See G.C. Hickey (1988), *Kingdom of the Morning Mist: Mayrena in the Highlands of Vietnam* (Philadelphia, University of Pennsylvania Press).

10. Condominas 1965: 131.

11. Condominas 1971: 139-40.

12. Hickey 1982a: 260-78.

13. Condominas 1971: 139.

14. F.M. Savina (1924), *Histoire des Miao* (Hong Kong, Imprimerie de la Société des Missions Etrangers), pp. 237-9.

15. Schrock 1966: 311-13, 350-51, 440, 482. For a fictional description of these 'zones of dissidence' after the First World War, see André Malraux (1930), *La Voie Royale* (Paris, Bernard Grasset).

16. Condominas 1971: 140; Condominas 1965: 137; Hickey 1982a: 337-40.

17. Schrock 1966: 656-8.

18. Hickey 1982a: 296-308.

19. Ibid.: 296-308; 334-7.

20. Schrock 1966: 771-72; Hickey 1982a: 343-58.

21. Hickey 1982a: 348-58.

22. Ibid.: 330-34.

23. Ibid.: 361-71.

24. Erwan Bergot (1975), *Commandos de Choc en Indochine* (Paris, Bernard Grasset), p. 60.

25. Schrock 1966: 164-6; 'Armed Uprisings by Ethnic Minorities along the Truong Son' (1974), *Vietnam Courier*, 28: 16.

26. Charles de Gaulle (1960), *War Memoirs: Salvation 1944-1946* (London, Weidenfeld and Nicolson), p. 225.

27. G. Bodinier (ed.) (1987), *La Retour de la France en Indochine 1945-1946*, Vol. I of *La Guerre en Indochine 1945-1954* (Vincennes, Service Historique de l'Armée de Terre), pp. 171-5.

28. Amiral Thierry d'Argenlieu (1985), *Chronique d'Indochine 1945-1947* (Paris, Albin Michel), p. 412.

29. De Gaulle 1960: 226.

30. Jean Sainteny (1967), *Histoire d'une Paix Manquée* (Paris, Fayard), pp. 195-216.

31. Bodinier 1987: my translation. Note that the term *moi* was the derogatory Vietnamese word, meaning 'slave', that was often used for the Montagnards of the Central Highlands.

32. Ho Chi Minh (1961), *Selected Works*, Vol. III (Hanoi, Foreign Languages Publishing House), pp. 62-3.

33. D'Argenlieu 1985: 298-9.

34. Ibid.: 298.

35. Front de Libération des Hauts Plateaux de Champa (1965), *Historique* (Phnom-Penh), p. 18; O'Sullivan (Hanoi) to Department of State, 20 May 1946, Paul Kesaris (ed.), *Confidential US State Department Central Files: Indochina, internal affairs 1945-1949* (Microfilm Project of University Publications of America), Microtext 4994.

36. Jacques Dalloz (1990), *The War in Indochina 1945–1954* (Maryland, Barnes and Noble), p. 73.

37. Hickey 1982a: 394–6; O'Sullivan (Hanoi) to Department of State, 27 June 1946, *Confidential US State Department Central Files: Indochina, internal affairs 1945–1954*: Microtext 4994.

38. J.T. McAlister (1967), 'Mountain minorities and the Viet-Minh: a key to the Indochina war', in Peter Kunstadter (ed.), *Southeast Asian Tribes, Minorities and Nations* (Princeton, NJ, Princeton University Press), Vol. II, pp. 804–9.

39. Hickey 1982a: 398–400.

40. Ibid.: 400–6.

41. Ibid.: 406.

42. Ibid.: 410.

43. Letter from Bao Dai to the High Commissioner of France in Indochina in 1951, in *Projet de plan d'équipment des territoires des 'Populations Montagnards de Sud' (PMS)*, p. 1: from collection of papers on the Central Highlands in the possession of G.McT. Kahin.

44. Norman Lewis (1957), *A Dragon Apparent* (London, Pan Books), pp. 120–6, 142–3.

45. Hickey 1982a: 407–9.

46. René Riesen (1957), *Jungle Mission* (London, Hutchinson), pp. 21–4; Bergot 1975: 200–5.

47. Bergot 1975: 217.

48. McAlister 1967: 816–20, 822–4.

49. Geoffrey C. Gunn (1987), 'Minority manipulation in colonial Indochina: lessons and legacies', *Bulletin of Concerned Asian Scholars*, 19(3): 27–8.

50. Vo Nguyen Giap (1965), *People's War, People's Army* (New York, Praeger), pp. 200–3.

51. *Times* (London), 30 June 1954.

52. *Manchester Guardian*, 30 June 1954.

53. Schrock 1966: 699–700.

54. Georges Condominas (1977), *We Have Eaten the Forest: The Story of a Montagnard Village in the Central Highlands of Vietnam* (London, Allen Lane), pp. xiii–xiv.

55. G.C. Hickey (1970), *Accommodation and Coalition in South Vietnam* (Santa Monica, Rand Corporation), pp. 23–4.

56. G.C. Hickey (1982b), *Free in the Forest: Ethnohistory of the Vietnamese Central Highlands 1954–1976* (New Haven, CT, Yale University Press), pp. 1–46.

57. Lewis 1957: 127–30; Hickey 1982a: 310.

58. Letter from Bao Dai to the Mission for United States Aid (Saigon) in 1951: from collection of papers on the Central Highlands in the possession of G.McT. Kahin.

59. J. Buttinger (1961), 'The ethnic minorities in the Republic of Vietnam', in Wesley L. Fishel (ed.), *Problems of Freedom: South Vietnam since Independence* (Chicago, Free Press of Glencoe), p. 109.

60. See, for example, a novel about the Montagnards at this time, written by Smith Hempstone (1966), entitled *A Tract of Time* (Boston, MA, Houghton Mifflin).

61. Bernard B. Fall (1966), *Vietnam Witness 1953–1966* (London, Pall Mall Press), pp. 191–3; Douglas Pike (1968), *Viet-Cong: The Organization and Techniques of the National Liberation Front of South Vietnam* (Cambridge, MA, MIT Press), p. 14.

62. Jacques Nepote (1993), 'Champa: propositions pour une histoire de temps long', in *Péninsule: Etudes interdisciplinaires sur l'Asie du Sud-Est péninsulaire*, xxive Année 2 (27): 115; Directorate of Intelligence, CIA, 'The situation in South Vietnam, 17–23 September 1964', in Paul Kesaris (ed.), *CIA Research Reports: Vietnam and Southeast Asia 1946–1976* (Microfilm Project of the University Publications of America, Microtext 4979).

63. Front de Libération des Hauts Plateaux de Champa (1965), *Historique* (Phnom-Penh), p. 15.

64. Gary D. Wekkin (1974), 'Tribal politics in Indochina: the role of highland tribes in the internationalization of internal wars', in Mark W. Zacher and R. Stephen-Milne (eds), *Conflict and Stability in Southeast Asia* (New York, Anchor Books), pp. 134, 144; 'Armed uprisings by ethnic minorities along the Truong Son (cont.)' (1974), *Vietnam Courier*, 29: 18–20.

65. Condominas 1971: 145; *Vietnam Courier* (1974), 28: 18

66. Neil Sheehan et al. (eds) (1971), *The Pentagon Papers as published by the New York Times* (New York, Bantam Books), pp. 120–1.

67. US Embassy (Saigon) to Department of State, 11 October 1961, in George C. Herring (ed.), *John F. Kennedy National Security Files: Vietnam, National Security Files 1961–1963* (microfilmed from holdings of the John F. Kennedy Library, Boston, MA, by Microfilm Project of University Publications of America, Microtext 5140).

68. *Foreign Relations of the United States (FRUS) 1964–1968* Vol. I: *Vietnam 1964* (1992), (Washington, US Govt. Printing Office), p. 786; US Embassy (Saigon) to Department of State, 7 November 1963, *John F. Kennedy National Security Files: Vietnam, National Security Files 1961–1963*: Microtext 5144.

69. *FRUS 1964–1968*, Vol. I: *Vietnam 1964* (1992): 503, 786.

70. Front de Libération des Hauts Plateaux de Campa (1965), *Historique* (Phnom-Penh), p. 19.

71. Hickey 1970: 24–5.

72. Hickey 1982b: 82–9.

73. *FRUS 1964–1968*, Vol. I: *Vietnam 1964* (1992): 786.

74. Ibid.: 785, 808–9.

75. Military Assistance Command Vietnam (MACV) to Commander-in-Chief Pacific (CINCPAC), 20 September 1964 (13.41 p.m.), in George C. Herring (ed.), *Lyndon B. Johnson National Security Files: Vietnam, National Security Files, November 1963 to June 1965* (Microfilmed from the holdings of the L.B. Johnson Library, Austin, Texas, by the Microfilm Project of the University Publications of America, Microtext 4965).

76. CIA Intelligence Information Cable, 20 September 1964, *CIA Research Reports: Vietnam and Southeast Asia 1946–1976*: Microtext 4979.

77. MACV to CINCPAC, 22 September 1964 (17.27 p.m.), *Lyndon B. Johnson National Security Files: Vietnam, National Security Files, November 1963 to June 1965*: Microtext 4965.

78. [Our aim is to defend our survival and our cultural, spiritual and racial patrimony, and thus the independence of our lands.] Front Unifié de Lutte de la Race Opprimée (FULRO) (1965), *Historique* (Phnom-Penh), p. 18.

79. FULRO (1965), *Historique* , p. 18.

80. Hickey 1982b: 90–8.

81. MACV to CINCPAC, 20 September 1964 (20.25 p.m.), *Lyndon B. Johnson National Security Files: Vietnam, National Security Files, November 1963 to June 1965*: Microtext 4965.

82. US Ambassador (Saigon) to US Secretary of State, 22 September 1964 and 23 September 1964, *Lyndon B. Johnson National Security Files: Vietnam, National Security Files, November 1963 to June 1965*: Microtext 4965.

83. US Ambassador (Saigon) to US Secretary of State, 2 October 1964, *Lyndon B. Johnson National Security Files: Vietnam, National Security Files, November 1963 to June 1965*: Microtext 4965; Directorate of Intelligence (CIA), 'The situation in South Vietnam 24–30 September 1964', *CIA Research Reports: Vietnam and Southeast Asia 1946–1976*: Microtext 4979.

84. Hickey 1982b: 109–13.

85. US Ambassador (Saigon) to US Secretary of State, 19 October 1964, *Lyndon B. Johnson National Security Files: Vietnam, National Security Files, November 1963 to June 1965*: Microtext 4966.

86. MACV to CINCPAC, 22 September 1964 (17.27 p.m.), *Lyndon B. Johnson National Security Files: Vietnam, National Security Files, November 1963 to June 1965*: Microtext 4965.

87. US Ambassador (Saigon) to US Secretary of State, 25 September 1964, *Lyndon B. Johnson National Security Files: Vietnam, National Security Files, November 1963 to June 1965*: Microtext 4965.

88. *FRUS 1964–1968*, Vol. I: *Vietnam 1964*: p. 1006; Special National Security Estimate (53–2–64), 'The situation in South Vietnam', submitted by Director of Central Intelligence, 1 October 1964, *CIA Research Reports: Vietnam and Southeast Asia 1946–1976*: Microtext 4989.

89. CIA Information Intelligence Cable from South Vietnam, 20 July 1967, in R.F. Lester (ed.), *CIA Research Reports: Vietnam and Southeast Asia, Supplements* (Microfilm Project of University Publications of America), Microtext 4986.

90. Hickey 1970: 26–7.

91. Front de Libération des Hautes Plateaux de Champa (1965), *Historique* (Phnom-Penh), pp. 16–17.

92. Jeffery J. Clarke (1988), *Advice and Support* (Washington, Center of Military History, United States Army), p. 73.

93. Schrock 1966: 95.

94. Hickey 1982b: xviii–xxi.

95. Grant Evans and Kelvin Rowley (1984), *Red Brotherhood at War: Indochina since the Fall of Saigon* (London, Verso), pp. 277–8.

96. Evans and Rowley 1984: 278.

5. Defining 'Self-Determination'

1. Frank L. Cooley (1962), *Ambonese Adat: A General Description* (New Haven, CT, Yale University Press), pp. 85–6; Paramita P. Abdurachman (1981), *New Winds, New Faces, New Forces* (Jakarta, Lembaga Research Kebudayaan Nasional, LIPI), p. 18.

2. Frank M. Lebar (ed.) (1972), *Ethnic Groups in Insular Southeast Asia* (New Haven, Human Relations Area Files), Vol. I, p. 116.

3. Lebar 1972: 118.

4. Richard Chauvel (1985a), 'Ambon: not a revolution but a counter-revolution', in Audrey R. Kahin (ed.), *Regional Dynamics of the Indonesian Revolution* (Honolulu, University of Hawaii Press), p. 239.

5. Chauvel 1985a: 239.

6. Ben Van Kaam (1980), *The South Moluccans: Background to the Train Hijackings* (London, C. Hurst), pp. 5–12.

7. Alfred Russel Wallace (1906), *The Malay Archipelago* (London, Macmillan), p. 230.

8. M.C. Ricklefs (1990), *A History of Modern Indonesia* (London, Macmillan), p. 106.

9. Cooley 1962: 87.

10. I.O. Nanulaitta (1966), *Timbulnja Militerisme Ambon* (Djakarta, Bhratara), p. 112.

11. Nanulaitta 1966: 114.

12. Nanulaitta 1966: 113; Robert Cribb (1992), *Historical Dictionary of Indonesia* (Metuchen, NJ, Scarecrow Press), p. 393.

13. Chauvel 1985a: 240–41.

14. R.Z. Leirissa (1991), 'Notes on central Maluku in the nineteenth century', *Prisma: The Indonesian Indicator*, no. 22, p. 64.

15. Cribb 1992: 200.

16. See Peter B.R. Carey (1981), *Babad Dipanagara: An Account of the Outbreak of the Java War 1825–1830* (Kuala Lumpur, Malaysian Branch of the Royal Asiatic Society Monograph); Sartono Kartodirjo (1966), *The Peasants' Revolt of Banten in 1888* (S'Gravenhage, Martinus Nijhoff).

17. J.A. Manusama (1960), 'Political aspects of the struggle for independence', in J.C. Bouman et al., *The South Moluccas: Rebellious Province or Occupied State* (Leiden, A.W. Sythoff), pp. 52–5.

18. Herbert Feith and Lance Castles (eds) (1970), *Indonesian Political Thinking 1945–1965* (Ithaca, NY, Cornell University Press), pp. 1–2.

19. Kaam 1980: 26–42.

20. Richard Chauvel (1985b), *The Rising Sun in the Spice Islands: A History of Ambon during the Japanese Occupation* (Clayton, Australia, Centre for Southeast Asian Studies, Monash University), p. 3.

21. Department of Education and Culture (1975–76), *Sejarah Daerah Maluku* (Jakarta, Pusat Penelitian Sejarah dan Budaya), p. 78; Chauvel 1985a: 242.

22. Kaam 1980: 43–53.

23. Dept. of Education and Culture 1975–76: 79.

24. Ibid.: 86.

25. Chauvel 1985b: 6–12, 15–21.

26. Chauvel 1985b: 31–2.

27. Kaam 1980: 53–9.

28. Ibid.: 244–5.

29. H.J. van Mook (1950), *The Stakes of Democracy in Southeast Asia* (London, George Allen and Unwin), p. 219.

30. Mook 1950: 180–81.

31. Ibid.: 212–13.

32. J.J.P. de Jong (1986), 'Winds of Change: Van Mook, Dutch policy and the realities of November 1945', in J. van Goor (ed.), *The Indonesian Revolution: Papers of the Conference held in Utrecht 17–20 June 1986* (Utrecht, Rijksuniversiteit Utrecht), pp. 166–7.

33. Chauvel 1985a: 245.

34. Mook 1950: 219–20.

35. Gunter Decker (1957), *Republik Maluku Selatan: Die Republik der Sud-Molukken* (Gottingen, Verlag Otto Schwartz), p. 113. Emphasis added.

246 NOTES TO CHAPTER 5

36. Chauvel 1985a: 248–9.
37. J. Prins (1960), 'Location, history, forgotten struggle', in J.C. Bouman et al., *The South Moluccas: Rebellious Province or Occupied State* (Leiden, A.W. Sythoff), pp. 25–7.
38. Chauvel 1985a: 249.
39. Mook 1950: 243, 257.
40. Ibid.: 255.
41. Ibid.: 259.
42. Cribb 1992: 402–4.
43. Decker 1957: 121, 124.
44. Kaam 1980: 73–7.
45. Prins 1960: 32.
46. Chauvel 1985a: 238.
47. Ibid.: 255–7.
48. Prins 1960: 35–7.
49. J.A. Manusama (nd), *De Strijd om de onafhankelijkheid der Zuid-Molukken* (Utrecht, Drukkerij Libertas), pp. 14, 54.
50. H.J. de Graaf (1977), *De Geschiedenis van Ambon en der Zuid-Molukken* (Franeker, Uitgeverij T. Wever), p. 281.
51. Chauvel 1985a: 259.
52. Prins 1960: 37–41.
53. Ibid.: 41–2.
54. Kaam 1980: 135–43.
55. Feith and Castles 1970: 170–1. Ben Anderson makes essentially the same point, but broadens his perspective in order to look at the less tangible areas of literature and culture; see B.R.O'G Anderson (1983), *Imagined Communities: reflections on the origin and spread of nationalism* (London, Verso).
56. Manusama 1960: 52–7.
57. Ibid.: 57–8.
58. Ibid.: 58–9.
59. Anthony Reid (1986), 'The revolution in regional perspective', in J. van Goor (ed.), *The Indonesian Revolution: Papers of the Conference held in Utrecht 17–20 June 1986* (Utrecht, Rijksuniversiteit Utrecht), pp. 183–99.
60. Dept. of Education and Culture 1975–76: 87.
61. Decker 1957: 140–41.
62. Manusama 1960: 60.
63. Dusan J. Djonovich (ed.) (1974), *United Nations Resolutions Series I: Resolutions adopted by the General Assembly* (New York, Oceana Publications), Vol. VIII (1960–62), p. 21.
64. H.J. Kruls (1960), 'The strategic importance in the world picture of past and future', in J.C. Bouman et al., *The South Moluccas: Rebellious Province or Occupied State* (Leiden, A.W. Sythoff), p. 131; see also Map 5.
65. Ricklefs 1990: 242, 250.
66. Cribb 1992: 137–40.

6. Islam, Ethnicity and Separatism in Southeast Asia

1. The extent and force of this Islamic revival will be shown in Chapter 7.
2. Although the majority of the Karens were Buddhist or animist, a vital leader-

ship role was, of course, played by the Christian Karens.

3. See glossary of terms at the end of this chapter.

4. 'Surely this is your nation (*umma*), one nation, and I am your Lord, so worship me.' The Al-Azhar approved edition of *The Bounteous Koran*, translated by M.M. Khatib (1986) (London, Macmillan), Surah 21: verse 92.

5. A distinction should be drawn here between an *Islamic* state as an ideal, and a *Muslim* state, where Muslims are in a majority, and where Islamic principles are important in the government and laws of the state, but where, for one reason or another, Islamic law does not absolutely dominate the political and social system.

6. Ali Shari'ati (1979), *On the Sociology of Islam* (Berkeley, CA, Mizan Press), p. 33.

7. Majid Khadduri (1955), *War and Peace in the Law of Islam* (Baltimore, MD, Johns Hopkins University Press), p. 141.

8. See, for example, the Qur'an, Surah 4: verses 97–101, and Surah 9: verse 20.

9. H.A.R. Gibb and J.H. Kramers (eds) (1961), *The Shorter Encyclopedia of Islam* (Leiden, E.J. Brill), p. 69.

10. See the Qur'an, Surah 25: verse 52.

11. See the Qur'an, Surah 9: verse 12.

12. Muhammad Ali (1983), *A Manual of Hadith* (London, Curzon Press), pp. 258–60.

13. Majid Khadduri 1955: 156, 173.

14. See translated documents in Truong Buu Lam (1967), *Patterns of Vietnamese Response to Foreign Intervention 1858–1900* (New Haven, CT, Yale University Monograph Series 11).

15. See the Qur'an, Surah 65: verse 7.

16. See the Qur'an, Surahs 65 and 66.

17. Ibrahim Alfian (1987), *Perang di Jalan Allah: Perang Aceh 1873–1912* (Jakarta, Pustaka Sinar Harapan), p. 235; E.W. Lane defines *taslim* as 'the abstaining from offering opposition in the case in which it is not becoming (to do so)'. See E.W. Lane (1967), *An Arabic–English Lexicon* (London, Williams and Norgate), p. 1413.

18. C. Snouck Hurgronje (1936), *Mekka in the Latter Part of the Nineteenth Century 1888–1889* (Amsterdam, Elsevier), p. 208.

19. Ibid.: 266. Concerning *taqlid*, see T.P. Hughes (nd), *A Dictionary of Islam* (London, Luzac), p. 628.

20. The Qur'an, Surah 60: verse 8; Muhammad Ali 1973: 253.

21. Majid Khadduri 1955: 157.

22. Albert Hourani (1970), *Arabic Thought in the Liberal Age 1798–1939* (London, Oxford University Press), Chapter 7.

23. W. Montgomery Watt (1968), *Islamic Political Thought: The Basic Concepts* (Edinburgh, Edinburgh University Press), pp. 130–34.

24. See St. Augustine (1972), *The City of God* (London, Penguin Books), particularly Book IV, where Augustine extols the benefits of a world composed of 'small kingdoms'.

25. Howard M. Federspiel (1970), *Persatuan Islam: Islamic Reform in Twentieth Century Indonesia* (Ithaca, NY, Cornell University Modern Southeast Asia Program), pp. 84–8.

26. See Ruth T. McVey (ed.) (1969), *Sukarno's Nationalism, Islam and Marxism* (Ithaca, NY, Cornell University Modern Southeast Asia Program).

7. Nationalism and the 'House of Islam'

1. See Denys Lombard (1967), *Le Sultanat d'Atjeh au temps d'Iskandar Muda 1607–1636* (Paris, Ecole française d'Extrême-Orient).

2. Richard V. Weekes (ed.) (1984), *Muslim Peoples: A World Ethnographic Survey* (Westport, Connecticut, Greenwood Press), Vol. I, p. 5; Mark Durie (1985), *A Grammar of Acehnese, on the basis of a dialect of North Aceh* (Dordrecht, Foris Publications), p. 3.

3. Examples of the kind of Acehnese-language publications available include collections of Acehnese *panton* (quatrains) and epics telling the stories of Acehnese heroes.

4. Amir Husin, Helmy Ali and Roger Burr (1986), *Aceh* (Banda Aceh, Tourism Office, Special Province of Aceh), p. 7.

5. Ali Hasjmy (ed.) (1983), *Kebudayaan Aceh dalam Sejarah* (Jakarta, Penerbit Beuna), pp. 98–9.

6. Ibid.: 195–204.

7. A. Popovic and G. Veinstein (1985), *Les Ordres Mystiques dans l'Islam: cheminements et situation actuelle* (Paris, Editions de l'Ecole des Hautes Etudes en Sciences Sociales), pp. 141, 144; W. Stöhr and P. Zoetmulder (1968), *Les Religions d'Indonésie* (Paris, Payot), pp. 335–7.

8. Syed Muhammad Naguib al-Attas (1970), *The Mysticism of Hamzah Fansuri* (Kuala Lumpur, University of Malaya Press), p. xvi.

9. Weekes 1984: 4, 8.

10. Anthony Reid (1969), *The Contest for North Sumatra: Atjeh, the Netherlands and Britain: 1858–1898* (Kuala Lumpur, University of Malaya), pp. 17–24, 25–30, 30–5.

11. James T. Siegel, (1969), *The Rope of God* (Berkeley, CA, University of California Press), p. 41.

12. Siegel 1969: 5.

13. Reid 1969: 91–7, 156–74.

14. Pusat Dokumentasi dan Informasi Aceh (1977), *Perang Kolonial Belanda di Aceh* (Banda Aceh), pp. 30–4.

15. Pusat Dokumentasi 1977: 33–4.

16. C. Snouck Hurgronje (1906), *The Acehenese* (Leiden, E.J. Brill), Vol. I, pp. 120–153; *ulema* is the Acehnese-language version of the Arabic *ulama*, or religious scholar.

17. Reid 1969: 201–7; Snouck Hurgronje 1906: 165–78.

18. Pusat Dokumentasi 1977: 45–8.

19. Ibrahim Alfian (1987), *Perang di Jalan Allah: Perang Aceh 1873–1912* (Jakarta, Pustaka Sinar Harapan), pp. 197–8, 233–4; M.H. Du Croo (1943), *Marechausée in Atjeh* (Maastricht, N.V. Leiter-Nypels), pp. 134–6.

20. From *Perang fi Sabilillah*, 'war in the cause/path of God'.

21. Ozay Mehmet (1990), *Islamic Identity and Development: Studies of the Islamic Periphery* (New York, Routledge), p. 27.

22. Ibrahim Alfian 1987: 231; Ali Hasjmy 1983: 410–16.

23. Ibrahim Alfian 1987: 268–9; Ali Hasjmy (ed.) (1971), *Hikayat Perang Sabi Mendjiwai Perang Atjeh lawan Belanda* (Banda Aceh, Pustaka Faraby), p. 70 ff.

24 Ibrahim Alfian 1987: 200–5.

25. Eric Morris (1985), 'Social Revolution and the Islamic Vision', in Audrey R.

Kahin (ed.), *Regional Dynamics of the Indonesian Revolution: Unity from Diversity* (Honolulu, University of Hawaii Press), p. 85.

26. Anthony Reid (1979), *The Blood of the People: Revolution and the End of Traditional Rule in Sumatra* (London, Oxford University Press), pp. 9–10.

27. Eric Eugene Morris (1983), *Islam and Politics in Aceh: A Study of Centre-Periphery Relations in Indonesia* (Ph.D. thesis, Cornell University, Ithaca, NY), pp. 70, 72.

28. T. Tjoet Ahmad (ed.) (1968), *95 Tahun Tantangan Ultimatum Keradjaan Belanda Terhadap Keradjaan Atjeh* (Medan, Seksi Publikasi/Dokumentasi Panitia Peringatan Pahlawan Nasional Dari Atjeh, Medan dan Sekitarnja), p. 69.

29. See Anas Machmud (1988), *Kedaulatan Aceh yang tidak pernah diserahkan kepada Belanda adalah bahagian dari Kedaulatan Indonesia* (Jakarta, Bulan Bintang), pp. 39–42.

30. Mahmud Junus (1960), *Sedjarah Pendidikan Islam di Indonesia* (Jakarta, Pustaka Mahmudiah), pp. 154–6.

31. Alfian (1985), 'The Ulama in Acehnese society', in Ahmad Ibrahim, Sharon Siddique and Yasmin Hussain (eds), *Readings on Islam in Southeast Asia* (Singapore, ISEAS), p. 84; Ali Hasjmy (1976a), *Peranan Islam dalam Perang Aceh dan Perjuangan Kemerdekaan Indonesia* (Jakarta, Bulan Bintang), p. 67; Pusat Dokumentasi 1977: 54.

32. Morris 1983: 88.

33. Siegel 1969: 56.

34. Ali Hasjmy 1976a: 12, 58.

35. Reid 1979: 28.

36. Ibid.: 25.

37. Ibid.: 30.

38. Ali Hasjmy (1978), *Bunga Rampai Revolusi dari Tanah Aceh* (Jakarta, Bulan Bintang), pp. 33, 36, 38; Morris 1983: 99.

39. C. van Dijk (1981), *Rebellion under the Banner of Islam: The Darul Islam in Indonesia* (The Hague, Matinus Nijhoff), pp. 270–3.

40. Reid 1979: 94–5.

41. Ibid.: 124–6.

42. Nazaruddin Sjamsuddin (1985), *The Republican Revolt: A study of the Acehnese Rebellion* (Singapore, ISEAS:), pp. 15–23.

43. Mohammed Ansori Nawawi (1968), *Regionalism and Regional Conflicts in Indonesia* (Ph.D. thesis, Princeton University, Princeton, NJ), p. 332.

44. Morris 1983: 118.

45. Reid 1979: 176–7.

46. See Ali Hasjmy 1976a: 71–2; Nur el-Ibrahim (1982), *Teungku Muhammad Daud Beureueh: Peranannya dalam Pergolak di Aceh* (Jakarta, Gunung Agung). In the latter work, the text of this declaration is printed, but without the statement 'bahwa perjuangan ini adalah perjuangan suci yang disebut Perang Sabil'.

47. Nazaruddin Sjamsuddin 1985: 24–6.

48. Dijk 1981: 273–84.

49. Mohammed Ansori Nawawi 1968: 314.

50. Nazaruddin Sjamsuddin 1985: 27.

51. Dijk 1981: 285–8.

52. A. Hasjmy (1976b), *Surat-Surat dari Penjara* (Jakarta, Bulan Bintang), p. 71.

53. M. Nur el-Ibrahimy 1982: Document 4, p. 245.

54. Morris 1985: p. 100.

55. Morris 1983: 160–61. One of these 'impure' practices was saint veneration, or *ziyarah*.

56. M. Nur el-Ibrahimy 1982: Document 15, pp. 266–8.

57. Nazaruddin Sjamsuddin 1985: 34–40.

58. Dijk 1981: 288–92; M. Nur el-Ibrahimy 1982: Documents 8 and 9, pp. 254–5, 256–7.

59. Ali Hasjmy 1976b: 71.

60. Mohammed Ansori Nawawi 1968: 317–18.

61. Nazaruddin Sjamsuddin 1985: 47–63.

62. See Ariffin bin S.M. Omar (1979), *The Masjumi and its Struggle for the Islamic State* (MA thesis, University of Singapore).

63. C.A.O. van Nieuwenhuijze (1958), *Aspects of Islam in Post-Colonial Indonesia* (The Hague, Van Hoeve:), pp. 169–70.

64. Dijk 1981: 92–3.

65. M. Nur el-Ibrahimy 1982: Document 11, p. 259.

66. Mohammed Ansori Nawawi 1968: 320–1; see proclamation in M. Nur el-Ibrahimy 1982: 1; *Darul Islam* is the Indonesianized rendering of *Daru'l -Islam*.

67. Letter from Hasan Muhammad Tiro to Prime Minister Ali Sastroamidjojo, 1 September 1954, in M. Nur el-Ibrahimy 1982: 14.

68. Herbert Feith and Lance Castles (eds) (1970), *Indonesian Political Thinking 1945–1965* (Ithaca, NY, Cornell University Press), p. 212.

69. David Brown (1994), *The State and Ethnic Politics in Southeast Asia* (London, Routledge), p. 123.

70. Feith and Castles 1970: 213.

71. Hasan Saleh (1956), *Revolusi Islam di Indonesia* (Aceh, Pustaka Djihad), p. 15.

72. Hasan Saleh 1956: 9, 10–11, 16–17. It is interesting to note that this is an essentially *Acehnese* interpretation of *Darul Islam*, since the *Darul Islam* revolt in West Java effectively began in 1948–49. Indeed, it could be argued that, like the communist-led Madiun revolt of September 1948, the West Javanese *Darul Islam* 'jumped the gun' in the struggle of ideologies.

73. Hasan Saleh 1956: 102.

74. Ibid.: 97–8.

75. Ibid.: 96–7, 112, 113.

76. Ibid.: 106.

77. Ibid.: 104, 105, 107.

78. Ibid.: 18.

79. Dijk 1981: 323–30.

80. Mohammed Ansori Nawawi 1968: 323.

81. Hasan Saleh 1956: 81–3.

82. Ibid.: 51. It is certainly true that, while the RMS rebels in the South Moluccas were able to survive in the interior of the island of Ceram, they were cut off from the villages of Ambon that alone could have sustained the revolt.

83. Nazaruddin Sjamsuddin 1985: 142–3.

84. Ibid.: 129–32.

85. Mohammed Ansori Nawawi 1968: 335.

86. See Ali Hasjmy 1976b.

87. Nazaruddin Sjamsuddin 1985: 212–30.

88. Herbert Feith (1962), *The Decline of Constitutional Democracy in Indonesia* (Ithaca, NY, Cornell University Press), p. 211.

89. Nazaruddin Sjamsuddin 1985: 132–9.

90. Howard M. Federspiel (1985), 'The military and Islam in Sukarno's Indonesia', in Ahmad Ibrahim, Sharon Siddique and Yasmin Hussein (eds), *Readings on Islam in Southeast Asia* (Singapore, ISEAS), pp. 155–6.

91. M. Nur el-Ibrahimy 1982: pp. 270–71, Documents 17 and 18.

92. Ibid.: 274–5, Document 20; Morris 1983: 230.

93. Ali Hasjmy (1989), '30 Tahun Daerah Istimewa Aceh' (typescript), 23.

94. See *INIS* (Indonesia–Netherlands Cooperation in Islamic Studies) (Leiden/Jakarta): (1990) Vol. 3, p. 16; Vol. 4, p. 32; (1991) Vol. 5, p. 29.

95. See, for example, Madjlis Ulama (1972), *Bagaimana Islam Memandang Kesenian* (Banda Aceh, Madjlis Ulama), pp. 41–57, 66.

96. Ali Hasjmy (1978), *Bunga Rampai Revolusi dari Tanah Aceh* (Jakarta, Bulan Bintang), pp. 107–11.

97. Deliar Noer (1978), *Administration of Islam in Indonesia* (Ithaca, NY, Cornell University Press), p. 35.

98. James Siegel (1979), *Shadow and Sound: The Historical Thought of a Sumatran People* (Chicago, University of Chicago Press), pp. 271–2, 279.

99. Majelis Ulama (1980), *Kesimpulan Seminar Sejarah Masuk dan Berkembangnya Islam di Aceh dan Nusantara* (Aceh Timur, Majelis Ulama Propinsi Daerah Istimewa Aceh), p. 14.

100. Michael Vatikiotis (1990), 'Ancient enmities: killings indicate revival of organized insurgency', in *Far Eastern Economic Review*, 28 June 1990, p. 13.

101. Michael Vatikiotis (1991), 'Troubled Province: Aceh unrest leads to mounting death toll', in *Far Eastern Economic Review*, 24 January 1991, pp. 20–1; 'Rumblings in Aceh', *TAPOL Bulletin*, no. 96 (December 1989), pp. 10–11.

102. *INIS* 1991: Vol. 6, p. 23.

103. Tengku Hasan di Tiro (1985), *The Case and the Cause of the National Liberation Front of Aceh, Sumatra*, 23 August 1985 (Goteburg, Sweden), pp. 10–11.

104. See Soedjakmoto (1960), *An Approach to Indonesian History: Towards an Open Future* (Ithaca, NY, Modern Indonesian Project, Cornell University Press), p. 15.

8. At the Frontier of the Islamic World

1. W.K. Che Man (1990), *Muslim Separatism: the Moros of Southern Philippines and the Malays of Southern Thailand* (Singapore, Oxford University Press), pp. 51–86.

2. Che Man 1990: 31–2.

3. Nagasura T. Madale (1984), 'The future of the Moro National Liberation Front as a separatist movement in Southern Philippines', in Lim Joo-Jock and S. Vani (eds), *Armed Separatism in Southeast Asia* (Singapore, ISEAS), 179–81.

4. Majid Khadduri (1955), *War and Peace in the Law of Islam* (Baltimore, MD, Johns Hopkins University Press), p. 173.

5. Moshe Yegar (1972), *The Muslims of Burma: A Study of a Minority Group* (Wiesbaden, Otto Harrassowitz), pp. 18–24.

6. Richard V. Weekes (ed.) (1984), *Muslim Peoples* (Westport, CT, Greenwood Press), Vol. I, p. 188.

7. Maurice Collis (1946), *The Land of the Great Image* (London, Faber and Faber), p. 250.

8. D.G.E. Hall (1968), *A History of South-East Asia* (London, Macmillan), p. 402.

9. Virginia Thompson and Richard Adloff (1955), *Minority Problems in Southeast Asia* (Stanford, CA, Stanford University Press), p. 151; F.S.V. Donnison (1956). *British Military Administration in the Far East* (London, HMSO), p. 17.

10. Moshe Yegar (1982), 'The Muslims of Burma', in Raphael Israeli (ed.), *The Crescent in the East: Islam in Asia Major* (London, Curzon Press), p. 109.

11. Yegar 1972: 95.

12. Col. Henry Yule and A.C. Burnell (1979), *Hobson-Jobson: A Glossary of Colloquial Anglo-Indian Words and Phrases* (New Delhi, Munshiram Monaharlal), pp. 594–5.

13. Yegar 1972: 29–31.

14. Thompson and Adloff 1955: 152.

15. C.E. Lucas-Phillips (1971), *The Raiders of Arakan* (London, Heinemann), p. 10; S. Woodburn Kirby (1958), *The War against Japan* (London, HMSO), Vol. II, p. 256; Donnison 1956: 20–21.

16. Frank Owen (1946), *The Campaign in Burma* (London, HMSO), pp. 31–2; Kirby 1958: 354.

17. Dorman-Smith to L.S. Amery, 8 April 1943, in Hugh Tinker (ed.) (1983), *Burma: The Struggle for Independence 1944–1948*, (London HMSO), Vol. I, p. 11; 'Report on Pyinnyathina', in *WO 203/6262A: SACSEA*.

18. Lucas-Phillips 1971: 24; HQ, Group 'V' Force, c/o HQ, 15th Indian Corps (SEAC) to HQ, Allied Land Forces (SEA), 8 January 1945, *WO 203/53*: Kirby 1958: 192–3; Donnison 1956: 21–2.

19. Anthony Irwin (1945), *Burmese Outpost* (London, Collins), pp. 40–1.

20. Irwin 1945: 64–6.

21. Ibid.: 77–8.

22. Lucas-Phillips 1971: 68.

23. Owen 1945: 50–54, 62; Donnison 1956: 64.

24. Owen 1945: 127–8; Donnison 1956: 106–7.

25. See Yegar 1972: 96, fn 2; and article by 'Asmi' (1954), 'The State of Arakan', *Guardian* (Burma), 1(10) (August), p. 27.

26. Irwin 1945: 86.

27. S. Woodburn Kirby (1965), *The War against Japan* (London, HMSO), Vol. IV, pp. 430–31; Donnison 1956: 72, 275–6.

28. Khin Maung Kyi (1955), 'The Mujahid Story', *Guardian* (Burma), Vol. 2, no. 3, (January), p. 38; Report by Brigadier Chettle on the Situation in Akyab District, 3 March 1945, *WO 203/5262A*; Donnison 1956: 349.

29. Tinker 1983: I, 152, 174–5, 205, 213.

30. Dorman-Smith to Secretary of State for Burma, 3 November 1945, in Tinker 1983: I, 529–30.

31. Hugh Tinker (ed.) (1986), *Burma: The Struggle for Independence 1944–1948*, (London, HMSO), Vol. II, pp. 77, 81, 111, 138, 171.

32. 'Asmi' (1954), 'The State of Arakan', *Guardian* (Burma), 1(10) (August), p. 29; Yegar 1972: 96–7.

33. Thompson and Adloff 1955: 154–5.

34. Yegar 1982: 123–6.

35. 'Asmi' (1954), 'The State of Arakan', *Guardian* (Burma), 1(10) (August), p. 28; Yegar 1982: 98.

36. Ba Chan (1953), 'Report on Arakan', *Guardian* (Burma), 1(1) (November), pp. 34–5; Weekly Intelligence Summary, no. 19/1947, *IOR M/4/2503*.

37. Ba Chan (1953), 'Report on Arakan', *Guardian* (Burma), 1(1) (November), p. 33; Note of Mass Meeting held at Rangoon, 15 June 1947, *IOR M/4/2503*; Governor of Burma to Secretary of State for Burma, 17 June 1947, *IOR M/4/ 2502: 1/46, pt. 1.*

38. Thompson and Adloff 1955: 153–64; *Guardian* (Burma) (1956), 3(3) (January), pp. 33, 38.

39. *Guardian* (Burma) (1956). 3(3) (January), pp. 37–8.

40. Thompson and Adloff 1955: 155–6; see comments by Burma Office officials in *IOR M/4/2503.*

41. Ba Chan (1953), 'Report on Arakan', *Guardian* (Burma), 1(1) (November), pp. 34–5.

42. Khin Maung Kyi (1955), 'The Mujahid Story', *Guardian* (Burma), 2(3) (January), pp. 38–40.

43. *Guardian* (London), 4 May 1988.

44. Yegar 1982: 128.

45. Yegar 1972: 105.

46. Ba Chan (1953), 'Report on Arakan', *Guardian* (Burma), 1(1) (November), pp. 34–5.

47. Moshe Yegar 1972: pp. 100, 128–9; *Times* (London), 9 May 1978; *Washington Post* report in *Guardian Weekly,* 16 February 1992.

48. Steve Coll (1992), 'Fugitives from Burma fight for food', in *Washington Post* report in *Guardian Weekly*, 16 February 1992.

9. Ethnicity, Islam and Irredentism

1. The Malay spelling of the name of the old kingdom and region is *Patani,* while the Thai spelling is *Pattani.* For purposes of consistency, *Patani* is used for the region as a whole, and *Pattani* is used for the modern-day province.

2. Letter, Tengku Mahmud Mahyiddeen to Barbara Whittingham-Jones, 21 January 1948, Barbara Whittingham-Jones Collection, SOAS Library, *MS 145982.*

3. Omar Farouk (1988), 'The Muslims of Thailand – a survey', in Andrew D.W. Forbes (ed.), *The Muslims of Thailand, Vol. I: Historical and Cultural Studies* (Gaya, Bihar, Centre for Southeast Asian Studies, Gaya), pp. 1–4.

4. Conner Bailey and John N. Miksic (1989), 'The country of Patani in the period of re-awakening: a chapter from Ibrahim Syukri's Sejarah Kerajaan Melayu Patani', in Andrew D.W. Forbes (ed.), *The Muslims of Thailand, Vol. II: Politics of the Malay-speaking South* (Gaya, Bihar, Centre for Southeast Asian Studies, Gaya), p. 151.

5. A. Teeuw and D.K. Wyatt (eds) (1970), *Hikayat Patani* (The Hague, Martinus Nijhoff), sections 1 and 2.

6. Ibrahim Syukri (pseudonym) (1985), *History of the Malay Kingdom of Patani* (Athens, OH, Southeast Asia Series, No. 68, Ohio University), p. 31; Virginia Matheson and M.B. Hooker (1988), 'Jawi literature in Patani: the maintenance of an Islamic tradition', *Journal of the Malaysian Branch of the Royal Asiatic Society,* 61(1): 10–13.

7. Matheson and Hooker 1988: 3–5.

8. Ibrahim Syukri 1985: 33–6, 43–4.

9. Thomas M. Fraser (1960), *Fishermen of South Thailand: The Malay Villagers* (New York, Holt, Rinehart and Winston), p. 49.

10. Donald and Elise Tugby (1989). 'Malay-Muslim and Thai-Buddhist relations in the Patani region: an interpretation', in Andrew D.W. Forbes (ed.), *The Muslims of Thailand, Vol. II: The Politics of the Malay-Speaking South* (Gaya, Bihar, Centre for Southeast Asian Studies, Gaya), pp. 73-4.

11. Tugby and Tugby 1989: 75-7.

12. Surin Pitsuwan (1985), *Islam and Malay Nationalism: A Case Study of the Malay-Muslims of Southern Thailand* (Bangkok, Thai Khadi Research Institute, Thammasat University), pp. 37-44.

13. Report by J.F. Johns, British Consulate (Singora), 9 March 1923, enclosed in letter, British Legation (Bangkok) to Foreign Office, 29 March 1923, *CO 717/31*.

14. A.J. Stockwell (1979), *British Policy and Malay Politics during the Malayan Union Experiment 1942-1948* (Kuala Lumpur, Malaysian Branch of the Royal Asiatic Society, Monograph 8), pp. 142-3. See report by J.F. Johns, 9 March 1923, *CO 717/31*.

15. Surin Pitsuwan 1985: 72-87.

16. Ruth T. McVey (1989), 'Identity and Rebellion among Southern Thai Muslims', in Andrew D.W. Forbes (ed.), *The Muslims of Thailand, Vol. II: Politics of the Malay-Speaking South* (Gaya, Bihar, Centre for Southeast Asian Studies, Gaya), pp. 38-9.

17. Bailey and Miksic 1989: 155.

18. Nantawan Haemindra (1976), 'The Problem of the Thai-Muslims in the Four Southern Provinces of Thailand, Part I', *Journal of Southeast Asian Studies*, 7(2): 205.

19. M. Ladd Thomas (1982), 'The Thai Muslims', in Raphael Israeli (ed.), *The Crescent in the East: Islam in Asia Major* (London, Curzon Press), p. 160.

20. Surin Pitsuwan 1985: 87-93; see also Scot Barmé (1993), *Luang Wichit Wathakan and the Creation of a Thai Identity* (Singapore, ISEAS)

21. H.E. Wilson (1989), 'Imperialism and Islam: the impact of "modernization" on the Malay-Muslims of South Thailand', in Andrew D.W. Forbes (ed.), *The Muslims of Thailand, Vol. II: Politics of the Malay-Speaking South* (Gaya, Bihar, Centre for Southeast Asian Studies, Gaya), pp. 59-60.

22. Ibid.: 62.

23. Nik Anwar Nik Mahmud (1987), *Anglo-Thai Relations 1945-1954* (Hull, U.K., Ph.D. thesis, University of Hull), pp. 154-60; Hugh Wilson (1992), 'Tengku Mahmud Mahyiddeen and the Dilemma of Partisan Duality', *Journal of Southeast Asian Studies*, 23(1): 41.

24. Wan Hashim Haji Wan Teh (1984), *Pejuang Gerila Force 136* (Grik, UMNO, Bahagian Grik), p. 25.

25. Ibid.: 8-13.

26. Ibrahim Syukri 1985: 67-8; Nik Anwar Nik Mahmud 1987: 151-4.

27. Anthony Eden to United States Ambassador (UK), 22 November 1944, in *Foreign Relations of the United States (FRUS) 1944*: (1965) (Washington, US Government Printing Office), Vol. V, p. 1320.

28. Anthony Eden to United States Ambassador (UK), 4 September 1944, in *FRUS 1944* (1965): Vol. V, p. 1317.

29. Ibid.

30. Stockwell 1979: 143; see also General C.D. Packard (WO) to G.F. Seel (CO), 16 June 1949, and attached correspondence, *FO 371/76291: 1949*.

31. Department of State to British Embassy (UK), 20 March 1944, *FRUS 1944*

(1965): Vol. V, p. 1314. The same ominous phrase was used by Churchill in relation to Italy in 1943. See Harold Nicolson (1967), *Diaries and Letters 1939–1945* (London, Collins), p. 321.

32. Surin Pitsuwan 1985: 111–14.

33. Quoted from 'Petition to the Right Honourable the Secretary of State for the Colonies, through the Commander-in-Chief, British Forces, Malaya', 1 November 1954. Barbara Whittingham-Jones Collection, SOAS Library, *MS 145 982* (see Appendix 6). See also Brain (HQ SACSEA) to Sterndale-Bennett (FO), 31 January 1946, *FO 371/54421*, f.2433.

34. Quoted from 'Petition', 1 November 1945, pp. 1–2 (see Appendix 6).

35. Ibid., p. 2 (see Appendix 6).

36. *Times* (London) 22 November 1945; HQ SACSEA to Sterndale-Bennett (FO), 31 January 1946, and enclosed correspondence, *FO 371/54421*, f.2433.

37. Nik Anwar Nik Mahmud 1987: 154–60.

38. *FRUS 1944* (1965): Vol. V, p. 1314; *Foreign Relations of the United States 1945,*(1969) (Washington, US Government Printing Office), Vol. VI, p. 1243.

39. *FRUS 1945* (1969): Vol. VI, pp. 1243-4.

40. Ibid.: pp. 1272–3.

41. Ministry of Foreign Affairs (1979), *Thai Muslims* (Bangkok, Ministry of Foreign Affairs), p. 6.

42. Ibid.: 5–6.

43. Ibid.: 5.

44. Virginia Thompson and Richard Adloff (1955), *Minority Problems in Southeast Asia* (Stanford, CA, Stanford University Press), pp. 158–9.

45. *Straits Times*, 4 February 1947, 5 February 1947, in Barbara Whittingham-Jones Collection (SOAS) *MS 145 982*.

46. Nantawan Haemindra 1976: 208.

47. Ibrahim Syukri 1985: 71–2.

48. *Straits Times*, 30 September 1947, in Barbara Wittingham-Jones Collection (SOAS) *MS 145 982*; Foreign Office minutes to G.H. Thompson (GB Ambassador, Bangkok) to Field Marshall P. Pibulsonggram (Prime Minister), 10 December 1948, *FO 371/70002*, f.17925.

49. Tengku Mahmud Mahyiddeen to Barbara Whittingham-Jones, 13 December 1947; Barbara Whittingham-Jones Collection (SOAS) *MS 145 982*.

50. Tengku Mahmud Mahyiddeen to Barbara Whittingham-Jones, 21 January 1948, Barbara Whittingham-Jones Collection (SOAS) *MS 145 982*.

51. Tengku Mahmud Mahyiddeen to Barbara Whittingham-Jones, 31 January 1948, Barbara Whittingham-Jones Collection (SOAS) *MS 145 982*.

52. Nantawan Haemindra 1976: 205–6.

53. Tengku Mahmud Mahyiddeen to Barbara Whittingham-Jones, 13 December 1947, Barbara Whittingham-Jones Collection (SOAS) *MS 145 982*.

54. Report by N.G. Norris, Assistant-Commissioner, Special Branch (Singapore), 6 December 1948, in G.H. Thompson (GB Ambassador, Bangkok) to P.F. Grey (FO), 24 December 1948, *FO 371/70002*.

55. Tengku Mahmud Mahyiddeen to Barbara Whittingham-Jones, 22 December 1948; Barbara Whittingham-Jones (1948), 'Patani Appeals to UNO', in *Eastern World* (April), pp. 1–8 in Barbara Whittingham-Jones Collection (SOAS) *MS 145 982*.

56. Tengku Mahmud Mahyiddeen to Barbara Whittingham-Jones, 13 December

1947, Barbara Whittingham-Jones Collection (SOAS) *MS 145 982*; High Commissioner (Malaya) to GB Ambassador (Bangkok), 22 November 1948, *FO 371/70002*.

57. *Straits Budget*, 19 February 1948; *Straits Budget*, 13 May 1948; *Scotsman*, 22 March 1948.

58. *Straits Times*, 23 August 1948.

59. G.H. Thompson (GB Ambassador, Bangkok) to Gurney (High Commissioner, Malaya), 6 December 1948; G.H. Thompson (GB Ambassador, Bangkok) to Marshal Pibulsonggram (Prime Minister, Thailand), 10 December 1948; G.H. Thompson (GB Ambassador, Bangkok) to P.F. Grey (FO), 24 December 1948, *FO 371/70002*.

60. Brain (Southeast Asia Command) to Sterndale-Bennett (FO), 31 January 1946. *FO 371/54421*.

61. J.J. Paskin (Colonial Office) to Sterndale-Bennett (FO), 7 May 1946, *FO 371/54421*; Memorandum by A.M. Palliser (FO), 2 December 1948: *FO 371/70002*.

62. General G.D. Packard (War Office) to G.F. Seel (FO), 16 June 1949, with enclosures, *FO 371/76291*.

63. Tengku Mahmud Mahyiddeen to Barbara Whittingham-Jones, 22 February 1948, Barbara Whittingham-Jones Collection (SOAS) *MS 145 982*.

64. A good example of this Jawi literature is the standard textbook history of Islam, *Ringkasan Sejarah Islam*, 3 vols, published in Pattani by the Saudara Press.

65. Ministry of Foreign Affairs 1979: 3; Andrew D.W. Forbes (1989), 'Thailand's Muslim Minorities: Assimilation, Secession, or Co-existence?', in Andrew D.W. Forbes (ed.), *The Muslims of Thailand, Vol. II: Politics of the Malay-Speaking South* (Gaya, Bihar, Centre for Southeast Asian Studies, Gaya), p. 179.

66. See, for example, the language used in Ministry of Foreign Affairs 1979, especially pp. 10–11.

67. Uthai Dulyakasem (1984), 'Muslim-Malay Separatism in Southern Thailand: Factors underlying the Political Revolt', in Lim Joo-Jock and S. Vani (eds), *Armed Separatism in Southeast Asia* (Singapore, ISEAS), pp. 222–4.

68. C.W. Watson (1989–90), 'Report on a Trip to Patani', in *Annual Report* (Canterbury, Centre of South-East Asian Studies, University of Kent at Canterbury), pp. 24–5, 27.

69. See Kusuma Snitwongse (1985), 'Thai Government responses to armed communist and separatist movements', in Chandran Jeshurun (ed.), *Governments and Rebellions in Southeast Asia* (Singapore, ISEAS); and Ministry of Foreign Affairs 1979: 19–20.

70. M. Ladd Thomas (1982), 'The Thai Muslims' in Raphael Israeli (ed.), *The Crescent in the East: Islam in Asia Major* (London, Curzon Press), pp. 165–9.

71. The province of Satun is divided from the Patani region by the largely Thai province of Songkhla. It is historically linked to Kedah and the west coast of Malaya rather than – as in the case of Patani – Kelantan and the east coast. Although they are overwhelmingly Malay in terms of ethnic origin, the majority of the people speak Thai and use it in their everyday lives. Even the religious shops – normally a repository of Malay culture – are filled with Thai-language books and periodicals. The explanation for this successful integration process probably lies in the fact that the main links of communications are northwards to Thailand – and particularly to the urban centre of Hadyai – while road and rail access to Malaya is minimal. Traditionally, the principal communication between Satun and Perlis has been by

boat, along a network of channels through mangrove swamps, and then through a formerly pirate-infested series of islands (personal observation from visit to Satun in August 1989).

72. Surin Pitsuwan 1985: 216–58.

73. Chaiwat Satha-Anand (1987), *Islam and Violence: A Case Study of Violent Events in the Four Southern Provinces of Thailand 1976–1981* (Tampa, Florida, University of South Florida Monographs in Religion and Public Policy, no. 2), pp. 8–13.

74. McVey 1989: 37; *Guardian Weekly*, 8 August 1993.

75. Arong Suthasan (1989), 'Thai society and the Muslim majority', in Andrew D.W. Forbes (ed.), *The Muslims of Thailand, Vol. II: Politics of the Malay-Speaking South* (Gaya, Bihar, Centre for Southeast Asian Studies, Gaya), 104–11.

76. Matheson and Hooker 1988: 10.

77. Surin Pitsuwan (1982), *Issues Affecting Border Security between Malaysia and Thailand* (Bangkok, Faculty of Political Science, Thammasat University Series No. 4), p. 33.

78. Norman Peagam (1976), 'Border pact under scrutiny', *Far Eastern Economic Review*, 21 May 1976, 92(21): 13; John McBeth and K. Das, (1980), 'A frontier of fear and factions', in *Far Eastern Economic Review*, 20 June 1980, 108(26): 16–18.

79. In 1989, the Malayan Communist Party reached an agreement with the Thai government that led to the ending of its guerrilla campaign. See *The Nation* (Bangkok), 28 August 1989.

80. Chaiwat Satha-Anand 1987: 35–9.

81. Geoffrey C. Gunn (1986), 'Radical Islam in Southeast Asia', *Journal of Contemporary Asia*, 16(9): 37–8.

82. John McBeth (1980), 'Separatism is the goal and religion is the weapon', *Far Eastern Economic Review*, 20 June 1980, 108(26): 21.

83. See, for example, Norman Peagam (1976), 'Boiling point in the troubled South', *Far Eastern Economic Review*, 21 May 1976, 92(21): 11.

84. Thomas M. Fraser Jr. (1960), *Fishermen of South Thailand: The Malay Villagers* (New York, Holt, Rinehart and Winston), pp. 40–5.

85. Chavivun Prachuabmoh (1989), 'The role of women in maintaining ethnic identity and boundaries: a case of Thai-Muslims in South Thailand', in Andrew D.W. Forbes (ed.), *The Muslims of Thailand, Vol. II: Politics of the Malay-Speaking South* (Gaya, Bihar, Centre for Southeast Asian Studies, Gaya), pp. 135–6; M. Ladd Thomas (1975), *Political Violence in the Muslim Provinces of Southern Thailand* (Singapore, ISEAS), pp. 5–6.

86. Uthai Dulyakasem 1984: 227–9; McVey 1989: 36–8.

87. See *Utusan Malaysia*, 24, 25, 26 July 1989 and 27 July 1989.

10. Conclusion

1. Ruth T. McVey (1984), 'Separatism and the Paradoxes of the Nation-State in Perspective', in Lim Joo-Jock and S. Vani (eds), *Armed Separatism in Southeast Asia* (Singapore, ISEAS), pp. 13–14. An extreme illustration of this tendency to differentiate between a territory and its population is provided by the Argentine attitude to the Falkland Islands. When a Falkland Islands delegation visited Argentina in March 1995, it was bluntly told at a meeting in Cordoba that Argentinians

were not interested in the Falklanders' views on 'nuestras Malvinas'. See *Falkland Islands Newsletter*, April 1995, p. 11.

2. McVey 1984: 12-13.

3. Karl D. Jackson (1985), 'Post-colonial rebellion and counter-insurgency in Southeast Asia', in Chandran Jeshurun (ed.), *Governments and Rebellions in Southeast Asia* (Singapore, ISEAS), pp. 17-20.

4. Jackson 1985: 15-17.

5. W.K. Che Man (1990), *Muslim Separatism: The Moros of Southern Philippines and the Malays of Southern Thailand* (Singapore, Oxford University Press), p. 179.

6. Gerard Chaliand (ed.) (1989), *Minority Peoples in an Age of Nation-States* (London, Pluto Press), pp. xii, 4.

7. Colonial Office (1949), *British Dependencies in the Far East 1945-1949*, Cmd. 7709 (London, HMSO), p. 52.

8. William P. Bundy (1971), 'New tides in Southeast Asia', *Foreign Affairs*, 2(49): 188-9

9. Richard M. Nixon (1967), 'Asia after Vietnam', *Foreign Affairs*, 1(46): 111-12.

10. See Samuel P. Huntington (1968), 'The Bases of Accommodation', *Foreign Affairs* 4(46): 648-52.

11. Early indications of the threat from Vietnam, both ideological and regional, can be seen in *Vietnam Courier* (1975) 37(6): 6-7; 37(8): 16 and in *Summary of World Broadcasts*, 6 May 1975, SU/4896/A3/2.

12. See Tim Kell (1995), *The Roots of Acehnese Rebellion, 1989-1992* (Ithaca, NY, Cornell Modern Indonesia Project, Cornell University).

13. Chandra Muzaffar (1987), *Islamic Resurgence in Malaysia* (Petaling Jaya, Fajar Bakti).

14. Leaving Burma to one side at this stage.

15. See Ibn Khaldun (1967), *The Muqaddimah: An Introduction to History* (London and Henley, Routledge and Kegan Paul with Secker and Warburg), pp. xi-xii.

16. '... *facilis descensus Averno ... Sed revocare gradum, superasque evadere ad auras, Hoc opus, hic labor est*', Virgil, *The Aeneid*, Book 6: lines 126-9 (Very roughly: 'The descent into hell is easy ... the real problem is getting out again').

Bibliography

Primary sources

Government archives

1. United States Archives collected by the *Microfilm Project of University Publications of America Inc.*, held at the Brynmor Jones Library, University of Hull:

a. *Central Intelligence Agency (CIA) Research Reports: Vietnam and Southeast Asia, 1946–1976*, ed. Paul Kesaris.

b. *Central Intelligence Agency (CIA) Research Reports: Vietnam and Southeast Asia, supplement*, ed. Robert E. Lester.

c. *Confidential United States State Department Files: Indochina, Internal Affairs, 1945–1949*, ed. Paul Kesaris.

d. *John F. Kennedy National Security Files: Vietnam National Security Files, 1961–1963* (microfilmed from the holdings of the John F. Kennedy Library, Boston, MA), General Editor, George C. Herring.

e. *Lyndon B. Johnson National Security Files: Vietnam, National Security Files, November 1963 to June 1965* (microfilmed from the holdings of the Lyndon B. Johnson Library, Austin, TX), General Editor, George C. Herring.

2. Archives in the Public Record Office, Kew Gardens, United Kingdom:

a. Cabinet Office Records: CAB 24/64

b. Colonial Office Records relating to Britain's policy towards Patani separatism: CO 717/31

c. Colonial Office Records relating to Britain's policy towards the Penang secession movement: CO 717/183/1/52928; CO 717/183/2/52928; CO 717/204/4/52928; CO 717/204/5/52928; CO 537/1556/50823

d. Foreign Office Records relating to Britain's policy towards Patani separatism: FO 371/54421; FO 371/70002; FO 371/76291

e. Foreign Office Records relating to activities of Karen politicians in the late 1940s: FO 643/66

f. War Office Records relating to The Second World War period and the immediate post-war period in the Arakan and Karen regions: WO 203/53; WO 203/58; WO 203/5262A

3. Records in the India Office Library, London:

a. India Office Records relating to the Arakan and Karen regions in the immediate post-Second World War period: IOR M/4/2502; IOR M/4/2503; IOR M/4/3023; IOR M/4/3025

Other archives and sources

1. Records in University Library, Universiti Sains Malaysia:

a. Microfilm of British Colonial Office Records, copied from the Public Record Office. (This is a very useful collection, and includes records on the Penang Secession Movement, 1948–51.)

b. A collection of microfilms relating to Penang, the Straits Chinese in general, and the Straits Chinese British Association in particular.
This collection includes a number of BA, MA and Ph.D. dissertations on the history of Penang, which are referred to in the general bibliography on secondary works and dissertations.

2. A collection of documents obtained under the Freedom of Information Act by Professor George McT. Kahin concerning the Central Highlands of Vietnam. These include Central Intelligence Agency, State Department and National Security Files referred to above, and some official correspondence by Bao Dai relating to the Central Highlands.

3. The Barbara Whittingham-Jones Papers in the Library of the School of Oriental and African Studies, University of London, MS 145 982. (Barbara Whittingham-Jones was a journalist who sympathized with the Patani separatist cause, and had extensive contacts with Patani Malay leaders in the immediate post-Second World War period. This invaluable collection has been extensively used in the chapter on Patani and the Patani Malays.)

Published documents

Allen, J. de V., A.J. Stockwell and L.R. Wright (eds) (1981), *A Collection of Treaties and other Documents affecting the States of Malaysia 1761–1963*, Vol. II (London, Oceana Publications).

Bodinier, G. (ed.) (1987), *La Retour de la France en Indochine 1945–1946: Textes et Documents*, Vol I of *La Guerre en Indochine 1945–1954* (Vincennes, Service Historique de l'Armée de Terre).

Burma Office (1947), *Burma: Report of the Frontier Areas Committee of Enquiry 1947*, Cmd. 7138 (London, HMSO).

Colonial Office (1949), *British Dependencies in the Far East 1945–1949* Cmd. 7709 (London, HMSO).

Department of Defense (1971), *United States–Vietnam Relations 1945–1967* (Washington, US Government Printing Office).

Department of State (1965), *Foreign Relations of the United States (FRUS) 1944*, Vol. V (Washington, US Government Printing Office).

Department of State (1969), *Foreign Relations of the United States (FRUS) 1945*, Vol. VI (Washington, US Government Printing Office).

Department of State (1992), *Foreign Relations of the United States (FRUS) 1964–1968*, Vol. I, Vietnam 1964 (Washington, US Government Printing Office).

Djonovich, Dusan J. (ed.) (1974), *United Nations Resolutions Series 1: Resolutions Adopted by the General Assembly*, Vol. VIII, 1960–1962 (New York, Oceana Publications).

Front de Libération des Hauts Plateaux de Champa (1965), *Historique* (Phnom-Penh), in Brynmor Jones Library, Hull University.

Front Unifié de la Lutte de la Race Opprimée (1965), *Historique* (Phnom-Penh), in Brynmor Jones Library, Hull University.

Ho Chi Minh (1961), *Selected Works*, Vol. III (Hanoi, Foreign Languages Publishing House).

House of Commons (1947–48), *Parliamentary Debates (Hansard)*, Vol. 443, First Volume of Session 1947–1948 (London, HMSO).

Penang Chinese Chamber of Commerce (1946–67), *Annual Reports 1946–1967*: reports kept in office of Penang Chinese Chamber of Commerce, Chinese Town Hall, Georgetown, Penang.

Sheehan, Neil, et al. (eds) (1971), *The Pentagon Papers, as published by the New York Times* (New York, Bantam Books).

Tinker, Hugh (ed.) (1983), *Burma: The Struggle for Independence 1944–1948*, Vol. I (London, HMSO).

Tinker, Hugh (ed.) (1986), *Burma: The Struggle for Independence 1944–1948*, Vol. II (London, HMSO).

Trager, Frank N. (ed.) (1971), *Burma: Japanese Military Administration: Selected Documents 1941–1945* (Philadelphia, PA, University of Pennsylvania Press).

Newspapers and journals

The main locations for these sources were: the Newspaper Library, Colindale, London; the British Library, London; the Georgetown Public Library, Penang, Malaysia; the microfilm collection on Penang and the Straits Chinese in the Library of Universiti Sains Malaysia, Penang, Malaysia; the Library of the School of Oriental and African Studies, London; and the newspaper file collection relating to Indochina and the Vietnam War in the Centre for Southeast Asian Studies, Hull University.

Far Eastern Economic Review (Hong Kong); *Financial Times* (Britain); *Glasgow Herald* (Britain); *Guardian* (Burma); *Guardian Weekly* (Britain); *Hu Yew Seah Magazine* (Malaya); *Indonesian–Netherlands Cooperation in Islamic Studies* (*INIS*) (Netherlands and Indonesia); *Malay Mail* (Malaya); *Malayan Chinese Review* (Malaya); *Manchester Guardian* (Britain); *Monde Diplomatique* (France); *Nation* (Thailand); *Observer* (Britain); *Penang Gazette and Straits Chronicle* (Malaya); *Scotsman* (Britain); *Straits Chinese Magazine* (Singapore); *Straits Echo* (Malaya); *Straits Times* (Malaysia and Singapore); *Summary of World Broadcasts* (Britain); *Sunday Gazette* (Malaya); *Tapol Bulletin* (Britain); *Times* (London); *Utusan Malaysia* (Malaysia); *Vietnam Courier* (Vietnam)

Secondary sources

Books or articles of particular significance will have accompanying comment in brackets.

Abdulrahman Abdul Kadir Kurdi (1984), *The Islamic State: A Study Based on the Islamic Holy Constitution* (New York, Mansell).

Abdurachman, Paramita R. (1981), *New Winds, New Faces, New Forces* (Jakarta, Lembaga Research Kebudayaan Nasional).

Alfian (1985), 'The Ulama in Acehnese Society' in Ahmad Ibrahim, Sharon Siddique and Yasmin Hussain (eds), *Readings on Islam in Southeast Asia* (Singapore, Institute of Southeast Asian Studies).

Ali Hasjmy (ed.) (1971), *Hikayat Perang Sabi Mendjiwai Perang Atjeh Lawan Belanda* (Banda Aceh, Pustaka Faraby).

— (1976a), *Peranan Islam dalam Perang Aceh dan Perjuangan Kemerdekaan Indonesia* (Jakarta, Bulan Bintang).

— (1976b), *Surat-Surat dari Penjara* (Jakarta, Bulan Bintang).

— (1978), *Bunga Rampai Revolusi dari Tanah Aceh* (Jakarta, Bulan Bintang).

— (1983), *Kebudayaan Aceh dalam Sejarah* (Jakarta, Penerbit Beuna).

— (1989), *30 Tahun Daerah Istimewa Aceh* (Banda Aceh, typescript).

Ali Shari'ati (1979), *On the Sociology of Islam* (Berkeley, CA, Mizan Press).

Alisjahbana, Sutan Takdir (1966), *Indonesia: Social and Cultural Revolution* (Kuala Lumpur, Oxford University Press).

Allen, Richard (1968), *Malaysia: Prospect and Retrospect* (London, Oxford University Press).

Amir Husin, Helmy Ali and Roger Burr (1986), *Aceh* (Banda Aceh, Tourism Office).

Ampalavanar, Rajeswary (1981), *The Indian Minority and Political Change in Malaya 1945–1957* (Kuala Lumpur, Oxford University Press).

Anas Machmud (1988), *Kedaulatan Aceh yang tidak pernah diserahkan kepada Belanda adalah bahagian dari kedaulatan Indonesia* (Jakarta, Bulan Bintang).

Anderson, B.R.O'G (1983), *Imagined Communities: Reflections on the Origins and Spread of Nationalism* (London, Verso and NLB).

Argenlieu, Thierry d' (1985), *Chronique d'Indochine 1945–1947* (Paris, Albin Michel). (This memoir contains some very useful documents outlining the evolution of d'Argenlieu's strategy towards Indochina, particularly in mid-1946.)

Ariffin bin S.M. Omar (1979), *The Masjumi and its struggle for the Islamic State* (MA thesis, University of Singapore, Singapore).

'Asmi' (pseudonym) (1954), 'The State of Arakan', *Guardian* (Burma) 1(10): 28–9.

Ba Chan (1953), 'Report on Arakan', *Guardian* (Burma) 1(1): 33–6.

Ba Maw (1968), *Breakthrough in Burma* (New Haven, CT, Yale University Press)

Ba U (1959), *My Burma* (New York, Taplinger).

Bailey, Conner and J.N.Miksic (1989), 'The Country of Patani in the period of re-awakening: a chapter from Ibrahim Syukri's Sejarah Kerajaan Melayu Patani', in Andrew D.W. Forbes (ed.), *The Muslims of Thailand*, Vol. 2 (Gaya, Bihar, Centre for Southeast Asian Studies).

Barmé, Scot (1993), *Luang Wichit Wathakan and the Creation of a Thai Identity* (Singapore, Institute of Southeast Asian Studies).

Baudesson, Henry (1932), *Au Pays des Superstitions et des Rites: Chez les Mois et les Chams* (Paris, Plon).

Benda, Harry J. (1958), *The Crescent and the Rising Sun: Indonesian Islam under the Japanese Occupation 1942–1945* (The Hague, Van Hoeve).

— (1985), 'Christian Snouck Hurgronje and the foundations of Dutch Islamic policy in Indonesia', in Ahmad Ibrahim, Sharon Siddique and Yasmin Hussain (eds), *Readings on Islam in Southeast Asia* (Singapore, Institute of Southeast Asian Studies).

Benda, Harry J. and Ruth T. McVey (eds) (1960), *The Communist Uprisings of 1926–1927 in Indonesia: Key Documents* (Ithaca, NY, Cornell University Modern Indonesia Project).

Bergot, Erwan (1975), *Commandos de Choc en Indochine* (Paris, Bernard Grasset).

Blythe, W. (1969), *The Impact of Chinese Secret Societies in Malaya: A Historical Study* (London, Oxford University Press).

Boland, B.J. (1971), *The Struggle of Islam in Modern Indonesia* ('s-Gravenhage, Smits).

Bouman, J.C. et al. (1960), *The South Moluccas: Rebellious Province or Occupied State* (Leiden, A.W. Sythoff).

Brown, David (1994), *The State and Ethnic Politics in Southeast Asia* (London, Routledge).

Bruce-Lockhart, R.H. (1936), *Return to Malaya* (London, Putnam).

Buck, Oscar T. (ed.) (1961), *America in the World* (Cleveland, OH, Meridian Press).

Bundy, William P. (1971), 'New tides in Southeast Asia', *Foreign Affairs* 2(49): 187–200.

Burton, Robert (1978), *The Anatomy of Melancholy* (London, J.M. Dent).

Buttinger, Joseph (1961), 'The ethnic minorities in the Republic of Vietnam', in Wesley Fishel (ed.), *Problems of Freedom: South Vietnam since Independence* (Chicago, Free Press of Glencoe).

Cady, J.F. (1958), *A History of Modern Burma* (Ithaca, NY, Cornell University Press).

Caply, Michel (1966), *Guérilla au Laos* (Paris, Presses de la Cité).

Carey, Peter B.R. (1981), *Babad Dipanagara: An Account of the Outbreak of the Java War, 1825–1830* (Kuala Lumpur, Malaysian Branch of the Royal Asiatic Society Monographs).

Chaliand, Gerard (ed.) (1989), *Minority Peoples in an Age of Nation-States* (London, Pluto Press).

Chandra Muzaffar (1987), *Islamic Resurgence in Malaysia* (Petaling Jaya, Fajar Bakti).

Chauvel, Richard (1985a), *The Rising Sun in the Spice Islands: A History of Ambon during the Japanese Occupation* (Clayton, Centre for Southeast Asian Studies, Monash University).

— (1985b), 'Ambon: not a revolution but a counter-revolution', in Audrey R. Kahin (ed.), *Regional Dynamics of the Indonesian Revolution* (Honolulu, University of Hawaii Press).

— (1990), *Nationalists, Soldiers and Separatists: The Ambonese Islands from Colonialism to Revolt 1880–1950* (Leiden, KITLV).

Che Man, W.K. (1990), *Muslim Separatism: The Moros of Southern Philippines and the Malays of Southern Thailand* (Singapore, Oxford University Press).

Cheah Boon-Kheng (1979), *The Masked Comrades: A Study of the Communist United Front in Malaya 1945–1948* (Singapore, Times Books International).

— (1983), *Red Star over Malaya: Resistance and Social Conflict during and after the Japanese Occupation of Malaya 1941–1946* (Singapore, Singapore University Press).

Chia, Felix (1980), *The Babas* (Singapore, Times Books International).

— (1983). *Ala Sayang! A Social History of Babas and Nyonyas* (Singapore, Eastern Universities Press Ltd.)

Christie, C.J. (1971), *The Problem of China in British Foreign Policy, 1917–1921* (Ph.D. thesis, Cambridge University).

— (1979), 'Marxism and the history of the nationalist movements in Laos', *Journal of Southeast Asian Studies* 10(1): 146–58.

— (1992), 'Partition, separatism and national identity: a reassessment', *Political Quarterly* 63(1): 68–78.

— (1994), 'British literary travellers in Southeast Asia in an era of colonial retreat', *Modern Asian Studies* 28(4): 673–737.

Clammer, John (1980), *Straits Chinese Society: Studies in the Sociology of the Baba Communities of Malaysia and Singapore* (Singapore, Singapore University Press).

Clarke, Jeffrey J. (1988), *Advice and Support: The Final Years* (Washington, Center of Military History, US Army).

Collis, Maurice (1946), *The Land of the Great Image* (London, Faber and Faber).

— (1956), *Last and First in Burma 1941–1948* (London, Faber and Faber).

Comber, Leon (1983), *13 May 1969: A Historical Survey of Sino-Malay Problems* (Kuala Lumpur, Heinemann Asia).

Condominas, Georges (1965), *L'exotique est quotidien* (Paris, Plon).

— (1971), 'Vietnamiens et Montagnards du centre et sud-Vietnam', in Jean Chesneaux, Georges Boudarel and Daniel Hemery (eds), *Tradition et révolution au Vietnam* (Paris, Editions Anthropos)

— (1977), *We Have Eaten the Forest: The Story of a Montagnard Village in the Central Highlands of Vietnam* (London, Allen Lane).

Cooley, Frank L. (1962), *Ambonese Adat: A General Description* (New Haven, CT, Yale University Press).

Cribb, Robert (1992), *Historical Dictionary of Indonesia* (Metuchen, NJ, Scarecrow Press).

Cromarty-Tulloch, T, (1946), 'Karens in the war in Burma', *Asiatic Review* 42(151): 248–9.

Cruickshank, Charles (1983), *SOE in the Far East* (London, Oxford University Press).

Dalloz, Jacques (1990), *The War in Indochina 1945–1954* (Maryland, Barnes and Noble).

Darwin, Charles (1913), *The Descent of Man* (London, John Murray).

De Gaulle, Charles (1960), *War Memoirs: Salvation, 1944–1946* (London, Weidenfeld and Nicolson).

Decker, Gunter (1957), *Republik Maluku Selatan: Die Republiek der Sud-Molukken* (Gottingen, Otto Schwartz).

Demariaux, J.C. (1949), *La Grande Chasse au Darlac Indochinois* (Paris, J. Peyronet).

Department of Education and Culture, Indonesia (1975/6), *Sejarah Daerah Maluku* (Jakarta, Pusat Penelitian dan Kebudayaan).

Dijk, C. van (1981), *Rebellion under the Banner of Islam: The Darul Islam in Indonesia* (The Hague, Martinus Nijhoff).

Dommen, Arthur J. and George W. Dalley (1991), 'The OSS in Laos: The 1945 Raven Mission and American Policy' *Journal of Southeast Asian Studies* 22(2): 327–46.

Donnison, F.S.V. (1956), *British Military Administration in the Far East 1943–1946* (London, HMSO).

Dorman-Smith, Reginald (1945), *Some Public Utterances 1942–1945* (Rangoon, Government Printing and Stationery).

Du Croo, M.H. (1943), *Marechausée in Atjeh* (Maastricht, Leiter-Nipels).

Dournes, Jacques (1980), *Minorities of Central Vietnam: Autochthonous Indochinese Peoples* (London, Minority Rights Group Report).

Dulyakasem, Uthai (1984), 'Muslim–Malay separatism in Southern Thailand: factors underlying the political revolt', in Lim Joo-Jock and S. Vani (eds), *Armed Separatism in Southeast Asia* (Singapore, Institute of Southeast Asian Studies).

— (1986), 'The emergence and escalation of ethnic nationalism: the case of the Malay-Muslims in Southern Siam', in Taufik Abdullah and Sharon Siddique (eds), *Islam and Society in Southeast Asia* (Singapore, Institute of Southeast Asian Studies).

Durand, Maurice M. and Nguyen Tran Huan (1985), *An Introduction to Vietnamese Literature* (New York, Columbia University Press).

Durie, Mark (1985), *A Grammar of Acehnese, on the basis of a dialect of North Aceh* (Dordrecht, Foris Publications).

Emerson, Rupert (1964), *Malaysia: A Study in Direct and Indirect Rule* (Kuala Lumpur, University of Malaya Press).

Evans, Grant and Kelvin Rowley (1984), *Red Brotherhood at War: Indochina since the Fall of Saigon* (London, Verso).

Fall, Bernard B. (1966), *Vietnam Witness 1953–1966* (London, Pall Mall Press).

—(ed.) (1968), *Ho Chi Minh on Revolution: Selected Writings, 1920–1966* (New York, New American Library).

Falla, Jonathan (1991), *True Love and Bartholemew: Rebels on the Burma Border* (Cambridge, Cambridge University Press).

Federspiel, Howard M. (1970), *Persatuan Islam: Islamic Reform in Twentieth Century Indonesia* (Ithaca, NY, Cornell University Southeast Asia Program).

— (1985), 'The military and Islam in Sukarno's Indonesia', in Ahmad Ibrahim, Sharon Siddique and Yasmin Hussain (eds), *Readings on Islam in Southeast Asia* (Singapore, Institute of Southeast Asian Studies).

Feith, Herbert (1962), *The Decline of Constitutional Democracy in Indonesia* (Ithaca, NY, Cornell University Press).

Feith, Herbert and Lance Castles (eds) (1970), *Indonesian Political Thinking 1945–1965* (Ithaca, NY, Cornell University Press). (An indispensable source for the history of Indonesia during the revolutionary period.)

Fistie, Pierre (1985), *La Birmanie ou la quête de l'unité* (Paris, Ecole française d'Extrême-Orient).

Forbes, Andrew D.W. (ed.) (1989a), *The Muslims of Thailand*, 2 vols (Gaya, Bihar, Centre for Southeast Asian Studies).

— (1989b), 'Thailand's muslim minorities: assimilation, secession or co-existence', in Andrew D.W. Forbes (ed.), *The Muslims of Thailand*, Vol. II (Gaya, Bihar, Centre for Southeast Asian Studies).

Fraser, Thomas M. (1960), *Fishermen of South Thailand: The Malay Villagers* (New York, Holt, Rinehart and Winston).

Freidus, Joy Alberta (1977), *Sumatran Contributions to the Development of Indonesian Literature 1920–1942* (Hawaii, University Press of Hawaii).

Furnivall, J.S. (1956), *Colonial Policy and Practice* (New York, New York University Press).

Gaudel, A. (1947), *Indochine française en face du Japon* (Paris, Susse).

Gellner, Ernest A. (1983), *Nations and Nationalism* (Oxford, Blackwell).

Gibb, H.A.R. and J.H. Kramers (eds) (1961), *The Shorter Encyclopaedia of Islam* (Leiden, Brill).

Glass, Leslie (1985), *The Changing of Kings: Memories of Burma 1934–1949* (London, Peter Owen).

Gobineau, Arthur de (1915), *Essay on the Inequality of Human Races* (London, Heinemann).

Gowing, Peter G. (1985), 'Moros and Khaek: the position of Muslim minorities in the Philippines and Thailand', in Ahmad Ibrahim, Sharon Siddique and Yasmin Hussain (eds), *Readings on Islam in Southeast Asia* (Singapore, Institute of Southeast Asian Studies).

Graaf, H.J. de (1977), *De Geschiedenis van Ambon en der Zuid-Molukken* (Franeker, T. Wever).

Guideri, Remo, Francesco Pellizi and Stanley J. Tambiah (eds) (1988), *Ethnicities and Nations* (Texas, The Rothko Chapel).

Gunn, Geoffrey C. (1986), 'Radical Islam in Southeast Asia', *Journal of Contemporary Asia* 16(9): 30–54.

— (1987), 'Minority Manipulation in Colonial Indochina: lessons and legacies' *Bulletin of Concerned Asian Scholars* 19(3): 20–8.

Haemindra, Nantawan (1976), 'The problem of the Thai-Muslims in the four southern provinces of Thailand' Part 1, *Journal of Southeast Asian Studies* 7(2): 197–225.

— (1977), 'The problem of the Thai-Muslims in the four southern provinces of Thailand', Part 2, *Journal of Southeast Asian Studies* 8(1): 85–105.

Hall, D.G.E. (1968), *A History of South-East Asia* (London, Macmillan).

Hamilton-Merritt, Jane (1993), *Tragic Mountains: The Hmong, the Americans and the Secret Wars for Laos, 1942–1992* (Bloomington, IN, Indiana University Press).

Hasan di Tiro, Tengku (1985), *The Case and the Cause of the National Liberation Front of Aceh, Sumatra* (Sweden, Goteburg, typescript).

Hasan Saleh (1956), *Revolusi Islam di Indonesia* (Aceh, Pustaka Djihad). (A key book outlining the case of the *Darul Islam* rebels in Indonesia in general and Aceh in particular.)

Hatta, Mohammad (1972), *Portrait of a Patriot: Selected Writings by Mohammad Hatta* (The Hague, Mouton).

Heinz, Wolfgang S. (1988), *Indigenous Populations, Ethnic Minorities and Human Rights* (Berlin, Quorum Verlag).

Hempstone, Smith (1966), *A Tract of Time* (Boston, MD, Houghton Mifflin). (A novel depicting the plight of the *montagnards* under Diem's regime, and the dilemmas faced by American advisers in the Central Highlands at that time.)

Heng Pek Koon (1988), *Chinese Politics in Malaysia: A History of the Malaysian Chinese Association* (Singapore, Oxford University Press).

Hickey, Gerald C. (1970), *Accommodation and Coalition in South Vietnam* (Santa Monica, Rand Corporation).

— (1982a), *Sons of the Mountains: Ethnohistory of the Vietnamese Central Highlands to 1954* (New Haven, CT, Yale University Press).

— (1982b), *Free in the Forest: Ethnohistory of the Vietnamese Central Highlands 1954–1976* (New Haven, CT, Yale University Press).

— (1988), *Kingdom in the Morning Mist: Mayréna in the Highlands of Vietnam* (Philadelphia, University of Pennsylvania Press). (Gerald Cannon Hickey and Georges Condominas are the key authorities on the Central Highlands of Vietnam during the colonial and the post-colonial periods.)

Hooker, M.B. (ed.) (1983), *Islam in Southeast Asia* (Leiden, E.J. Brill).

Hourani, Albert (1970), *Arabic Thought in the Liberal Age 1798–1939* (London, Oxford University Press).

— (1991), *A History of the Arab Peoples* (Cambridge, MA, Harvard University Press).

Hughes, T.P. (nd), *A Dictionary of Islam* (London, Luzac).

Huntington, Samuel P. (1968), 'The bases of accommodation', *Foreign Affairs* 4(46): 642–56.

Ibn Khaldun (1967), *The Muqaddimah: An Introduction to History* (London and Henley, Routledge and Kegan Paul with Secker and Warburg).

Ibrahim Alfian (1985), 'The Ulama in Acehnese society', in Ahmad Ibrahim, Sharon

Siddique and Yasmin Hussain (eds), *Readings on Islam in Southeast Asia* (Singapore, Institute of Southeast Asian Studies).

— (1987), *Perang di Jalan Allah: Perang Aceh 1873–1912* (Jakarta, Pustaka Sinar Harapan).

Ibrahim Syukri (pseudonym) (1985), *History of the Malay Kingdom of Patani* (Athens, OH, Ohio University Southeast Asia Series)

Irving, R.E.M. (1975), *The First Indochina War: French and American Policy 1945–1954* (London, Croom Helm).

Irwin, Anthony (1945), *Burmese Outpost* (London, Collins). (Memoirs of British officer who fought in Arakan with the Arakanese of 'V' Force during the Second World War.)

Ismail Lutfi (nd), *Ringkasan Sejarah Islam*, 3 vols (Patani, Saudara Press and Darulikhwan Press).

Jackson, Karl D. (1980), *Traditional Authority, Islam and Rebellion: A Study of Indonesian Political Behaviour* (Berkeley, CA, University of California Press).

— (1985), 'Post-colonial rebellion and counter-insurgency in Southeast Asia', in Chandran Jeshurun (ed.), *Governments and Rebellions in Southeast Asia* (Singapore, Institute of Southeast Asian Studies).

Jaspan, M.A. (1970), 'Recent developments among the Cham of Indochina: the revival of Champa', *Asian Affairs* 57: 170–76.

Jong, J.J.P. de (1986), 'Winds of change: Van Mook, Dutch policy and the realities of 1945', in J. van Goor (ed.), *The Indonesian Revolution: Papers of the Conference held in Utrecht, 17–20 June 1986* (Utrecht, Rijksuniversiteit Utrecht).

Kaam, Ben van (1980), *The South Moluccans: Background to the Train Hijackings* (London, C. Hurst).

Kahin, Audrey (1979), *Struggle for Independence: West Sumatra in the Indonesian National Revolution, 1945–1960* (Ph.D. thesis, Cornell University Press, Ithaca, NY).

Kartodirdjo, Sartono (1966), *The Peasants' Revolt of Banten in 1888* ('s-Gravenhage, H.L. Smits).

Kedourie, Elie (1974), *Nationalism* (London, Hutchinson Library).

Kell, Tim (1995), *The Roots of Acehnese Rebellion 1989–1992* (Ithaca, NY, Cornell Modern Indonesia Project, Cornell University).

Kelly, Francis J. (1991), *The Green Berets in Vietnam* (Washington, Brassey's).

Khin Maung Kyi (1955), 'The Mujahid story', *Guardian* (Burma) 2(3): 38–40.

Khun Yi (1988), *The Dobama Movement in Burma 1930–1938* (Ithaca, NY, Cornell University Press).

Kirby, S.W. (1957–69), *The War against Japan*, 5 vols (London, HMSO).

Kroef, J.M. van der (1976), 'Separatism in Indonesia', *Southeast Asia Spectrum* 4(4): 9–19.

Kruls, H.J. (1960), 'The strategic importance in the world picture of past and future', in J.C. Bouman et al., *The South Moluccas: Rebellious Province or Occupied State* (Leiden, A.W. Sythoff).

Lane, E.W. (1967), *Arabic–English Lexicon* (London, Williams and Norgate).

Larteguy, Jean (1965), *Un Million de Dollars le Viet* (Paris, Solar).

Lebar, Frank, Gerald C. Hickey and John K. Musgrave (eds) (1964), *Ethnic Groups in Mainland Southeast Asia* (New Haven, CT, Human Relations Area Files).

Lebar, Frank M. (ed.) (1972), *Ethnic Groups in Insular Southeast Asia* (New Haven, CT, Human Relations Area Files).

Lebra, Joyce C. (1977), *Japanese-Trained Armies in Southeast Asia* (London, Heinemann).

Legge, J.D. (1961), *Central Authority and Regional Autonomy in Indonesia: A Study in Local Administration 1950–1960* (Ithaca, NY, Cornell University Press).

Leirissa, R.Z. (1991), 'Notes on Central Maluku in the Nineteenth Century', *Prisma: The Indonesian Indicator* 22: 53–66.

Leng Hin-Seak (1969), *Political Leadership in a Plural Society: Penang in the 1960s* (Ph.D. thesis, Australian National University).

Lenin, V.I. (1947), 'Preliminary draft of theses on the national and colonial questions', in V.I. Lenin, *Selected Works*, 2 vols (Moscow, Foreign Languages Publishing House).

Lewis, Norman (1957), *A Dragon Apparent* (London, Pan Books).

Lim Beng Kooi (1974), *The Japanese Occupation of Penang, 1941–1945* (BA dissertation, University of Singapore).

Lim, Lilly (1960), *The Municipal Government of Georgetown, Penang 1946–1957* (Singapore, University of Malaya Press).

Ling, Trevor (1979), *Buddhism, Imperialism and War* (London, George Allen and Unwin).

Lintner, Bertil (1990), *Land of Jade: A Journey through Insurgent Burma* (Edinburgh, Kiscadale).

Loh Fook Seng, Philip (1975), *Seeds of Separatism: Educational Policy in Malaya 1874–1940* (Kuala Lumpur, Oxford University Press).

Lombard, Denys (1967), *Le Sultanat d'Atjeh au temps d'Iskandar Muda 1607–1636* (Paris, Ecole française d'Extrême-Orient).

Lucas-Phillips, C.E. (1971), *The Raiders of Arakan* (London, Heinemann).

McAlister, J.T. (1967), 'Mountain minorities and the Viet-Minh: a key to the Indochina war' in Peter Kunstadter (ed.), *Southeast Asian Tribes, Minorities and Nations* (Princeton, NJ, Princeton University Press).

McCoy, A.W. (1973), *The Politics of Heroin in Southeast Asia* (New York, Harper and Row).

Machiavelli, Niccolo (1950), *Discourses on the First Ten Books of Titus Livius* (New York, Random House).

MacMahon, A.R. (1876), *The Karens of the Golden Chersonese* (London, Harrison).

McVey, Ruth T. (1989), 'Identity and rebellion among the Southern Thai muslims' in Andrew D.W. Forbes (ed.), *The Muslims of Thailand* Vol. II (Gaya, Bihar, Centre for Southeast Asian Studies).

— (1984), 'Separatism and the paradoxes of the nation-state in perspective', in Lim Joo-Jock and S. Vani (eds), *Armed Separatism in Southeast Asia* (Singapore, Institute of Southeast Asian Studies).

Madale, Nagasura T. (1984), 'The future of the Moro National Liberation Front as a separatist movement in Southern Philippines', in Lim Joo-Jock and S. Vani (eds), *Armed Separatism in Southeast Asia* (Singapore, Institute of Southeast Asian Studies).

Madjlis Ulama (1972), *Bagaimana Islam Memandang Kesenian* (Banda Aceh, Madjlis Ulama).

Madmarn, Hasan (1990), Traditional *Muslim Institutions in Southern Thailand* (Ann Arbor, MI, University of Michigan Press).

Md. Salleh bin Md. Gaus (1984), *Politik Melayu Pulau Pinang 1945–1965* (Kuala Lumpur, Dewan Bahasa dan Pustaka).

Mahmud Yunus (1960), S*edjarah Pendidikan Islam di Indonesia* (Djakarta, Pustaka Mahmudiah).

Majid Khadduri (1955), *War and Peace in the Law of Islam* (Baltimore, MD, Johns Hopkins University Press).

Malraux, André (1930), *La Voie Royale* (Paris, Bernard Grasset)

Manusama, J.A. (1960), 'Political aspects of the struggle for Independence', in J.C. Bouman et al., *The South Moluccas: Rebellious Province or Occupied State* (Leiden, A.W. Sythoff).

— (nd), *Om Recht en Vrijheid: De strijd om de onafhankelijkheid der Zuid-Molukken* (Utrecht, Drukkerij Libertas).

Marshall, Harry Ignatius (1922), *The Karen People of Burma: A Study in Anthropology and Ethnology* (Ohio, Ohio State University Press).

Matheson, Virginia and M.B. Hooker (1988), 'Jawi Literature in Patani: the maintenance of an Islamic tradition', *Journal of the Malaysian Branch of the Royal Asiatic Society* 61(1): 1–85.

Matthews, Bruce and Judith A. Nagata (eds) (1986), *Religion, Values and Development in Southeast Asia* (Singapore, Institute of Southeast Asian Studies).

Maududi, S. Abul A'la (1982), *Rights of Non Muslims in Islamic State* (Lahore, Islamic Publications).

Means, G.P. (1970), *Malaysian Politics* (London, University of London Press).

Mercado, E.R. (1984), 'Culture, economics and revolt in Mindanao: the origins of the MNLF and the politics of Moro separatism', in Lim Joo-Jock and S. Vani (eds), *Armed Separatism in Southeast Asia* (Singapore, Institute of Southeast Asian Studies).

Mill, John Stuart (1946), *On Liberty, and Considerations of Representative Government* (Oxford, Blackwell).

Ministry of Foreign Affairs, Thailand (1979), *Thai Muslims* (Bangkok, Ministry of Foreign Affairs).

Mohamed Noordin Sopiee (1974), *From Malayan Union to Singapore Separation: Political Unification in the Malaysian Region 1945–1965* (Kuala Lumpur, University of Malaya Press).

Mohammed Ansori Nawawi (1968), *Regionalism and Regional Conflict in Indonesia* (Ph.D. thesis, Princeton University Press, Princeton, NJ).

Mook, H.J. van (1944), *The Netherlands Indies and Japan: Their Relations 1940–1941* (London, Allen and Unwin).

— (1950), *The Stakes of Democracy in Southeast Asia* (London, George Allen and Unwin).

Morris, Eric E. (1983), *Islam and Politics in Aceh: a study of centre-periphery relations in Indonesia* (Ph.D. thesis, Cornell University, Ithaca, NY).

— (1985), 'Social revolution and the Islamic vision', in Audrey R. Kahin (ed.), *Regional Dynamics of the Indonesian Revolution: Unity from Diversity* (Honolulu, University of Hawaii Press).

Morrison, Ian (1947), *Grandfather Longlegs: the life and gallant death of Major Seagrim* (London, Faber and Faber). (The biography of Major Seagrim, who organised a Karen resistance movement in Burma after the British retreat in 1942.)

Muhammad Ali (1983), *A Manual of Hadith* (London, Curzon Press).

Naguib al-Attas, Syed Muhammad (1970), *The Mysticism of Hamzah Fansuri* (Kuala Lumpur, University of Malaya Press).

Naidu, Ratna (1980), *The Communal Edge to Plural Societies: India and Malaysia* (India, Vikas).

Nanulaitta, I.O. (1966), *Tibulnja Militerisme Ambon* (Djakarta, Bhratara).

Nazaruddin Sjamsuddin (1985), *The Republican Revolt: a study of the Acehnese Rebellion* (Singapore, Institute of Southeast Asian Studies).

Nepote, Jacques (1993), 'Champa: propositions pour une histoire des temps long', *Péninsule: Etudes interdisciplinaires sur l'Asie du Sud-Est péninsulaire* 24(27): 65–119.

Nguyen Khac Vien (ed.) (1968), *Mountain Regions and National Minorities* (Hanoi, Xunhasaba, Vietnamese Studies no. 15).

Nguyen Trac Di (nd), *Tim Hieu Phong-Trao Tranh-Dau FULRO (1958–1969)* (Saigon, Ngoc-Hung).

Nguyen Van Khon (1991), *Tu Dien Viet Anh* (TP Ho Chi Minh, Nha Xuat Ban Tre).

Nicolson, Harold (1967), *Diaries and Letters* (London, Collins).

Nieuwenhuijze, C.A.O. (1958), *Aspects of Islam in Post-Colonial Indonesia* (The Hague, Van Hoeve).

Nik Anwar Nik Mahmud (1987), *Anglo-Thai Relations 1945–1954* (Ph.D. thesis, Hull University).

Nixon, Richard M. (1967), 'Asia after Vietnam', *Foreign Affairs* 1(46): 111–125.

Noer, Deliar (1972), *The Modernist Muslim Movement in Indonesia 1900–1942* (Kuala Lumpur, Oxford University Press).

— (1978), *Administration of Islam in Indonesia* (Ithaca, NY, Cornell University Press).

Nu (Thakin) (1954), *Burma under the Japanese* (London, Macmillan).

Nur el-Ibrahimy (1982), *Teungku Muhammad Daud Beureueh: Peranannya dalam Pergolak di Aceh* (Jakarta, Gunung Agung).

Ooi, Diana (1967), *A Study of the English-Speaking Chinese of Penang* (MA thesis, University of Malaya).

Ooi (Tan), Diana (1978), 'The Penang Straits Chinese British Association', *Malaysia in History* 21(2): 43–55.

Orwell, Sonia and Ian Angus (eds) (1970), *In Front of Your Nose: The Collected Essays, Journalism and Letters of George Orwell*, Vol. IV, 1945–1950 (London, Penguin Books). (Pp. 325–6 contain some comments made by George Orwell in February 1947 on the Karen problem in Burma.)

Omar Farouk (1988), 'The Muslims of Thailand – a survey', in Andrew D.W. Forbes (ed.), *The Muslims of Thailand*, Vol. I (Gaya, Bihar, Centre for Southeast Asian Studies).

Owen, Frank (1946), *The Campaign in Burma* (London, HMSO).

Ozay Mehmet (1990), *Islamic Identity and Development: Studies of the Islamic Periphery* (New York, Routledge).

Pandey, B.N. (ed.) (1979), *The Indian Nationalist Movement 1885–1947: Select Documents* (London, Macmillan).

Pike, Douglas (1968), *Viet-Cong: The Organization and Techniques of the National Liberation Front of South Vietnam* (Cambridge, MA, MIT Press).

Pitsuwan, Surin (1982), *Issues Affecting Border Security between Malaysia and Thailand* (Bangkok, Thammasat University, Faculty of Political Science Monograph Series).

— (1985), *Islam and Malay Nationalism: A Case Study of the Malay-Muslims of*

Southern Thailand (Bangkok, Thai Khadi Research Institute, Thammasat University).

Png Poh Seng (1969), 'The Straits Chinese in Singapore: a case of local identity and socio-cultural accommodation', *Journal of Southeast Asian History* 10(1): 95–114.

Po Chit (1947), *Karens and the Karen State* (Burma, Karen National Union). (A key pamphlet, arguing the case for an independent, or at the very least fully autonomous, Karen State. Two copies of this pamphlet exist in the records of the India Office Library, in IOR M/4/3023.)

Po, San C. (1928), *Burma and the Karens* (London, Elliot Stock). (Dr – later Sir – San C. Po has been regarded as the 'father' of the Karen nation. In this book, he outlines the political aspirations of the Karens in the inter-war years.)

Popovic, A. and G. Veinstein (1985), *Les Ordres Mystiques dans l'Islam: cheminements en situation actuelle* (Paris, Editions de l'Ecole des Hautes Etudes en Sciences Sociales).

Porter, A.N. and Stockwell, A.J. (1987–1989), *British Imperial Policy and Decolonization 1938–1964*, 2 vols (Basingstoke, Macmillan).

Prachuabmoh, Chavivun (1989), 'The role of women in maintaining ethnic identity and boundaries: a case of Thai-Muslims in South Thailand', in Andrew D.W. Forbes (ed.), *The Muslims of Thailand*, Vol. II (Gaya, Bihar, Centre for Southeast Asian Studies).

Prins, J. (1960), 'Location, history, forgotten struggle', in J.C. Bouman et al., *The South Moluccas: Rebellious Province or Occupied State* (Leiden, A.W. Sythoff).

Purcell, Victor (1954), *Malaya: Communist or Free?* (Stanford, CA, Stanford University Press).

— (1975), *The Chinese in Malaya* (London, Oxford University Press).

Purser, W.C.B. and A.M. Knight (1911), *Christian Missions in Burma* (London, SPG).

Pusat Dokumentasi dan Informasi Aceh (1977), *Perang Kolonial Belanda di Aceh* (Banda Aceh).

Qur'an (1986), *The Bounteous Koran*, Al-Azhar approved edition, trans. M.M. Khatib (London, Macmillan).

Raja, Ananda (1990), 'Ethnicity, Nationalism and the Nation-State: The Karen in Burma and Thailand', in G. Wijeyewardene (ed.), *Ethnic Groups across National Boundaries in Mainland Southeast Asia* (Singapore, Institute of Southeast Asian Studies).

Reid, Anthony (1969), *The Contest for North Sumatra: Atjeh, the Netherlands and Britain 1858–1898* (Kuala Lumpur, University of Malaya Press).

— (1979), *The Blood of the People: Revolution and the End of Traditional Rule in Sumatra* (London, Oxford University Press).

— (1986), 'The Revolution in regional perspective', in J. van Goor (ed.), *The Indonesian Revolution: Papers of the Conference held in Utrecht 17–20 July 1986* (Utrecht, Rijksuniversiteit Utrecht).

Renan, Ernest (1939), 'What is a Nation?', in Alfred Zimmern (ed.), *Modern Political Doctrines* (London, Oxford University Press).

Ricklefs, M.C. (1981), *A History of Modern Indonesia* (London, Macmillan).

Riesen, Rene (1957), *Jungle Mission* (London, Hutchinson).

Roff, William R. (1967), *The Origins of Malay Nationalism* (New Haven, CT, Yale University Press).

— (1974), *Kelantan: Religion, Society and Politics in a Malay State* (Kuala Lumpur, Oxford University Press).

Sacks, I. Milton (1960), 'Marxism in Vietnam', in Frank N. Trager (ed.), *Marxism in Southeast Asia: A Study of Four Countries* (Stanford, CA, Stanford University Press).

Sainteny, Jean (1967), *Histoire d'une Paix Manquée* (Paris, Fayard).

Santa Maria, Bernard (1982), *My People, My Country* (Malacca, np).

Sarkisyanz, E. (1965), *Buddhist Backgrounds of the Burmese Revolution* (The Hague, Martinus Nijhoff).

Satha-Anand, Chaiwat (1987), *Islam and Violence: A Case Study of Violent Events in the Four Southern Provinces of Thailand 1976–1981* (Tampa, Florida, University of South Florida Monographs in Religion and Public Policy).

Savina, F.M. (1924), *Histoire des Miao* (Hong Kong, Imprimerie de la Société des Missions Etrangers).

Schrock, Joanne L. (1966), *Minority Groups in the Republic of Vietnam* (Washington, Department of the Army). (A comprehensive study of the different *montagnard* groups of South Vietnam, prepared for the use of the US armed forces in Vietnam.)

Selth, Andrew (1986), 'Race and Resistance in Burma 1942–1945', *Modern Asian Studies* 20(3): 483–95.

Short, Anthony (1975), *The Communist Insurrection in Malaya 1948–1960* (London, Muller).

Siegel, James T. (1969), *The Rope of God* (Berkeley, CA, University of California Press).

— (1979), *Shadow and Sound: The Historical Thought of a Sumatran People* (Chicago, University of Chicago Press).

Silcock, T.H. and Ungku Aziz (1950), *Nationalism in Malaya* (New York, Institute of Pacific Relations).

Silverstein, J. (1960), *Burmese Politics: The Dilemma of National Unity* (New Brunswick, Rutgers University Press).

Simandjuntak, B. (1969), *Malayan Federalism 1945–1963* (Kuala Lumpur, Oxford University Press).

Smeaton, Donald M. (1887). *The Loyal Karens of Burma* (London, Kegan Paul Trench). (An important book making the case that the Karens should be allowed a large measure of autonomy from Burma proper.)

Smith, Anthony D. (1986), *The Ethnic Origins of Nations* (Oxford, Blackwell).

Smith Dun (1980), *Memoirs of the Four-Foot Colonel* (Ithaca, NY, Department of Asian Studies, Cornell University).

Smith, Donald E. (1965), *Religion and Politics in Burma* (Princeton, NJ, Princeton University Press).

Smith, Martin (1991), *Burma: Insurgency and the Politics of Ethnicity* (London, Zed Books). (This provides the most comprehensive analysis of the interraction of ideological, strategic and ethnic issues in the history of modern Burma.)

Snitwongse, Kusuma (1985), 'Thai Government responses to armed communist and separatist movements', in Chandran Jeshurun (ed.), *Governments and Rebellions in Southeast Asia* (Singapore, Institute of Southeast Asian Studies).

Snouck Hurgronje, C. (1906), *The Achehnese*, 2 vols (Leiden, E.J. Brill).

— (1936), *Mekka in the Latter Part of the Nineteenth Century 1888–89* (Amsterdam, Elsevier).

Sochurek, Howard (1968), 'Vietnam's Montagnards: caught in the jaws of a war', *National Geographic* 133(4): 443–87.

Soedjakmoto (1960), *An Approach to Indonesian History: Towards an Open Future* (Ithaca, NY, Cornell University Press).

Soh Eng Lim (1960), 'Tan Cheng-Lock: his leadership of the Malayan Chinese', *Journal of Southeast Asian History* 1(1): 34–61.

Soulie, M. (1927), *Marie, 1er. Roi des Sedangs 1880–1890* (Paris, Marpon).

Ssu-yu Teng and John K. Fairbank (eds) (1969), *China's Response to the West: A Documentary Survey 1839–1923* (New York, Atheneum).

Steenbrink, Karel (1993), *Dutch Colonialism and Indonesian Islam: Contacts and Conflicts 1596–1950* (Amsterdam, Editions RODOPI).

Stenson, M.R. (1974), 'The ethnic and urban bases of communist revolt in Malaya', in J.W. Lewis (ed.), *Peasant Rebellion and Communist Revolution in Asia* (Stanford, CA, Stanford University Press).

Stevenson, H.N.C. (1944), *The Hill Peoples of Burma* (Calcutta, Longmans Green and Co.).

Stockwell, A.J. (1979), *British Policy and Malay Politics during the Malayan Union Experiment 1945–1948* (Kuala Lumpur, Malaysian Branch of the Royal Asiatic Society Monograph).

Stohr, W. and P. Zoetmulder (1968), *Les Religions d'Indonésie* (Paris, Payot).

Stowe, Judith A. (1990), *Siam becomes Thailand: A Story of Intrigue* (Hurst, London).

Suthasana, Arong (1989), 'Thai society and the Muslim majority', in Andrew D.W. Forbes (ed.), *The Muslims of Thailand*, Vol. II (Gaya, Bihar, Centre for Southeast Asian Studies).

Tan Chee-Beng (1979), *Baba and Nyonya: A Study of the Ethnic Identity of the Chinese Peranakan of Malacca* (Ph.D. thesis, Cornell University, Ithaca, NY).

— (1987), 'Structure and change: cultural identity of the Baba of Melaka', *Bijdragen* 144(2): 297–314.

— (1990), *The Preservation and Adaptation of Tradition: Studies of Chinese Religious Expression in Southeast Asia* (Columbus, OH, Anthony R. Walker).

— (1992), *Bibliography on Ethnic Relations with Special Reference to Malaysia and Singapore* (Kuala Lumpur, Institute for Advanced Studies, University of Malaya).

Tan Cheng Lock (1947), *Malayan Problems from a Chinese Point of View* (Singapore, Tannso).

Taouti, Seddik (1985), 'The forgotten Muslims of Kampuchea and Vietnam', in Ahmad Ibrahim, Sharon Siddique and Yasmin Hussain (eds), *Readings in Islam in Southeast Asia* (Singapore, Institute of Southeast Asian Studies).

Taufiq Abdullah (1947), *Schools and Politics: The Kaum Muda Movement in West Sumatra 1927–1933* (Ithaca, NY, Cornell University Press).

Taylor, Robert H. (1987), *The State in Burma* (London, Hurst and Co.).

— (1984), *Marxism and Resistance in Burma 1942–1945: Thein Pe Myint's 'Wartime Traveler'* (Athens, OH, Ohio University Press).

Teeuw, A. and D.K. Wyatt (eds) (1970), *Hikayat Patani* (The Hague, Martinus Nijhoff).

Thomas, M. Ladd (1975), *Political Violence in the Muslim Provinces of Southern Thailand* (Singapore, Institute of Southeast Asian Studies).

— (1982), 'The Thai Muslims', in Raphael Israeli (ed.), *The Crescent in the East: Islam in Asia Major* (London, Curzon Press).

Thompson, Virginia and Richard Adloff (1955), *Minority Problems in Southeast Asia* (Stanford, CA, Stanford University Press).

Tjoet Ahmad (ed.) (1968), *95 Tahun Tantangan Ultimatum Keradjaan Belanda Terhadap Keradjaan Atjeh* (Medan, Seksi Publikasi dan Dokumentasi Panitia Peringatan Pahlawan Nasional Dari Atjeh, Medan dan Sekitarnja).

Truong Buu Lam, (1967), *Patterns of Vietnamese Response to Foreign Intervention 1858–1900* (New Haven, CT, Yale University Monograph Series).

Truong Vinh Ky, J.-B. Petrus (1910), *Dictionnaire Franco-Annamite* (Paris, Librarie Larousse).

Tugby, Donald and Elise (1989), 'Malay-Muslim and Thai-Buddhist relations in the Patani region: an interpretation', in Andrew D.W. Forbes (ed.), *The Muslims of Thailand*, Vol. II (Gaya, Bihar, Centre for Southeast Asian Studies).

Turkoly-Joczik, Robert L. (1986), *The Military Role of Asian Ethnic Minorities in the Second Indochina War, 1959–1975* (Ph.D. thesis, University of Wales at Aberystwyth).

Vahid, Syed Abdul (ed.) (1964), *Thoughts and Reflections of Iqbal* (Lahore, Ashraf Press).

Vasil, R.K. (1980), *Ethnic Politics in Malaya* (New Delhi, Radiant Publishers).

Vaughan, J.D. (1971), *The Manners and Customs of the Chinese of the Straits Settlements* (Kuala Lumpur, Oxford University Press).

Vo Nguyen Giap (1965), *People's War, People's Army* (New York, Praeger).

Wallace, Alfred Russel (1906), *The Malay Archipelago* (London, Macmillan and Co.).

Wan Hashim (1983), *Race Relations in Malaysia* (Kuala Lumpur, Heinemann).

Wan Hashim Haji Wan Teh (1984), *Pejuang Gerila Force 136* (Grik, UMNO, Bahagian Grik).

Watson, C.W. (1990), 'Report on a trip to Patani', in *Annual Report of the Centre of South-East Asian Studies 1989–1990* (Canterbury, University of Kent at Canterbury).

Watt, W. Montgomery (1968), *Islamic Political Thought: The Basic Concepts* (Edinburgh, Edinburgh University Press)

Weekes, Richard V. (1984), *Muslim Peoples: A World Ethnographic Survey*, 2 vols (Westport, CT, Greenwood Press).

Wekkin, Gary D. (1974), 'Tribal politics in Indochina: the role of the Highland Tribes in the internationalization of internal wars', in Mark W. Zacher and R. Stephen-Milne (eds), *Conflict and Stability in Southeast Asia* (New York, Anchor Books).

Wijeyewardene, Gehan (1990), *Ethnic Groups across National Boundaries in Mainland Southeast Asia* (Singapore, Institute of Southeast Asian Studies).

Wilson, H.E. (1989), 'Imperialism and Islam: the impact of "modernization" on the Malay-Muslims of South Thailand', in Andrew D.W. Forbes (ed.), *The Muslims of Thailand*, Vol. II (Gaya, Bihar, Centre for Southeast Asian Studies).

— (1992), 'Tengku Mahmud Mahyiddeen and the dilemma of partisan duality', *Journal of Southeast Asian Studies* 23(1): 37–59.

Winzeler, Robert L. (1985), *Ethnic Relations in Kelantan: A Study of the Chinese and Thai as Ethnic Minorities in a Malay State* (Singapore, Oxford University Press).

Wu, David Y.H. (1982), *Ethnicity and Inter-Personal Interaction* (Singapore, Maruzen, Asia).

Wurfel, David (1985), 'Government responses to armed communism and secessionist rebellion in the Philippines', in Chandran Jeshurun (ed.), *Governments and Rebellions in Southeast Asia* (Singapore, Institute of Southeast Asian Studies).

Yegar, Moshe (1972), *The Muslims of Burma: A Study of a Minority Group* (Wiesbaden, Otto Harrassowitz).

— (1982), 'The Muslims of Burma', in Raphael Israeli (ed.), *The Crescent in the East: Islam in Asia Major* (London, Curzon Press). (Two important works by the foremost authority on the Arakanese Muslims.)

Yeap Joo Kim (1975), *The Patriarch* (Singapore, np).

Yoon, W.Z. (1973), *Japan's Scheme for the Liberation of Burma: the role of the Minami Kikan and the 'Thirty Comrades'* (Ohio, Ohio University Papers in Southeast Asian Studies).

Yule, Henry and A.C. Burnell (1979), *Hobson-Jobson: A Glossary of Colloquial Anglo-Indian Words and Phrases* (New Delhi, Munshiram Monaharlal).

Yusuf Qardhawi (1985), *Minoritas Non-Muslim di-dalam Masyarakat Islam* (Bandung, Mizan).

Index